*

*

*Laurette*

*

*

*

# Laurette

BY

MARGUERITE COURTNEY

*

*Introduction by Samuel Hopkins Adams*

RINEHART & COMPANY, INC.   NEW YORK   TORONTO

*For My Daughter, Marguerite*

# Introduction

Whether or not Laurette Taylor was the greatest actress of her day is not within the present writer's competency to determine. That she was perhaps its most shining personality, he can testify from long acquaintanceship. Her rise from the tawdriest purlieus of the theater to its summit had in it a touch of the miraculous.

My own association with Laurette, which developed into a firm friendship, was in a sense a secondary relationship, adjunct to her devotion to my wife who was her oldest and closest friend. She was then at the height of her loveliness and charm. The hazards of melodrama and the rigors of barnstorming which had constituted her harsh apprenticeship were all in the past. She had broken off an unhappy marriage and was approaching a happy and successful one. She was the toast of New York. Lights flashed her name across Broadway. The world was her oyster.

Nobody could have enjoyed its flavor more than she did. There was no element of surprise in her deep satisfaction. She had a fanatic belief in herself. Success was her natural element. She was mirthful, arrogant, capricious, ill-disciplined, avid of intellectual stimulus of whatever kind, with a flashing and acquisitive intelligence and an insatiable curiosity which fed it. And she was self-centered in a way that was almost selfless. Laurette Taylor's world revolved like a multicolored pinwheel around Laurette

Taylor, the actress, rather than around Laurette Taylor, the person. The center and core of her life was the stage. Her one unwavering devotion was to her calling.

Nothing else mattered in comparison. She became rich. Money counted for little with her. She became a shining figure in the social life of New York and London. The important, the near-important and the self-important crowded to her doors. They never touched her nearly. There was in her no taint of snobbery. The people who interested her, of whom she talked in her reminiscent moments, were primarily her associates of the stage; secondarily writers, artists, scientists, the creative element.

She had a double standard of morality. Her friends might do as they pleased. She never sat judgment on them. Their behavior was their own business. For herself, it was different. She could be quite startlingly free of speech. But her conduct was circumspect to the verge of being puritanical. There must have been thousands of men in love with her in those days. Scandal did not touch her.

Such was Laurette Taylor as I first knew her.

Twenty years later her world had fallen away from her. Her husband was dead. Her fortune had dribbled away. Her beauty was gone. Broadway had forgotten her. She was deep-sunk in alcohol. But the unshakable confidence in herself was still there. I have seen her enter a drawing room, fat, flabby, dowdy, worn, yet still invincibly certain of herself. And, sure enough, before the evening was over and without manifest effort on her part, she would be the center of interest, with everyone hanging on her words.

Because that spirit was indestructible, she was able to make the most triumphant comeback in the annals of the American stage. It rejoiced her soul; she would have been less than human had it not. When it came, she accepted it as a matter of course. At the worst she had never lost that superb confidence in herself.

At the ebb of her fortunes, when she was visiting us, she confided to my wife that she was making notes for an autobiography. Jane encouraged her. A month later she had dropped the project.

"It seemed simple enough, Jane," she explained. "But when I

got into it, I found the character just too damn' complicated for me to handle."

She would have been, I think, astonished at what her daughter has made of that complicated character; astonished and, for the most part, gratified. It would not have been an easy task for an impersonal biographer; it must have been peculiarly difficult for one so close to the subject. In the opinion of one who knew Laurette well, Marguerite has given a masterly presentation not only of a luminous figure but also of the glittering world in which she played so conspicuous a part.

—SAMUEL HOPKINS ADAMS.

# Acknowledgments

Because my mother destroyed virtually all family records—including press books, letters, programs, photograph albums and other memorabilia of her theatre and private life—I have had to rely to an unusual degree upon the records and personal recollections of others. When I began work on this biography it was my good fortune to find many still alive whose close association began on 125th Street, New York, where my mother was born and raised as a child, also many who vividly recalled her early melodrama and Western stock days. Certain key figures, both in and out of the theatre, were valuable sources of material, others gave me perhaps a moment here, a moment there, an incident, an impression, a mood . . . but the picture grew, vivid and true, and consistently challenging and exciting.

My debt is very great. The following is a partial list of those to whom I owe much, some of whom have passed away. *Members of the family:* Bessie Cooney Owens, Mabel Pearsall, Charles Edward Taylor, Dwight Taylor. *One Hundred and Twenty-fifth Street and Melodrama Days:* Margherita and Elsa Steinert, Frank Kemper, Hugo and Mignon Ziegfeld, Mary Farrell Foy, Walter Moore, M. C. Zumwalt, Bartley Campbell, Walter Scott, John Briscoe, Joseph Santley, Daisy (Mrs. Joe) Humphreys. *The Prosperous Years:* Elsie Janis, Ethel Barrymore, Lynn Fontanne, Lillian Kemble Cooper, Geoffrey Kerr, Field Marshal Earl Alexander of Tunis, Lily McCormack, Grace George, Zoe Akins, Elsa Ryan, Lester Donahue, Rollo Peters, King Vidor, Louis Calhern, Cedric Gibbons. *Years of Defeat and the Comeback Years:* Mary Morley, Elizabeth (Buff) Cobb, José Ruben, Jessie Royce Landis, Otto Preminger, Vincent Price, Edith Barrett, William A. Brady, Anthony Ross, Willis Gould, Tennessee Williams, Dr. Paul De Santo.

For valuable assistance in research I am indebted to George Freedley and his associates, Theatre Collection, New York Public Library; Glenn Hughes, Director of Drama, University of Washington; May Davenport Seymour, Museum of the City of New York; Mrs. Arnold Rattray of the East Hampton Star; author Stewart H. Holbrook; Dorothy York for generous use of her biography in work of Charles A. Taylor. And of great help were my mother's own recollections in the form of notes and articles, both published and unpublished, which she was preparing under the title "Stars That Crossed Mine."

Particularly I want to express my gratitude to Samuel Hopkins Adams, who painstakingly passed along an expert's knowledge in the compilation of biographical data, and ceaselessly goaded me to come through like a "pro" during the long years it took to complete this task; to Ashton Stevens who, until the day of his death, demonstrated an unwavering faith and warm encouragement once he believed me capable of telling a story so dear to his heart, and who with the active participation of his wife, Katherine, made available news columns and personal letters; to George Cukor for the generous use of his correspondence, and the many penetrating insights on the work and temperament of an artist he revered; to Eloise Sheldon Armen who recreated so sensitively many moments of my mother's life I could not know; and to Harold Clurman for a stout critical staff to lean on during the final stages of cutting an overlong biography.

Lastly, to William H. Courtney, my husband, I bow low. His all-round editing skill and critical acumen were put entirely at my disposal, as well as much of his precious time. No task was too menial to perform if it forwarded my work, no obstacle so great that a way was not found to surmount it. His patience, deep understanding, and belief through six difficult years kept my course steady. It would be superfluous to say that with a lesser man my goal would never have been reached.

MARGUERITE COURTNEY.

Idyllwild, California
November 12, 1954

*

*

*Laurette*

*

*Laurette Taylor who made history in the theatre over a span of fifty years with the luminous truth of her acting, spent most of her time as a child weaving luminous lies around her everyday life. She did so, by her own statement, because her life bored her. "It was so easy to think of things that pleased me far better than the facts," she said. Perhaps one who is to turn the world of make-believe into a world of truth must start early to switch those two worlds around. Whether or not this is so, the record shows that Laurette as a child and adolescent spent most of her time in a world of her own fancy. And this fancy—gossamer and born of nothing—was to press itself upon the lives of those around her, changing them and disrupting them, so that in the end one purpose was served: that the child took her fertile imaginings into the theatre and there created the truth which in everyday life she found so unbearable.*

*The why of it, like the why of all magic, cannot be known. One tells the story and the threads weave the pattern, dimly or clearly, gloriously or shabbily—the pattern of a life.*

*

# *Elizabeth Cooney*

A little girl, fists punched into cheeks, sits on the high stone stoop of her home at 52 West 125 Street and finds her life utterly boring. It is, she considers, in need of much embroidery to make it bearable, and she devotes a great deal of time to this mental needlework. Having a fertile imagination she is rarely at a loss for an exciting design, and she never hesitates to substitute fancy for fact.

Why Loretta Cooney looked on her childhood with so jaundiced an eye is not clear. It was a pleasant way of life as it was lived in the quiet streets of Harlem in the 1880's. One Hundred and Twenty-fifth was a street of three-story residences and the Irish, German and Italian families who lived there enjoyed for the most part a modest financial security. The children had pretty clothes and many playmates. Parents—with nerves untorn by speed and telephones and a too-crowded city—opened their homes to their children's friends, or with confidence sent the youngsters into the streets and parks to play. There was usually a grandparent or two from the Old Country who could remind the grownups to be grateful for their opportunities, and the grandchildren of the virtues of work and discipline and daily prayer. The horsecar traveled as fast as anybody wanted to go; the parks were full of leisurely cyclists, tandem and single. With the first snowfall you

3

could take your bobsled down a hilly New York street, clearing your path with a shout. It was a city that had grown just enough for neighborliness but not so much that the neighbor was a stranger's face in an elevator.

True, an elegance of living that was not theirs surrounded the children who lived on One Hundred and Twenty-fifth. The really swank residential street in Harlem was One Hundred and Twenty-third with its row of brownstone fronts overlooking Mount Morris Park. The "swells" lived there. They had drawing rooms while One Hundred and Twenty-fifth had parlors. They patronized different stores, dined at different restaurants at prices beyond the range of the thriftier families of One Hundred and Twenty-fifth. But elegance in those days was looked up to and aspired to rather than envied. The children of immigrants dreamed that someday it would be theirs. Elizabeth Cooney, Loretta's mother, dreamed it when she set up in dressmaking on One Hundred and Twenty-fifth Street; and Loretta dreamed it sitting on the high stoop of her home.

Most of the families on the street, like Mrs. Cooney, conducted their small businesses right in their own homes. The Repetti's ran a candy kitchen in their basement and made chocolates which in time became nationally famous. The widowed Mrs. Lombardi operated a hairdressing parlor, in which her two daughters helped after school. Mr. Henkle, a lithographer, turned out handbills and theatrical posters in his basement; and Mr. Otto Frank, his neighbor, had a small photo studio at the corner of Lenox Avenue. The Cooneys lived in the middle of the block between Lenox and Fifth Avenue. Across the street Miss Ida Whittington gave piano, harp, singing and dancing lessons in her parlor. Miss "Whitty" had been in vaudeville but everyone in the neighborhood overlooked that fact because she really behaved in a most ladylike fashion.

When Elizabeth and James Cooney moved from Newark to New York, Elizabeth, not yet twenty, was already the mainstay of the Cooney finances. The whole top floor of Number 52 was converted into the workroom of her dressmaking establishment and in the basement was a millinery shop for which she made the hats. The first and second floors were reserved for family living. Elizabeth thought she had laid her needle aside when she married James. When they first met he was earning a respectable income as a harness and saddle maker. Unfortunately he was cursed with the dreaming Irishman's aversion to work and preference for good whiskey and good talk. As a result his harness business languished long before the smell of the first gasoline engine could have blighted it, and to meet the mounting bills Elizabeth once more became industrious with her needle. The shifting of the main burden of breadwinner had been gradual and neither of them minded very much considering their respective natures.

James was a well-educated man with little or no ambition in life. He was handsome, albeit on the short round side, with the Irish charm that covers many weaknesses. He had small, well-made hands and feet, large expressive eyes and a finely chiseled nose. To Elizabeth's sorrow none of their three children inherited his nose but all got her short, turned-up one. He sang, played the piano, read omnivorously, and recited not very classical poetry in a beautiful Irish voice. A rather ferocious red mustache belied these more amiable qualities and when he stood over his children in anger, he could chill their blood. The only real determination he had was on his most unpleasant side; he was a fanatical Catholic. He swung between an easygoing nature with a poet's view of life, and the mean suspicion and temper of the bigot; the pendulum being kept in motion by his Catholicism on the one hand and whiskey on the other. He never went into a theatre in all his life and considered all theatre people, *a priori*, damned.

Elizabeth had no formal education whatsoever. Her central characteristic was a driving ambition to improve herself and the position of her family in the world. She loved gaiety, bright lights and music and an occasional beer. She adored the theatre and as a young girl had had her dreams of being an actress, but unrelieved poverty and a stern Catholic mother had prevented her from realizing them. She was a passionate woman without any capacity for the amiabilities of affection. It was this quality that attached her to James long after she had lost respect for him, and made it possible for her to leave him with scarcely a backward glance once her passion was dead. Both husband and wife were tempestuous in nature and their strong physical attraction had in it a considerable degree of cruelty. In an argument James would taunt his wife because she could neither read nor write. Her love of pretty clothes he construed, when it pleased him, as lightness of character, and he went into jealous rages if he thought she looked too pretty. When she slipped out for a beer or to the theatre, under the pretense of delivering a dress or chaperoning one of her young assistants home, she was in James' book eternally damned for a frivolous, Devil-serving woman. Because she was terrified of lightning, he delighted in forcing her to stand at an open window during thunderstorms. His petty tyrannies grew worse as he became more shiftless and she more successful. She on the other hand jibed at him for his lack of success. His superior education combined with lack of ambition infuriated her. When she found him reading, she would seize the book and burn it in the stove. Later, when he brought books home for his children, she did the same thing; reading was in her mind concomitant with laziness.

These two natures in their different ways were to contribute an explosive force to the career of their daughter Loretta. From the outset she had the hard-driving will of her mother behind her, and sharpened her own determination upon the rocklike opposition of her father to her course.

Hard-driving Elizabeth was born Elizabeth Dorsey in Somerset County, New Jersey, in 1863. She was the tenth of eleven children born to Patrick and Bridgett Dorsey, who emigrated to America from Galway, Ireland, in the early 1850's. Patrick had been a gatekeeper on a large estate outside of Dublin, and it may well have been while watching the carriages drive in and out, and bowing to the gentry, that Bridgett took it into her head America would offer finer opportunities to the Dorseys. Be that as it may, Pat set out for the New World at the urging of his wife. Bridgett followed sometime later with their three infant sons, and the family settled in the small Irish community of Peapac, New Jersey.

Their first years in America, like those of most immigrants, were years of grinding poverty. Bridgett baked bread to sell and practiced midwifery. Pat got what work he could as a stonemason. The babies came year after year. It seemed the Dorseys could never get any money ahead with all the mouths to feed. As soon as the children were old enough they went to work. Bridgett, a devout Catholic, accepted her poverty as she accepted her children, as a gift from God. "If God closes one door He will open another," she used to say to her sometimes rebellious brood. Occasionally she would sing and jig in the liveliest manner, making her children laugh with delight, but more often was weighed down by her troubles and a chronic pessimism characteristic of the Irish.

With the eleventh baby on its way, John, the eldest child, had had enough. "Sure, if I have to slave all my life, it's for a family of my own I'll do it!" he said in disgust. He picked himself a strong young colleen, and off he went to make his own way. Within the year he was back, a widower, with the baby that had taken the life of the young mother. Bridgett accepted them both and raised her son's baby daughter as her own.

Elizabeth and Nellie, Bridgett's youngest, early showed an aptitude with the needle, and when still mere children began earning money as seamstresses. Pat took the credit for that. "My two sisters were the finest seamstresses in all Galway," he would recall, "and all the grand ladies of the county brought them cloth to cut and sew for their fanciest dresses. Bridgett, now, she can't sew a patch on straight—God love her soul!"

Bridgett was a peppery little woman and no stranger to an argument. But arguments in the Dorsey household, by her order, took place behind closed doors. It was no business of the neighbors what troubles the Dorseys were having; nor could she be provoked to a quarrel outside her home. In the traditional uproar of Irish communal life, it was one of the wonders of the town to see little Bridgett turn on her heel and close her door with a bang on an argumentative neighbor. She shut her mouth tight, kept her own counsel, and asked help from no one but God.

The best of times were none too good for the Dorseys. Pat's health failed, and the family moved to Newark where the children had better opportunities to ply their various trades. It was there that Elizabeth, age fifteen, met James Cooney, age twenty, of the beautiful eyes and the soft brogue of the Old Country. It was not at all difficult to persuade herself that he was the Prince Charming of her dreams.

Bridgett thought otherwise. She called James "a good-lookin' dish with nothin' in it." Learning that they were to be married in spite of her disapproval, Bridgett went to the church and at the conclusion of the ceremony made known her presence to the abashed couple. "It's been done in the Holy Church, and I'm grateful to God for that," was her one comment.

James was fond of whiskey then, but Elizabeth overlooked it because it brought out his genial side; he would recite poetry in a lilting Irish voice, and sing the Irish ballads that she loved. Whiskey relaxed his jealousy—in those days at least—and he could admire his wife in a new hat without becoming suspicious of her motive in buying it. His easygoing nature might even have seemed an asset to Elizabeth because, being a forceful woman, she preferred having things done her way. When his business slackened off and she found herself earning a substantial part of the family income by dressmaking, she was not unduly upset; it gave her a certain control over him, and made her not quite so vulnerable to his charms.

By the time they had settled in New York they were jogging along well enough together. From the Mount Morris district, Elizabeth acquired a wealthy clientele which gave her a steady and lucrative trade. In busy seasons she had as many as eighteen girls working for her in the big airy room on the top floor, and two to run the millinery shop in the basement. James made the long tables where the girls worked, putting a deep groove along the edges to hold the pins. He turned to and cut patterns for his wife, working in a small back room, singing in a pleasant baritone, occasionally strolling in to tease the girls at the long tables. He also kept the books and delivered the clothes. Now and then he'd stop at a saloon after making a delivery, and by the time he got home the money would be gone—not only on whiskey, but into the pockets of all sorts of people whom he found deserving of his liberality. It was not too hard for Elizabeth to forgive him. These expansive moods were far easier to take than his bigotry and suspicion. He was full of love and Irish blarney and delighted to bring home gifts purchased with her hard-earned money. One time it was a pony—"a mite of a pony" said he, leading it into the bedroom and making a determined effort to put it into the bed beside her. Elizabeth even forgave him that. She made herself pretty clothes and James was proud to take her to All Saints Church of a Sunday. They were, everybody said, "a handsome couple."

One by one the Dorsey clan moved from Newark to New York City. Bridgett continued to keep a sharp eye on her brood, particularly Elizabeth, to see that the easier life did not loosen her morals or weaken her faith. When the first child was born to the Cooneys on April 1, 1884, Bridgett Dorsey attended as midwife. The baby was born with a caul. Elizabeth named her—rather too fancily everybody thought—Loretta.

There is every evidence that from the time Elizabeth knew she was pregnant, her girlhood dreams of the theatre reawakened. It was common and somewhat scandalous knowledge in the family that time and again she braved James' displeasure to slip away and see the shows. Lily Langtry had made her American debut in "She Stoops to Conquer" and, enthralled by her beauty and charm, Elizabeth went half a dozen times or more to see her. Very possibly she hoped that the child within her would one day illumine the American Theatre as did the Jersey Lily. Whatever her dreams they closed themselves tight around her first-born. When the two other babies came along they were christened in quite pedestrian style, Elizabeth and Edward, and no trailing fancy came to light upon their heads.

At five, Loretta was already prone to fits of melancholy. There is a picture of her at that age. The large brown eyes with their extraordinary elevation of brow, gaze superciliously at the photographer. His blandishments do not move her; the sprig of holly he gave her lies forgotten in her hand. One senses a disenchantment with the world around her; only the white fur skin, on which she reclines so languorously, sends by secret channels a faint tingling to the center of her tiny being where, because of it, a small new dream of grandeur is about to be born. . . .

Loretta was chubby at five; she might have been ordinary-looking except for the eyes which mirror either intense expectation or tragic disappointment in what life has to offer. And what life has to offer is often relatively unexciting compared to what her fancy can manufacture. . . . She trots to the corner on an errand . . . often she goes on a mission for her mother to pick up pins or

thread or perhaps take a note to a neighbor. On her return
Grandma Dorsey asks pleasantly what she has been doing. Loretta
looks up with large solemn eyes which gradually light with pleasure. Errands she can tell about any day . . . this is something
special. "I went to the corner," she breathes, "and do you know
on the way home the grocer stopped his wagon and gave me a big
*pickle!*" Her eyes dance and she smiles at this triumph of adventure. "Child, child," says her grandmother, "I watched you
from the window every step of the way and surely no one stopped
you or gave you anything at all!" And the saints are called upon
and the Holy Virgin invoked to save the child from the sin of a
lyin' tongue.

Mount Morris Park was a fairyland for a child of five to play
in. In winter its hill (which was the most of it) sparkled with snow
and papa pulled you round and round on a little sled with curved
runners. You shoved your hands deep in the little fur muff mother
had made, and you wore a mystic smile. You were a princess and
this was your domain. In summer you pedaled a tricycle around
it, occasionally bumping the other children quite deliberately.
They were interlopers, they didn't really belong; you tolerated
them and that's about all. The bell in the old fire tower fascinated
you. It didn't toll for fires any more, but rang out curfew at nine
each night. Sometimes you waked up and heard it—Bong—Bong
—Bong—nine thunderous strokes. When you were five you liked
the sound for that meant the older kids were scurrying home
leaving your park quiet under the stars; enchanted, of course,
with its enchanted bell. Later when you were old enough to stay
out until nine, the bell became your enemy; especially on the long
summer evenings "when the beautiful dusk was falling and you
wanted to stay up in it and experience the dark that followed."
Bong—Bong—Bong! Whatever you were doing you had to stop
and fly like the wind, for if you were not home on the last stroke
a stern and righteous father was waiting, a father whose arm could
swing as hard and relentlessly as that bronze bell.

People began to fascinate you as you grew older. They were
like places—all different; some enchanting, some not. Their man-
nerisms fascinated you—the way their mouths opened, their heads

set, their hands moved. Chubby, almost stolid-looking, you would watch them, fists digging into either cheek and elbows riveted on knees in your concentration; only the eyes—windows of the imagination—dilated and at the same time veiled themselves, as though you were peeking out from behind a curtain the better to see what people did when they didn't think they were being watched. You began to be different "characters." Teachers knit their brows over the little girl who one day was excitable, highly animated, in true Latin style like her neighbors the Repetti girls, and who on the next was plunged in gloom, perhaps copied from Grandma Dorsey on one of her "bad" days. Then as likely as not as soon as school was out it was thirty double-skips without stopping, gloom forgotten in the joy of being the best skipper on the whole block.

Mother got onto your ways faster than anybody, but she didn't give you away—even to yourself—and you loved her for that. The day a bitter winter wind whipped tears from your eyes, you cupped hands over them and ran, preserving the little watery globes until you got home so you could throw yourself on mother's lap and pour out a tale of woe. She patted your shoulder and gently wiped the tears away and said, "There, there now!" so soothingly; and you knew, and she knew, it was a beautiful story to match those beautiful tears, and it was a favor you were doing to make anything so beautiful in a drab world.

Papa didn't understand at all. "They're lies-lies-lies!" he'd shout and pound his fist on the table. "You'll confess to the good priest, and promise the Holy Ghost to mind that lyin' tongue, or I'll . . ." It was a fearful temper he had and he towered over you with his red mustache working, eyes flashing. But you stiffened your spine and glared defiance. And presently you heard him saying, "It's work for the priest," and you knew that you were safe, for the time being at least.

The priest was another matter. He was a holy man sitting behind his curtain in the confessional, and you could tell him fearful tales of your sins and transgressions, knowing he was bound by holy vows to be silent. He always gave the same penance of five "Hail Marys" which you said with extravagant contrition before the altar at All Saints Church, and relished your saintliness as a

moment before you had relished your sins. Then one day he
passed you on the street and tweaked your ear and said, "And
have you been stealin' more apples from the pushcart, Loretta?"
and he wasn't a holy man any more, but a tattletale, a sinner himself against the Holy Ghost, who was the sacred repository of
your crimes. . . .

At an age when most children shake the fancies from their heads
and try to find themselves in the crude but very realistic social
structure of grade-school life, Loretta was simply spurred on to
greater imaginative endeavors. She decided to pick for herself
the "type" that would have the maximum social success. A little
French girl in her class at school enjoyed tremendous popularity.
Her accent was fascinating, her quick Gallic gestures adorable.
When Loretta was shifted to another school she remembered
these shining successes and introduced herself to her new classmates as "Laurice" who had not been long in this country from
"Gay Paree." It was so "difficile" to make oneself understood.
. . . Helpless little shrugs and quick fluttering hands made the
predicament charmingly clear. A group of breathless grade-school
males surrounded her and—as she had hoped—followed her home.
Unfortunately James was at the front door. She tried to pass him
with a friendly nod; but no. "Where is the door key, Loretta?" he
said very distinctly. "Under ze doormat, fazzer," she replied very
indistinctly. "Take out whatever is in your mouth," he roared,
"and speak plainly!" Her beautiful dream was pricked and her
followers melted away, snickering. Inside the house papa did not
wait for the priest to dole out penance; he administered it himself
with a heavy hand.

Papa was fun when he wanted to be. In certain moods he could
be as affectionately demonstrative as a giant puppy; Elizabeth
could not. She could work her fingers to the bone, be passionately
protective of her child, but she could not show affection. She had
the attitude of many who toil hard all their lives, that affection
is a luxury along with many other things that they cannot afford,
and to see another relaxed enough to give it, wrought a bitter
jealousy of the one whose emotional granaries were so easily filled.
This bond which might have been between father and daughter
was discouraged by Elizabeth because she could not participate;

and the one other—their mutual love of books—was also the cause of jealous pain to the mother. Though tolerant of her daughter's "imaginings," she flew into a rage if she found Loretta with her nose buried in a book, following the imaginings of another. It was then that her child was suddenly "good for nothing . . . lazy . . . coming to no good end." Didn't she know "there was work to be done" instead of "mooning over a book" and "growin' pale from the lack of the outdoors and healthy exercise?"—and all the rest of the endless embroidery of words the Irish use to cover the truth, which in this case was fear that her own illiteracy would expose her to ridicule from her daughter as it had from her husband.

Loretta found haven in the public library and there became a familiar hunched little figure as she devoured the works of Dickens, Sir Walter Scott and Mark Twain, the authors her father taught her to love. For hours the child would read, head lolling on crooked arm, as though it was not print she saw but a miniscule show played out before her on the long library table. The librarian came to look upon her as a fixture. A gentle nudge was often necessary to break her trance, and once while reading "Oliver Twist," Loretta sobbed so long and violently the good woman was forced to send her from the building.

It is a pity that what James could have given to his daughter was withheld, the companionship of their mutual interest in books and the warmth of easy affection, for it might have had a stabilizing influence on a nature which developed such stark singleness of purpose that many of the simpler havens of the spirit were never established. In later years, when that nature lost its home in the theatre, it wandered in an unmarked desert, and was without one single retreat to solace it.

Fancy wove into fancy, making a delightful prison from which on startling occasion Loretta would burst with a wild undreamlike energy to be the best skater on the block, the fanciest swimmer. Elizabeth had purchased a house at Spring Lake, New Jersey, where she took the children during the summers. It was there that Loretta, Bessie and Eddie had learned to swim. Characteristically, Loretta used the "overhand" stroke adding a back-feathering of the fingers which was very pretty if not particularly propulsive. She preferred to play with boys. She was healthy and strong and had the rough-and-tumble approach of the tomboy to all games and fun in general. Her romantic and glamorous musings were strictly reserved to her dreams and her play-acting.

At first James took this by turns boisterous and daydreaming child in stride except when she stirred her mother up to argument with him. "It's beautiful poetry she makes," Elizabeth would say after Loretta had finished some long fanciful tale of something that had never happened, "which ye can't appreciate because it's not in your books!" And her defense was not casual but violent, as though the child's fancy took root in her like another child and cried to be born. "They're lies I tell ye," James would shout back, "and it's nothin' but confession and penance on the floor of All Saints till her knees ache will cure the child!" And Loretta's knees did ache many a time with the cure. But it was a cure that didn't last. She'd be dreaming again, sitting on the high stoop of the Cooney house with eyes large as saucers, telling a breathless tale of an event too shining ever to be quite possible in mortal affairs.

The coquetry of the character "Laurice" had stirred something in James that had slumbered for a while—his suspicion of the arch and the gay in females. Physical chastisement became more and more frequently the end of each adventure for Loretta. He hung a whip on the back of his bedroom door; it was an ugly-looking whip with a knot from which spread separate leather thongs, a domestic version of the cat-o'-nine-tails. The younger children knew instinctively the whip was not for them, but to play absolutely safe were careful not to do anything to deserve it. Not so Loretta. The whip was her special property. If she dawdled after school and came home late, or went coasting or cycling when she had been told not to, or broke any one of the dozen rules her father laid down for her deportment, she made no attempt to cover up the delinquency or talk herself out of trouble. She would walk in the door, take down the whip and hand it to James with a hard bravado. Once she tied a crisp pink bow around the knot from which the thongs spread out. The ridiculous idea of the bow flipping up and down through the air as he applied it to her back made her laugh—in his face, of course. But he did not laugh. He was humorless about his daughter; if he had not been, he would have known that the whip would do no good. It brought out the rebel in her as nothing else could. One time as he reached for it she ran to the window and shouted at the top of her lungs, "Help! Police! Murder!"—not because she was afraid but because she wished to humiliate him. She never let him see that she was hurt. Many a time after a whipping she would climb into bed beside her younger sister Bessie, whose comforting hand could feel the rising welts on Loretta's back, her whole body racking with suppressed sobs. But Loretta never let her father see or hear her cry. She never gave him that satisfaction.

Loretta grew prettier as she approached her teens and was physically well developed for her age. Her childhood chubbiness had left a dimple in her cheek, but a burst of string-bean growth momentarily triumphed over its hold on the rest of her body. The eyes, when not veiled for inward visions, sparkled with mischief and fun, and bursts of irrepressible energy were always suggesting wild adventures.

These adventures, while they incensed James, primarily tickled Elizabeth's risibilities. She could hardly wait to regale her brothers and sisters with stories of what "that loon, Loretta, has been up to now!" She handled her daughter with humor—a quick, mordant, laughing humor which worked wonders. When it failed, the punishment was to lock Loretta in her room. That was *real* chastisement. Alone and with nothing to do, her imagination devoured her.

A major excursion into fantasy when she was twelve inadvertently became her first step toward the stage. The composition teacher at school asked her pupils to write the story of their lives. Loretta as usual considered the facts of her life too dull to bear repeating. "All the other children have fathers," she wrote, "but I have none. I am the illegitimate child of a Spanish count. When you look into my mother's great eyes you may realize at times that she is longing for faraway Spain."

The teacher asked her to read her composition to the class. If she thought Loretta would hesitate to brand herself publicly as a bastard, she was badly mistaken. Loretta read with such a wealth of feeling that she had herself in tears, and her audience visibly shaken. The news spread quickly through the neighborhood, and

James became acutely conscious of the rougher elements making the cuckold sign just out of his line of vision and the more sophisticated members of the grade-school set tittering and nudging each other as he passed.

The teacher hurried to Loretta's mother and explained she had not meant to embarrass the Cooney family but had hoped by a public exposure to shame the child into admitting her fabrications. Her intentions had boomeranged. She would like to help in some way if she could; the child was not really bad; she suffered from an overactive imagination and an effort should be made to employ that imagination constructively; she suggested singing, dancing, elocution, writing—anything that would utilize this power.

With the teacher's backing Elizabeth went to Ida Whittington to arrange for singing and dancing lessons for Loretta after school hours. Then she faced up to James. While he fulminated, she stood in front of him smoothing her sewing apron and straightening her spine, which was the way she had of riding out a storm once she was dead set on a course. It made her feel better to know she had an ace up her sleeve. "James," she said when he stopped for breath, "with a girl like that comin' into her womanhood, it's a good thing to see that she's properly occupied." She paused significantly. She knew James very well. She knew how his mind worked.

Loretta began her lessons with the grudging consent of her father. The teacher was delighted with her new pupil.

Miss Whitty was a big dark-skinned woman with thick mobile lips and a healthy animal vitality which gave a boom to her voice and triumphed over the limp of a crippled leg. She had never got vaudeville out of her blood. When Loretta went through a tap routine or delivered a song, she spotted the natural élan, the instinctive brightening and fusing of the whole personality which belongs to the born performer. Watching her, Miss Whitty felt like an old circus horse sniffing the tanbark; the child became not only pupil but protégé, and the teacher and Elizabeth schemed in secret how best to promote Loretta's chances in the theatre.

Loretta lost no time acquiring an audience for her flowering talents. She began to enliven the neighborhood with what became locally famous as "Vestibule Shows." "Hey, want to see a show?" she'd whisper to her classmates at recess. Then she'd tell them to come to the vestibule of some building at a discreet distance from the Cooney home. Those who gathered got a real show— costumes (rapid changes for each act behind the stairs), singing, dancing and recitations. Grownups stopped to watch and threw pennies and nickels. Loretta was proud as Punch. Sometimes she wandered home in a daze of success, costume still on. It might very well be a new dress belonging to one of Mrs. Cooney's customers, filched from a box and returned surreptitiously, pinholes around the waist, hem soiled. Elizabeth knew, but said nothing. One day she came on her daughter in the street, cheeks flaming with red paint extracted by vigorous licking from the rose petals on Elizabeth's hat, and hair glinting a brassy gold from flakes of radiator paint brushed through with a lavish hand. "Holy Saints!" breathed Elizabeth, looking quickly around for the fateful figure of James and propelling her bedizened child toward home as fast as she could. The important thing to Elizabeth was not why Loretta was so flamboyantly made up—she knew why; but that James should not see his daughter and punish her.

Elizabeth was vigilant as to Loretta's moral conduct, not as James was with the rack and the screw of suppression, but with a dynamic vigilance which usually managed to find harmless and satisfactory outlets for her daughter's terrific energies. In watching over the deep dreams of her own heart, she guarded and guided Loretta with instinctive wisdom; for Elizabeth's daughter and Elizabeth's dreams were, or soon became synonymous.

Years later, Loretta wrote: "It is a wonder I didn't end in prison instead of on the stage. And the reason I did not was because of my mother's patience and understanding. Bless her."

But not all Loretta's vagaries could be shielded from James, and the whip was a more and more frequent end of a lively adventure. What was worse for James' temper, mother and daughter became partners in crime. They took to going to see the shows at the Harlem Opera House on One Hundred and Twenty-fifth Street once a week, leaving the house at six and standing in line for two hours to get twenty-five-cent seats in the gallery. Their exits from home were tempestuous and their returns sheepish, but it made neither mother nor daughter less determined. All the stage favorites of the day played a week's engagement at the Harlem after their Broadway runs, and Elizabeth and Loretta saw the best of the theatre there: Joseph Jefferson (then a very old man) in "Rip Van Winkle"; James K. Hackett in "The Rivals"; Mrs. Leslie Carter—a beauty with long flaming hair—in "The Heart of Maryland." Ada Rehan, De Wolf Hopper, Anna Held, Ellen Terry and Sir Henry Irving all came to the Harlem.

Once the curtain rose Loretta grew oblivious to everything but the drama taking place upon the stage. Unconsciously she would begin to participate, mumbling and jabbering along with the actors, flinging out her arms in sudden gestures; until Elizabeth was forced to take hold of her and whisper sharply, "Shut up, you darn fool!" If the excitement grew too intense, the child would slide slowly down in the seat until almost resting on the back of her neck, as though to remove herself as far as possible from what was going on. When emotional impacts became unbearable, hands would press over ears and eyes would close. "You'd wonder who was givin' the show," Elizabeth would recount to her brothers and sisters, eyes dancing with mirth, "that darn fool Loretta or the performers!"

The two came home from these expeditions groggy with visions. Elizabeth rode out whatever storm was brewing in James' breast, laid her head upon her pillow unrepentant, and schemed far into the night how to give her daughter a chance in the bright exciting world of the theatre.

But the tension told on Elizabeth. She had never been physically strong. Headaches had racked her since she was a young girl. Despite her bravado, she feared her husband's outbursts which were growing increasingly violent, and still was bound to him with that strange passion that never was gentle, never bred understanding between them. She became Machiavellian in plotting to forward her daughter's career, and enjoyed a few small successes. At twelve, in the demurest costume in the world, Loretta sang at a church bazaar; and in another, quite as demure, recited "How Salvador Won" at a Knights of Columbus benefit. The cause being worthy, James conceded the point. But he didn't like it. And for mother and daughter a Knights of Columbus benefit was a long way from the glories of the Harlem Opera House.

"Mine was not a placid family," Loretta wrote years later, which was a considerable understatement. As a child and adolescent her life was almost pure of any example of emotional discipline. Her mother's temper was as violent as James' although it was quick and over in a flash—"like a summer storm," Loretta recalled. "Count ten before you lose your temper!" admonished Elizabeth one day, slapping her daughter smartly on the cheek. "Count it yourself before you lose your own!" answered Loretta, holding her aching jaw. And the next minute both of them were laughing. James *held* his anger—fed it for hours, even days. He had an unpleasant habit of scolding his daughter for some misstep and then saying, ". . . and tomorrow you'll have the whippin' for it." Knowing this, Loretta improved the shining hours in between by breaking all the rules she could think of, figuring she might as well be hanged for a sheep as a lamb.

All the emotional upheavals in the family centered around the one child; both parents seemed singularly indifferent to the two younger children. Loretta grew up finding a natural habitat in the center of an emotional storm. All of her life she had a tendency to brew them herself out of nothing, as though force of habit made her feel at home in them. With her own children, later in life, "scenes" took the place of any real discipline; in fact she mistook scenes for discipline, and in their absence felt vaguely that she was neglecting her duty as a mother.

If there was any peace left in the household when the Cooneys got through with their various forms of self-expression, a visit from Grandma Dorsey was sure to rile up what was left. Bridgett never ceased to sorrow that so many of her children were, in her estimation, lukewarm in their faith. "God is letting me live so long," she would say, "so that I can bring my children back to the Church." She was quite fiery in her crusade, and a visit to the Cooney ménage rarely ended without a blowup over theological matters. So cantankerous was Bridgett on the subject of the Catholic Church that even James, who alone could match her fervor, was driven to exclaim, "Ye'd think it was a corn on her toe the way she carries on about it!" Loretta when plagued by the dullness of life could always start some fireworks by shooting a

few theological questions at her grandma. Bridgett accepted everything Catholic, and could explain nothing. Questions posed by
her granddaughter such as, "How do you explain the Trinity?
How can there be Three in One?" sent her hopping up and down
with fury. How dare the child question the Holy tenets of the
Church! Another time, Loretta sidled up to her and asked blandly
why priests wore skirts. "Elizabeth!" Grandma shouted to her
daughter. "Are you going to let this little heathen question a holy
man?"

"I'm not," Loretta replied, "I'm asking you."

"You can't question a holy man!" bellowed Bridgett.

Elizabeth rushed her daughter from the room with a firm hold
on the ear. But she couldn't rob Loretta of her exit line; just as
she went over the doorsill, Loretta bellowed back, "Couldn't he
be just as holy in his pants?"

"I confess I conjured up these doubts because Grandmother
got so violent," Loretta said later. "I thought she was so fanatical
that even the Pope would object."

Years later when Loretta was a grown woman the two got to
be great friends. Each had an admiration for the stubborn spirit
of the other; apart from that neither gave an inch. Bridgett never
saw her granddaughter on the stage, and never referred to her
theatrical pursuits. When Loretta at last achieved stardom in 1910,
she made a special trip to see Bridgett at Spring Lake, hoping to
find her attitude slightly softened toward the theatre. The old
lady had not been well and was sitting in a rocking chair staring
gloomily out the window. "Well, Grandma!" Loretta called out
in a voice vibrant with the warmth and happiness of her success.
The old lady did not react. "Well, Loretta," she responded with
a sour commiseration that had a vibration all its own, "and how
does it feel to have your face on all the ash cans of the city?" That
was the only direct reference she ever made to her granddaughter's fame.

Bridgett lived to be almost a hundred years old and every day
of her life until she died recited a rosary for her actress-grand-
daughter's soul.

When her fingers grew too stiff to close round the small agate
beads, Loretta had a rosary specially made with beads of ivory so

large that when Bridgett first saw them lying in the box she cried out with childish delight, "Oh, look! Candy Easter eggs!" They hung from the arm of her rocker, and later by the side of her bed, and the clawlike fingers would close over them one by one and the lips move in prayer. Bridgett stored up benedictions a-plenty in Heaven for Loretta's soul, but not one ever passed her lips for her granddaughter's earthly career.

*

## La Belle Laurette

At last Loretta's opportunity came, not from the blue, but from the connivance of Elizabeth and Miss Whitty. A letterhead was printed by Mr. Henkle, announcing in large black letters: LA BELLE LAURETTE WILL GIVE IMITATIONS, RECITATIONS AND SING SONGS. It was embellished with four beautiful pictures of Loretta in a variety of costumes, one a military outfit to go with a song composed by Miss Whitty, "Military Molly." This was a tight-fitting blue coat with a double row of brass buttons and short pleated skirt, finished off with white busby and boots and little white drum slung from a shoulder strap. The letterhead was then mailed to every manager large and small listed in the New York *Clipper*, a paper covering news of the melodrama and variety circuits.

To their complete surprise an offer was received from Lynn, Massachusetts, for a one week engagement. Armed with this official document Elizabeth faced up to James; it was a real professional opportunity for Loretta to show what she could do, and it was only fair to the child, after all the lessons, to let her accept. Mother and daughter packed up with dour predictions from James as to what happens to a family that a mother deserts ". . . leavin' two birds in the nest cryin' out for a mother's care and no answer . . . encouraging a vain and lyin' child to expose

herself to the vulgar gaze of every Tom, Dick and Harry . . ."
etc., etc. Off they went—as innocent a pair as ever tried to carve
a career in the theatre, but ruggedly determined.

When Elizabeth discovered that the engagement was at a nickelodeon, she burst into tears and wanted to go home. In the strati-
fied popular theatre of the day the nickelodeon was next to the
lowest rung, that is, one rung above the curio hall of the dime
museums where freaks, sword swallowers and mummies were exhibited. There were the "Ten-twent-thirts," the variety shows
(forerunner of vaudeville), and at the top of the ladder, the fifty-
cent circuits which booked the best of the melodramas.

Nickelodeons did not even enjoy the blessings of a theatre;
they were a variety type show given in converted storerooms and
unoccupied buildings. A platform was erected and an improvised
curtain banged up and down between the acts. The audience paid
ten cents to sit down, a nickel to stand up. It meant ten or eleven
performances a day. It meant a noisy audience demanding every
penny of their money's worth and generally feeling they weren't
getting it. A piano player pounded away at an upright and to
discuss music cues with him was like trying to talk to a Hottentot
in Darkest Africa. Everybody—piano player, manager, fellow
Thespians—spoke in a vernacular that was totally incomprehensible to the two shaking neophytes. Elizabeth's grit deserted her;
she begged her daughter to go home, but to no avail.

The act did not go over at all. It consisted of an imitation of
Anna Held singing, "You're Just a Little Nigger But You're Mine
All Mine," in a fetching black poke bonnet with a rose over the
ear; and, after a rapid change of costume, a stirring recitation
of "How Salvador Won"—Loretta's old Knights of Columbus
stand-by.

The manager was kind, but at the end of the week advised Elizabeth to take her daughter home. "Neither of you know anything
about the theatre," he said.

They took his advice. Elizabeth put Loretta back in school and
went on an extended tour of the Catskills with James. Loretta was
thirteen years old.

When another offer came sometime later for a week's engagement at Gloucester, Massachusetts, Loretta trembled for her future. Would her mother go?

Elizabeth didn't know that she would; but then, the two younger children were looking peaked . . . there was no reason at all why James shouldn't take them down to the summer home at Spring Lake and give them a romp in the sun . . . school would be out next week. . . . "It's *customers* ye talk about instead of your own flesh and blood!" she said, raising her voice because James had begun to rumble. "I notice ye take no heed of the customers when it's your vacation that's in question! And besides —if you must know—the customers are all fitted to their summer wardrobes . . . the ones that count anyhow . . . and the divil take the rest!" And so it went, the "Irish embroidery" as Loretta called it, to hide the central fact that one's mind has been made up to pursue a certain course against all opposition.

James lost the argument, as he did most of them. Nonetheless he issued an ultimatum of his own: if this happened once again he would walk out and never return. Never! Was that clearly understood? Elizabeth had the grace to weep, but she and Loretta went.

Gloucester was a fisherman's town and the "theatre" was a storehouse by the wharves. Again "La Belle Laurette" was a flop. As she put it succinctly, "It was a question of who smelled to high heaven the most—the audience or my act." After the first performance the manager came around and reduced her salary from twenty-five dollars to fifteen dollars, and said if she didn't improve her act, he'd fire her. Elizabeth wanted to go home.

The Bernard Sisters (really mother and daughter) were the hit of the show. They wore identical white organdy dresses with large blue sashes and sang saucy songs. The mother had a diamond set in her front tooth. In the "spots" it gleamed like a tiny headlight. They tried to help Loretta with her act. "Military Molly" was Loretta's first song; it had plenty of *esprit de corps* but no sex appeal, according to the Sisters. "Give 'em a smell of the petticoats," the mother said. "Never mind the saluting!"

At the night performance Loretta delivered the song as follows:
They call me Military Molly (*Petticoats tossed up back instead of salute*)

I'm always bright and jolly (*Petticoats tossed up
    front instead of salute*)
I'm a patriotic soldier girl (*Wink at audience*)
Of good true blue (*Another wink*)
Etc., etc. . . . .
The Sisters contributed some of their old jokes:
        (To the piano player) "How many keys have you
            got there, professor?"
    "All that I need," sez he.
    "There's one missing," sez I.
    "Oh," sez he. "What one?"
    "The one to my room," sez I.
Elizabeth wanted to go home, but the "improvised" version of
the act did a little better and they stayed on to do four weeks
through the mill towns of Massachusetts, seven performances
a day. The manager from a burlesque house offered Loretta fifty
dollars a week if she would wear tights. That finished Elizabeth.
This time she did go home taking her daughter with her.

After the mill towns, Elizabeth was a chastened woman. She
applied herself to her languishing dressmaking business, and even
let her husband win a few arguments. Loretta pined. School was
impossible after her brief adventure in the theatre. She tried to
apply herself to her study books, but across the printed page two
saucy figures in organdy and wide blue sashes kicked and pranced,
footlights glowed and blobs of faces laughed. Her head filled
with rising volleys of applause and the stamping of booted feet,
and she would come to, staring into the stern face of a teacher
whose repeated commands to recite had been drowned out by the
inner hubbub. How to explain these things to people who didn't
understand what a wonderful and exciting place the world could
be? She began to relish the hours of the night when fancies were
undisturbed. She schooled herself to dream sequences of glamorous
adventures in which she was the heroine. Each night she took up
the story where it had been left off, unrolling it like a movie serial
to a finale of unprecedented splendor. Her days by comparison
were inexpressibly dull.
    When not absorbed in her fancies—either waking or sleeping

—she was terribly bored. And boredom made her do unpredictable things.

One summer evening walking listlessly down a hot Harlem street she saw a horse drooping between the shafts of an empty buggy. There seemed to be not a sound, not a movement, up and down the whole street—just the horse looking like the embodiment of the lifelessness that permeated the entire neighborhood. Without preliminary thought of any kind Loretta seized the buggy whip from its socket and brought it down smartly on the animal's flanks. He took off with a loud clatter of hoofs and crash of wheels against the cobblestones, and Loretta took off after him shrieking in demoniacal excitement "Runaway horse! Runaway horse!" The whole street came alive like an overturned anthill, and Loretta forgot her boredom in the glorious thrill of the chase.

By fourteen Loretta had grown extremely pretty. The little girl legs had filled out, and she was in rightful possession at last of many of the desired curves. Her nose was tiptilted, not fine-cut but saucy, and dark eyebrows contrasted strikingly with red-gold hair. Hers was a delightful femininity combined with a kind of little-boy forthrightness that was irresistible. Her beaux were legion. She tacked a list of their names on the wall of her room and it ran from ceiling to floor. She checked them off as in favor or out with extravagant whimsy as to reason. This highhandedness was mostly bravado; she was not really sure of herself with the opposite sex. Any display of feminine allure was pounced upon by her father as an indication that she was "no good." Swinging over to her mischievous tomboy side she met with the same disapproval and suspicion. She was neither fish nor fowl. Her moods of profound futility increased. More and more she gave herself to daydreams wherein she was glamorous and desirable. In real life she felt on surer ground with her beaux if she swam with them, cycled with them, played the rowdy for all it was worth. If one offered an awkward expression of puppy love, he ran the risk of a devastating laugh or a biting sarcasm. Occasionally she was smitten, and was more often than not abject about it. Papa with his bigotry had stamped her charms with a sense of guilt; and guilt does not mix well with confidence in love.

When Loretta was dismissed during her first year of high school as an intractable pupil, James abruptly took over her career. He enrolled her in a nearby business school for a stenographic course. She was to make herself useful, by God, or else! Elizabeth protested wildly, and for Loretta it was like being buried alive. But James was adamant. Singing and dancing lessons stopped. He saw to it personally that she got off to school on time and came home directly it was over. Every infraction of discipline won for her a sound whipping. If there was any loitering on the way from school it was taken for granted she'd "been up to no good." One evening he waited while skies darkened and the last of the school children scurried by with their books. No Loretta. At last it was completely dark and James set out to look for her. Fresh snow had fallen that day and coming to a hilly street James heard the gay excited cries of youngsters coasting. A sled slithered toward him piled four deep with kids "belly-whopping"; it seemed as if the driver was trying to steer between his legs. The next thing he knew James was flat on his back with the human pyramid tumbling off the sled beside him. On the bottom was his daughter! She had recognized him, knew she was in for a licking and decided to have some fun while she could.

He pulled her all the way home that night by the ear—seven long humiliating blocks. She never forgot it nor the whipping afterward; but she didn't cry.

Whippings are humiliating experiences for any adolescent child, all the more so for one who so often was a queen in her fancies, who had played to audiences obviously delighted by her feminine charms. There was a defiance that grew, and combined with the defiance was a deep unsureness of those charms; a definite split that the child preferred to widen between a world where she was constantly humiliated and a world where the dreams she had of herself were safe, where the illusion held, and even met with vociferous approval. And as time went on those two worlds developed one clear line of demarcation: the footlights of a stage.

Miss Whitty was not deterred by losing her pupil. More cards were printed and sent around to the agencies. This time they bore a verse composed by Loretta.

"What! Haven't you heard of Laurette?
The charming and gay soubrette,
Whose singing and dancing
Is simply entrancing.
What! Haven't you heard of Laurette?"

No response. Then Miss Whitty read in the *Clipper* that auditions were being held at Keith's vaudeville on 14th Street and told Elizabeth. Secretly they made preparations for the event. The act decided on was elaborate and much too long. First would come "Military Molly" in the little blue coat with the brass buttons (the tame version). Then, dressed in an organdy frock, "You're Just a Little Nigger But You're Mine, All Mine," recited for some obscure reason to a huge bunch of violets. After that a quick change into black plumed hat and short-skirted black taffeta dress and the rendition of a song (with French accent) that had been composed by a friend of Miss Whitty's. The lyrics were as follows:

"Laurette
My Pet
They tell me you are but a gay soubrette
And yet
I've set
My heart on winning yours, Laurette."

Miss Whitty's music was in kind.

With rugged optimism the three women decided on yet another number. As a finale Laurette was to appear in a padded gingham dress in *black-face* and sing a coon song. This staggeringly ambitious program was rehearsed assiduously by the three connivers.

Auditions at Keith's were harrowing affairs. The audiences, consisting entirely of agents and managers, gave short shrift to performers who did not immediately catch their interest. Many a young tyro who had barely begun a verse or started a dance routine was forced to flee the voluble disapproval of the audience or be jerked unceremoniously from sight by a long hook from the wings. Yet when the fateful moment arrived for Loretta she unrolled her full repertoire without interruption and in dead silence. At the finale the two women perspiring in the wings—more covered with burnt cork than the bouncing "mammy" on

the stage—thought surely a star had been born. Years later Loretta
met one of the agents who had been in the audience that day. The
truth was, he said, they all were so completely astonished at her
nerve, youngness, and the elaborateness of the presentation that
they had literally sat spellbound for the duration.

The seed of Loretta's talents scattered so lavishly at the Keith
audition fell on stony ground. No offer came. Elizabeth applied
herself to dressmaking and Loretta went back to her dreams. The
dreams were tinged now with melancholy, that haunting adolescent fear of being a misfit. "Nobody wants me in the theatre,"
she brooded sitting on the brownstone steps of her home, "I'm no
good at school any more. . . . I hate typing. . . . I hate business.
. . . I'm neither a child nor a woman—just an old lady of fifteen!"

Some younger kids bounced up and down on the pavement below her, skipping rope. "Salt—pepper—mustard—vinegar. . . ."
She used to be the best double-rope skipper on the block but she
was too old for that now. . . . "Laurette . . . My Pet. . . ." She
saw herself doing that little back flip with her skirt which the
Bernard Sisters had taught her . . . heels together . . . bounce
up . . . flip . . . down. . . . Blobs of faces over the footlights
laughed and hands clapped delightedly. She turned and winked.
"I'm a patriotic soldier girl . . . Of good true blue. . . ."

Loretta stamped her foot sharply on the stone stoop and dug
her fists into her cheeks. What was the good of thinking about
that?

. . . She remembered she'd sent a "Black Hand" note to the
new boy down the street—a crudely printed warning that if he
didn't notice her she would do something desperate. . . . He
hadn't answered—and he hadn't noticed her. And to that other
one—he must be eighteen or more—she had mailed a picture of
herself in one of her stage costumes inscribed "The One and
Only Laurette." He had returned it without comment and turned
his head the other way when he saw her on the street. Dead ends
. . . all dead ends. . . . "Why, my parents won't let me marry
'til I'm eighteen—three years 'til I can have a baby!"

Slap-slap-slap went the ropes on the pavement. Suddenly with
one of her lightning changes of mood Loretta was down the
steps, grabbed the rope from one of the kids and was jumping

like mad! "One-two-three-four . . ." She used to do a hundred with a double jump at every ten. . . ."Thirty-six, thirty-seven, thirty-eight . . ." She was beginning to puff. Time was a termagant making her blow at fifteen as she never had done at twelve! "Sixty-two, sixty-three"—oh, to heck with it! She didn't want to skip anyway, she was too old.

Out of the corner of her eye she saw an elegant pair of boots standing stock-still beside her. She followed them up to well-pressed trousers, a tan frock coat, a vest to match with imposing watch chain, satin lapels, and the handsomest face she had ever seen, under a tan sombrero! And he was watching *her!* She skipped like one possessed—double jumps at every five instead of every ten! At last she reached the coveted hundred, and handed the rope back to its owner. The stranger turned and gravely watched the other child jump. Loretta stood spellbound. She had never seen anyone so elegantly dressed. She thought he must be a Frenchman—or a cowboy. Suddenly he turned back and asked her a question: could she tell him where Miss Whittington lived? Loretta must have looked slightly demented—and *very* beautiful. She couldn't speak, what with her astonishment and the hundred skips; her cheeks were flushed and her eyes were wide at this apparition of elegance; dumbly she raised a finger and pointed to Miss Whitty's house. He doffed his sombrero with great gallantry and departed across the street.

Loretta flew into the house, madly brushed at her disheveled locks, pinched her cheeks, although they were already flaming, and tore over to Miss Whitty's. But there was no answer to the bell. Apparently teacher and visitor had departed.

The next day as soon as she had an opportunity, Loretta was back again inquiring about the handsome stranger. His name was Charles Taylor, Miss Whitty said, a playwright and producer, and an old friend of hers. He had just returned from the West for a production of one of his melodramas on Broadway. Did Miss Whitty think he would give her a part? Miss Whitty did not. He was one of the top writers of melodrama, and could have his pick of the actors trained in that school.

Loretta lingered just long enough to wangle Charles Taylor's address, a theatrical boardinghouse in the Bowery. Then, with-

out returning home, she was off on foot to find him. To take a
horsecar that distance was a long trip; to walk took the better part
of the afternoon. When she pulled up in front of Charles Taylor's
door, it was already growing dark. One look at the young blonde
head, the blurted confession that she had come all the way from
Harlem to offer her services as an actress, and Charles was out the
door steering her firmly by the elbow into the first cab he could
find. The trip uptown was made at record speed. Even with such
expedition, they arrived at the Cooney doorstep long after the
curfew had tolled its final warning.

James met them at the door. There was a fearful scene. Elizabeth was away and could not intercede. At first he insisted upon
an immediate marriage, but Charles, always a glib talker, managed
to convince him of his entire innocence in the matter. James
turned on Loretta. Everything he had predicted for her had come
true . . . she was a strumpet and a hussy, runnin' after men and
her own dishonor like a common streetwalker! It all came of
traipsin' around in the low theatrical circles she and her mother
seemed to prefer . . . she might be fifteen and think she was a
woman grown, but, by God, he'd whip her so she'd never forget
this night!

While the tirade raged Charles beat a strategic retreat.

Something stopped James from carrying out his threat. There
was in Loretta all her life an extraordinary innocence that never
left her; it was one of the most palpable facets of her personality,
and this night it must have been obvious with the obviousness of
a shining light, even to the thick-headed James. He compromised.
With some dim elephantine sense that he might be laughed at for
this sudden tolerance after all his outbursts, he swore Loretta to
absolute secrecy about the day's events. It was not to be mentioned,
especially to her mother. "It would break her heart most surely,
and bear on her conscience for the loose ways you've learnt pur-
suin' your unholy mummeries . . ." and so on, and so on.

Loretta promised. If she had known how soon she would see
Charles Taylor again and with what a dizzying effect on her
career, she might not have mounted the stairs that night to her
room with the words "dead end . . . dead end . . ." punctuat-
ing each lagging footfall.

Several long, long months later, into Loretta's bleak life shot a ray of hope: an offer came by mail to play a week's engagement at the Boston Athenaeum. This time it was up to Elizabeth to choose between her husband and her daughter's career. There was no question about it; if she went with Loretta, James walked out. To his lasting chagrin his wife chose to go with her child. What's more she took him at his word, closed the house, and sent the two younger children down to her sister Kate's at Lake Como. Perhaps he had intended to return after a bout of drinking to drown his humiliation, perhaps he did return to the house to find it dark and ghostlike with shades drawn and sheets covering the furniture. Poor James! who had only his easygoingness to offer his family, and had even that torn up into so useless and valueless a thing by the almost mechanized drive of his wife's and his daughter's ambition.

At the Athenaeum, Loretta stuck to her tried-and-true numbers: when she recited "How Salvador Won," she wore a white silk jockey outfit, whipping a little quirt against her boots; for a sweet-young-girl number, pink organdy; and lastly there was the peppy version of "Military Molly." She came on just after an exhibition bout by James J. Corbett, and launched into her first number over the din of scuffling boots as half the audience unceremoniously took leave following this main event. It was an unpropitious start. But, although Loretta was unaware of the fact, Fate sat in the audience that night in the form of none other than the handsome Charles Alonzo Taylor.

Taylor was known at the turn of the century as "Master of Melodrama." Along with half a dozen other prolific writers, he strewed the country with melodramas. In 1898, he had five shows running on Broadway simultaneously and half a dozen companies on tour. His royalties were $1,250 a week from the Broadway shows alone, a top sum for a playwright at that time. Currently, he was casting a number one road company for one of his most popular shows, "King of the Opium Ring." Accompanied by his young son, Charles Edward, he had come to see the one-act thriller "The Dope Fiends" played by Hosmer and Ross, old friends of his. They slipped into their aisle seats just as La Belle Laurette pranced onto the stage snapping her riding whip, flashed

a brilliant smile and launched into "How Salvador Won." Charles
was transfixed. He recognized her immediately as the youngster
who only a few months before had stood on his doorstep. He sent
his card backstage and as soon as the act was over went around to
sign her up for forty weeks as soubrette for his show.

Taylor was a complete stranger to Elizabeth but there were
unmistakable vibrations in the dressing room between Charles
and Loretta. Neither, for obvious reasons, gave any indication of
having met before, but Elizabeth sensed something. At this crucial moment in Loretta's career Elizabeth turned narrowly suspicious. She wanted no part of Taylor's offer. She eyed his fawn-
colored coat, his fancy vest, and fawn-colored sombrero with ill-
concealed disapproval; he was far too resplendent a figure to be
respectable to her way of thinking. "My girl's too young to be
traipsin' round the country without a chaperon," she stated with
an air of finality. Loretta groaned. "You have a wife who travels
with you, I suppose?" Elizabeth suddenly shot at him, glancing at
the fidgeting boy at Charlie's side.

No, replied Taylor, his wife was dead, but there would be an
older woman in the company; in fact he had come to Boston to
sign Harriet Ross and her husband Bert Hosmer, for the show.
Mrs. Hosmer was a woman of splendid character, an old friend,
and she would see to it that the girl was chaperoned at all times.

Elizabeth set her lips in a thin line. "Deed's not done," she
snapped, "and besides I know nothing of the woman—except that
at the moment she plays a dope fiend." Loretta wanly rubbed the
make-up from her face, stealing desperate glances now and then
at Taylor. Elizabeth took a deep breath, smoothed down the
front of her dress and straightened her spine. She had made a decision. "Can't be done," she said, "unless you sign me to a forty-
week contract, too."

"If that's the only way I can get her, you're signed," Taylor
said. And the deed was done.

Elizabeth toured the forty weeks. "King of the Opium Ring"
billed as the genuine "inside story" of life in San Francisco's
notorious Chinatown, was the worst kind of claptrap but very
much what the audience demanded in the popular theatre of the
day. Its most sensational scene was the rescue of the heroine from

a second-story window by a trio of Chinese acrobats standing on each other's shoulders. To quote an enthralled reviewer: "The topmost man receives the form of the unconscious heroine into his arms from the second-story window of a Chinese den, the living column moves across the stage, and the lady is thrust through another second-story window into the arms of her friends."

Besides the acrobats, a Chinese family—mother, father and two babies—traveled with the company; also two Shetland ponies, forty-three inches high. Before each performance the babies, dressed in native garb, were driven round the town behind the ponies to advertise the show. Family and ponies also took part in the big Chinese festival scene in the last act. Taylor hired fifteen or twenty extras in each town to augment this scene. He passed out firecrackers, and inflated pig bladders for performers to whack over each other's heads or deflate to make a rude *who-oo-oshing* sound. He instructed the crowd to "make merry." Occasionally the scene got completely out of hand, the merrymakers throwing firecrackers into the audience, chasing each other with the pig bladders, and pulling the queues of the Chinese actors with more realism than art. Loretta played Lizzie Mulvey, a tough urchin of Chinatown, and won a nice notice as a "beautiful and clever little soubrette whose work is praised by the most competent critics."

Taylor was charmed by his soubrette. His next play was written for her, and he had it ready at the end of the forty weeks. It was called "Child Wife." Elizabeth was to sign another forty-week contract immediately—a double one for mother and daughter if that was the way it had to be.

But Elizabeth had had enough. No, she couldn't go. She had neglected her other two children long enough and had her own livelihood to make. "And I'd just as soon do it without Chinese babies in my lap and ponies and acrobats for travelin' companions! Besides, how do I know if that good-for-nothing James can get along without me? I'll wager as soon as I open my door he'll blow in like an old newspaper." No, it couldn't be done; that is, unless—Elizabeth was about to play her ace. If her daughter was married now . . . *that* would be another matter entirely. All Charles needed was a hint. And to Loretta with star dust in her eyes and the glamorous figure of the "Master of Melodrama" at her feet, it was the easiest solution in the world. They were married early in the year 1901 and immediately went on tour with his new opus "Child Wife." The title was eminently appropriate. He was a man of thirty-six, already twice married, with a ten-year-old son, and Loretta was sixteen. Both his and Elizabeth's savings were in the show, and the program read, "Costumes by Madame Cooney."

*

# Charles A. Taylor— "Master of Melodrama"

Charles Alonzo Taylor had had a checkered career before he brought his effulgent presence backstage at the Athenaeum to dazzle La Belle Laurette. He was the son of Dwight Bixby Taylor, a successful photographer of Greenfield, Massachusetts, veteran of the Grand Army of the Republic and old Indian fighter. The Taylors were proud of being related, through Dwight's mother, Dorothy Bixby, to the Mrs. Bixby to whom Abraham Lincoln wrote his famous letter of condolence upon hearing of the loss of her five sons in the Civil War. While Mrs. Bixby's sacrifice was not as heroic as was first believed, two of her sons having deserted and one returned wounded, she nonetheless became a symbol in American history of a mother's sacrifice in war, and the Taylors remained proud. They were also related to Emily Dickinson through a branch of the family which resided, and lived to vast and respectable ages, in Amherst. Zachary Taylor, doughty soldier and President of the United States, was supposedly on the family tree, but this was vigorously questioned by one upright member of the Amherst clan. "I can't believe it," wrote the lady.

"They say his vest was always stained with tobacco juice, and all the Taylor men—regardless of occupation—were so neat."

Dwight was born in Amherst. According to family records, his grandfather, Moses Taylor, owned part of the land on which Amherst College was subsequently built, and he and his son Stillman, Dwight's father, planted the big elms that grace the Amherst campus. The Taylors were of stern Puritan stock—sea captains, soldiers, and in trade. From their portraits it is clear that each would look askance at a descendant who sought his fame and fortune in the theatre.

Charles' father loved the out of doors and his wife, a frail woman, needed it for her health. Dwight Bixby Taylor constructed what he called a "View Wagon" in which he could expose and develop his photographic plates, and in this the whole family took to the road each summer as soon as the weather was clement. Those early years of traveling around the lovely New England countryside behind Old Maud, the gray mare, and camping at night on some likely spot, imbued young Charles with a love of travel and of the wide-open spaces that remained in him all his life. In 1869, the family uprooted and went West because of his mother's failing health. Dwight Bixby settled in Oakland and became chief operator for Bradley and Rulofson, photographers well known in San Francisco. Charlie's mother died in Oakland when he was thirteen.

The West was a magical place for Charlie and the most magical thing about it was the little "Iron Horse" still pushing its way through valley, desert and mountain. He used to go down to the marshes where they were building a roadbed across the Oakland Mole and stand close to the tracks to watch the engines go by. He made friends with the engineers, and occasionally they would hoist him aboard and let him ring the bell and throw wood into the firebox.

He loved to tell of the engineer Johnny Bigbeard, who could spit a stream of tobacco juice out the cab window and turn over a tarantula crawling beside the track better than a boy could do it with a blowgun; of Dan Driscoll who was pinned under his engine in the marshlands and drowned as the tide rose while the crew stood helplessly by. They were fascinating tales. He was a romantic kid, and his imagination cut truth and fancy to a beautiful pattern, each improving on the other as he recalled the past. He and Laurette were well matched in that if nothing else.

He began to pick up odd jobs around the yards. One was to couple and uncouple the cars. The men in the yards got youngsters like Charlie to do it because in those days the operation had to be done by hand and it was a distinct advantage to be small and agile when the heavy couplings came together. Once he had to finish a job for a predecessor who hadn't been quite agile enough. The coupling was still covered with blood.

The first locomotive Charlie rode hauled gravel for the roadbed. He called it the little "Carry Pebbles." It was a six-ton engine with a four-wheel drive; he and the engineer used to push it off the turntable together. Later he was made assistant fireman on the "Little Felton" that ran from Oakland to Los Gatos, the head of the rail line at that time. "I fired her with two-foot and four-foot wood picked up along the track. As we started up the long grade the engine would talk to me, slowly and laboriously, 'Oh, Charlie Taylor, four-foot logs— Oh, Charlie Taylor, four-foot logs——' Then as she pushed over the top and started down grade she began to chatter, 'Two foot'll do! Two foot'll do! Two foot'll do!' "

He loved the little locomotives he rode in the early days. They were alive to him.

In the year 1883, he took boxcars jammed with Chinese out onto the desert to help build the railroad from the Mojave to Needles, and later was put in charge of the water train that kept them alive. His experiences in those days formed the basis for many of his melodramas afterwards. Life was cheap and water was precious on the desert. You had to be tough to survive. He learned a lot from the Chinese; he ate their rice and drank their tea and saw many a white man older and tougher than he break under the desert heat. The few human indentations made on the desert by a railhead or a water-supply station like Daggett or Hinckley, consisted of a saloon, an eating place, and a "hotel." Amusements were drinking, gambling, fighting and—if a woman of any description were adventurous enough to be around—lively shooting affrays over her favors.

When the road was finished, he collected fares and made a lot of money. The fare was ten cents a mile on a strictly cash basis. There were few ticket agents as yet. Charlie's bosses instructed him to "leave the rails and enough to run the railroad" and no questions asked. Fares were often paid in twenty-dollar gold pieces by restless adventurers and others who found it expedient to move on in a hurry; and there was no change.

Charlie was an astonishing boy for one living in such a milieu. Exposed to every temptation of this rough and lawless life of the West—saloons, women, easy money, the chicanery of gang bosses; the hardening spectacle of the Chinese workers herded like beasts under the torturing desert sun—entirely undisciplined within himself and with no discipline over him, he yet maintained a personal detachment from his surroundings, and above all, an eye for life as an essentially humorous spectacle which kept him free from the debaucheries of spirit that such a life might easily have engendered.

Another faculty which operated as a balance wheel was his love for, and remarkable affinity with, the dumb creatures of the world. In the caboose in which he lived on the Mojave he kept a pet fox, a Gila monster, some horned toads and several snakes for company. He slept with the fox, which he tied up in a canvas bag with only its head out, so the claws wouldn't scratch him. The snakes he kept for "watch dogs"; they would hiss and stir long before the human ear caught the sound of someone's approach. A friend, Joe Janes, who worked with him on the railroad, remembered a pet badger that followed Charlie from car to car as he collected fares. All during his life it was characteristic of him, when he got any money ahead, to buy a farm or a piece of land, someplace where he could have animals around him.

His children remember him at his best: walking to a streetcar in a small New Jersey town every morning, his little black and white pig, "Trotty," tagging behind him to "see him off" at the corner; riding like the wind bareback down a Long Island lane—"Indian style" he called it—one hand lightly twisted in the horse's mane, horse and rider, one; holding Biddy, the buff-colored bantam cupped in one hand, talking to her—and Biddy talking back, until her husband grows jealous and jumps up in Charlie's other hand and all three of them talk together. He could stand in a barn and call a mouse no bigger than a blown dandelion head, and after she appeared, call her mate—both by name, of course. They would sit side by side on a beam looking at him with beady little eyes as much as to say: "Well, Charlie, what's new?" He claimed there was only one creature in the world that never developed a personality no matter how long you lived with it and that was a side-winder. He knew, because he tried to make pets of them on the desert. "They never learned to tell me from a stranger, and I never could tell one of them from another."

While still in his teens he became passenger conductor on the Oakland-Tulare run; the youngest conductor in California. In Tulare he was known as "Handsome Kid Taylor." Women adored him. His attitude toward them was a mixture of gallantry, humor and arrogance which, along with his handsome looks, apparently was irresistible.

His hearing was impaired in a railroad wreck at Tehachapi while still a young man. Instead of shaking his confidence, it bolstered a natural arrogance and as time went on he used his deafness more and more as a convenient device for maintaining the center of the stage. By the time he met Laurette it had become a club for silencing others and had not a little to do with their many spats; Laurette also liked the center of the stage.

It was another railroad wreck that served as a stepping stone to his writing career. He was conductor on a Pullman that was carrying Governor Leland Stanford on a speaking tour throughout the state. In the party was Senator George Hearst, father of William Randolph Hearst. Making up lost time outside of Modesto, the train went out of control. Charlie's quick action in applying the emergency brake saved the rear Pullman, in which the governor's party was traveling, from leaping the track. Charlie and the governor became fast friends. Hearst gave him a one-hundred-dollar bill, and told him, "If you ever need a job, go see my son Billy in San Francisco."

As a boy Charlie was fascinated by the theatre. He met many of the stage celebrities of the day when they came to his father's studio to be photographed, and he and his father were often guests of the stars at shows at the Market Street Theatre in San Francisco. He was a natural showman himself and, after becoming a railroad conductor, put on skits and minstrels in Tulare between runs. The S.P. shops were located there and the town was full of lively young men whom he recruited for his productions. Charlie was himself an excellent singer and dancer and his audacious manner on the stage captivated his audience. It was after one of these shows that he met his first wife, Emma McNeill—"a little Irish girl with a sprinkle of freckles across her nose and a twinkle in her eye." He fell in love with her at once and they were married the third of June, 1888. Theirs was a tragically brief life together; she died on Christmas Day, 1890, shortly after the birth of her son. After her death Charles sold his home in Tulare and gave up railroading. Remembering the senator's suggestion, he went to see William Randolph Hearst about a job on the San Francisco *Examiner*. The city editor put him to work as a special-feature writer.

One thing became quickly evident: Charlie couldn't stick to facts; he couldn't even stick to the story he was supposed to report. Sent to cover a fire he came back and wrote two columns on a kitten he had found stuck in a tree and the efforts of the citizenry to get it down. Before he had finished with this simple tale he would as likely as not have a family of Chinese acrobats forming a ladder of mercy (à la "King of the Opium Ring"), a rich old lady promptly endowing a home for cats—with this particular cat the first inmate—and, possibly, a young virgin on her way to a nunnery, pausing with moist eyes to view this last heart-warming scene before convent walls close round her.

The editor took it like a man the first two or three times— after all, the senator had asked him to be nice—but finally he exploded. "Young man," he said in a voice of ill-concealed exasperation, "you've missed your calling. Go write melodrama!" Those were fateful words.

Where truth stopped and melodrama began from then on would be difficult to say. Charlie made many claims to adventure and it is hard to sift them all. He became quite a figure in the Yukon where he took hardy troupes of players into the gold towns. He claimed to have met the daughter of the captain of the *Mary Dear,* the "only living person who knew where the treasure of Cocos Island was buried"—and that together they sailed to the Island. As many times as he told the story the outcome remained obscure. In an interview he gave in his late sixties, when he had made a short comeback in motion pictures, he again recounted this tale. This time he decided to write *finis* to it. With the calm of a man who has seen everything, he announced to the startled reporter, "We found the treasure."

There was really no need to paint the lily. His life held color and excitement a-plenty.

He relished melodrama. Melodramas were stereotyped in form. Plot, characterization and dialogue served merely as a rigging for physical heroics and mechanical effects. Villainy was punished and virtue triumphed. Besides the hero and heroine, there was the adventurer, the rube and the foreigner—each character behaving one hundred per cent true to type. No subtlety was needed or required. Charles rapidly became a leader in the field. It was natural for him to think in terms of "stalwart heroes" and "trembling virgins"; a black-and-white code of morality fitted neatly over his past experiences. Tarts, gang bosses, gamblers, unprotected young girls and bewildered old ladies were the everyday cast of characters in his early adventures in the West. He himself was the dashing young man of unassailable honor, and the Chinese laborer, whom he knew so well, the natural toby * of the piece. All the ingredients of melodrama were there. Charles had only to stir the pot, dip in his pen, and win for himself the enviable title, "Master of Melodrama."

He produced his first melo at the Bijou Theatre in San Francisco in 1891. It was called "The Devil's Punch Bowl," and later became one of his big successes under the title "Yosemite." He claimed he got his inspiration while sitting neck deep in a water-tank car gazing out over the austere majesty of the Mojave Desert. Charles staged the production, managed the front of the house, posted the bills, and netted $3.25. In the next fourteen years he wrote twenty melodramas. All but one made money.

* Melodrama lingo for *Patsy*.

# Child Wife

At the time he met Laurette, Charles exuded the plush well-being of the successful playwright and producer. He was tall—over six-foot-two—and lanky. His features were sharply defined, with the rocklike cast of his Puritan ancestors. In repose his face was deceptively solemn, which made his ribaldry and flashes of humor come as a surprise to those who did not know him well. Poor or rich he was a natty dresser. Women besieged him. His manner toward them was a mixture of lofty arrogance and sentimental worship in the rather phony "Meet-Me-Tonight-in-Dreamland" tradition. Laurette's extreme youth and inexperience awakened the latter emotion, while his arrogance took the form of wishing to "mold her nature," place her at the top of the acting profession as his "creation." He referred to her as "this child whom I have rescued from the wolves of Broadway." He thought her large eyes and awe-struck admiration denoted a nature soft and malleable. He was to find out his mistake. And she was to suffer some cruel disillusionment through him. However, for the moment she accepted his adoration at face value, and the day they were married all was syrup and light. It must have seemed to Laurette that from that day forward her path in the theatre would be upward. In high spirits husband and wife set out in Taylor's *chef-d'œuvre* "Child Wife."

It is not altogether clear why "Child Wife" failed so dismally. Maybe it was because Charles, carried away by the sweetness of his young bride-to-be, had written a sentimental little play with —as one critic put it—"no shooting, no fireworks and no red fire." The audience, used to being "hopped up" by mock heroics, may have found it too tame.

Misadventure dogged the tour. After several performances outside of New York the title of the play was changed. Handbills announcing its advent on Broadway read: "Introducing La Belle

Laurette in 'Daughter of the Diamond King.' " There was a picture of Laurette looking incredibly young and moonfaced. Actually, Newark was as close as the company ever got to Broadway.

Charles courted disaster throughout the tour by using, in a big classroom scene, fifty school children, recruited locally. In Butte, Montana, some of the boys found their stage debut on the opening night a heady experience, and the next night they played hookey to kibitz the scene from the gallery. They razzed their erstwhile stage classmates all through the schoolroom scene, and one of the group, feeling an urge to express his dramatic instincts, lay in wait for the hero in the big climax of the show.

The hero is an electrical inventor who loses his reason but regains it just in time to exonerate himself from the calumny of the villain, win back the love of his child wife and prove the success of his invention. This scene, as one reviewer put it, had the audience on the "nettles of suspense." Slowly the actor spoke his lines: "My reason has returned. My wife has come back." He reached to throw the switch of his machine. At this point the would-be Booth could contain himself no longer. "My contract is fulfilled!" he yelled, leaving the actor literally speechless, and the audience in hysterics. Backstage, Laurette was blazing with fury. As soon as the curtain fell a terrific commotion started in the gallery. Charles sprinted up the stairs and found his young wife attempting singlehanded to eject the culprits from the theatre. In reminiscing he used to say, "That took real courage. I never saw anyone so tough!" But at the time he roundly scolded his wife for being the biggest "hoodlum" of the lot.

The piece continued its forty-week tour across the country. It was scheduled to play the Cordray Theatre, Portland, Oregon, on September 14, 1901, the day President McKinley died. The performance was called off that night out of respect to the murdered President.

The fifty-cent circuits could be the slowest death in the world because as long as a half a dozen customers paid the fifty cents you played the show. Maybe you skipped town afterward, leaving the hotel bill unpaid, and had to soothe the unpaid actors with promises of riches in the next town, but you played the show.

Like showfolks everywhere the troupe buoyed itself with the hope that the next stand would be better and the show would click, and went on. But in Deadwood, South Dakota, financial strangulation overtook the "Daughter of the Diamond King." *

Taylor got the remnants of his company to Seattle, put on a series of shows trying to recoup his losses. Laurette went into the leads.

Laurette, seriously tackling the histrionics of melodrama, was soon disillusioned. Scenes were stilted and lifeless, virtually unplayable. The imp got the better of her and she would play them for laughs. Charlie lectured her. You believed completely in what you were saying and doing, and made the audience believe, no matter how silly it seemed. "Believe it, and the audience will believe it." She learned the lesson well. In 1905, when she was on tour in one of Charlie's most popular successes, "Queen of the Highway," a distinguished Eastern critic wrote: "Miss Taylor has arrived just in time to prevent the word ingénue from passing into a term of contempt, for too many of the actresses who afflict this line of business are remarkable only for their affectation and . . . shrill discordant voices. . . . Miss Taylor is a charming contrast to this ilk. She is delightfully natural and artless and apparently unconscious of her many attractions and the effect she is producing." But that was later. Those first attempts in 1901 to struggle with Charlie's lurid prose got Laurette's funny bone. Their initial production was "Escaped from the Harem" and one of its more pulsating moments was a scene between the Oriental Prince and the lovely Lola Montez (Laurette), his unwilling captive.

Prince (hand on Lola's shoulder): "What are you gazing at, my dear?"

Lola (drawing herself to her full height): "I—prefer—to—bathe—in—private!"

For two nights Laurette read it as written, then the line stuck in her throat. "I couldn't have said it again for a five-dollar raise.

---

* Later William Koegh produced the play in New York starring his wife, Dolly Kemper, a Harlem neighbor of Laurette, who went on the original tour. It was then financially successful and toured for a year.

When the Prince said his slaves would prepare me for the plunge, I walked over to him and in the friendliest spirit in the world replied, 'It's a funny thing—but I'm a funny girl—I always lock my bathroom door when I take a bath.' "

The audience roared with astonished laughter, then applauded. Charlie was furious when she came off. She had r-r-ruined his piece. She said she hadn't; the audience had both laughed and applauded; what more did he want? She read the line the same way the next night and asked him to listen. With a showman's acumen and no humor (he never had any about his own melo-drama), he realized the torrid moment had turned to one of laughter *and* a more limpid virtue. "Go ahead, Laurette," he told her. "It will bring in a better class of people."

But Laurette chafed under the restrictions of these pieces. She wanted to test herself in a role with real dramatic opportunities. She made a compromise with her husband; she would play his melodramas with absolute seriousness if he would let her do a straight dramatic role. Charles conceded the point. He put on a pirated version of Goethe's "Faust" and Laurette played Mar-guerite. She never forgot the thrill of her first "long dress" part.

Shortly after this portrayal Laurette found she was pregnant, and these two major events in her life became inseparable in her mind. In her spare time she began making baby clothes and on each garment embroidered the name "Marguerite." She played leads until her pregnancy could no longer be adequately con-cealed. Then she took small walk-on parts of maids and messenger girls, carrying trays and bundles to disguise her condition.

Although artistically successful the Seattle venture never got off the "cuff." It was the depth of the theatrical depression in the Northwest. Charlie, moreover, was not one to stint on production or "effects." He poured money into them, letting the actors go unpaid from week to week. In this instance the payroll was never met and finally amidst ominous rumblings from the unhappy troupe Charlie was forced to close up. With a certain sense of rough justice he invited them to one square meal before abandon-ing them to their fate. He had come upon an old law that said a hotel could not refuse to serve a pregnant woman, so Laurette ordered quantities of food sent to their room and the actors gathered for one last feast. Charlie also ascertained that it was illegal to lay hands on a woman carrying a child. Every time there was a knock on the door Laurette jumped upon the one trunk in which all their belongings were packed. When it came time to board the train Charlie and a friend carried the trunk down the stairs and out the door, Laurette still perched on top.

In Chicago they ran out of funds. Laurette wired her mother for the fare to New York. She was terribly tired and had to have rest before going on, so Charles got a room at a cheap hotel. Again a frustrated management, learning that the couple had no money, besieged the room trying to throw them out. The weary Laurette took up her vigil on the trunk. In Seattle it had seemed a lark; in Chicago it was torture. Elizabeth sent the fare but there was not enough to pay the hotel. This time the trunk had to be left behind. In it were all the baby clothes embroidered with the name "Marguerite."

The ride from Chicago to New York was made on a slow train, in a crowded, poorly heated, day coach. Laurette was ill and in pain with every jounce. The conductor allowed her to lie down in the aisle, and took off his coat, folding it under her head for a pillow. Then he stood guard to make sure that her rest was undisturbed. If it had not been for that conductor Laurette's baby would undoubtedly have been born before the train reached New York.

It was the thirty-first of December when Elizabeth met her daughter at the station. Snow was falling and the thermometer was dropping toward zero. Laurette still wore the taffeta skirt, inset with bands of white lace, and the short taffeta coat in which she left Seattle. She was shivering uncontrollably and her face was drawn with pain. It was obvious to Elizabeth that the birth of the baby was imminent. They rushed home where Laurette was put into the same big yellow oak bed in which she had been born, and the doctor was called. The pains were growing worse and the fortitude that had kept her going until she got home was beginning to break. She was screaming so loudly that her younger sister Bessie took refuge under the kitchen table in fright. Bridgett Dorsey had come over and was fuming at the slowness of the doctor's arrival. "I'll deliver the child myself. Sure, I delivered the child's mother and what's wrong with her I'd like to know!"

But Laurette for all the pain didn't want the child delivered—not in the year 1901! It had been too dreadful a year—all the drudgery and failure and disappointment, the hunger and exhaustion. No, this child would be born in the New Year and have a clean slate to write her luck on. Of course it would be a girl and have that beautiful name Marguerite which had been so carefully embroidered on all the clothes. True, the clothes had been left behind in Chicago but she would make others and mother would help her. The pain was pretty awful, but not as awful as the year she wanted to kick into oblivion first, before her baby came. Laurette held her breath and listened for the whistles of the New Year but heard nothing . . . only the ordinary hum of a city street at night. Then she screamed again.

Bridgett went to the kitchen where water was heating on the stove. She plunked a big enamel pan on the table under which Bessie was cowering and complained to no one in particular, "You'd think she was givin' birth to the President of the United States the way she's screamin'." Bessie shivered with excitement and pulled the red-and-white-check cloth closer to the floor so that her grandmother wouldn't see her. Still muttering to herself Bridgett went back to the bedroom. The child under the table heard her sister cry, "No-*no*-no!" in a rising crescendo. Suddenly the whistles began blowing, a few preliminary pipings in the snow-blanketed streets, then happy blasts of sound from all directions. A long high scream drowned them out. Then Bessie heard them again merrily tooting in the New Year. Inside the flat there was silence. Presently Bridgett came grumbling in on quick feet and put something in the enamel pan on the table and went out again. Just above Bessie's head came the thin wail of a new-born child. . . .

In later years Laurette would tell over and over the story of how she had embroidered the name "Marguerite" on all the garments for her first-born child, and how that child had turned out to be a boy instead. She would tell you, with her chuckling laugh, that in this case at least prenatal influence was a complete flop. But there were very few people who ever heard the story of the train ride from Chicago, and the conductor who watched over her distorted little body as she tried to rest stretched in the aisle of an unheated day coach. She could always give you the laugh on the story, but she couldn't handle the other part. The things that hit her emotionally she buried. If you wanted to know about them you had to watch her on the stage, where she felt safe and shielded, where she told the truth which she somehow couldn't bear in real life.

In that first heartbreaking year with Charlie, Laurette had carried her childhood dreams far from the quiet Harlem Street and her mother's protective love. She had tested them in the toughest of all tests where glamour and fantasy must triumph over a hungry stomach and bone-deep exhaustion and the small bickerings of discouraged people. And she had met the test. In an interview after she had achieved stardom on Broadway, she said of this period, ". . . I looked upon it as a sort of armor to fit me for the fighting I expected and still expect to do . . . working hard, never shirking [I looked] upon its hardships as the test of my ambition, its quality and its quantity." Such determination goes deeper than a dream; it uses every adverse experience as a step toward the goal that is dreamed of; it makes a woman of a child, a worker of a dreamer. It was the foundation of an Art which seemed to take its life effortlessly from the empyrean, but its roots were in struggle and hardship and suffering.

## Rags to Riches

Charlie announced the birth of his son, Dwight Oliver Taylor, in *Theatrical News*, published by his friend Charles Blaney, as follows:

> Charles A. Taylor wishes to announce to his many friends in the profession that on the morning of January 1st, 1902, "The Daughter

of the Diamond King" presented "The King of The Opium Ring" with a ten-pound comedian, and that his wife, the charming little actress, Laurette Cooney, is the most interested and happiest of all parties concerned; he furthermore wishes it to be known that he is now engaged upon a domestic drama entitled "The Floorwalker" and is nightly rehearsing the star part.

A pretty picture, but whether it was quite accurate might be questioned. Bridgett and Elizabeth managed this particular show, and Charlie was definitely a super. However, he did go to work to restore the family fortunes. Within the next two years he turned out four melodramas, each phenomenally successful. They were: "Queen of the Highway," "Through Fire and Water," "The White Tigress of Japan," "Rags to Riches." This was the peak of his fame as a dramatist and also the peak of popularity for melos in America.

Although there was little or no literary distinction to melo-drama, some authors depended more than others on developing plot and characterization. Charles preferred to base his reputa-tion on "effects." These he achieved without regard to expense by great mechanical ingenuity and the sheer muscular prowess of his hero and heroine. Profits from one melodrama would be poured into the next. Only when others took over his shows did he make money.

"Queen of the Highway" was produced early in 1902 by James Wallack and toured the country for two successful seasons. Then came "Through Fire and Water" based on Charles' railroad ex-periences. The title was not allegorical: it derived from a scene where the hero drives his locomotive across a burning bridge and through a flood. In the grand climax the hero is shown being swept to his death over a waterfall, while the heroine suspended head down from an overhanging branch waits to pull him to the safety of her arms.

Laurette, recuperating after the baby's birth, was quite con-tent to let Charles' sister, Helen Hunter, play the lead in this strenuous opus. Helen had kicked over the family traces and fol-lowed her adored brother into the theatre. By the time the sec-ond company of "Queen of the Highway" was formed, Laurette was her energetic self once more and took the part of the ingénue, Jess Miller. The part by melo standards was not physically exacting. Laurette's big scene came at the end of the third act when, dressed in man's attire, she volunteered to carry Uncle Sam's mail pouch, after her lover had been captured by Black-foot Indians. Mounting a wiry little pony she gallops into the night. There were always several curtain calls showing the pony at full gallop, Laurette clutching his mane; but other than that the role was not too strenuous. The leading lady, as Belle Diamond, had to be made of far sterner stuff. It was her job to persuade her horse to walk a narrow trestle while the hero, roped to the saddle, was slowly pulled from a ravine where ravening wolves howled for his blood. According to a newspaper account she was sent to the hospital twice and one horse had to be destroyed.

"The White Tigress of Japan," inspired by the Russo-Japanese situation, opened on Broadway, August 20, 1903. To advertise it Charlie walked down Broadway with a live leopard on a leash. The pyrotechnics of this piece were so concentrated that one critic remarked, ". . . the smell of gunpowder doesn't leave you 'til the next day." Another headlined his review: *Forty-second Street Torn Up Again--This Time by a Melodrama!*

Charles' most successful melodrama, and the one which introduced "Laurette Cooney" to Broadway in the fall of 1903, was written on commission for Frank MacIntyre who had produced "Through Fire and Water." MacIntyre had just had a big success with a new child actor, Joseph Santley, in "An Affair of Honor," and was looking for another vehicle in which to star the boy. Charles turned out "Rags to Riches" in three weeks. Still considered a classic of the melodramatic form of playwriting it was one of the biggest money-makers of the day, and to quote Alexander Woollcott, established the thirteen-year-old Santley as "the darling of the fifty-cent circuits from the Bowery to Kansas City." Laurette also won acclaim for herself all along the line.

Charles was busy with his own productions during the rehearsals and run of "Rags to Riches" and was seldom in the theatre. The few times he appeared the company observed that the usually exuberant Laurette grew subdued. Her wit was not so ready; the wonderful smile and ebullient spirit seemed under a cloud. She had already learned some bitter lessons. Being hard of hearing, Charles was suspicious of merriment unless he was quite certain what it was about. The essence of Laurette's wit was a quick spontaneous outburst—her sallies sprang from her conversation like jack-in-the-boxes, and others would laugh suddenly and long as much from surprise as anything. It was the type of laughter that made a deaf man nervous. Many a time Charles turned on her, tongue-lashing her without mercy in front of an assembled company at rehearsal, or with their friends at a dinner or show: she was loud, flippant, impudent—anything he could think of to crush her because he thought he had been made the butt of a joke. His fury had a brutal finality about it which showed no kindness but only the cruel, sharp edge of a vain man's hurt vanity. Laurette was growing afraid of him and his outbursts. As with her father, she was outwardly defiant, sullen, or brash, but inwardly young emotions shriveled in a winter cold. She was learning the special loneliness of a wife who is a "creature" rather than a person to her husband. She had accepted his "adoration" and "worship" naïvely at first as part of the whole dream fabric of her make-believe world. Now she was coming to know the underface of such hollow concepts: neglect, sexual indulgence without tenderness, sentimentality without feeling, a blind arrogance that took no heed of the emotional insecurities bred in adolescence and the deep timidities which the lash of her father's whip had engendered.

The Taylors had a small apartment on Tenth Street but seldom occupied it. Charles was out of town much of the time visiting one or another of his touring companies, and at such times Laurette preferred to stay with her mother. These trips of Charlie's became protracted if and when one of his leading ladies fell in love with him, which frequently happened. He had an aptitude for a curiously lofty form of dalliance with the fair sex, a somewhat evangelical approach to extramarital affairs which justified them in his own mind at least. It was a quality that outraged Laurette even more than the infidelities themselves. She was learning to hate well before she had properly learned to love.

Early in 1904, Laurette left the cast of "Rags to Riches" to await the birth of her second child. By this time the Taylors were more than flush financially and, when Charles heard the news, he bought a big white frame house on a tree-lined street in Mount

Vernon, New York, moved his family there, and came home from his travels. The baby was born in August and this time the name Marguerite could alight at last on a child of the proper gender.

Ironically, there was much bitterness in the young mother at the birth of this child. There was every opportunity now to lavish on it the luxuries and attentions that had been denied the first, to surround it with all the comforts that had not been possible before. But not one garment was now embroidered "Marguerite"; Laurette almost apathetically turned the baby's care over to an Irish nurse, Bertha, who was also general factotum of the household. In later years Laurette could not recall what time of day the baby was born or any of the circumstances, while her first she always remembered vividly. "You did not hurt like the first," she would say when her daughter asked for details, "maybe that's why I don't remember." She chuckled of course when she said it, and slid a quick impish, somewhat abashed look at her daughter's face. But *something* hurt—so much, that her mind drew a veil over the episode.

The baby, as if in response to the thinness of the climate that received it, was sickly from the start. Its eyes ran when it was brought into the light and no formula could be found that would agree with it. Against the doctor's orders Bertha threw out all other prescriptions and fed it a grayish gruel, which she kept warm in a big pot on the back of the stove. She took the little creature into her bed at night, warming it like a half-dead kitten.

One day Bertha got it into her Irish heart that the baby might die and rushed off to a priest to have the child baptized. Mary, she named it, Mary Estelle Taylor. When she told Laurette, the young mother for the first time showed some real fire. "Her name is *Marguerite!*" she said. "How dare you christen her Mary! It's Marguerite—a beautiful name!" And she took the child and looked down at it for a long time. . . . Perhaps she was thinking of a cruel train ride and the trunk with all the baby clothes left in Chicago . . . of the hopes she had had of a fine baby girl when it would have mattered . . . when she had *wanted* a baby. But this baby she had not wanted. It had been conceived in hate and revolt. It was a tiny galleon come into port too late; the riches had been squandered, the hopes were ashes; only the name was left, that beautiful name of her first "long-dress" part . . . Marguerite.

*

# *Mount Vernon*

One might assume that the big white house in Mount Vernon, with its large and comfortably furnished rooms and fresh lace curtains at each window, would be a milestone worth noting in Laurette's life. It was the first and only real home she had during her married life with Charlie. Bertha was there to keep the place tidy and do all the household chores that Laurette disliked. After two arduous years Laurette had leisure, and it might well have seemed good to rest.

But actually the place had little meaning for either of the Taylors. Charlie, who by his own count established (and broke up) over a dozen beautiful homes in his lifetime, was not by nature a homemaker. His homes like his melodramas were "productions" and suffered from some of the same faults; the "effects" were good but the main protagonists were stereotypes that never came to life. Charlie, the husband; Laurette, the housewife, were parts indifferently played, and lacked the ring of truth. As for leisure, it had little meaning for Laurette except as it served as preparation for work. And leisure with Charlie she found quite unendurable. Almost before they had moved into Mount Vernon the Taylors were ready to move out again.

Charlie, after a few weeks of hanging around the house in a velvet smoking jacket and carpet slippers, daubing at an oil painting—a project in oils was always a sign that Charlie had gone domestic—tired of the role of family man and began spending more and more time in New York.

Even before the furniture had been moved in Al Woods was up from the city to discuss a production with him and Hugo Ziegfeld, who had put on Charlie's first New York show, "The Derby Mascot." The three men perched on packing boxes in the hall. Laurette, heavy with child, was, perforce, relegated to the side lines; she sat on the hall stairs listening rather wistfully to an argument. Woods had a blind eye, Ziegfeld stuttered, and Charlie, of course, was deaf. The argument seemed to intensify these infirmities. One by one the men rose and stood in a taut group. Woods began leveling his good eye in the direction of first one adversary then the other, Hugo pursed his lips in an "o" shape which delivered nothing but frustrated consonants into the air, while Charlie attempted to ride down all opposition with a loud and toneless monologue. Suddenly, Laurette, whose expression had grown increasingly lugubrious, could stand it no longer; without lifting her chin from between cupped hands she announced in dismal accents, "This is going to be one helluva play. The producer can't see, the author can't hear and the manager can't talk!"

She was glad when Charlie took his surplus energies into town. He was an exhausting man to live with, even for Laurette who had developed considerable resistance to the impingement of other egos on her own. He spent most of his hours in town at H. C. Miner's Lithographing Company, the popular meeting place for many of the theatrical brains of the day. Harry Miner was a friend of his, and Charlie and the other "blood and thunder boys" who wrote the melos could blow off steam at Miner's when not funneling it into their work.

While she idled, waiting for the birth of her second child, Laurette had filled the house with family and friends for diversion. People (if they were entertaining), rich food, late hours, lots of laughter, were Laurette's highroad over the boredom that assailed her when faced with everyday living. That is not to say these things sufficed; they only diverted, when she was not acting. Laurette had made a choice early in life, if choice it could be called. The roots of her growth were not in ordinary soil. Her sources of renewal and sense of well-being were in a world of her own cultivation: the world of her imagination. She found few havens in reality. It was either boring or unbearable. More and more she farmed the soil and subsoil of her own fancy to feed the basic impulses of her nature. In life they strangely withered; in the theatre they grew, effulgent and enduring.

There is a picture of Laurette that remains from the days at Mount Vernon which otherwise make no impress whatsoever on her story. It is a memory portrait by a sensitive Irish girl, Laurette's favorite cousin, who came frequently to visit. A city-bred child, Mabel loved to walk in the woods on the outskirts of the small country town. Laurette joined her in the spring days before the baby came. They would wander for hours, Mabel looking for jack-in-the-pulpits and Laurette searching for violets, calling back and forth to each other of their discoveries, forgetting time. It is a picture that stays in the mind because it is so unlike Laurette. For once the powerful drive shaft of her ambition idles. She is content to live in the moment; to feel the soft spring air upon her cheek, call through the dapple of sun and shade, bend down and snap the stem of a violet, as cool and fragrant as the earth itself. It was perhaps a reality that did not press her too closely for answers. Even the weight of the child within her may well have seemed momentarily benign—a comfortable extension of self rather than a confinement of self, and for that reason acceptable. Such moments were to be rare, her approach to them diffident, inconclusive, the approach not of a stranger but of a prodigal who squanders his birthright in a far land.

It was far more typical to find her making two magnificent Japanese kimonos for the role of Empress in "The White Tigress," which she hoped to play in the autumn, or acting out Japanese dramas with sister Bessie and Dolly Kemper in a storeroom the girls had painted white, and where, with some of the Japanese bric-a-brac and two bamboo screens from the props of "The White Tigress" they achieved stage settings of notable simplicity. Or, when Charlie was home there was play-reading in the den, Charlie declaiming in his pseudo-dramatic style, Laurette unerringly pulling a thin thread of credibility from the hodgepodge of histrionics. Margherita Steinert, opera singer and close family friend, recalling these readings stated emphatically, "Laurette was *never* an amateur! Charlie was an amusing ham when he read his plays, but Laurette made them live."

Play-reading and planning a future in the theatre was about the only language husband and wife still had between them.

In February, 1905, "Queen of the Highway" went on tour with Laurette playing her old role of Jess Miller. The show was in Newark on her twenty-first birthday April 1, 1905. It made the circuit of the Pennsylvania coal towns, ending up at Mahanoy City, April twenty-ninth; from there to Hartford and New Haven, the tour closing the middle of May.

About the same time, Henry Miller was introducing Margaret Anglin to New York City as a star in a play called "Zira" written by a young Englishman, J. Hartley Manners, who had come to America with the Miller company the previous year. But these well-groomed doings were far removed from the frenetic activities of Jess Miller riding her pony through South Bethlehem, Allentown, Pottsville, Hazelton, Ashland and Mahanoy City; and Hartley Manners was six years away from writing his smash hit "Peg O' My Heart" for that energetic little soubrette.

Just after the close of the "Queen of the Highway" tour Charlie ran into an old friend, William Russell, affectionately known as "Daddy" Russell to Seattle theatre audiences. He had just taken over the Third Avenue Theatre there and was in New York looking for talent. In a matter of minutes Russell had persuaded Charlie to take actors, scenery, properties, costumes and plays for an entire season of stock to Seattle. Three days after the meeting the entire enterprise, including Charlie and Laurette, was in motion toward the Pacific coast.

Bertha saw them off from the porch at Mt. Vernon, holding little Marguerite, trig and neat as a valentine, in her arms, while Dwight, standing close to Bertha's skirt, shot out his underlip in a brave effort not to cry. The children would follow later with Bertha, after the Taylors were settled in the West. The beautiful house at Mount Vernon would be sold, and all the beautiful furnishings with it.

Charlie was exuberant. During the long, dusty hours of the trip he recounted anew to Laurette his early successes in the West. He had always considered himself a Western dramatist. The West had the vigor of mind necessary to appreciate his plays. The East was becoming effete under the influence of English drawing-room drama, the new so-called "realism" that was taking hold. As she listened, Laurette's mouth was a little sullen—not characteristic of the lovely lips at all—a little pouting and questioning. She had thrown in her lot with him and would not know where to turn in the theatre if she left him now; it wasn't a question of love any more but expediency. Perhaps he would come through yet. Perhaps this play of his, "Yosemite," which had fired her imagination, would be the one. He had promised they would do it in Seattle. The lovely leaf dress her mother had made was in her trunk. . . . That delicious scene where, as a wild untrammeled child of the woods, she steps with the quick, instinctive vigilance of an animal to the edge of the pool and gazes at her reflection . . . innocently pleased with her beauty . . . innocently unafraid in the vast silence of the forest that surrounds her, the only home she has ever known . . .

Laurette's eyes grew soft, the pupils dilated and her hands lay quiet in her lap. The *click-clack* of the train wheels blended with the sound of the lapping waters of the forest pool; the soot raining down from open ventilators, cinders tattooing against the sides of the train were lost in the stillness of Yosemite's grandeur. . . . She was playing a great part, breathing the life of her belief into Lone Star before a spellbound audience. . . .

Charlie slipped out to the smoking car to find another audience. The little woman was her most charming self—quiescent—moldable. She had a simplicity, a directness that made every mother's son in an audience want to claim her as a daughter, a sweetheart, a wife, worship her as a symbol of pure womanhood; BUT—Good God!—you had to project these human values on a grand scale, paint the canvas with broad bold strokes, give 'em thrills—action—or you didn't have a show! That's what these realists forgot! He was glad to be leaving the East. It was finished. Three years in the West would put his "little darling" on the top and Broadway would come crawling on its knees over the Rockies to find her!

Back in the coach Laurette, a box of chocolates forgotten at her side, gazed out the window deep in reverie.

*

# *Seattle Stock*

William Russell had assured the Taylors that Seattle could be an Eldorado for a good stock company. They needed that reassurance. When they had floundered into it in 1901 with the remnants of their "Child Wife" company, it was still suffering the aftermath of the panic of 1893. Once it had been a top show town; now few traveling road companies went to the expense of moving the scenery to play there. Cordray, builder of Seattle's first stock house, had been driven to the wall; John Cort and Robert Considine, the two other big theatre men, had moved out to more profitable areas. Variety was the only type of entertainment to survive, and did so more by virtue of a free flow of beer to the customers than the quality of the acts.*

The curative effects of the gold strike in Alaska in 1897 were not felt until the century was well over its hinge. Then "wealth such as never before had come into an American City began to flow into Seattle." ** The assay office in a single day received nine hundred thousand dollars in gold dust and nuggets. Cort and Considine returned when gold returned, and began programs of expansion that made them the theatre giants of the Northwest. Alexander Pantages came down from the gold fields where he had worked in a honky-tonk as a waiter, and with the money he had saved opened his first theatre on Second Street. Between 1902 and 1904 eleven theatres were built in Seattle. This time the Taylors arrived to find the veins of the metropolis well infused with gold, business booming, several stock houses open all season, and the town looking for good entertainment.

Russell and his partner, Edward Drew, were shrewd operators. They had weathered the depression, and with the importation of the Taylor Company were making their bid to have the Third

* Cf. "A History of Variety—Vaudeville in Seattle," Eugene Clinton Elliott. Pp. 24–25.
** Ibid.

Avenue Theatre become the top-ranking stock house on the Pacific Coast. Stated the *Argus:* "The eyes of the entire theatrical
profession are focused upon (the enterprise). Seattle cannot afford
to be considered but what it was in the past—the best show town
on earth."

After leaving their luggage at the hotel, Charlie and Laurette
went to look at the theatre which was to be their home off and on
for the next two years. It had the rather gloomy, uninhabited look
of the storehouse which it originally had been. But with the company bannerhead stretched across one side of the building displaying Charlie's Black Cat trademark ("I'm a man with nine
lives," he used to say), eight-sheet posters of Laurette as Sparkle
in "Escaped from the Harem" and two lines of small American
flags gaily snapping in the breeze, the dark, cavernous structure
took on a festive air. Laurette felt an involuntary thrill. *Her* theatre. *Her* picture. Her pick of the parts she wanted to play. This
was, after all, quite a way from that childish performance five
years ago in Boston of "How Salvador Won," when she had
snapped her little whip against her riding boots and lifted her voice
valiantly trying to be heard over the scraping boots of the departing customers.

She persuaded herself that Charlie was right; it would be bad
business to start off with the classics she so longed to do. "They're
still picking the gold dust out of their teeth around here, little
darling," he told her. "We want to get them coming in first with
the popular stuff, then we'll spoon them the class. You stick with
Charlie and you'll be the queen of them all!"

During these days of Seattle stock Laurette established a method
of rehearsing to which she adhered all her life. She was never a
good study. With a different part to learn each week while giving two shows a day there was never time to learn the lines verbatim, even if she had had the aptitude. She worked instead to get
the general sense of each scene, achieve a consistent character, and
let the words fall where they would. Mumbling the gist of a
speech, feeling out "business," watching the other players, seeming more intent upon their parts than her own, she was establishing a relationship—a very real relationship—between the character she played and those which were contingent upon it. She

bothered not at all with the precise script until these relationships, the motivations of scenes and speeches, were well rooted in her mind. Then at the last minute, if necessary, she would sit up all night and work away at the actual lines as though she were finishing off the last details of an edifice already solidly standing on its foundation. In stock days this was a necessity; it became a lifelong habit.

Seattle was delighted with the Taylor Company's initial efforts. "Looks Like Old Times" headlined the *Daily Times*. ". . . all the stage business is quick and snappy, the people don't bump into each other in getting around the stage, and there are no tedious waits." Poor Seattle! How it had suffered. For the present it was quite uncritically pleased just to find itself back in the ranks of respectable theatre towns.

It was a strenuous and profitable season. They put on ten different plays in twelve weeks, all but two written by Charles. In spite of the hard work there was an air of pleasurable excitement backstage. The costumes were fresh, scenery new, the audiences enthusiastic. Klondikers, still drifting down to Seattle to spend their gold, added a special air of celebration to the performances. Vociferously enthusiastic, they were as like as not to give advice to the actors from their boxes, comment loudly on the beauty of the heroine, adjudicate the rights and wrongs of a situation. They brought their ladies with them, easily distinguished from the rest of the sober populace by their attar of roses perfume, their scented cigarettes, fine raiment and easy laughter. Laurette's sister Bess, a new member of the company, acquired an admirer from the gold fields who used to pelt the stage with nuggets by way of showing his enthusiasm. On one occasion he made the mistake of hurling these gold bouquets while she was onstage with Laurette. "You go tell your friend," Laurette snarled between clenched teeth, "if he throws one more nugget, I'm going to have him thrown out."

The only ruffle on the smooth passage of the first season was Laurette's refusal to take her status of permanent leading lady of the Taylor Company with the seriousness and dignity which Charlie thought the position warranted. She insisted on playing the parts that would give her the greatest contrast from week to week whether they were starring roles or not. Her ambition was not reaching for stardom; it was reaching for the ability and the versatility that would make her a star. Charlie scolded and scolded but to no avail. "He tried to impress upon me," Laurette wrote later, "the dignity and importance of my position as a leading woman. But I had long observed that leading women with an overwhelming sense of their dignity and importance lacked the human quality in their acting. . . ." Laurette never forgot this "long" observation of her youth.

When the Taylor Company went on tour at the close of the season many patrons of the Third Avenue Theatre expressed the hope that Russell & Drew would see fit to bring them back. Undoubtedly it was the intention of the management to do so but Charlie, as soon as he had money in his pocket, itched to become his own boss. As they started off on their tour of Portland, San Francisco and Los Angeles he was laying plans for his own productions the following season.

Road business was good. Charlie alternated his two biggest money-makers "Held for Ransom" and "Queen of the Highway." In Portland the Fair was in full swing and many old friends of Charlie's railroading days were given boxes for the shows, introduced to his "talented little wife," wined and dined royally at the best restaurants. In San Francisco the Taylors were joined by their two children and Bertha. In Los Angeles they had a corner suite at the Hollenbeck overlooking Second and Spring, just a short walk from the Los Angeles Theatre on Main. Charlie invited in the newspaper men, served sandwiches and beer, told of the big things that he and his wife were going to do in the West. Laurette had a feeling of solid ground under her feet. There were fine clothes, good food, parties, laughter and many compliments upon her acting and her beauty.

When Charlie stepped up to the Hollenbeck bar in the late afternoon and in a voice with just the right resonance to carry the length of the room, ordered, "One Martini, please, with—(*pause*)—an *olive* in it," he was being his showman self. He believed in self-advertising as part of show business. His elegant clothes, his at times deliberately dudelike ways, along with his extreme good looks attracted attention wherever he went, and he used this to his business advantage. A slow stroll through a hotel lobby greeting friends; the suave approach of the connoisseur in ordering food and wine; a few anecdotes (and he was a master of these) in a voice that carried beyond the bounds of the immediate listener; in all these things he was acting as advance man for his own shows. "Who's that?" "Why, that's Charlie Taylor. He's putting on a show here tomorrow night." The Martini-with-an-*olive*-in-it was just the note to strike in this "cow-town," as he designated the City of Angels in the year 1905.

Charlie was gratified to note a stir among some of the patrons downing their ponies of red-eye. At the end of the bar a big handsome brute of a man in slouch hat and flowing tie stopped abruptly in his conversation with Rol King the hotel manager, and stared. A word to his companion and the two men moved down the bar and stood beside Charlie. Rol King made the introductions. "Charlie, I want you to meet a friend of mine, Walter Scott. Walter, this is Charlie Taylor."

No one had to be told who Walter Scott was. As Death Valley Scotty his doings had been headline news since he had started on his romp through the states a few months before, spending a supposedly inexhaustible supply of gold taken from his Death Valley mine. It had begun with his chartering a special train from the Santa Fe for a trip from Los Angeles to Chicago. Scott paid forty-five hundred dollars for the ride and tipped the crew another thousand. In New York he gave twenty-dollar gold pieces to bellboys for tips, bought newspapers and shoeshines with hundred-dollar bills, saying "Keep the change." With such doings he put the newspaper bannerhead to his everyday use. Upon his return to Los Angeles, Scotty was content to peel off one-dollar bills from rolls of the proverbial horse-choking size, but by this time the legend was secure, and the size of the roll, not the denomination of the bill, still made the headlines.

A natural polarity immediately exerted itself between these two showmen. Within the next few minutes, Laurette's future, as she envisioned it, was sold out to the freak whim of Walter Scott who decided to become an actor under the banner of Charles A.

Taylor. Before the men left the bar a three-way contract had
been signed between Scotty with King as his manager and Charlie.
Charlie was commissioned to write a play in which Scott was to
play the lead depicting "Death Valley life as it really is." The
opening was scheduled for New York, January 15, 1906. "As an
earnest of his intentions," reported the Los Angeles *Express,*
"Scotty handed Taylor $10,000 to buy stationery on which to
write the play, and before they left the bar all hands were called
by Scotty to drink on his new venture. Before the toasts were
over $400 more of Scotty's money lined the till of the Hollenbeck
saloon."

It must be said in Charlie's favor that he probably sincerely
thought he was shooting the Taylor fortunes off in a new and
highly profitable direction; even an artistic one. He had a blind
spot in his nature that made it impossible for him to differentiate
between the real and the fake, between theatre and show. He
believed in Scotty, he thought the story of the Death Valley mine
a good one.

No amount of loud talk back in their suite at the Hollenbeck
could convince Laurette that Charlie had made a theatrical coup.
She was as acute in these matters as he was blind.

He waved a pile of telegrams under her nose—"offers from all
over the country—three thousand dollars for a one-night stand—
Topeka—Kansas City!—we can't handle them they're coming in
so fast. It's another gold mine, little darling—with Scotty's fame
and my reputation as a playwright we'll clean up. We'll hit New
York like all twenty Borax mules at once, and you'll be on the
front mule!" But he could not make her laugh.

"What about 'Yosemite'?" she asked.

" 'Yosemite'—my masterpiece! I'll put every cent I make into
it. We'll take it to New York ourselves. A million-dollar production! They'll never see its like again. Bridal Veil Falls tumbling in
a diamond-flecked mist before their very eyes . . ."

But his wife's mouth stayed sullen. Charlie picked up his small
son and threw him astride his shoulders. "Jing-a-long-a-Joesy,
Jing-a-long-a-Joe! Jing-a-long-a-Joesy," he sang in a pleasing
voice, prancing up and down the sitting room. The child shrieked

with joy but Laurette sat silent. Was it always to be like this? The cheap, the obvious, working the thin line between show business and side show?

As soon as the tour closed in Los Angeles, Charlie left for the East to make the bookings and work on the play. Laurette returned with Bertha and the children to a little place in the White River valley near Seattle, where following the Taylor Company's successful season he had bought another of his many homes.

No sooner was Charlie out of town than Scotty got himself broken up in an accident driving his "juice wagon." Charlie wired frantically from the East and was assured that Scotty would recover in time for the New York opening. But his injuries were extensive and the January opening and Eastern bookings had to be canceled. In February, Scotty recovered sufficiently to travel to Seattle for rehearsals.

All of Laurette's worst fears were realized with this production of "Scotty, King of the Desert Mines." Walter Scott had no serious intention whatsoever of becoming a real actor. It was simply a new and diverting means of keeping himself in the public eye. He made no attempt to learn his lines, strode out on the stage issuing a string of oaths and shooting off his gun, mugging at the audience, kidding his fellow actors or ignoring them as the mood struck him. It was by any standard of theatre a disgraceful exhibition; as Laurette had feared, a side show.

The play was as phony as its protagonist. The *Argonaut* (March 31, 1906) termed it "one of the worst melodramas that has ever insulted the stage." It included by contract Scotty's mule, Slim, and Scotty's bodyguard, one S. Jackson, a dour, wooden-faced gentleman who stood behind Scotty during the entire course of the play smoking a big black cigar and fingering his gun. The team of Malemutes used as sled dogs was, according to the program, the original U. S. Mail Team from Nome, Alaska, "their storm leader, a full-blooded timber wolf, the only one ever broken to harness." There was a sandstorm (this got out of hand the first night and enveloped the audience), a railroad wreck, a blizzard and endless gunplay which Scotty augmented at will with his six-shooter.

In the midst of this welter of bad taste, one who looked sharply could see "a little bit of pink-and-white soubrette" earnestly going about her business of "supporting" Scotty.

One who did look sharply and so described Laurette in San Francisco was Ashton Stevens, a young critic for Hearst's *Examiner*. The play he aptly labeled "a perfect measles of melodrama" and could say nothing good of it, but the pink-and-white soubrette was something else again. "The only human that did not seem to belong to the outfit was Miss Laurette Taylor." He found it "a shock" to see her in the midst of such doings.

Stevens further recollected how he went backstage after the performance, "as much in my capacity of red-blooded male as energetic critic." There wasn't much he could say for the play, but he could and did congratulate the author—with a wink stageward—on having a mighty pretty little soubrette. "Yes," answered Charles without encouragement, "she's my wife."

"That," added Stevens in concluding his reminiscence, "is one reason why I did not marry Laurette Taylor."

There was some metal in Laurette's art that no circumstance could corrode. While Scotty clowned and cursed his way through the show, she played the little soubrette as though it were the crowning glory of her career instead of its lowest ebb. In San Francisco she took herself out into the streets to watch the laborers at work so that she could more accurately and authentically swing her sledge hammer in the scene where she mended the torn up rails of the Santa Fé just before the train thundered across the trestle. Offstage she might be surly, in her hotel room wrapped in furious despair; but once on the stage nothing could uproot her from the character she was playing, giving her very best to her audience, with whom, it seemed, no amount of personal despair could make her break faith.

She probably was not conscious of any code, but developed and clung to one as easily as she breathed; years later, when she did break faith with her audience for the first and only time, the whole edifice of her world came down in ruins around her head as though she had struck at its keystone.

It would be better to draw a merciful veil over the remainder of this road tour. It went on and on. There were always the morbidly curious to fill the seats and watch the freakish doings of the leading man. On a postcard sent from Kansas City May 7, 1906, Laurette scribbled to her friends the Steinerts in New York: "Still supporting Scotty and awfully tired of her job." The play's only asset was the dubious fame of its principal, and as the novelty of being an actor wore off and Scotty frequented the show less and less, or walked out before it was over, audiences began to fall off. Finally, in what Midwest town is not recorded, "Scotty, King of the Desert Mines" folded, and the company came home to Seattle.

Charlie was in a mood to make amends. He hired the Seattle Theatre and put on "Yosemite," temporarily entitled "Stolen by Gypsies" for the purpose of titillating melo audiences. Laurette's belief in the play was justified in that it was rated among the top five successful Seattle productions of the year, and Charlie's most distinguished play.

This small ray of what the theatre might be was soon blacked out by mounting misfortunes. In the fall the Taylors returned to Daddy Russell's Third Avenue Theatre, but the regrading of the steep hill on which the building was located forced its closing a few weeks after the season began.

Charlie met the crisis head on. He took over an old Methodist church building at the corner of Third and Pine and remodeled it into a theatre. Called Taylor's Castle Garden it was, according to Charlie, to provide entertainment for everybody; there would be freaks, vaudeville, carnivals, fruit and grain exhibits, baby shows, tugs-of-war, banjo and mandolin clubs, trained animals—even a petrified man. Charlie drew the line at one thing: a chamber of horrors. He thought it unwholesome.

Laurette threw herself into the project with her usual vigor. She trained a corps of pony dancers, made carnival costumes, brushed up on her act of "imitations and songs," which was to be one of fifteen specialty numbers in the first production.

Seven days after the remodeling started the Grand Opening took place. It began with a "Frolic of Clowns," then came the specialty numbers, ending with "artistic poses by Ada Gautiers under a powerful calcium light." The main spectacle was the carnival "Cinderella" in which over one hundred performers took part. Laurette as Cinderella rode in a huge pumpkin surrounded by acrobats and tumblers.

Seattle flocked to the doors. The only hitch was that by the end of the third week Charlie had run out of money. Creditors for props, furnishings, electrical equipment, carpenters, feed merchants, animal trainers, actors—in fact almost everybody but the petrified man—closed in for payment. The theatre was closed and all goods attached. Charlie promptly collapsed with a nervous stomach and was whisked off to the White River farm and put to bed. Laurette in desperation went to the box office, broke a bottle of ammonia under the nose of the law enforcement officer, grabbed up some personal belongings and fled.

During a winter of interminable rain Laurette nursed her sick husband back to health. Both children had chicken pox. When a succession of uncommunicative gentlemen arrived from town with long white pieces of paper she chucked them in a bureau drawer and forgot about them. Apparently it was an excellent way to handle subpoenas for she heard nothing further from the law.

When spring came, Charlie began to feel better. Growing expansive one day on the beauties of the still rain-soaked farm, he suggested Laurette give it a name. "Why not," she answered sourly, "call it Stuck Valley?"

Seattle friends helped the Taylors make another start. A syndicate of businessmen, headed by Russell and Drew, reactivated the old church property as their new Third Avenue Theatre, put Charlie in charge as manager but wisely held onto the purse strings.

This, announced Charlie proudly, was to be "little darling's" theatre, and it was—with a vengeance. She dyed curtains, patched plaster, mended seat covers, tacked down the frayed carpet in the auditorium. Productions were done on a shoestring, the same costumes recut and resewed, scenery repainted for a dozen different productions. When props were needed, Charlie sent Laurette out to beg and borrow them from Seattle merchants on the strength of a smile and promise of a free ad on the canvas drop. When he was busy elsewhere, she sold tickets at the box office, dashing backstage just in time for the show. Her costumes were beautiful, her performances as near perfect as she could make them. Given carte blanche on plays, she tackled the heavily dramatic roles of Carmen, Camille, Marguerite in "Faust," Ayesha, Queen of Kor in "She," and enchanted her audiences anew. If a technical difficulty arose, the play was not scheduled until she had mastered it. Before Carmen she lived with castanets tied to her wrists, clacking them double time as she ate, studied, lay in bed at night, falling asleep with them still between her fingers. "One of the peskiest things I ever tried to learn," she recalled years later. She studied Spanish for the role and sang "La Paloma" with such dash and fire, despite her lack of voice, that it won an ovation.

Seattle was in its heyday as a show town in 1907; many ranked it next to Broadway as a theatrical center. The ramshackle church building on the wrong side of town, badly ventilated, seats improperly tiered, acoustics poor, would have been hopelessly outclassed had it not been for the sterling qualities of its leading actress, and the undeniable flair for showmanship of its manager.

Hard work could not break Laurette's morale in the theatre but on the domestic side it was at a low ebb. There were many hours when Charlie absented himself, visiting with other showfolks, mixing business with pleasure. There was always someone to mention innocently the fact that the handsome Mr. Taylor had been seen at another stage door, squiring the reigning queen of a traveling troupe to supper. His excuses were invariably on a high level: Laurette had her duties as a mother, but a man couldn't be expected to hang around between matinee and night while the kids mewled and puked over their food.

On the second night of "She" everything blew apart backstage. Laurette was in her costume, her fingers wired for the sparks that would flash the divine fire by which Ayesha continually renews her youth. Something had gone wrong with the electrical circuit against which she pressed the metal tip on her shoe in order to spark. It was a sweltering July night. The airless closet which served as a dressing room, the scratchy net and tinsel in which Laurette was swathed, the constricting wires on her fingers seemed unbearable. The three hundred sides of the exacting part, never fully memorized, beat on her brain in fragments which suddenly she felt she could never coalesce. Charlie slipped into the theatre, thinking the performance had started, only to find a frantic electrician still looking for the break in the circuit, a wife on the verge of hysterics. By the time the break was mended and Laurette took her place in the wings she was trembling from head to foot. As the curtain rose she *sank* in a crumpled heap of net, tinsel and wires to the floor.

Bessie understudied her sister that night and more and more frequently after that. Laurette had a series of fainting spells, usually after blowups with Charlie. The company kept a healthy distance from the embattled Taylors, and the children, whose daily playground had been backstage, were despatched to the hotel room and left in care of the floor maid for longer and longer intervals.

In the autumn of 1907, Minnie Maddern Fiske came to Seattle on tour. She was a lone holdout in the ranks of stars against the powerful theatrical syndicate which at that time had gained control of the major theatre circuits in the Northwest. As a result even the most important stars were compelled to submit to the terms and time schedules of the syndicate or they found themselves without theatres in which to play. In time most of the stars had succumbed to the syndicate, but Mrs. Fiske, backed by her husband, Harrison Grey Fiske, remained defiant to the end. She had toured the country playing in draughty, ill-lighted halls and skating rinks. In Seattle only one theatre was available to her; the Third Avenue. She took one look and pronounced it "impossible."

Mrs. Fiske was barely a name to Laurette; she didn't know where or what Mrs. Fiske had played, and Laurette herself had never acted in a first-class theatre in her life. All Laurette knew was that she had sweated and slaved over the remodeled church; she had painted and sewed, scrubbed and hammered, and now Mrs. Fiske called it "impossible." "Think of it! My theatre!" Laurette exclaimed. But then she had to admit when she really looked at it, it was just that, impossible.

"What broke my heart," Laurette recalled afterward, "was to think that I had only reached impossible in my three years of hard work in Seattle."

She took up the long and taxing part of Camille and tried to forget this careless summation of her life's work. She was skin and bones—"or as near that as I ever could be." Rehearsals, combined with daily performances of "East Lynne" in which she played a dual role, were exhausting. But it was Laurette who had demanded "Camille," sensing it would be her farewell to Seattle.

After the first night she told Charlie she was through, she could not go on, and the week was played out in bitter silence between them.

The last performance of "Camille" was given on December 14, 1907. Laurette told Charlie quietly of her plans. She was going East to try her luck in the legitimate theatre. Charlie was stricken. "What can they do for you in the East, little darling, that I can't do for you here?" he pleaded. "In two or three years Seattle will be the greatest theatre center in the country—it's growing all the time. We'll grow with it. Don't leave me now, little darling—my little dream wife—that I've loved so!" His voice broke with emotion, color drained from his face, and the hand he placed on her arm in a pleading gesture, shook.

But Laurette's heart was frozen. She had waited too long for kindness and consideration, real or feigned. She had been shouted at, lorded over, sent out to cadge and beg like a pauper, left alone in a hotel room after exhausting performances, to drink coffee and sew and cry; not tears—never tears—but little dry, half-strangled cries of outrage and fury because her pride and self-esteem were hurt. She was sick of the sentimentality with which he covered his lack of feeling either for her or for his children, indifference toward every need but his own. No, there was no forgiveness, only sullen hate because she had been used and abused so callously.

Marguerite would go with her mother and the boy would come on later by himself after Laurette was settled. That's how it was to be.

Seattle friends were saddened by the breakup. Their good friend Frank Eagan, who ran a theatrical school, gave a farewell party the day before Laurette left for New York. The boys and girls of the school were included as well as the Taylor children. With the sensitive antennae of the young, Marguerite and Dwight picked

up and stored in their memories the haunting sadness of that last
party. . . . A gloomy hall with one electric-light bulb illuminat-
ing a table on which are piled a heap of dusty dominoes . . . each
guest donning one before entering the room used for dancing
classes . . . Black masks with lips smiling—some unsmiling—beneath. Who is this? thinks Dwight, My mama? She is leaning
down, masked face close to his. The small boy is filled with an
ungovernable sorrow. His lovely mama has disappeared under the
black mask with the cut-out eyes. "Mama, mama!" he cries, "is it
you?" and he raises his hands and touches her cheeks.

"Of course, darling!" The curving lips part in the fun-loving
smile he knows so well. But the child has a sense of loss, and he
weeps and will not be comforted. . . .

. . . In another corner of the big room, a tall austere-looking
man is surrounded by children. He holds his three-year-old
daughter with one hand and with the other makes eloquent gestures as he sings. The song is about the famous race of two pad-
dleboats, the *Robert E. Lee* and the *Natchez* on the Mississippi
River. He is "hamming it up" and the children love it. "Look!
Watch! You can plainly see . . ." He shades his eyes and peers
far off, leaning forward with one knee slightly bent, "Smoke from
the Natchez"—he points a long finger—"and the Robert Lee!"—
points again in another direction. Some of the smaller children
involuntarily turn and follow his gaze, but the little girl continues
to peer up at her father's face. He repeats the verse over and
over, each time dropping his voice lower until it is barely a
whisper, pointing each time. The children are spellbound. As the
last whispered phrase fades away one can hear a pin drop. Suddenly he straightens up and squeezes the little girl's hand. "Your
poor old deaf father!" he says with mocking self-pity. "Everybody
can hear Charlie Taylor sing but Charlie Taylor!" Then he
laughs. He is quite pleased with the performance really. He is, of
course, exaggerating his deafness; he can still hear, a little, and his
voice remains true and melodious in the songs he learned in his
youth.

His daughter, solemn as an owl, continues to stare up at his
face. . . .

# Shabby and Anxious

The young woman who turned her back upon Seattle and headed for Broadway was not given to speculations on Destiny, nor could she have realized that she was making the right move at the right time. Melodrama was at its cusp in the West. With the opening of the first moving-picture house in Seattle in September, 1907, the "thrillers" received a body blow which, although not felt immediately, would within two years have them on the ropes. Road shows fell off rapidly, and by 1912 the principal houses in Seattle were dark twelve to twenty weeks out of the year. On Broadway there was a whole new impetus away from histrionics toward subtler and more sincere dramatic forms. A vogue of naturalism was in favor in both playwriting and acting. Ethel Barrymore, Margaret Anglin, George Arliss, George Fawcett were some of the new talent popularizing a far greater degree of realism in acting than had ever obtained before. Like a needle to a magnet, the young actress whose genius for imaginative realism on the stage was to be unequaled and unchallenged in her time in the American theatre, was heading, quite blindly, for the climate in which that genius could best flower.

The move was a blind one not only because Laurette was not one to analyze her steps, but because she was at the time almost totally ignorant of the broad trends in the theatre. She had had her nose too close to the grindstone to know what was going on around her. As she said herself, "Bernhardt and Mrs. Fiske were barely names to me. I hadn't been inside a first-class theatre since my mother took me to the Harlem." She had developed an acting style of her own that had absolutely no relationship to the stilted, lifeless medium in which she worked. Like the Topsy which she sometimes played, it had "just growed." She had breathed such miraculous life into the mummified corpses of the melos that many in the audience, who like herself knew nothing else, were given their first insight into what the living theatre could be. She had no idea where she fitted in the theatre of the twentieth century as it was evolving in the East; that she fitted so well never even entered her head.

Destiny, if Destiny it was, did not at once benignly smile. A handful of notices and three years of Western stock opened no doors on Broadway to a shabby young actress. All through the spring and the long hot summer of 1908 Laurette haunted the managers' offices, wore out the leather of her shoes on the Broadway pavements. "I was shabby, I was anxious—and an actress should never look either." Elizabeth, with whom Laurette was living in an apartment near the Hippodrome, had nursed her through a nervous collapse when she first arrived from the West. "I shook when I asked for a part, and I never got a part in my hands to show that I could stop shaking and act. My nerves had nothing to do with my assurance but no one gave me a chance to prove it." In the Leibler office she plucked desperately at the sleeve of a florid young man named George Tyler, then steaming along at the beginning of his own successful career as producer. He freed himself from her importunate grasp with a brusque, "Can't do a thing for you, young lady—I'm just the office boy!" Six years later she got her revenge. Hearing that her contract with Oliver Morosco was broken, Tyler cabled to London where she was playing "Peg O' My Heart" asking her to sign with him. She cabled back: "If you want my signature, come over and get it." He did.

Laurette had a letter or two of introduction. One was to Henry Savage who was producing Molnar's "The Devil" on Broadway and was casting a number two company for Chicago. She stood in line with twenty other aspirants to try out for the small part of Mimi, the artist's model. Five were auditioned and Laurette and another girl were given the chance to rehearse. Both were told to go and watch the actress playing the role in the New York production and copy everything she did. Laurette thought the woman's performance very bad. The part was that of a young girl, simple, brave, affectionate, without any deep capacity for suffering; her big speech came in the last act when she likened a girl's heart to a railroad station where transitory idols (loves) come, stop awhile, and go away. "The voice of the woman playing the part," Laurette recalled, "shook with self-pity and her body drooped with despair as she read the speech." Laurette found it impossible to make herself do it this way "because it was wrong." The director sent her back after each rehearsal, to study the original Mimi, but it did no good. Finally, with great sarcasm, he asked her to go *once more*, and see how closely she could approximate Miss So-and-So's excellent performance. Was that clear? Yes. This time Laurette studied her model with great care. At the next rehearsal every sigh, every droop of despair was in her performance, an exact take-off. The cast howled with laughter. Laurette was promptly fired.

But when the glow of how right she had been in her interpretation wore off, Laurette suffered black discouragement. The only part she had even had a chance to read since coming East—a small soubrette role—and she had failed! It did not help that Charlie appeared at that moment from the West, and raged at what he called her "lack of dignity." Tramping from office to office like a thousand other down-at-heel actresses, doors being slammed in her face, when she had been, and again could be, the star of his company! What was she thinking of? When he saw that this tack only made her defiant he took another approach. He begged her as his wife, the mother of his children, to come back to him.

The decision was not easy. Separation was a serious matter for a young Catholic woman. There had been nothing but closed doors and discouragement since she had left Charlie. But she could not go back. She was groping for some position in the theatre that she felt he could not give. Until she found it she could take no more of his battering ego. She would never love him again—if she ever had except for those first dazzling moments—but divorce she had never even considered. No, she would establish herself in her profession in the way she wanted to and then, please God, she would be able to stand the rest.

In September of the same year Laurette had the rare experience of being vindicated in her interpretation of the role from which she had been fired. Another producer, Will Block, finding that "The Devil" was not protected by copyright, hastily gathered a company in an effort to beat the Henry Savage production to

Chicago. This time Laurette got the part. The two versions opened within twenty-four hours of each other, and critics reviewed both performances. Percy Hammond wrote: "Miss Nordstrom (of the New York company) failed to appreciate the bit of the model, Mimi, and plays it with so much affected sweetness that it goes for nothing. Even the naïve speech comparing man to a railway train and his discarded sweetheart to the station left behind is a blank." He advised the actress to go and watch Miss Taylor in the same role in Mr. Block's company "and learn the value of simplicity, the heartbreak of the valiant."

It is interesting to note that Hammond in the same review makes mention of the fact that the leading lady of the Block Company "retains her bad stock-company habits of excess." Laurette, with only stock-company training, never acquired such habits.

She seemed to know from the beginning just what she wanted to do on the stage and how she wanted to do it, and this basic concept was little changed throughout her career. When she became associated with Daniel Frohman in "Seven Sisters" he quickly came to respect this knowledge. "She just does things the way she feels them and she is usually right," was his philosophical comment. "There isn't the least use trying to get her to do them in another way. She simply will not."

"The Devil" was a short-lived triumph. The Block Company was attached after five days, and Laurette was left stranded in Chicago. Elizabeth wired her the money to come home.

There was a surprise waiting for her when she returned to New York. Charlie had rented sumptuous quarters in a new apartment building and furnished them himself with the help of the Taylors' faithful family friend, Margherita Steinert. "Perhaps if I make her a home," he had said brokenly to Margie, "she will come back to me." He had lavished upon it his keen productive sense; everything from the tall iron sconces in the hall with electric bulbs shaped like flames, to the willow-pattern plates decorating the living room walls, the blue of their design picking up the blue of the deep-piled carpet, was charming and keyed in a soft harmony that spelled *home*. It could not but seem inviting to a very weary little actress just returned to New York in the sweltering heat of mid-September.

The children were there too, in the charge of a birdlike Frenchwoman, who stepped forward, wearing matching cap and apron, and dropped a respectful curtsy to "madame." It was a typical Charles A. Taylor production, no expense spared.

Charlie was making a real effort at reconciliation. In his peculiar way he loved his wife, and still thought it possible for them to make a future together in the theatre. He was under no illusions; a future in the theatre was more important than the home if husband and wife were to stay together. That next step he had carefully worked out as well.

He had revised "Yosemite," Laurette's favorite play, to bring it up to the standards of the first-class theatre. Color transparencies, which had been made for the original production in San Francisco with funds advanced by Charlie's friend, James Flood, were used as base sketches for the scenery. Again no expense had been spared. The sets were ready, the cast assembled. Would Laurette play the dual role of Mercedes and Lone Star in a New York production?

In Laurette's answer was both her woman's decision to do her part to keep the family together, and the decision of the actress, still reaching blindly for her place in the theatre. The answer was *yes.*

\*

# Yosemite

"Yosemite" opened in Buffalo, December 8, 1908. What happened there was typical of the near-farce which so often threatened Charlie's most serious productions. Sober criticism of the play and of Laurette's performance was lost in an uproar over the leaf costume she wore as Lone Star, and the fact that she played the part barefooted. Civic rectitude protested, police officers were sent to monitor each leaf the second night. The newspapers had a field day kidding civic rectitude. What should a child of the wilderness wear? Pantalettes? Rubber boots? Galoshes, perhaps?

Laurette, taken completely by surprise, pleaded with the public to be fair. No type of criticism could have hurt her more or hit her in a more vulnerable spot. An excessively modest woman because of strict Catholic training and lack of confidence in her physical attractiveness, Laurette's basic conception of the use of clothes was that they were made for concealment. She loved pretty clothes, but she loved them as adornments to hide rather than reveal physical attributes. Anyone who had watched her at her favorite pastime of ripping a dress apart and putting it together again knew this. Cap sleeves on an evening gown: "My upper arm is overdeveloped from swimming." Flowers or ruffles across the front of a yoke: "Too much bosom." Panels added to a skirt: "Too clinging."

As in so many other ways, the requirements of the theatre were an entirely different matter. What Laurette Taylor wanted did not exist; nor any of her phobias. For Lone Star the leaf costume had been right and all personal concerns were overridden by that simple fact. Her letter to the Buffalo *Courier* has more than a degree of pathos:

Editor *Courier*

I must protest and protect myself against the articles appearing in your paper regarding my attire in the last act of "Yosemite." Had I worn this dress of leaves with the idea of creating any discussion, I might long ago have been a rival of Gertrude Hoffman or Eva Tanguay by doing a nature dance in vaudeville. I have no ambition along the Salome line—I want my competency as an actress not my ability to wear few clothes to be considered. . . . I want to say the part appealed to me strongly.

Can you imagine or have you ever seen, Innocence depicted as wearing shoes and stockings? Then why tights? This child has been guarded like a rare flower for her lover who is to come and claim her. In her primitive way, she figures, even as a modern woman, that to find favor in his eyes she must be beautiful but modest. Therefore instead of dirty and tattered rags, she has dressed herself in leaves and flowers, the best of Nature's adornments.

The scene is the spirited perfection of human love, beautifully written by the author, and I think Mr. Durkin and myself grasp its delicate symbolism enough to convey the idea to the audience without being vulgar.

Be just to me. I ask your consideration.

Respectfully,

LAURETTE TAYLOR

Hurt and disturbed by the unwelcome notoriety, Laurette was tempted to give notice, but realized it would be cowardly to quit. Besides, she believed in the part. They finished the Buffalo engagement. There had been compensatory developments. The brothers Shubert, Lee and Jake, heard excellent reports of Laurette's work, went to see the play and took careful note of the star's talents other than her ability to wear leaves charmingly. As a result they booked the show into Washington, D. C.

Leading Washington critics exercised mature judgment in assaying the value of the play and Laurette's performance. Almost without exception she was labeled a discovery.

But the fulsome praise was again buried under a continued uproar, by more sensational elements of the press, over the leaf costume and the bare feet. Alice Roosevelt Longworth sat in a box and with her rapier tongue guyed an entire performance. She sent violets to the star afterward but that did not heal the wounds. "Instead of fame, I achieved notoriety," Laurette said bitterly in one of her few references to the ordeal. After two weeks in Washington she gave her notice. "The criticism was so strong, so unkind, I could not bear it any longer."

Actually that was not the whole story. Laurette knew that "Yosemite" was Charles' best effort. For all the deep sincerity of his attempt he had not been able to free himself from the stereotype handling of character, the wooden dialogue of the melos. Given a powerful theme, he had failed to achieve depth and realism. The flaws in his work were those to be found in his own character. Through some fatal catalytic in his make-up, feeling deteriorated into sentimentality, sentiment into bathos, comedy into buffoonery. When Laurette appeared in his plays, it was only her consummate skill which permitted her to extract a core of reality from the sentimental and often near-farcical claptrap. It was when she realized that these elements had soured his most serious attempt at legitimate drama that the breach between husband and wife became widest.

"Yosemite," from which both Laurette and Charlie had hoped

so much, like the crags and gorges of its settings, became the im-
passable terrain between the two artistically. Never again did she
play in one of his plays or under his management. And "Yosemite"
was the last play Charlie ever completed. It was, he said to the end
of his life, his masterpiece.

A week after Laurette left Washington she had signed with the
Shuberts for three years. Within the month she was rehearsing in
"The Great John Ganton" by J. Hartley Manners, an up-and-
coming young English playwright. "Yosemite," without its star,
lost the interest of its audiences and the brothers Shubert too, and
quickly folded.

*

# *"Discovered"-1909-1911*

In the next three years Laurette was discovered, mislaid and discovered again so many times that one critic referred to her as the
"most discovered actress" of her time. She appeared in six plays,
all but one produced on Broadway. She flunked the test of stardom, then promptly shone with the effulgence of a star in a lesser
role. Both the Shuberts and David Belasco threatened to sue her
for breach of contract. A lot was happening to the little leading
lady from Western stock.

Through it all Laurette went doggedly on, taking what came,
good and bad, working because it was "my need to work." If
ever she showed her work-horse habits, learned in those grueling
days of stock, it was in this period. But that was all she showed of
her stock training.

New York critics enjoying the crisp and penetrating portrayals
of Mrs. Fiske, the glowing maturity of Margaret Anglin, the brilliant playing of Ibsen by the young Nazimova, began dissecting
the style of this newcomer with all the enthusiasm of entomologists
examining a new kind of bug. From the beginning they were baffled, bemused, and for the most part entranced by her technique.
Or was it technique? No one could quite decide.

James O'Donnell Bennett, eminent Chicago critic, announced his discovery with a discreet roll of drums after the opening of "The Great John Ganton" in April, 1909: "She had not been on the stage ten minutes when she gave the judicious cause to rejoice. . . . Nobody on that night seemed to know just who the young lady was, though several ventured the statement that they had 'seen her in something.' It will not be difficult to recall her another time. Prophecy relative to players is always dangerous because the stage as a profession renders careless and sluggish more minds than it develops; but . . . there is a temptation to say that the future must hold something for this fresh, luxuriant and youthful talent. It is difficult to resist the glow of spontaneous feeling intelligently directed in a day when so much acting is intensely matter of fact and extremely deficient in initiative."

Other critics gazed into their crystal balls and found them not too clouded. The word "genius" is used more than once. All of them considered her "a find."

Laurette had read the part of May Keating in "The Great John Ganton" at the Shuberts' New York office for the author, Hartley Manners, just two weeks after she left "Yosemite." When she first saw him, she thought that he was a priest. His large brown eyes were unusually gentle in aspect, his whole face possessed the rather grave and tranquil look of a cleric. When he spoke his voice was "a benediction." She read well. What nervousness she felt had been quickly calmed by his quiet attention and the courteous and sincere way he told her after the reading, "Very nice, Miss Taylor, really very nice indeed." She found herself wishing that she had stopped to black the tips of her shoes that morning and wondering if the light from the office window showed up the shine on her otherwise smart redingote suit coat. To hide these distracting concerns she gave him a quick smile that had a friendly little "Ha!" beneath it, and almost dipped him a curtsy when she took his hand. She noticed the faintest twinkle in the brown eyes as he said good-by, and the strand of dark hair that curled rebelliously over the calm brow from an otherwise perfectly groomed head. She decided he was Irish.

She was told to be at the theatre at two to meet the rest of the company.

Laurette did not bother to return to her mother's, but gulped a bowl of soup for lunch and walked the streets until the appointed hour. A bitter February wind lifted the tails of her redingote and stabbed across her stomach where the coat was stylishly cut away. She arrived at the theatre chilled and shivering.

The very first person she saw was a beautiful woman "with glinting brown eyes and burnished brown hair" swathed in a gorgeous mink coat with hat and muff to match. This paragon of style and beauty was standing to one side of the bare stage chatting in intimate tones with the author and the star, George Fawcett. Laurette shrank up against the radiator and tried to stop her teeth from chattering. The lady in the mink coat swept her with a quick, appraising glance and in a tone far from inaudible remarked to the author, "Do you think I'm going to play *second* to that?" while Fawcett demanded querulously, "Why couldn't they have got someone that somebody knew?"

The author made the introductions and the reading began. All confidence had oozed away through the tips of Laurette's unshined shoes. Her hands shook, her voice was lost somewhere behind chattering teeth. Before she had finished her first scene the beautiful Titian was heard to remark, again with crushing audibility, "But, Hartley, the girl has no voice!"

"But I assure you," the author replied earnestly, "she had a most lovely voice when she read for me this morning. She's frightened, that's all——"

Laurette blessed him and cursed the Titian all in one breath. She hated that brown-eyed, mink-coated hussy as she had never hated anybody before in her life. Maybe if *she* had only a bowl of soup under her ribs and a coat stylishly cut away where you needed it most, instead of all that mink, she wouldn't have a voice either!

Sick with despair, Laurette read on. At last she came to her big scene. She could feel herself getting mad—fighting Irish mad. As she launched into the long excoriating speech in which she called Fawcett a pig, Laurette gave it everything she had. It was an invective worthy of her fighting Dorsey blood. At the conclusion there was no further question on the part of any member of the company as to her ability to play the part.

Jane Peyton, the lady in mink, became in time Laurette's closest friend, but the change was gradual. It was not conducive to
friendship to notice that almost every day Miss Peyton was taken
to lunch by Mr. Manners and that her vivacious charm and aristocratic deportment obviously had his unqualified admiration.
That the relationship was purely friendly and of long standing
escaped Laurette's fevered notice. The author's interest in Laurette seemed to be confined to taking great pains to see that she read
his lines correctly. On the opening night in Chicago Laurette
was thrilled to find a basket of flowers in her dressing room with
the card: "Good luck. From the author." On making a quick tour
of the other actresses' dressing rooms she found identical baskets
in each with cards identically inscribed, except for Miss Peyton's. Her card read: "To Jane—with love, Hartley."

An unpleasant incident at the outset of the play's road tour
paved the way for better relations between the two women. To
save money Laurette roomed with a young woman playing a
minor role. In one of the first towns their hotel room was little
more than a cubbyhole on an air shaft. Shortly after arrival, the
roommate, clad only in a shift, began grooming her long tresses
before the open window, and from time to time gaily waved her
brush at someone across the areaway. Laurette saw an eager gentleman at the window opposite, straining over a trunk tray full of
shoes. Presently the wall telephone jangled. After a series of giggling "yeses" the girl hung up and turned to Laurette. "You
shouldn't jump to conclusions," she said with considerable hau-
teur. "That was an old friend. He has a friend and they want to
take us to dinner. We'll have a good meal and not have to pay
for it."

Laurette believed her momentarily. But when the two men
arrived, there was small doubt in her mind that a payment of
sorts was expected. To Laurette, the aspect of evil had no nuances;
if they had sported forked tails and billy-goat horns her reaction
could not have been more violent. Assuming a slight football
crouch, and muttering something that was supposed to be an
apology but sounded more like the growled warning of a cornered
animal, she dove between the two and fled down the hall.

The fear of the easy-sister and the two callers overcame Laurette's coldness toward Jane. After a lonely dinner she went to her dressing room and asked for advice. Jane graciously offered to share her suite, and Laurette moved in after the performance that night. This arrangement continued for the duration of the road run.

Jane Peyton, in private life Mrs. Guy Bates Post, had countless friends. She used the theatre more as a springboard for her social life than as a profession. Moreover, as Laurette termed it she was a "creative meddler." As Jane learned more of the one-time Western soubrette with the brilliant smile and cocky manner, she found it quite complicated enough to appeal to her love of drama and courageous enough to be worthy of her best efforts to unravel the complications. She had not missed a trick when the shy, aloof Hartley—a determined bachelor for all the years she had known him—had allowed his gentle brown eyes to rest for long spaces of time on Laurette's face when the latter wasn't looking, and had seen Laurette hopefully turn her most devastating smile on him, only to despair when she received not the slightest sign of encouragement. Jane was determined to bring the two together at the first opportunity and laid her plans carefully and well.

"The Great John Ganton" went into New York in May after ten weeks on the road. Again Laurette was acclaimed as "a find." So pleased were the brothers Shubert that they voluntarily raised her salary from seventy-five to one hundred dollars. But the play closed in June and after that her career hit another doldrum. She spent a hot summer in a dull and pretentious play called "The Ringmaster," in which she was badly miscast. There was first a tryout in Washington stock, then a New York production.

Elizabeth had designed and made three lovely costumes for "The Ringmaster," but the Shuberts said positively that they would not do. Laurette was put in the hands of a costumer known for his "chic" creations.

Laurette tells of the lugubrious results: *

> In the first act I was discovered dictating letters. For this Mr. Ellis wrapped me in a slate-colored satin dress. The busiest dress ever seen. White polka dots from pin point to dollar size galloped

* "Critics" by Laurette Taylor. *Town & Country*, March, 1942.

from the waistline down to the small train. My hat . . . had an enormous rose-colored velvet bow with two enormous square rhinestone ornaments in front like headlights on a car. For the second act . . . I had another busy dress . . . a blue foulard patterned with what seemed to be little jiggly black worms. The train had weights in it so it would stay out behind me. There was no carpet on the floor so, as I walked, the train would go "clatter clatter" across the boards. I felt like turning on it and saying "Shush— Shush—You!" Instead I moved only when necessary. In the last act I had to denounce my father. For this, I had a dinner dress of salmon-pink covered from head to foot with tiny, bugle-like spangles. I would shake the newspaper in my father's face and "tinkle-tinkle" would go all the spangles. My big speech went something like this:

"I have just read in this paper (tinkle-tinkle) of your dastardly robbery of widows and orphans (tinkle-tinkle). You are no longer my father" (throwing the newspaper on the table which brought forth such a tinkle as spangles had never made before). From then on I tried to hold my body rigid and let my voice take care of my emotions. All this made me appear a pretty bad actress.

I may not have been chic in the clothes my mother made for me, but they didn't talk back!

Charles Darnton reported in his review of "The Ringmaster": "Miss Laurette Taylor was so completely at sea in the role of Eleanor Hillary and so loaded with clothes of strange design that you felt like throwing her an anchor." The notice almost broke Elizabeth's heart.

The wardrobe cost four hundred dollars. In those days, before Equity, actors furnished their own costumes, so it was arranged that Laurette pay the Shuberts back at the rate of twenty-five dollars a week. As the play closed in three weeks she was left owing them over three hundred dollars. Later, when the Actor's Equity Association was being organized and Laurette made speeches for the cause, she used to cite this incident as an example of what could happen to the unprotected actor.

After "The Ringmaster" came a tryout of Hartley Manners' comedy "Miss Brown—Burglar." Lee Shubert watched from a box and decided Laurette was not a comedienne. Next came "Mrs.

Dakon," another tryout on the road, in which Laurette played the sixteen-year-old daughter, Ruth Dakon. Again she received such critical acclaim that the Shuberts hastily changed the title to "Dakon's Daughter" in order to feature her. A play scout for Rejane, Miss Daisy Andrews, whose dramatic opinions carried great weight in Europe, saw the play on the road and termed Laurette's performance nothing short of "colossal." But the play was a failure and never went into regular performances in New York.

After these two flops the Shuberts seemed to have no further ideas as to what to do with their young actress and loaned her to Leibler Brothers for a relatively small role in "Alias Jimmy Valentine," in which H. B. Warner starred. The part of Ruth Dakon was forty-five sides; the part of Rose Lane a bare seventeen. To everyone's astonishment, except possibly Laurette's, she ran away with the show. Again the critics were hard pressed to convey just how she did it. James O'Donnell Bennett who had followed her career with an increasingly benign eye had more success than some.

> In the hands of a conventional actress the character would be extremely insipid. Whatever Miss Taylor may be she is not conventional, and her manipulation of the role is strikingly in point. Her treatment of it recalls the absorbing spectacle . . . of a woman doing things to a last season's hat—pulling it aslant in one place, bestowing a fresh touch of color in another, toying in meditation, that still seems not especially purposeful, with a piece of velvet, or restoring a feather to its original piquant significance. . . . Some such ingenuity of procedure and such freshness of touch Miss Taylor has exercised in her acting. . . . Audiences follow her maneuvers with intense interest for she exercises in an almost uncanny way the faculty of riveting attention upon herself; and observation is constantly rewarded by the disclosure of fleeting bits of detail, swift changes of mood, little quizzical touches of emphasis and tricks of facial play that are as unexpected as they are right and charming. . . . It has been suggested that perhaps this actress has not yet acquired a method. . . . But when you note the excellence of her pauses . . . or when you listen with her while she listens with an eloquence more illuminating than a dozen sentences would

be—then you are constrained to believe that here is either an extraordinarily subtle method or an intuitive gift for expression that amounts to genius.

The criticism is interesting because in it Mr. Bennett might be describing Laurette at the height of her career rather than the beginning. Her basic approach to acting does not change. There was to be a rounding and smoothing of her talent, and a disciplining of it under Hartley Manners' tutelage. Her voice also was to be improved to correct a certain harshness and occasional flatness caused by incorrect production. But it was fruitless, then as later, to look for a method. Her infallible sense of the theatre sprang from a deep creative rightness with which she was in tune, and which, in its essence, was as much a part of her at sixteen as it was at sixty.

Laurette enjoyed all the attention she received. But however serious about her work, she did not make the mistake of taking herself seriously. She was beginning to bubble again with that excess of good spirits which was the natural inheritance of her tremendous vitality and buoyant Irish nature. After repressive years with the deaf and domineering Charlie, she was laughing again, and it felt good to laugh.

Ashton Stevens in a delightful interview at the time catches her charm, her gaiety, her mischievous sallies, and predominantly this desire to laugh and have others laugh with her. Oddly enough, when Stevens saw Laurette in "The Great John Ganton" he had forgotten the impact of the "little pink and white soubrette" in "Scotty." He wrote that as Ganton's daughter he found Laurette "mild and forgettable." Subsequently at a supper party Laurette joshingly reminded him of the earlier meeting in San Francisco. In his review of "Jimmy Valentine" he gave himself an anonymous kick for his myopia: "An impertinent critic [once] wrote that she was mild and forgettable. Either he or Miss Taylor has greatly improved since then." Stevens and Laurette became the best of friends and their friendship was lifelong.

Here is what he said of her, and what they laughed about in 1909:
This is the way it started—over the telephone.

"It's awfully kind and flattering and such—but, you know, I'm not the star of 'Alias Jimmy Valentine'. I'm only the leading woman who pursues Jimmy. Mr. Warner is the star and really—well, you know—"

"I don't know a thing about it. Mr. Warner is a noble young star . . . but everybody is talking about you and I'm sure that everybody wants to hear you talk—"

"But surely you understand the professional etiquette! You ought to. You must be old enough. You gave me my first rhetorical bouquet when I was a stage child; you gave me my first 'roast' when I was an adult." . . .

Did I say she is very pretty? No; not yet. But she is. At least she was that afternoon when she came into the Annex for talk and tea, and I hope it is habitual. She was wearing, among other things, a down slanting hat of elephant blue, and under the eaves of it you could see a tiny tumble of hair of the color of honey. Under that was a most animated brow and two (2)—let us be accurate even though descriptive—of the most animated hazel eyes that ever looked at you. A little lower was one of those irregular, charming and absolutely irrelevant noses that belong to the American race alone. And just under that was an irregular mouth broken into the quaintest little-boy smile you ever saw. It was half smile, half grin. Barrie could write a play around that grin. Mark Twain may have seen it in a vision when he gave us Tom Sawyer.

"The first time I saw that grin, Miss Taylor," I said by way of being impersonal, "was when you were trying yourself out with Scotty, the spendthrift from Death Valley, in a melodrama."

"You can't surprise me with my past. I remember it terribly. Scotty didn't always appear. One evening in Denver the newspapermen came to me and asked if the real live Scotty surely would appear. I promised him to them body, boots and mule. And then they wrote that the man who pulled a Stetson over his eyes and rode the mule and shot the gun was only the sedentary manager who a few minutes earlier had been taking the money at the door—and that was the truth, too.

"To hear Lee Shubert laugh as you are laughing now would be the greatest symphony I ever heard—if he laughed at me," she said. "That's my tragedy. I can't make my manager laugh."

". . . Then you're really serious about wanting to be funny on the stage?"

"Why drag in that awful word serious? I don't want to be serious on the stage. I want to make people laugh. I want to be funny. When you use that word serious you remind me of Lee Shubert breaking my heart. After he saw me play comedy in Washington he didn't leave a whole bone in that heart. . . . I had such a funny part and was so funny in it—believe me *so* funny—even the audience was heard to laugh. But Mr. Shubert—there he sat in a box looking about as lively as Edgar Allan Poe, who is dead. That is 'true appreciation,' I said to myself; he feels it not in his face, but deep within.

"I felt sorry for Marie Dressler and May Irwin. I hoped they had saved enough to retire in comfort. And then I woke up, as they say in the two-a-day. I was called to consciousness by the small cool voice of Mr. Shubert. He was shaking his head from east to west and back again and saying, 'But you are not funny. But you are not funny.' It seemed to me that he said it a thousand times, and meant it two thousand.

"No—I did not swoon. I smiled. Maybe it was a ghastly smile, but I smiled it, and then I commenced to argue with him. Did you ever argue to anybody how funny you are? But of course you never did. In your profession you must be solemn and grave—the undertaker. But I must be funny. It is my mission. I don't care who does the voting if somebody only will let me be funny.

" 'Didn't you hear the audience laugh?' I said to Mr. Shubert. He only wagged his head from east to west, and said, 'But you are not funny.' 'I may not have been funny to them, Mr. Shubert; I may not have been funny to you—you, who are a business man, a person of affairs, one who never has had the time or environment for fun— but to myself I was funny; oh, I knew that I was funny. I felt my soul rock with it.' "

Laurette Taylor bewildered poor me as she must have bewildered poor Shubert. For all this came in passionate gusts through a twisted little-boy smile.

". . . And you do get the strangest surprises," she went on with eyes as straight as her mouth was crooked. "Now, when I asked Mr. Shubert for my first pair of corsets——"

"Your first?"

"Yes," she said simply, "the first. I'd never worn them till last season. And then the dressmaker insisted. She said she couldn't fit me without them. I told her that I would see Mr. Shubert about it. I hastened to him. I was agitated. 'I guess you will have to get me a pair,' I said to Mr. Shubert.

" 'Get you a pair! Me get you a pair! . . . Why in the name of heaven should I get you corsets?'

" 'Because I haven't got any; we never use them in our family.'

" 'I furnish costumes, I furnish properties, but corsets—a corset is a purely private matter, Miss Taylor, believe me.'

" 'Believe me, Mr. Shubert, a corset in this instance is not at all a private matter; it is a property. A property is something you use on the stage, but not off.' "

"What did Shubert do?"

"Bought 'em. And I returned them to him as soon as the part was over. You see, they were really no affair of mine at all."

I put down my cup to keep from spilling the Oolong. I felt as young as Miss Taylor's little-boy grin. I laughed all over the place. . . . I said to her:

"I've got to shut my eyes to 'see' you on the stage. There, you are smart. It would seem that Fifth avenue rather than melodrama had been robbed. There's an urban tune in your voice, and your diction is a lesson in English. But here—now—you *are* funny. I swear you are!"

"Of course I am. I've known it all along. You have survived a real test of your intelligence. And if you're anything like as friendly as you look you'll promise to send the news on a postcard to Lee Shubert."

The promise was made and kept.*

The Tom Sawyer grin was an apt description; it was just that. There was a little-boy quality about her sense of fun and mischief; she was almost as ingenuous as the Mark Twain character and certainly as unconventional. This quality combined with her beauty, and a wistfulness that would ride over her gaiety at times like mist over summer fields, held a special kind of enchantment for those who met her at this period. These were the days before Hartley Manners' influence had come strongly to bear upon her character, and as a person she had a greater clarity of outline than she later possessed. It was a shame to teach Tom Sawyer the arts of gentility; it muddled his direction, took away some of his instinctive ability to get in and out of mischief and keep going on his golden adventures.

She far preferred to laugh than to talk of her troubles. Few knew that she had any. But Jane Peyton knew. Jane could see

* (*Chicago Sunday Examiner*, January 9, 1910)

the funny side of things but had a sharp eye for the shadows too. She had watched Laurette sitting in the late hours while on tour with "Ganton" composing fairy stories for her children in New York. They were continued stories to be read each night by the French nurse at bedtime. It made "the kids" seem closer. She knew that most of Laurette's paycheck went for their care and the upkeep of nurse and apartment. Charlie was in Toronto with a new stock company, a new leading lady, and home ties, financial and sentimental, were slack.

Then came news that the family doctor had stopped in on a routine call to find Dwight and Marguerite ill and unkempt, the nurse sodden with drink. Laurette had the children sent to her as soon as they could travel and Jane helped her care for them while on the road.

Four days after "Ganton" opened in New York came word that Charlie had taken off for the wilds of Alaska with his leading lady and the receipts of the Toronto stock company, leaving the rest of the outfit, including Sister Bessie and her brand-new husband, stranded.

Jane suggested there was nothing to salvage from such a marriage and urged Laurette to get a divorce at once. What's more she was convinced that her young friend was on her way up, and warned that Charlie, exercising his rights, might very well return someday to cash in on her fame.

But Laurette did nothing. Divorce was a disgrace in the Dorsey code, and Grandma Dorsey had suffered enough having a granddaughter become an actress. Add "divorcée" to that and Bridgett would be praying night and day for an erring granddaughter's soul.

For almost a year Marguerite and Dwight went wherever Laurette traveled. It was a life of hotel rooms, and trains, and backstage dressing rooms. The smell of grease paint was more familiar than fresh air. It was a life that swung bewilderingly between the carnival excitement of the theatre with its bright lights, music and laughter, where storybook people with paint on their faces always had time to play with a child, and the loneliness and severity of a hotel room where only a weary floor maid paid an occasional call through many a long and tedious hour.

Jane admonished Laurette that she was not being fair to her

children dragging them around the country; they should be put in boarding school where they could have the proper care. But Laurette would not consider it. She was lonely and wanted them close. Charlie's sudden return in February, 1910, almost a year to the day after he had left New York, quickly changed her mind. His prodigious adventure in Alaska, where he was the first to take a traveling company through the gold towns of the Yukon, had palled—and, by inference, so had the charms of his leading lady.

Laurette knew nothing of his return until a call came from the lobby of the apartment house where she lived with Elizabeth that Charlie was on his way up to see the children. Terrified, she rushed them from their beds, and fled with them down the back stairs to Jane's.

Elizabeth tried to stop Charlie at the door, telling him the children were in the country, but he pushed past her into the bedroom, felt under the crumpled sheets and cried out, "Their little beds are still warm! My God! How can she do this to me?"

Distracted with grief—now that he was back in the role of faithful husband and devoted father—he rushed into the night, fairly galloping to the bosom of his adoring sister, Helen Hunter, and put on such a show of despair that her loving heart never forgot it. Even as an old lady she could not speak Laurette's name without her lips trembling with fury at "how she treated poor Charlie." A magician of the emotions, Charlie drew them like rabbits from a hat at will. What explanation he gave of his year-long desertion while he tarried under the Northern Lights with the current lady of his fancy, can only be imagined.

Jane won her two points after that: Marguerite and Dwight were placed in a boarding school in Connecticut, and Laurette started divorce proceedings in New York.

The skein of Charlie's life unwinds completely from Laurette's after this. Jane had been mistaken. The illusion of his own grandeur was too strong ever to allow Charlie to put himself in the position of supplicant or leech on another's fame and reputation. He never made any further attempt to interfere with Laurette's life or associate himself with her success. Streaked through the crazy hodgepodge of his temperament—a mixture of barker, Munchausen, Francis of Assisi, adventurer and egotist supreme—was the pride, independence, and courage that Yankee sea-captains had left in his blood. He steered his crazy ship alone, stayed on the bridge no matter what the weather, and somehow made port. Laurette never saw him again.

After the divorce Charlie became a part of her life which she never discussed. When she achieved sufficient prominence to be interviewed and was asked about her early struggles, she never referred to him except as "the manager" or "the producer." When at last she could bring herself to mention him at all as her husband, she blandly had him "die" in 1910, the year of the divorce. As far as she was concerned he did. Actually he lived to the ripe old age of seventy-six and died in California in 1942. But Laurette felt more comfortable having him dead, so she "killed" him in 1910.

She never lost an almost childish fear of her first husband. When Charlie visited New York in the early 1930's after some twenty years in the West, Laurette's children were amazed to find her in a highly agitated state. She was afraid he would "make trouble," cause her some kind of "unwelcome publicity," try to see her. It was difficult to convince her that he was a harmless, fantasy-ridden fellow in his mid-sixties, almost entirely forgotten by the theatre world. Her picture of him was that of a ruthless, domineering man, still callously indifferent to her welfare. There was obviously some wound that never closed.

The last two typed pages of Laurette's unfinished recollections were devoted to "Charles A. Taylor." She was proud of the objectivity she had finally attained and said to her daughter on one of their last visits together, "I think I have the perspective now to see how he fitted into my life, and to say what he taught me in the theatre." It was a perspective that had taken her thirty-five years to achieve.

The young and energetic producing team of George M. Cohan and Sam Harris did not agree with Lee Shubert that Laurette was "not funny." They took over Hartley Manners' comedy "Miss Brown—Burglar" from the Shuberts, retitled it "The Girl in Waiting," and offered Laurette a five-year contract which stipulated stardom at the end of three years. She said yes. The Shuberts said no. There were claims and counterclaims as to obligations fulfilled and unfulfilled. Laurette felt that the Shuberts, after two bad plays and apparently no ideas on developing her career, except to state that she was not to play comedy, had no further claims on her services. Her Irish was up. "I walked into their offices with my shabby shoes and my flat purse, and I said to them, 'I'm going to fight you—I can't be any poorer than I am, so I'm going to fight you!'" The fight was brief. A court ruled that the Shuberts by raising Laurette's salary voluntarily when she made her first success with them, had automatically abrogated the terms of the original contract. "We parted company, the best of enemies, never to meet again."

"The Girl in Waiting" opened in Philadelphia, April 19, 1910. It was Philadelphia's turn to "discover" Miss Taylor, "hitherto unknown and unheralded." The notices were pallid compared to those she had received previously in far less important roles, but Philadelphians liked her and the play well enough to demand thirteen curtain calls on the opening night. Cohan and Harris were sufficiently pleased to elevate her to stardom then and there instead of waiting the stipulated three years. The first Laurette knew of it was when she turned into the street where the Garrick Theatre was located and saw her name in electric lights over the marquee. Completely dumbfounded, she said to Harris, "Don't you think you've picked me a little green?" To which Harris replied: "Like a bunch of bananas, you'll ripen." He went on to explain that he and Cohan had decided she might just as well take the plunge now as later, that it was easier to advertise a star than a leading lady. Laurette didn't give it much thought one way or the other except that it would mean an opportunity for better parts.

When the Chicago opening drew near after a two-month summer layoff, the full implications of what stardom meant dawned upon Laurette. All over the town which had received her so cordially in "Ganton" and "Jimmy Valentine" were eight-sheet posters with her picture; electric lights spelled her name in two-foot letters over the Olympic Theatre. Theatrical columns were full of happy anticipation at seeing the young actress whom

Chicago had "discovered" blossom into a full-fledged star.

Suddenly—and for the first time in her life—Laurette knew panic!

On opening night she was taut with nerves and from the outset keyed her performance impossibly high. An individual little chuckle which had characterized her performance in Philadelphia and which had been termed "most effective," became so insistent as to sound like the prelude to hysteria. At the close of the performance it was obvious to all that she was in a state bordering on collapse. No one knew better than Laurette that she had failed to meet the test of stardom. On her curtain call she stepped to the footlights and in a breathless and completely disarming little speech told her audience, "Those twinkling little lights are very hard to live up to—I know tonight I have not done so . . ."

Her friends, the critics, mourned. Mr. Hammond wrote: "In the course of the proceedings last night Laurette Taylor made the suggestion which stifles, if it does not altogether choke, the words of criticism which we otherwise should utter. This suggestion was to the effect that . . . her elevation to stellar glory had stampeded her and left her dazed artistically. It becomes our painful duty to report the unusual possibilities indicated by previous performances were not realized." After remarking on the unhappy chuckle he went on to say, "We beseech Miss Taylor to return to the refreshingly unmannered manner of her minor career. All we ask is that she give her best to everything she does."

Mr. Bennett was inconsolable: ". . . here we get not the Laurette Taylor of the wonderful facial play in the 'Great John Ganton' nor the wonderful pauses and the searching emotional thrust in 'Alias Jimmy Valentine,' nor yet the Laurette Taylor of the still pathos of Mimi in 'The Devil.' Instead it was a Laurette Taylor thrust into the role of hoyden and enacting it along conventional lines neither much better nor any worse than scores of smart girls on the American stage could." Faint praise indeed from one who had been urging Laurette to essay Shakespeare and take her place with the great ones of the theatre.

Laurette joined in the wake. She beat her breast in public with a will. "All the lovely things that had been said about me in the papers before the opening instead of encouraging me made me tremble. I knew that I could never live up to the idea the critics had of me—and I didn't. I really don't know what they wanted me to do, but whatever it was it seems that I did not do it. . . ." She noted that all the nice things they did have to say had ended with a "but." "I'm going to make them say all those lovely things about me someday without any buts. I have all the ambition in the world. I've made the plunge and after the first shock the water's fine."

Ashton Stevens came backstage to offer suggestions. He made the mistake of criticising the play. Laurette flew at him. She had fallen more than ever in love with the author and nothing he could do—including his playwriting—could be wrong. Her problems had nothing whatever to do with the play, she stated flatly. It was entirely her fault. "The play," she told Stevens, "was obviously written by someone with a knowledge of inherited silverware—and I don't know anything about inherited silverware. That's the trouble."

She was more defensive than right about the play. Hammond thought it written in the author's usual "bright and alert fashion," but Bennett found it a "tedious and incredible farce" and felt his protégé wasted in it. Mr. Manners was heard to grumble rather peevishly, "They talk as though Sarah Bernhardt had been asked to play in 'Charley's Aunt.' " Maybe only Mr. Shubert was happy.

"The Girl in Waiting" closed after only so-so success on the road. It was not good enough to warrant bringing it into New York.

*

# Hartley Manners

It was like Laurette to characterize Hartley's playwriting as that done by a man with a knowledge of inherited silverware. She thought she knew whereof she spoke. . . . Jane had managed to get the two of them together at last—during the two months' summer layoff of the play before the opening in Chicago—and it had been a little bit like trying to join a quiet brook with a highly agitated arm of the sea; the result had been more of a whirlpool than the hoped for confluence of their two personalities. Possibly only such an arch matchmaker as Jane would ever have thought of trying.

Hartley was forty years old that summer in 1910 which marked the beginning of their courtship. Laurette was twenty-four. Where she was undisciplined and impetuous in her emotions, he was disciplined and deliberate. His manners were perfect, Laurette had none. He abhorred "scenes" of any kind; Laurette lived by them. Laurette was disorderly in her habits, he was methodical in the extreme. In some ways he was as bound by tradition as the proverbial Englishman who dresses for dinner every night in the depth of the jungle. His morning bath, the press of his trousers, the proper strength of his tea were all ritual with him. Laurette was right; the air of "inherited silverware" sat easy on him.

No one knew a great deal about Hartley's past. He had cronies rather than close friends: those with whom he played bridge regularly, tipped a friendly glass at a bar, or exchanged anecdotes by the hour while sitting in the deep chairs of his various clubs —anecdotes of the theatre, or prize fighting, of which he was extremely fond, or the position of an Englishman in the world, or the intransigence of the Irish—but never confidences. Few had knowledge of him beyond the bare facts of his career as an actor and playwright, which began in 1898 when he was twenty-eight. In that year he served his apprenticeship as an actor, touring Australia with Charles Cartwright for six months. His first London appearance was in 1899 at the St. James Theatre with Sir George Alexander and he remained with that distinguished actor's company for two years. He wrote "The Queen's Messenger" as a curtain-raiser for Sir George, and it became such durable dramatic fare that for the next eighteen years it was the most frequently performed one-acter by amateurs, playing in all parts of the world, and eventually was the first dramatic production to be given on the new medium, television, in 1928. He made his playwriting and acting debut in America in 1902 with Lily Langtry in "The Crossways" which they co-authored. Jane did not meet him until he returned to America in 1904 with Henry Miller with whom he appeared in the original production of Henry Arthur Jones' "Joseph Entangled."

Not even Hartley's best friends could say that he was a good actor. It can only be said he was thoroughly "exposed" to the great actors of the day—Charles Hawtrey, J. Forbes-Robertson (he played Laertes in the latter's production of "Hamlet"), Herbert Beerbohm Tree. The theatre, however, was part of his blood. His broad experiences in it were to make him one of the best directors and all-round theatre men in the business, but his acting remained consistently abominable. His style was wooden and to hide a chronic stage fright he tended to become stiffly declamatory in speech. It was a sort of slow rigor mortis which overtook a naturally easy and beautiful delivery.

Hartley's acting career was mercifully brief—1898 to 1905—but his playwriting continued to flourish.

In this he was indefatigable, turning out script after script. Many of his earliest efforts he took to a young friend, Ethel Barrymore, for criticism. A quiet, "No, Hartley," from Ethel sent him off again to write another. He had great respect for her judgment. "They were very English, Pinero-like plays," Ethel recalled. "He didn't really hit his stride until he met Laurette. That was the great explosion of his life. We all knew him as Jack Manners in London when he was an actor. He became J. Hartley when he turned playwright."

Half a dozen Broadway productions soon established him on the American scene as a dramatist of note. The year of "The Great John Ganton" he had two other plays running in New York: "The Patriot" with William Collier, and "The House Next Door," which served the highly expert comedian J. E. Dodson for three seasons.

The first twenty-eight years of Hartley's life remain a mystery. Few people felt they knew him well enough to ask about them. In his "Who's Who" biographical sketch, this period is covered with the phrase "privately educated." The only bit of information ever dredged up was that somewhere in his young past a Jesuit priest had exerted a strong influence in his life; so strong that at one point he had begun a course of training for the priesthood, but this training had stopped short of entering a seminary. Other than this, those twenty-eight years are a blank. Jane, a born intrigante, was sure that he was the illegitimate child of some noble house of England. If true, the secret was well kept. He not only died with it locked in his bosom, but in a final fillip to the mystery—after a lifetime of impenetrable reserve and with absolutely no compulsion to do so—revealed in his will the names of one Martin and Annie Dunne of London, England who, Laurette subsequently learned, were Hartley's brother and sister and to whom he left a considerable sum of money. This might be considered to have solved the mystery, but upon taking a look at Martin and Annie Dunne, it only became deeper. They were sandy-haired, sandy-complexioned, spindly little cockneys, twenty years or so younger than Hartley; and only if the whole theory of heredity was abrogated, could they pass as brother and sister to the Hartley Manners of the black waving hair and white Irish skin; of the strongly established structure of brow and nose and width of eye that no set of genes could throw out and then so completely forget in subsequent progeny of the same parents.

If anyone could pry out a secret it was Jane, but she made no headway with Hartley on this one. She remained convinced that he was hiding a royal if slightly irregular ancestry. Laurette, surprisingly enough, asked few questions. Hartley's reticence in itself was almost as mysterious to her as any explanation of it could be. She was fascinated by it and accepted it as an integral part of his personality. It was part of living with him to know nothing about him. You could not be intimate with the deepest aspects of Hartley's nature. You could be intimate with his kindness, his humor, his gentleness, and his love, but in this intimacy he reserved his personal history and, in a large measure, what that history had done to his soul. Laurette did not press. To her the demarcation between being born to the purple, if such he was, or being sufficiently absorbent to acquire all the attributes of one so born, was faint. Her theatre sense made the two things equally impressive, and to separate the true from the false in the matter would have been as depressing and thankless a job as unraveling truth from fantasy in her own life. His "gentleman ways" were all of one piece whatever their origin; they came with him along with his extraordinary reticence as to where he had acquired them. Were they a compound of the parts he had played?—Lord Scarlett of "The Crossways"?—Lord Chetland in "The Squire of Dames"?—or perhaps the elegancies of Croker Harrington in Pinero's "Iris"? Who knew? Who cared? was Laurette's attitude. When you loved him, you lived with this distinct pattern and you never questioned it. His reserve was as much a part of him as his fine, slim feet, his beautiful hands and his extraordinary gentleness of manner; so much so that if one circumstance had chipped the smallest piece from this pattern, she would have felt a little bit as though the world were coming to an end. Indeed, in the last year of his life when mental and physical suffering cracked ever so slightly his poise and inner reserve, it did seem to Laurette that the world was falling in ruin. And when he was gone, chaos came and sat on her shoulder, an intimate and horrific bird, as though it had broken from the strong cage which Hartley had built to hold it prisoner.

But the end of the love story of Hartley and Laurette was a long way off in the summer of 1910, and the beginning had not yet begun.

It was middle June when Laurette stepped off the train at Winsted, Connecticut, and was met by Jane in a smart two-seater buggy with a lively chestnut mare between the shafts. They bowled off down the road and presently turned off onto a hard dirt road along which they went for several miles. Only an occasional cow peered through scrub woods. As they passed a group of farm buildings Jane sang out a "Hullo-oo, Pa Dew!" to a lean man in the yard. Pa Dew was the only human imprint on the land until they arrived at Jane's big rustic lodge overlooking a mirror-clear little lake skirted by trees.

Jane did not announce at once that Hartley was coming. First, Laurette was to greet her children, who had been visiting at Lake Wonksonkmonk since the closing of school, then she was taken out on the broad veranda of the lodge. Jane wanted to have the quiet sylvan beauty of the place exert its full charm before showing Laurette the cabin she and the children were to occupy for two months. "High Rock Cottage" was on the shore just opposite Jane's, and was more rock than cottage. The huge boulder upon which it was built formed a hazardous hump in the center of one of the two tiny rooms; a couple of iron beds filled the other. An afterthought of a kitchen, broom-closet size, and supported by stiltlike posts, jutted from one wall. They had scarcely begun their inspection when Jane, to forestall any disappointment in the cottage, broke the news that Hartley would be one of several guests for the week end. Jane's offstage timing also was perfect.

"Quiet sylvan beauty" is only a relative term when applied to any landscape Jane inhabited; in no time, that landscape would be crawling with celebrities, semi-celebrities, the social and the antisocial. Jane loved human beings, and in her company even the most inimical personalities behaved humanly toward each other. Her rough château was the focal point of the social activities of the surrounding countryside. Hidden away down narrow rutted lanes along the lakeside, and back on wooded knolls were various writers and artists, pursuing a *yin* existence through the summer to reinvigorate their *yang* activities during the winter. There was Edward Sheldon, the playwright; Edward Childs Carpenter, poet and playwright; Willard Metcalf, the painter; Channing Pollock; the Charles Rann Kennedys (she, the lovely Edith Wynne Matthison); the emotional actress, Helen Ware, whose specialty was tearful heroines. Shelley and Henry Hull lived down in Pleasant Valley, a mile or two away. On week ends, Jane's rambling abode was filled with house guests: Carl Van Vechten, Will Irwin, Amy Lowell, Clara Louise Kellogg, the opera diva (both women smoked black cigars), Doris Keane, Samuel Hopkins Adams (who was to be Jane's fourth husband) and scores of others.

Laurette felt like a rather small frog in this impressive social splash, but was determined to make the most of the week end that Hartley was to spend at Jane's. She tore up and resewed a couple of tired-looking dinner dresses, one green and the other yellow; she did her hair a new way, adding a long switch and wearing the heavy mass low on her neck; and she practiced up on her swimming. This latter was the easiest part; the children lived in the lake, and she adored the water.

Hartley arrived with a flock of other guests and Laurette began a headlong pursuit. Hartley was extremely popular with the ladies. He listened most effectively with large gentle brown eyes fastened upon his feminine vis-à-vis, a slightly melancholic look from time to time creeping into his gaze; they were never quite sure at the end of the evening whether he had fallen half in love with them, or half asleep. It generally titillated them to further efforts to find out. He was an excellent bridge player. Laurette's game was aboriginal, but finding that he liked to play, she played too. He offered to teach her some of the rules of the game. Heaven! Then he offered to teach two other ladies. Heck! The four sat at a table. Laurette was the least apt of his pupils. When this became painfully obvious, she decided she didn't want to play any more and walked away. If she had been an expert knife thrower, she would have hurled a couple of knives over her shoulder to pinion the two "apt" pupils left behind.

The next afternoon some of the women guests were to swim to the end of the mile-long lake. The men were to follow, each in a rowboat, in case someone couldn't make it. Laurette thought: Now, ladies, watch my smoke! She stayed as close as possible to Mr. Manners' boat, feathering her fingers prettily on her backstroke, and getting her mouth full of water smiling up at him. Her showing off soon had her exhausted.

The swimmers were allowed to stop at any point and rest. As rest was becoming imperative for Laurette, she decided to use it for a test of Mr. Manners' interest. Everybody was going down one side of the lake. Laurette thought: "I'll swim to the other side to rest; if he doesn't follow me, I'll know he doesn't care a darn." She pulled away for the opposite shore and presently heard oars splashing untidily behind. Her heart leapt excitedly.

A very flushed Mr. Manners drew alongside with his black curly hair for once not neatly in place. "Are you all right, Miss Taylor?" he asked.

"Quite," said Laurette.

"Good!" said he.

Some of the other swimmers started over.

"I thought you were in trouble," he said.

"I was—and am," Laurette said—with a look.

"What can I do? Shall I row you back to the house?"

The others arrived:

"So, Hartley Manners, little you care about us," they shouted. "Your rowboat is supposed to follow all of us, dearie. If Laurette's quitting, let her be. We don't want to be at this all day!"

Laurette drew herself up on one of the many rocks that jutted out of the water by the shore. "Go along if you want to," she said to Mr. Manners.

If she thought that he would stay, she was mistaken. He set off briskly down the lake with the rest of his charges splashing and laughing around him, and Laurette was left to brood in solitary glory on the hazards of sportsmanship when one is trying to charm an Englishman.

The week end was almost over. On the last evening everybody played bridge. A thunderstorm was brewing and Laurette, who had commandeered the seat opposite Hartley, grew more and more nervous. There was a sudden clap of thunder and she jumped up, scattering her cards. "Here we sit playing the devil's game with God's anger all around us!" she cried, and fled into a small heavily curtained den off the living room.

The game broke up and Hartley followed her into the den. "Come and look at it," he said, making a gesture toward one of the curtained windows. "It's really beautiful."

"No-no-no!" Laurette cried with rising emphasis, shrinking back. All her coquetry was gone. It was a real and deadly fear she had of thunder and lightning. "My grandmother used to say you could see the face of God if you looked," she murmured in a small scared voice, "and that it cured some and blinded others according to the state of grace you're in. . . ." She smiled uncertainly at Hartley, her fingers weaving together in a small fluttering movement as she tried to conquer her fear.

Hartley let his eyes rest on her face for a long, long moment; then he reached out and briefly touched her hand. "You're a curious child, Laurie," he said with great gentleness. . . .

He was gone the next morning early. Jane pronounced the week end an unqualified success. Laurette didn't know. The melody of that voice calling her "Laurie" stayed with her, the beauty of his face that bore at times so melancholy a look, as though he sought access to some lost world of his youth. She had never known such gentleness of spirit. In his presence she felt like a wild untrained puppy, and, like a puppy, brimming over with an undisguisable love. Many a night for the remainder of her stay at the lake she went into her tiny cottage, drew tight the curtains, lit the lamp, and buried her head in a book. She did not want to see the moon on the quiet surface of the lake or hear the murmur of the leaves in the soft night breeze, for they were all part of the melodic voice, the beautiful face, and the gentle spirit that she was still not at all sure could be won.

Jane had no doubts. Hartley was invited again later in the summer and from this week end Jane plucked a sign which she considered the brightest harbinger for the future of the romance. Hartley, attired in a borrowed bathing suit, allowed himself to be strapped into a large cork life-preserver and, with feet encased in immaculate white sneakers, plunged off Jane's dock into the lake where Laurette and various house guests were disporting themselves. It was the one and only time that Hartley was known to immerse himself in water outside of a bathtub. This courageous effort to enjoy what Laurette enjoyed proved almost fatal. In some inexplicable manner the life-preserver became firmly wedged around his head, and with the feeblest flipping motion of sneakered feet he revolved helplessly in slow circles. He was so frightened that even his instinct to survive was half paralyzed. Jane considered this a demonstration of love equal to that of Leander swimming the Hellespont. And even Laurette was impressed.

Before leaving to resume her role in "The Girl in Waiting" in August, Laurette told Jane that she was returning the next summer. Marguerite and Dwight, in spite of string-bean structures inherited from their father, had put on weight thanks to Pa Dew's cream and milk and eggs; they hadn't had shoes on their feet the entire summer and were supremely happy. Laurette was determined they should have more of it.

"Perhaps Hartley will come too," Jane said archly.

"Not him," replied Laurette. "His idea of roughing it is to change from a double-breasted blue serge suit to a pair of perfectly pressed white flannels. What would he do on this lake all summer?"

"That would depend on you," replied Jane. Jane's laughing eyes and lips could make you feel a romance was three quarters settled before it was even begun. But you couldn't hang a romance on the one word "Laurie" and a jump in the lake, no matter how optimistic you were.

*

# ". . . *Nothing Half so Sweet in Life* . . ."

How much Laurette saw of Hartley that winter is not a matter of record. Probably not as much as she wanted to, and certainly not enough to be sure that he was as much in love with her as she was with him. Hartley was infinitely shy of the feminine and more than a little attached to his bachelorhood. This, with his extreme reticence, kept Laurette in considerable doubt as to the degree of his devotion. Moreover, she was used to forthright and immediate expression; anything else bewildered her. It is not inconceivable that many a tentative advance on Hartley's part went unnoticed in her own somewhat whirlwind approach to their romance. The sea and the brook; the same element, but so differently paced in their rhythm!

Undoubtedly there were scenes. It was Laurette's firm conviction, reaching back to her childhood, that differences of opinion made life exciting, and that the stormier the expression the greater the degree of one's affection. If Hartley was tardy in keeping an appointment—and next to Laurette he was one of the tardiest of human beings—she would berate him, not so much because she was angry as because she was anxious for some revealing fervor on his part. The invariable and rather pallid excuse that he was "finishing a rubber at the club, old dear," was to Laurette altogether unsatisfactory. By her own admission she indulged in many a scene of anger and jealousy.

"My only rival seemed to be bridge, but I attacked it as I would a flesh and blood one."

Hartley was not an easy man to provoke. He would reason but would not argue. If she persisted in argument he would very politely take his hat, gloves and cane and return to his club.

"You have an undisciplined tongue, Laurie," he once told her, "and it would be sad if you said something you would regret."

"I never regret anything I say," she responded hotly.

"It would be even more sad if I could not *forget* something you would say. I believe I would forgive anything you said, but forgetting is something else again."

This was new kind of talk for an Irish girl who had exploded into speech on every and any occasion, whether it hurt somebody or not. She was baffled, fascinated and often miserably unsure as to whether he loved her or not.

"Aren't you going to stay and argue with me?" she would almost plead at times.

"You'll lose him with that tongue of yours," Elizabeth would caution. "He's a fine gentleman, and he won't stand for any of your sass, I'm warning you now. . . ."

Laurette would bite her tongue and the next time Hartley was late would wonder if he would come at all, at all.

She opened in New York in "Seven Sisters," February, 1911. Before leaving for Chicago in April her uncertainty had largely vanished. Hartley had outlined a play with her in mind, and asked Jane to find him a place on the lake the next summer, to work on it there. For a shy, conservative Englishman, Laurette considered that tantamount to a proposal.

"Seven Sisters" was another astonishing success.

Quite solemnly Producer Daniel Frohman had warned, "I'm not going to star you, Miss Taylor."

"That's quite all right, Mr. Frohman," replied Laurette. "Mici is the part—whether I'm starred or not doesn't matter. It's the chance of a generation—a white Topsy. I can't miss!"

And she didn't.

"Oh, what a jolly mix-up!" crowed Stevens in his review. "When she was a star, she wasn't, and now that she isn't, she is! She wanted to be funny you may remember . . . they made her a star for a teacup comedy by Hartley Manners and she tried very hard to be but wasn't at all funny. Her starship seemed to scare all the fun out of her. But Charles Cherry's starship relieved her of fright as completely as she relieves him of starship."

Here and there a reviewer managed to maintain a sober critical faculty in the face of the whirlwind impudence of her performance. There were minor dissonances in the chorus of praise; a "carelessness of speech" was noted, a growing "excess of zeal for natural effects." There was the impression of a lack of discipline and control; as Laurette put it, "Before I knew Hartley I tended to 'spill over' in everything I did."

But Laurette was in no mood to be admonished. Life was beginning to expand after years of grinding work. She was free of Charlie, and was at last making progress with the shy Mr. Manners. She was "spilling over," and it was not unnatural that it should take on the tomboy quality of her youth. The survival instincts of the tomboy had been hardy; the tenderer emotions were in abeyance waiting the proper soil and climate. Now that she was in love she was reaching out, but tentatively. She still found it safer to laugh, and she wasn't going to let a mere bunch of critics take the soul-saving grace of laughter away from her.

There is great insouciance in the picture of Laurette at this period in her life. A child released from certain irksome fetters insisting upon enjoying herself and still not too particular about dignity and importance. The role of the romping fourteen-year-old Mici fitted her mood perfectly.

"Seven Sisters" was still doing good business in Chicago when she left the cast in June, 1911, and went immediately to Wonksonkmonk. Hartley was already occupying what Pa Dew had rather grandly described as a seven-room cottage called Sunset Lodge. Actually it was one room which could be divided into seven compartments by drawing a number of faded gingham curtains. The bed occupied one compartment, a wash bowl and pitcher another, oil stove and table another, and so on. There were kerosene lamps, and an outhouse reached by a path through the woods. When Laurette saw Sunset Lodge, she was more certain than ever that Hartley must be in love with her.

Hartley never indicated in any way that the place was less than a palace, and in these rustic surroundings proceeded to conduct his life exactly as he would have in the heart of London or New York. Every morning at nine A.M. a flat-bottomed boat was rowed down the lake by one of the Dew boys, with a large copper tub of steaming hot water on the back seat for Hartley's morning bath. An hour or so later an elderly Frenchwoman was similarly transported bearing in her arms piles of snowy laundry including his perfectly ironed shirts. The *Tatler*, the *Sketch*, the *London* and the *New York Times* appeared regularly in Pa Dew's mailbox, and these also were water-borne the half mile down the lake to the Lodge. Visitors coming by rowboat or along the lane by the lake shore would find Hartley attired in immaculate white flannels and custom-tailored shirt, wearing, perhaps, a checked cap as his one concession to rustic life. With quiet enthusiasm he would demonstrate to those interested the exact manner in which the limply hanging curtains could be pulled in order to avail oneself of the ultimate privacy they afforded. Many a morning Laurette stood at her window at High Rock Cottage, watched the steaming copper tub rowed by, and chuckled with delight. "I felt like Delilah," she said, "having wooed my Englishman so far from his native haunts—if not his habits."

It was at Sunset Lodge that Hartley wrote "Peg O' My Heart." It took him four months. He carefully explained to Laurette his working methods. His scripts were completely rewritten four times. The first version was formal and didactic. In the initial stages the story was pushed along, the scenes laid out more or less mechanically. Gradually with each rewriting the script became more supple and alive. Work on the dialogue came last. For this reason he would not read the play to her until it was virtually completed.

But this, of course, would never do for Laurette; she must hear it as soon as it was down on paper. So one afternoon, with considerable reluctance, Hartley gave in. They sat on the porch of

Sunset Lodge, author with cap pulled low over his eyes to shade them from the sun, pipe in the corner of his mouth. Once again Laurette was warned not to expect too much; then Hartley began to read. He grew absorbed. His beautiful voice went on and on, muted music, the diction impeccable. At last it was finished. "How do you like it?" he asked.

"Hartley, it's *awful!*" came Laurette's prompt reply.

So ended the first reading of "Peg O' My Heart," the play that was to make the fame and fortune of both.

Hartley vowed that he would not let Laurette see the play again until it was finished. But she was persuasive. He would admit to having completed a couple of scenes, and the next thing he knew they would be walking through the woods arm in arm to Sunset Lodge so that he could read them to her. Each time there was an argument—or at least, Laurette did everything she could to start an argument—until finally the readings were given up because Hartley found them "too discouraging." Laurette felt like a little girl being punished. But Hartley was adamant. It was his brain child and she could wait until it was completed.

Nevertheless, he was absorbing much of the living spirit of "Peg" through Laurette. On many a star-studded night they strolled and talked, and many a long, lazy afternoon sat on Jane's wide porch while Laurette told tales of her childhood, her Irish family, particularly her peppery little grandmother; the turn of phrase Bridgett used, so essentially humorous and invariably delivered without humor; her steadfast religion; her tart and immediate summation of character; her pride and peasant sense of her place in the world, the dignity of being "a decent, God-fearing human soul." Hartley found in Bridgett Dorsey's granddaughter many of the characteristics that made "Peg" loved by millions throughout the entire world; the spirit of youth, both the directness and the clear innocence of a child, the penetrating wisdom of one who remains simple in heart and unsuborned by compromise.

"Peg, if ye must know, is my grandmother," Laurette once told a reviewer. But Peg also was Laurette.

Hartley did his writing at night. It was a habit formed during years of city living, and even here in the quiet of the woods he would wait until there were only the deep-throated comments of the frogs to keep him company before taking up his pencil to work. From midnight on were his working hours. At five in the morning he would retire, with breakfast at eleven or later.

Jane and Laurette spent their mornings in a strict regimen of health. Observing that Laurette was beginning to curve a little too much for beauty, Jane quoted Dion Boucicault's three rules for an actress—First Rule: Keep your figure. Second Rule: Keep your figure. Third Rule: Keep your figure.

As Laurette said: "I was born round. Everything. Eyes. Cheeks. Lips. Figure." That summer saw the tentative beginning of Laurette's relentless fight with fat. If the Manners family had been entitled to a coat of arms the word "*reducing*" would have been engraved upon it. Every summer for sixteen years family life revolved around Laurette's reducing. She did not go about it quietly or unobtrusively. It was as dramatic a performance as she ever put on. A favorite quotation was Irvin Cobb's retort to a friend who asked if he hadn't lost a few pounds. "Hell! What do you mean *lost?* I went to the mat with it and *won!*" But these herculean efforts were to come later. The mornings at the lake were not too strenuous: a swim in the lake and a delightful if unsatisfying lunch on Jane's screened dining porch.

By the time Hartley appeared on the scene, Laurette was, in the words of "Peg," "sick for the sight of him."

In the afternoons people came from all points of the compass irresistibly drawn into the orbit of Jane's sunny sociability. They appeared along faintly marked paths through the woods, or by rowboat, or canoe. Some came by car, some were met at the railroad station by any number of swains who sat about waiting to do Jane's bidding. There were swimming and games and hours of talk. It was talk that was animated and entertaining, engaged in by some of the most brilliant minds of the day. At any other time Laurette would have been in the center of it, reveling in the quick play of ideas, contributing her own highly original, if not always informed, remarks on any and all subjects that might be introduced. But lovers are self-absorbed. Hartley and Laurette listened mainly to each other. He recounted stories of the great actors with whom he had played, the techniques and manners of another era in the theatre, while Laurette regaled him with tales of Western stock and early family life. They walked together, rowed together—he was too terrified of the water ever to try the more romantic canoe—played bridge together.

In the evening they sat on High Rock Cottage's rickety bird's nest of a porch, with the children asleep inside. He read aloud from his favorite authors, George Meredith, Thackeray, Anthony Trollope, Kipling. Solemnly he advised, "When you feel like reading a new book, read two old ones instead and you will be well read."

He gave her a Victor talking machine, introduced her to the voices of Melba, Caruso, Scotti, Sembrich. When he was not there, Laurette read passages from the books to her children, played the records again and again. It brought him close. But it was so tenuous and shy a courtship, with so much left unsaid. She often wondered what was going on in that gentle mind of his, behind that infinitely gentle gaze. She loved to see the look of tender astonishment spreading over his face at something she would say; in that look was the wonder of discovery, of pure delight, that a musician might have on hearing an infinitely pleasing chord, or a poet, catching the worded rhythm of an innermost revelation. But oh, so, so gentle. How was she to encompass this love, or be encompassed by it? It made her feel clumsy and awkward; and because it still was not declared in word or action other than this look of wonder and adoration, she was afraid to approach too close lest it shatter or dissolve before her very eyes.

Many a night Laurette saw Hartley off down the tree-lined lane by the lake, watched him disappear swinging his lantern with the finicky step of a man who prefers pavements, then went back to her own little porch to stare for long minutes across the star-bright waters of the lake. There were times when, in all that quiet, she seemed to be holding her breath to listen to the beat of her own heart. The tiny waves, lapping the pebbled shore, echoed the sound, faintly, sibilantly, as though they carried it out through the night to be lost on some distant sill of infinitude. Laurette. . . . Laurette. . . . Who is she?

For the first time Laurette tried to answer that question. She had run away from it all her life in stormy revolt or dreamlike projections of her fancy. But because of her love for Hartley an answer seemed now imperative. She had measured herself by storms: opposition, failure, her ability to survive emotional turmoil in herself and in those around her. But in Hartley there was no such turmoil. In a way she felt more lost than ever surrounded by his quiet and selfless devotion. She wanted more than anything else in the world to become a part of it. But how? Her aggressiveness covered a multitude of bewilderments about him. She tried to test him with scenes, but he would not have scenes; she demanded passionate declaration, but it was not in his nature to so declare himself. She found herself waiting with a humility quite unlike her to be shown the life he would make for them both.

As she stood listening to the beat of her heart and the tiny echo of the waves, she was conscious for the first time of the great swinging rhythms in life that can come flood tide without violence and without destruction, and of which there is no reason to be afraid. Laurette was leaving a childish confusion about such matters behind. She had waited a long time to give herself to love neither defiantly nor cravenly, but proudly and with deep confidence. She waited now, impatient, somewhat bewildered, to be shown the way. . . .

Inside, one of the children stirred on the iron cot. She had almost forgotten them. They were off most of the day, fishing from the rocks, rounding up cows with the Dew children, or watching the milking in the late afternoon. Jane's young daughter, Mildred, taught them French, took them off on picnics, blackberrying. Laurette hardly saw them except swimming, and when they came home to roost at night, dog-tired, sun blisters as big as half dollars on their shoulders, scratches on their legs, and splinters in their leather-hard feet. Her heart suddenly sank. Her children! It had never occurred to her: the hazard to a man of Hartley's sybaritic habits of taking on a ready-made family!

He had always been excessively polite to Marguerite and Dwight as though they were adults in miniature, but she had never observed any particular demonstration of interest in them, even the usual sycophantic efforts on the part of a courting male to win favor. No candy, or jouncing on the knee, or chucking under the chin; just a "How do you do?" and a "So long for now," with cap doffed each time and a slight bow from the waist. And what must he think of their appearance? Their perennial costume of bathing suits, hair dry as straw and streaked from sun and water, eyes bloodshot and noses running from numerous underwater exploits in the lake? Not very attractive, she had to admit. . . . She went inside, turned up the lamp in the front room and took a long look that was meant to be appraising. Dwight was clutching a small glass jar in which he had imprisoned numerous fireflies. Most of them had given out their last flicker but a few were still glimmering their weird green-white light against the glass. She remembered how proudly the boy had told her of this night light he had fashioned for Marguerite to use when the covers slipped off. "See! See! All she has to do is shake the bottle and she's got a light to find the covers with." Apparently on this particular night he had used the light of the flickering bugs to pull the sheet completely over himself and off his sister. Marguerite was rolled in a ball like a pill bug, knees pulled up under her, and only the almost black soles of her feet showing beneath her small rump. Laurette felt a sudden ferocity standing there by the bed. They had all come a long rough road. She wanted peace and security for her children as well as herself, as an animal wants these things for its growing litter. Would Hartley love them? Could she ask him to love them? It seemed suddenly to Laurette that they might belong to a part of her that Hartley could not understand, an unruly, primitive part which, perhaps, he did not—could not—love. She didn't know. There were so many things she didn't know. . . .

It was on one of these questioning nights that Hartley sat at his writing table, pondering the dedication for the finished manuscript of "Peg." Presently, from the loose sheaves of paper scattered about the table he pulled a clean white sheet toward him and, after a long moment of thought, wrote in his small meticulous script:

To
LAURIE

"—— in that which no waters can quench,
No time forget, nor distance wear away."

*

# The Bird of Paradise

"Peg O' My Heart," neatly bound, was Hartley's betrothal present to Laurette. With it went a modest little ring of small sapphires and diamonds. Their marriage waited only on the play's New York production.

Laurette was enchanted with the finished script and there was no question in her mind that this was the play she would do next. They took it at once to Cohan and Harris. After Hartley had finished reading two acts Cohan stopped him.

"I don't want to hurt your feelings, Hartley," he said, "but no matter how good the third act is, it couldn't save the piece." He turned to Harris. "There's nothing to it, is there, Sam?"

"Not a thing," concurred Harris. "No punch."

Undaunted, Laurette proceeded to read the play to every Broadway producer who would listen. Her own soft brogue, as yet barely eradicated from her natural speech, must have carried extra persuasions to the producers' ears but she fared no better than Hartley. The play was too mild . . . syrupy. . . . No punch.

It was hard to discourage Laurette with "no" but, as time drew on, the thinness of her purse and shoe soles accomplished it. Poverty was too familiar to be pleasant. On her rounds with "Peg" she began to skip lunch, and more and more frequently dropped by to see her friend, Jane Peyton, at the dinner hour. After a six-month layoff it was imperative she find a job.

Oliver Morosco, ex-acrobat, who had come into the theatre on a shoestring and built up a number of successful stock houses in the West, was eagerly eying Broadway as his next field of conquest. For his debut on the Great White Way he shrewdly chose a play called "The Bird of Paradise." It had enjoyed a successful run at his Burbank Theatre in Los Angeles with Lewis Stone starred, and the popular Western actress Bessie Barriscale as leading lady. The New York production waited upon the casting of a Broadway "name" in the role of the tragic Luana to replace Miss Barriscale.

There are different stories as to how Laurette came to get the part of the little Kanaka girl who takes a white man for a lover and, eventually spurned, flings herself into the crater of a volcano. Guy Bates Post, under contract to play Ten-Thousand-Dollar Dean, the beachcomber, claimed that he noticed the lean and hungry look when Laurette came to his wife's apartment, and penciled in her name for the unfilled role. Another story is that Annie Morosco, the producer's wife, made the suggestion, having greatly admired Laurette in "Seven Sisters."

However it came about, Morosco wired Laurette from the Coast offering the part. On the bare outline of the play provided by Mrs. Morosco, Laurette accepted. She was immediately intrigued by the idea of playing a Hawaiian princess. It would be a break from the comedy and ingénue roles which had made her reputation in the East, and as early as this in her career Laurette was determined not to be typed. That she would once again forfeit stardom was of minor importance.

Hartley was not at all happy when he learned of Laurette's quick decision. And when he found she was to play a native girl who takes a white lover, wears a grass skirt and does a hula, he was acutely distressed.

"Really, Laurie, I think this is most unwise," he told her. But he knew better than to press.

Elizabeth was frankly shocked. She was broad-minded up to a point but considered Luana an "outlandish" part and highly immoral. "I'll never hold my head up with my friends again, and that's the truth!"

But Laurette had made up her mind. In Luana she found what had been only crudely suggested in the character of Lone Star in "Yosemite," around which her first dreams of legitimate theatre had clung. At last she could realize such a character, a child of nature, artless, passionate, delighting in her lover without sense of sin or shame.

She immediately set to work to master the special skills required for the part. A fat little Hawaiian who in Laurette's words "moved like a fat little wave" came to teach her the hula. When she could

balance a gourd full of water on the back of each hand and un-
dulate her hips without spilling a drop, he pronounced her pro-
ficient. Four dusky musicians whom Morosco had brought from
the Islands came to her apartment every evening after rehearsal,
sat cross-legged on the floor of the parlor and strummed their instruments while teacher and pupil danced. They would call to her
over the music, strange guttural words of encouragement and
praise, and Laurette learned to answer back in their native tongue.
Eyes flashing, teeth gleaming, smile more brilliant than ever, it
would seem at times as she danced that her skin had already taken
on a darker hue. Hartley sat rather correctly in one corner of the
room, chain smoking, not saying a great deal and not very happy.

Elizabeth stayed as far away as possible, working in a back
room on Laurette's grass-skirted costume, all doors closed between
her and the atavistic cries and whining guitars of the little brown
men in the parlor. Sometimes, according to her daughter, she wept
as she sewed.

Tenants in the walk-up apartment house began to complain.
The spinster singing teacher downstairs, whose chandelier swayed
under the nightly stompings, informed the landlord that five
colored men were being entertained nightly by "that actress and
her mother upstairs." The landlord told Laurette she would have
to move. Laurette appealed to Hartley for advice. He suggested
that she use a little tact and ask the singing teacher to coach her
in Luana's Hawaiian love song; in that way the lady would realize that the dancing each evening was part of her job, not a nightly
bacchanal.

"It was a wonderful idea," Laurette recalled. "I went down
every morning before rehearsal for a lesson. She withdrew her
complaint and I learned my song. I had the great satisfaction of
singing the words directly at her in Hawaiian. I knew the translation. She didn't. If she had, she would have swooned."

When Richard Walton Tully, the author, came from the West,
Laurette ran into further opposition. He said she wouldn't do at
all for the part; she was too tall, too blonde, had a distinct Irish
accent and had never been to Hawaii. Laurette promptly offered
to buy the dinners of any two Broadway actresses who had been
there. Tully, rough-spoken, quick-tempered, made no attempt to

conceal his displeasure. "If he could have kept me out of the part, he would have," Laurette said. "How he didn't want me!"

Throughout rehearsals he continued to squabble with Laurette. Superciliously he advised her to merely "indicate" the hula with a few motions as she could never give it proper authenticity; when he stripped off his coat to demonstrate the basic steps, Laurette watched without comment. Dutifully she confined herself to these basic motions, reserving her growing virtuosity for the evening sessions with her teacher. On one occasion Tully snapped that she was much too sure of herself, that it was the nature of the Hawaiian to be apologetic for everything—for living, for loving, even for every word uttered. Laurette took this as a valuable key to the projection of the character. "To know that about the Hawaiian even improved my accent and helped soften my vowels," she commented blandly. That it had been delivered more as an insult than a suggestion was quite beside the point; it could be utilized in her work, and that alone was important.

No amount of opposition could hold Laurette back. She was in love, her whole world expanding. Luana was the perfect part to express her sense of physical well-being, of joy, to slough off the many emotional deprivations she had suffered as she climbed the hard road to success. Life beckoned, and many hungers long suppressed flowed from Laurette into the primitive Luana, who was not afraid to give herself to life and to love. Even Hartley in time was wooed from tacit disapproval and, although he never considered Luana a proper role for Laurette, freely acknowledged the consummate skill of her portrayal.

"The Bird of Paradise" opened at Daly's Theatre, January 8, 1912. As a play it received mixed notices. The seasoned principals, Theodore Roberts, Lewis Stone, Guy Bates Post, individually gave good performances but failed to recreate the subtle magic of the Pacific Island paradise upon which the play largely depended. Laurette's Luana, however, was considered one of the memorably authentic portraits in the theatre. Stated one review:

> It is an impersonation that for beauty of treatment, sensuous grace and charm, innate dignity, feminine coquetry and poignant pathos deserves a place among the ambitiously great accomplishments of the modern stage.

There was the familiar uproar over stardom but this did not excite Laurette half so much as the enthusiastic reception of her hula. "Miss Taylor's interpretation of the hula has captured New York. . . . By painstaking study and care she has reached past imitation to the spirit of the thing."

The hula caught on like wildfire. Society belles flocked to learn the "dances of the Pacific"—and who should be teaching them but Naiche Kaiawe, the fat little man who moved like a fat little wave.

Laurette had not forgotten "Peg." During the week's tryout of "The Bird of Paradise" in Rochester, she invited Morosco to her dressing room between matinee and night. Hartley was there, having come up for the opening, and Laurette introduced the two men. Mr. Manners, she said, had written a marvelous play and she wanted Morosco to read it; it would be the making of him on Broadway. Morosco thanked her, but "The Bird" was to do just that for him. As good as "The Bird" was, Miss Taylor stated, this play was infinitely better; wouldn't Morosco read it? No, he did not wish his attention distracted from his present production even by a good play. Laurette, with an impatient shrug, subsided.

Hartley had his own methods for handling such matters. After the night performance he took the midnight train to New York with Morosco, discussing everything but his play. Ascertaining that Morosco would return to Rochester for the Saturday performance, Hartley was on hand at the station bright and early with a drawing room reserved for the two. Morosco scowled at the unusually chipper Englishman, and warned him, "Don't you talk about your damn play!" The author promised.

As soon as they were in the drawing room Hartley settled down for "forty winks" on the divan. Then apparently as an after-thought he raised up on an elbow and pointed to his brief case.

"By the way, old boy, in that little bag of mine over there you might find a play or two to amuse you."

"You go to the devil!" was Morosco's reply.

But Fate was on Hartley's side. Morosco tried unsuccessfully to buy a newspaper, fingered through all the guides and maps in the car, then shooting a look of deep distrust at Hartley's broad and inoffensive back, also settled down for a nap. But sleep would not come. Finally in desperation he opened Hartley's bag, pulled out the first script that came to hand and after a page or two became so engrossed that he did not look up until the conductor called the change at Schenectady. Hastily he wrote out a check for five hundred dollars, drew up a short option, shook Hartley by the shoulder, and before the author was half awake shoved the check and option into his hand. Hartley, rubbing his eyes, looked at the check and shouted, "Whoops, you want my play, do you? This calls for a drink."

"When I alighted from the train," Morosco concluded in his account of this incident,* "I had under my arm . . . 'Peg O' My Heart' which, as is so often the case with theatrical producers, I had found quite by accident, and which was ultimately to make me over five million dollars."

"The Bird of Paradise," after a slow start in New York, began to build steadily and after several weeks looked as though it were in for a run on Broadway. Sometime in March, with the house selling out nightly, Laurette received a letter in a wild erratic scrawl stating she was "marked for death." A Mrs. Helen Taylor had been killed several weeks previously by a bomb sent through the mails. The writer said that he had perpetrated the crime and Laurette would die in the same manner because "she was too beautiful to live."

Laurette was convinced the killer would hurl his bomb from the audience. Detectives were planted through the house. Spotting these burly gentlemen through the peephole before making her entrance seemed to afford Laurette a small degree of comfort. The police were sufficiently impressed to assign two bodyguards to escort her to and from the theatre and stand guard outside her apartment through the night.

Her performances became highly erratic. Once a man half rose in the front row to remove his coat and Laurette raced for the wings. During a scene with the tribal priest, a black feather came loose from his robe and floated through the air; catching sight of

* "The Oracle of Broadway," Helen Morosco and Leonard Paul Duggan. Caxton Printers.

the dark spiraling object above her head, Laurette was offstage with dressing room door slammed shut before anyone knew what had happened. The other actors played their scenes as far away from her as possible. She claimed there was only one line she could really put her heart into during those frightening hours and that was when Luana passionately exclaimed, "I want to live, live, live!"

Gradually, as nothing untoward happened, everyone regained a certain amount of composure. Then a second letter repeated the threat and demanded money. Then a third. Laurette's nerve deserted her completely. She wired Morosco begging him to bring her West. Giroux, Morosco's general manager, sent word that she was "bordering on collapse," it would be senseless to make her continue. Morosco agreed. The understudy was hastily rehearsed, Laurette's children were brought from their Baltimore schools to a rendezvous at a midtown hotel, and amidst the greatest secrecy Hartley saw the family off on a night train for Chicago. During a short stopover there Laurette received a fourth letter. "I have found out you have two small children," it read in the erratic scrawl of the previous notes. "HAVE NO FEAR. I will not rob them of their mother."

There was not a drop of comfort in this communication for Laurette. The fact that the killer for all the secrecy had traced her to Chicago only terrified her the more. She sped on to Los Angeles.

Shortly after her arrival the writer of the letters was apprehended in a Harlem cellar actually putting together crude bombs. He was hopelessly insane. Laurette's comment: "He must have been to think I was too beautiful to live."

Upon arrival in California Laurette took a bungalow on the ocean front at Venice to recover from the ordeal. The children, abruptly uprooted and finding little companionship, spent much of their time wandering about the nearby amusement pier. The forlorn off-season aspect of the numerous closed and deserted booths was mitigated by the endless opportunity to munch on popcorn, spun candy and hot dogs. It was in the course of one of these peregrinations that Dwight and Marguerite first experienced the cold and cheerless side of being the children of a celebrity.

Late one afternoon they decided to go through the House of

Fun. Inside was a maze of dimly lit passageways, filled with phosphorescent skeletons, dangling spiders, loud buzzers and collapsing floors. The children were only part way through when the operator, apparently forgetting the two small customers within, decided to close up and go home. With the pulling of the main switch everything inside ceased to operate and the place was plunged in Stygian darkness. After what seemed an eternity of stumbling through the blackness, Marguerite and Dwight emerged to find an iron gate drawn and padlocked across the entrance. A passer-by seeing their plight called the police and eventually the terrified youngsters were released and escorted home. At the sight of her children flanked by blue-coated officers and a group of curious stragglers, Laurette paled. Alone with them, it was not the thought of the ordeal but the possibility of the unwanted publicity to follow which occupied her mind. Instead of comfort it was a sound scolding they got, and for the first time they were conscious of that clammy spectre "Unwanted Publicity" which was to haunt and make miserable much of their childhood.

There is no indication that with the production of "Peg" in Los Angeles any of the principals sensed that they were about to find their El Dorado. It was scheduled at Morosco's Burbank Theatre as a regular stock-company production. Hartley arrived from the East just in time for rehearsals. Laurette sent a businesslike post card to Elizabeth in the East: "Ran 7 Sisters two weeks— Peg will go 4—I go to San Francisco after this for 4 weeks— then to Europe until October. Laurette"—a schedule which was to be considerably upset by the unobtrusive opening of "Peg" on May 12, 1912.

"Peg" was a winner from the start, smashing the record for stock runs in Los Angeles by playing 101 performances to standing room only. The reviewers were cautious; not much of a play said some, but they enjoyed it. As for Laurette, she was completely charming and the "Peg of Everybody's Heart." Morosco was undisturbed by the so-so notices. Audience reaction was what counted. He was quite confident that he had a hit and began laying plans for a New York opening.

Big, handsome John Cort was in the audience the first night

and laughed and cried until the tears ran down his cheeks over the adventures of the warm-hearted colleen who comes to live by the terms of an uncle's will in the unfriendly household of her aristocratic English relatives, the Chichesters. He saw the show five or six times. Then at the peak of his career, Cort was constructing the magnificent theatre on Forty-eighth Street in New York, which was to bear his name. Morosco made up his mind that "Peg" should open that theatre, but when he sounded out Cort the answer was no, Peg was not "big enough"; Cort intended to open with a lavish musical. His plans, however, were to go awry and "Peg" was to be the first and most illustrious tenant of the Cort Theatre.

Laurette had moved to a bungalow on the grounds of the Sunset Apartments convenient to the Burbank. Hartley took a room in the main building. Every evening he came for early dinner. Louise, the West Indian maid, slicked up the children, urged them to sartorial efforts from which in the ordinary course of events they were happily free. Laurette inspected them, gave implicit instructions as to their deportment. It was evident that all sorts of things never given much thought before in the Taylor ménage suddenly assumed considerable importance when Mr. Manners was about to appear. Because the rules were relatively new and in force for so small a portion of the day, the briefing generally took place just prior to his arrival. Once or twice he walked in before it was over and a small panic seized the children as though the curtain had been inadvertently raised before the stage was quite set. Supper was an agony of trying to remember the only half-assimilated rules.

Marguerite and Dwight were no more used to the low-spoken and formal courtesy of Hartley Manners than was their mother. Family life as they knew it consisted of a series of tempestuous, untrammeled emotional outbursts and arguments, a general free-for-all and the devil take the hindmost. Here was someone who seemed to be part of the family and yet wasn't, or, that is, didn't act as though he were. One day the uncertainty became too much for Marguerite to bear any longer. An urgent need for clarification was brought about by the sight of an almost empty vegetable dish being presented to her by Dwight, which she was to pass next to Mr. Manners, sitting on her left. "Never, *never* take the last of the vegetables if there is a guest," was one of Laurette's injunctions on proper table deportment. Marguerite looked in the vegetable dish, then at Hartley, then at her mother, and decided it was now or never to clear up her confusion.

"Mother," she quavered, waving the dish in the general direction of Mr. Manners, "is he still a *guest?*"

Another new member of the family circle was Peg's dog, Michael. The animal used until dress rehearsal died suddenly. A frantic stage manager rushed to the pound to find a substitute. The only dog suitable for the role (the playwright's description: a shaggy, unkempt, and altogether disgraceful-looking Irish terrier) was a female puppy about to be put away. As there was no time to coach the cast in a new name, the female continued to bear the name of Michael. After the Los Angeles run another of suitable gender could be procured in New York.

At first sight the puppy seemed eminently expendable, but looks proved deceiving. From the beginning Michael exhibited a captivating *sang-froid* toward the audience, combined with a burning devotion for his mistress which made his performance unforgettable. When rehearsals started in New York, Laurette tried out half a dozen dogs but not one of them could emulate these stunning virtues. Michael was hastily expressed across the country and arrived just in time for the opening night. He had developed a bad pleurisy in the unheated baggage car and had to wear a flannel band around his stomach and commute from a hospital, but his performance was quite unaffected by these unfortunate circumstances.

Anyone who ever saw Laurette as Peg saw Michael. From the opening in Los Angeles in 1912, through the New York and London runs, and again in the 1921 revival, Michael played every performance of "Peg." His is an unbeaten record for a stage dog of one thousand two hundred and fifty performances. In his own dog way he stands with Peg as an immortal of the theatre.

Laurette's tribute to Michael's acting talent was concise and admiring: "Like all good actors he ignores the audience. He scorns dog tricks. His temperament is buoyant and imaginative, and this he successfully projects across the footlights." So perfect was the stage illusion that, despite obvious female endowments and numerous litters of pups over the next twelve years, Michael was never once referred to in the feminine gender. Years later Percy Hammond was to speak of him as that "veteran male impersonator."

Michael's story weaves in and out of the story of Laurette and Hartley for the next seventeen years. They both came to look on the shaggy little mongrel as a barometer of their own well-being. From the outset he seemed to symbolize the fickleness of fame and fortune to them, his ups and downs became a sobering yardstick of their own.

"With us," Laurette explained to a reporter shortly after the brilliant success of "Peg" in New York, "it's like it is with Michael. We paid a dollar for the poor little mutt and took him out of the pound the day before he was to be killed. And now Mike has been a great success. That's how it goes. . . . I believe one comes to the top like a cork if it is to be. . . ."

*

# Peg O' My Heart

Veteran theatregoers have remarked upon the air of expectancy and excitement that imbues a first-night audience about to witness a theatrical event of the first magnitude. The penumbra of the event seems to cast a glow upon those who are assembled to witness it. This was so on the evening of December 21, 1912, as the smartly dressed crowd flowed under the Louis Seize portals of the Cort and were escorted down the aisles of the magnificent rose-and-gold auditorium by usherettes dressed in the period of Marie Antoinette.

Hartley in full evening regalia, looking a trifle pale, came early, flanked by his good friends Melville Stone, president of the Associated Press, and financier, Eugene Meyer. He need not have worried. When the performance was over another first-night "great" had become a part of theatre history and Peg a beloved immortal of the stage.

As the lovable Peg, Laurette came into her own. It had been a hard-earned success and shone with the special luster of a golden talent, hammered and worked and polished by ceaseless effort. The critics of the day not only recognized her success, but almost to a man paid homage to the hard work that had gone to make that success, and this last appreciation was not lost on Laurette. Her prayer had been: "Deliver me from being a personality. Let me be an actress." And her prayer had been answered.

Listen to Louis Sherwin in the *Globe:*

> To see a new star who had a right to be a star was so astonishing that we all lost our senses last night and roared at Laurette Taylor! She proved that (she) is now the best comedienne on the American stage. In 10 minutes she gave us more acting than we have been accustomed to seeing in 10 months. No wonder we were amazed. After years . . . of bungling, half-trained young women who have been pitch-forked into stardom for the sake of a few "cute" mannerisms masquerading as personality . . . it was almost bewildering to gaze upon a young actress who is now a star by right of conquest. . . . People will talk of "sudden rise"—"luck"—"Personality." Bosh! This woman has worked and striven as few persons on the stage have had to work . . . for years she struggled in the most obscure branch of her profession, playing vile parts in cheap melodramas, learning her trade in the most unpromising surroundings. You must admit she has . . . earned her position. Personality she has—but it is personality which is an outward and visible manifestation of brains, character and temperament. . . .

And Burns Mantle paid this tribute:

> During . . . long, hard grinding years she dragged the Taylor talent through the back country and whipped it into service with the cheaper dramatic fare of the road. The tricks are hers—but she uses them artfully. Back of the tricks is a technique polished by that same experience, and back of the technique is a curiously impressive personality—the Laurette Taylor of the big staring wistful eyes; the swift and haunting smile; the curious plaintive, skillfully modulated voice. . . . She can hold her audience tense at will or she can set it laughing at nothing. She does not portray youth; she

projects the spirit of the heart of a child and the wisdom of the
centuries seem to be hers. . . . She is a thorough actress, mistress
of the art . . . and deservedly entitled to the position she has won.
We welcome and congratulate her most heartily.

The play which was to slip into immortality along with its chief
character did not fare so well. It was a "fragile little play" . . .
"carpentered by ancient rule of thumb." "Its color," according to
Alan Dale, "was not champagne, but sarsaparilla." Laurette's art
was under "heavy pressure to rescue it from oblivion."

Laurette was horrified to read these reviews; all praise for her,
all blame for Hartley. Not only was this a new theatre partnership, but "Peg" launched them as husband and wife as well; just
before the New York rehearsals started they had slipped off to
Philadelphia to be married. "How terrible some of you critics
made me feel!" she moaned. "The perfectly horrid things that
were written about Hartley's play! And here we are newlyweds
with a fine excuse for a quarrel right at the beginning."

It was a needless concern. Hartley was delighted with her triumph. He loved her, he loved "Peg." All was right with his world.

The fragile little play never hesitated for a second on its journey to immortality. There were packed houses at the Cort for
the next year and a half, and all existing records for long runs
were broken. When "Peg" closed in the spring of 1914 it was only
because Laurette was tired of the role, not that the public was
tired of Peg.

Hartley and Laurette were feted as Broadway's newest successful team and most charming married couple as well. Career and
home life were one brilliant burst of new people, new experiences,
a whole new adventure the like of which neither of them had
known before. It was as though the world was "goin' round in
one grand waltz," as Peg would put it.

Laurette met and entertained Hartley's friends of his bachelor
days: Melville Stone and Eugene Meyer; handsome George Mac-
Donald, pioneer in the public utility field, hereditary Papal Mar-
quis; Charles M. Schwab, living in the lonely splendors of his vast
château on Riverside Drive where Hartley played a weekly game
of bridge. In the theatre: Wilton Lackaye, De Wolf Hopper,
Nat Goodwin and Laurette's favorite, J. E. Dodson, the expert
comedian of incisive style.

The role of hostess in her own home was a relatively untried one for Laurette, and she suffered the usual nerves of the young bride. Serving punch and passing popcorn to the customers of the Third Avenue Theatre in Seattle, or sulking through a dinner during which Charlie held forth as sole entertainer, was as near as she had come to a social life. In her eagerness to acquit herself with honor she made mistakes and she and Hartley had their misunderstandings.

Soon after their marriage they had as dinner guests ten of Hartley's closest friends from the Lotos Club, who had presented them with a magnificent damask cloth as a wedding present. Leonardo da Vinci's scene of "The Last Supper" was woven into the cloth. There were only two in existence, and the other was in a museum. During dinner Hartley, engrossed in an anecdote, failed to notice that his cigarette had rolled from the ash tray onto the cloth and burned a small hole. Laurette discovering the damage set up a clamor that stopped all conversation. Hartley tried to make light of the matter. "Don't feel so badly, Laurie. I only burnt a hole in the eye of Judas, and as a good Catholic that should please you."

But Laurette continued to scold. "I wanted to show the guests how highly I prized the cloth, and I thought that by going on and on like Tennyson's brook I would leave no doubt in their minds."

Finally it was time for her to leave for the theatre. Host and friends settled down to an evening of bridge. When Laurette returned, Hartley chided her for making such a fuss over a triviality to the embarrassment of the guests. That started her off all over again. A triviality? Ruining a cloth, the only one of its kind outside a museum, a triviality? He tried to reason with her but to no avail. He tried to make her smile but she would not. Finally he said with great sobriety, "My dear child, what is more important, a happy marriage or a tablecloth? A first-class weaver can stitch the eye of Judas."

"*Weave* is the word, Mr. Manners, not stitch. And don't call me child. I'm a grown woman. You haven't adopted a child."

"I think I have," said Hartley gently, and left the room.

They were living in an apartment on West End Avenue. Elizabeth lived with them and she thought Hartley "the grandest gentleman in the world." These were serene days for her; the reward of her faith and the long hard fight to place her daughter at the top in the theatre. What's more, "Peg" was on the White List of the Catholic Church and Elizabeth breathed a sigh of relief. To her mind it expunged the disgraceful Luana from the devil's records, and she could hold her head up once more with her Irish Catholic friends. When she looked around at the luxuries that now surrounded Laurette, on the rich velvets and brocades of the living room, the bearskin rugs on the floor, the gleaming mahogany furniture, the marble and crystal lamps, she was content with these as the accouterments of success for which they had struggled so hard; but instinctively she knew the bond between them was in work, and always would be.

Off the kitchen was a little room which Elizabeth fitted up for a sewing room. There she could be found almost any time of the day working on Laurette's party dresses; there were many of them now for the many parties, and Elizabeth made them all. Also she was sewing Marguerite's First Communion clothes, camisole and panties as well as dress, and even little doeskin slippers with a tiny design of white beads embroidered on the toes.

"It's not the first time I've played cobbler," said Elizabeth, cocking her head robin-fashion to catch a glimpse of her grandchild's astonished face. "Your Uncle Eddie could never bear to wear his shoes, and as soon as he was out of my sight at Spring Lake they'd be under a bush at the side of the road and him barefoot all the day. It was a shame and disgrace to me, the neighbors whispering the Cooneys had no money to buy shoes. Be that as it may, I thought it was the hardness of the leather might be troublin' his feet, so I took an old felt hat of mine and made him the finest little pair of shoes you ever did see. Not that he wore them. Eddie always liked his feet out, poor boy. I think surely it must have been that he breathed through them, what with his lungs bein' so delicate and all. . . ."

A child could steal away before the story was finished and Nana would take no notice, bending over her sewing with a smile on her face, continuing to herself. It was all a grand new world for her, one she had dreamed of as a child, and it had come true at last for her beloved daughter.

Elizabeth made herself a gray silk party dress with fine tucking from shoulder to waistline and white ruching on the high-boned collar. Her dark hair was swept up softly into a bun on top of her head; it was graying a little at the temples, adding distinction to her fine brow. She sat on the side lines at the parties Hartley and Laurette gave at Sherry's and went occasionally to the Sixty Club gatherings on Sunday nights where the "tangoing stars," as they were called, danced until dawn. She met all the grand people Laurette was seeing: John and Lily McCormack; Cissie Loftus; the Nash girls, Mary and Florence; Cyril Maude; Francis Starr; Fannie Ward; Grace George; Bill Brady; Bruce McRae; Elsie Janis. It was How-do-you-do, Mrs. Cooney? . . . And how does it feel to have your daughter the toast of Broadway? And Elizabeth a little bewildered and self-conscious, tidying her hair and bursting out with some such downright Dorsey-ism as, "The darn fool will dance her feet off this night!" as she watched Laurette twirl with one partner after another until the wee hours of the morning.

Elizabeth was very happy in these days. The rising wave of success had not as yet taken her daughter far from her side.

Laurette adored to dance. At the beginning of their married life Hartley had made an attempt to master a few ballroom steps, just as he had tried to take to the water because Laurie loved it so; but the results were quite as dismal.

"You had better stick to your bridge, Hartley," Laurette told him after trying him out on the dance floor, "and I'll stick to my dancing."

Just as "finishing a rubber" was Laurette's only rival, "finishing a dance" was Hartley's.

"If I found a good dancer," said Laurette, "I'd stick to him all evening if I could. Hartley had to learn that it was the dancing, not the man, just as I had to learn that it was the bridge, not the woman, that kept him out so late."

By November, 1913, Laurette had broken the record for continuous performances. Maude Adams was the previous title-holder with three hundred performances as Lady Babbie in "The Little Minister" in 1897. Laurette was growing restive. Peg was "all right for a starter" she said but she hadn't worked all these years for success to have it imprison her forever in one role. She was, as Burns Mantle put it, "threatened with the curse of popularity."

She would as soon have joined the waxwork figures of Eden Musée as let her fame rest with "Peg." Her admiration was for the innovators, like Alla Nazimova who introduced Ibsen's plays to New York. "There was courage," said Laurette, "courage of one who was willing and able to tread unknown paths." Sarah Bernhardt was her idol. Playing a young man in "L'Aiglon" at the age of fifty-five with astounding success, triumphing in a dozen roles of every variety. "I studied Bernhardt," said Laurette; "no, not studied her, I drank her in."

There was no question in Laurette's mind which course she was going to pursue in the theatre.

Laurette's first meeting with the great French tragedienne was unpropitious. Bernhardt was playing scenes from her successes at the Palace Theatre in the spring of 1913. As a publicity stunt a high-powered press agent sought three prominent Broadway actresses to walk on with her in a scene from "Phèdre." Only Laurette and Marguerite Clark, then starring in "Prunella," accepted. A stenographer in the agent's office was recruited at the last minute as the third "prominent actress." The three women were pinned into ill-fitting robes over once-pink tights; wreathes of enormous pink roses were placed on their heads, and on their feet shapeless gilt sandals. Then they were taken to the great one's dressing room. The ailing Bernhardt apparently had not even bothered to inquire as to the identity of the two young actresses or what they were playing in New York, but on meeting Laurette a spark of interest lit for a moment behind the curiously slanted, catlike eyes.

"Tragic actress?" she asked in English.

"No, madame. Comedienne."

Bernhardt looked puzzled, muttered something in French, then swept her hand across Laurette's eyes. "Non—non!" she said emphatically. "Tragique actress!"

The brief appearance of Phèdre's handmaidens was as near farcical as the costumes, but Laurette remembered only the matchless thrill of "walking on" with Bernhardt, the weight of those "divine bones" leaning on her arm as the procession slowly made its way to Phèdre's throne.

A week later Bernhardt sent word to the Cort that she would like to see Laurette play. Because of Madame's daily matinees a special performance of "Peg" was arranged for eleven o'clock in the morning. A souvenir program was printed in French, an armchair placed in the aisle. At the sight of the chair Bernhardt had a tantrum, insisted on sitting in an aisle seat; there, bright-eyed and eager as a child she waited for the curtain to rise. Thus, for the immortal Sarah, Laurette played her immortal "Peg."

At Bernhardt's specific request not a line of publicity was given the event. Over her signature had been issued a bewildering number of statements on everything from the health value of lemon juice before breakfast to the plight of the immigrant. Witnessing Laurette's Peg the French actress seemed to touch bedrock in publicity quicksands. She wrote in an article syndicated all over the country:

> One young artist in New York has not allowed herself to be blinded. She has worked hard and is still working, although she is already a very agreeable comedienne, possessing humor, emotion, and a rare thing for her age—power. I speak of Laurette Taylor who will become within five years the foremost actress in this country. . . . All aspirants for the stage should take this young actress as their model.

Three years later, on another farewell tour, Bernhardt again asked to see Laurette play. This time she was grievously ill and, because of the ailing leg, forced to use a wheel chair. To permit her to retire backstage between acts, the two sets of "The Harp of Life" were moved from the Globe to the Empire where she was playing. The performance was given at one P.M. This time there was no embargo on press or public and the audience came by special invitation. It was one of the most brilliant professional assemblages in New York theatre history.

Due to difficulties in getting Madame's wheel chair in and out of the box, prolonged retirements backstage to sip hot milk and rest, the second act was not finished until almost six o'clock. Bernhardt stayed in her place until the audience had left, then asked the company to play the last act. But there wasn't time. She thanked the cast, patted Laurette's cheek, and was wheeled off to prepare for her evening performance.

Asked what it was like to play for Bernhardt Laurette said, "It was like playing to royalty and a little child."

Bernhardt was Laurette's lodestar, the great inspiration of her acting life. "But I could never be a Bernhardt," she once said. "There just isn't enough of me."

After "Peg" had run a year, four road companies were sent out and promptly broke all records. Four more companies went out, playing to standing room only. Laurette announced in the spring of 1914, "The fattest and oldest of the road company Pegs has just been heard from, and she is duplicating the success of all the others. It would seem that I've been wise in not giving my very competent understudy a chance, for then she, and not I, might have been the star."

Hartley was garnering up to ten thousand dollars a week in royalties from the road companies alone. He was, of course, pleased by their success but was a jealous guardian of Laurette's fame as the originator of the role. By his order each road company poster carried Laurette's name above that of the company star, and in larger type, as the creator of Peg. For this reason literally millions of people who never saw Laurette in the part thought that they had. Another factor which helped create this mass illusion was the publication of the popular song "Peg O' My Heart" which sold over a million copies. It had no connection whatsoever with the play and was, in fact, a matter of infringement litigation by Hartley, but as each copy carried photographs of Laurette on the title page and credited her as the star of "Peg," the illusion grew. It is impossible to claim—and Laurette never wanted to—that Peg's immortality stemmed from Laurette alone. Peg was intrinsically a creation of such humanness and warmth that a vast audience throughout the entire world took her to its heart for herself alone.

Michael also achieved an enviable niche in the theatre. He received flowers and presents from people and dogs. He learned to take his own curtain call. Entering downstage left, he made a circuit of the stage at a brisk canter, exiting through the garden door upstage right. Invariably as he came flush with the footlights he rolled a laughing, roguish eye in the direction of the audience which won him a crescendo of applause.

The fragile little play went on and on. "We don't mention 'Peg' at home any more," Laurette told a reporter in the spring of 1914, "not even the royalties from the road companies." When Morosco had come East in the early part of the year to launch the road companies, he discussed the playing of Chicago and the other big cities which had been reserved for Laurette and the original cast after the run at the Cort was finished; but both Hartley and Laurette were decidedly cool to the idea. They wanted to go to England first. Playing "Peg" in London had prestige value, and besides, Hartley was eager to introduce his bride to the country of his birth. The decision on the road tour was held in abeyance until the New York run was through.

But as the spring drew on there was no letup of the heat or the public's interest in "Peg." Laurette had taken one night off in a year and a half—a busman's holiday when she went to see Elsie Janis give an imitation of her. She and the cast were mentally exhausted. Laurette decided to call a halt to the show.

Morosco was decidedly upset when he received the news in Los Angeles. He visualized a whole summer's run lost, and the lush fields of Chicago, Boston, Philadelphia and Baltimore lying fallow until Laurette chose to return from European triumphs. He told her she was making the gravest mistake in not establishing her popularity throughout the United States before going to Europe; that by the time she returned Peg would be "too dated" for a city like Chicago which demanded first returns from New York. But Laurette was adamant. "Ye can't cage the Irish," she quoted to him in Peg's own words. "They'll die on your hands."

He tried to make her jealous by predicting she would forfeit her American popularity to Peggy O'Neill, a little Irish miss of seventeen, who was packing them in on the road.

"I don't care who you send out, or how many," Laurette told him. "They can explore the whole Western Hemisphere for all of me. I know all about it, because I've traveled over it in one-night stands. I want a chance to see if I am an actress or just lucky. And if I can't do it now, when I am on the top, when can I do it?"

"Peg O' My Heart" was still playing to packed houses when

it closed on the thirtieth of May, 1914, after 604 performances. The final program was printed on gold silk, and an album containing pictures of the cast was presented to each member of the audience. Laurette made a disarming little speech after the final curtain, holding Michael in her arms. She told the audience how tired she was of playing "Peg." "We've made a lot of money, but even money gets very monotonous," she confided. At this point she noticed that Michael had gone to sleep. "You see, even Michael gets bored with talk of money. Now I'm going to say something very new and bright." As though on cue Michael promptly woke up and wagged his tail. Laurette laughed, the audience laughed, and broke into that wonderful applause, which Laurette once characterized as "affectionate as well as admiring" and which thrills the heart of an actor as nothing else can in the theatre. Then they stood and cheered and cried. And Laurette cried. And Michael wagged his tail.

*

# *Peg in London*

Laurette and Hartley sailed for England on the *Aquitania* on June tenth. No sooner were they on the high seas than Morosco, in violation of his contract, pulled Peggy O'Neill from one of the touring companies and prepared to open in Chicago. Upon receiving news of this on shipboard there was nothing for Hartley to do but take the first boat back to America and fight. It was a wretched decision for husband and wife to make. They had been looking forward to this vacation in England before opening "Peg" in the fall. The keenness of their disappointment is clear in the letter Hartley posted as soon as he docked in New York on July fourth:

Dearest Laurie:
    At last the awful journey is over. The only nice things were your letter and your wireless. I read your letter every night. It was

sweet of you to write it under all the stress of my last night in London. . . . I will cable you tonight and write you every night what happens. I do hope the wretched thing can be settled and that we may settle down in London and have a real home. I can't tell you how I've missed you. I never thought I would have a journey without you. But your letter was so courageous and so like you that it helped me very much. . . . I am wondering if you are in the country and if you like it and if you are contented and if you are better and less nervous. If I can hurry back we can still have some kind of holiday in England. . . . I think of you all the time.

My deepest love to you my dear wife,
Hartley

Hartley and his lawyers went directly to Chicago to meet with Morosco and his attorney. The weather was torrid and there were hot tempers and bad feelings on both sides. Hartley resented what he termed Morosco's "cheap trick" of waiting until he was on the high seas to put a company in Chicago. Morosco felt that he was being cheated of road revenues simply because of a whim of Laurette's and had a right to protect himself.

While the immediate point in controversy was an injunction whereby Hartley prevented the Chicago company from playing, the whole matter of contract rights was wrung out in a series of negotiations marked by increasing bitterness. Morosco was loud and abusive, using the strong-arm tactics of many of the pioneers in the early hurly-burly days of the theatre, while Hartley was a cold and deadly fighter once he made up his mind that he had been wronged, and no detail or point of harassment was too small for his attention.

Morosco fought to obtain one half of the European rights which originally had been reserved entirely by Hartley. In the eventual settlement Hartley continued to hold these rights, and Morosco the United States and Canadian rights, subject, however, to the author's royalties of seven to ten per cent of the gross. Also the new agreement, like the original, specified that neither party was to use "Peg" in moving pictures without the consent of the other. Sometime later Morosco violated this provision and Hartley immediately brought suit to restrain him. The bitter litigation lasted six years. Although defeated in the lower courts, Hartley fought all the way to the Supreme Court of the United States where he finally won. Justice Oliver Wendell Holmes delivered the opinion in typical Holmes-ian language: "Indeed by providing, under certain stipulations, for release of the play for stock company presentation the author showed the lowest point to which he was willing to let it go."

The unhappy negotiation concluded, Hartley caught the Cunard liner *Aquitania* on her next trip, July twentieth, and arrived in England just as the drumbeats of World War I sounded low but ominous in Central Europe.

It had been a blow to Laurette when Hartley was forced to return and fight Morosco. "It's a fine thing ye do, Mr. Manners, leaving me and Michael with the cold unfriendly English just like ye leave Peg in the play," she told him in the soft Irish brogue she often used when joshing with him. "I'll be scared to death of them without you to mind my manners for me, and that's no pun, believe me."

Hartley rallied Frank Kemble Cooper to help out—a friend since their early acting days with George Alexander at the St. James. Frank had three lovely daughters. The eldest, Violet, had played Ethel for a number of performances toward the close of the New York run and would assume the role in London. Hartley was quite sure that in their company Laurette would not be homesick.

The Kemble Coopers came from a long line of distinguished theatre folk. They were direct descendants of the renowned Fanny Kemble of the English stage, and Mrs. Sarah Siddons, one of the great beauties of her day and considered the greatest Lady Macbeth of all time. The inheritance had not been lost on Frank Cooper's girls. Violet, the most striking of the three, had a profile of classic strength and beauty. Greta's head might have been sculptured by Praxiteles for the god Hermes—its conformations had been achieved with a total disregard for the stingy and ignoble line; only in Lillian, the youngest, was the magnificent bone structure slightly diluted by the inroads of prettiness. They were tall, strong-limbed, and carried themselves instinctively with that noble bearing which England sometimes bestows on bloodlines, as though quality is established over the centuries rather than by a fly-by-night affair of the genes. All three, and their handsome brother Anthony, eventually chose the stage.

Their father motored Laurette to the country the day after Hartley set sail for America. "They were staying in the tiniest cottage you could possibly imagine all covered with pink roses," she recalled. "I stooped under a low doorway, and there they all were looking like trapped gods!"

Whatever fear Laurette had of the English broke down immediately in their company. The girls were fun-loving, warm and friendly. Although they preferred to understate their godly appearance by wearing rough tweeds and plain soft felt hats— Greta even sported a monocle—and conducted themselves with a forthrightness more characteristic of the opposite sex, they were, in fact, intensely feminine, preoccupied with clothes, gossip and romantic intrigue. Immediately, Laurette was taken to their hearts and she reciprocated. It was an association that was to be professionally as well as personally close. Violet, Greta, and Lillian each played Ethel in "Peg" at one time or another, and Hartley's productions for the next nine years invariably had a part for one of the Cooper girls.

While Hartley was away Laurette spent most of her week ends at Houghton-Huntingdonshire, taking rooms in the village close to the rose-covered cottage where the Kemble Coopers lived. Time passed quickly. With her new-found friends she walked over the lovely English countryside trying to keep pace with their long strides, laughing at Greta who would pop her monocle in her eye absent-mindedly and whistle the most intricate arpeggios in tones so liquid as to shame the English meadow lark. They would stop at St. Ives for cakes and tea, linger along the banks of the river Ouse. Sundays they took hamper lunches to a houseboat tied at the water's edge. Called the *Sir Reginald de Grey*, it seemed to have been moored there expressly for their pleasure, for no owner or watchman ever came to disturb them during the long lazy afternoons.

Several overnight visits with Elsie Janis and her mother provided another pleasant interlude. Elsie had made her English debut in April in "The Passing Show of 1914" and was living on a houseboat at Datchet on the Thames. Windsor Castle was across the river, and in the hush and quiet of the evening hours one could hear the big clock at Eton striking.

Both Elsie and the Cooper girls noted with wonder Laurette's quiet confidence in her coming London stage debut; all her nervousness was engendered by the thought of meeting the English socially. These week ends were an idyllic prelude to that meeting, and during them Laurette fell in love with the best of England, as found in her tiny hamlets and along her placid low-lying rivers where time, that has marched so riotously through her history, curls up to sleep a little in a landscape brushed with centuries of beauty.

But when Hartley returned there was still that other England to be met. It was the England of titles and rigid formality; of luncheons, where who sits next to whom was of the utmost importance and even the chitchat seemed more prescribed than spontaneous; an England of theatre names which rang pontifically in Laurette's brain; Sir Herbert Beerbohm Tree, Mrs. Patrick Campbell, Gerald du Maurier, Sir George and Lady Alexander. She would meet them all. She was sure she could charm them as Peg O' My Heart, but that opening was three months away in October, and in the meantime it was up to Mrs. Manners to win them.

In his concern to have Laurette acquit herself well, Hartley proscribed her one sure weapon, her incredibly swift mind and tongue which worked so well in double harness, and could deliver a highly original viewpoint on almost any subject before most people could clear their throats. To this, Laurette's only social technique, Hartley ill-advisedly said no.

"You have an Irish tongue, Laurie," he warned her. "Speak in haste to the English and you'll repent in solitude."

He begged her to count ten before she spoke.

"If I stop to count ten," Laurette told him, "nothing seems worth saying." But she promised to try. She knew it meant a lot to Hartley that she make a good impression on his beloved London.

His advice, however, proved almost fatal.

The first luncheon given in her honor was at the Berkeley Hotel in Piccadilly. Listed as guests were a princess, a marchioness, a duchess or two, and several brilliant men of letters; but of all the names on the list the one that struck terror into Laurette's heart was that of Mrs. Patrick Campbell. Stella Campbell was famous for her cruel wit which, Laurette had heard, quickly reduced her victims to quivering jelly.

To give herself courage Laurette went out and bought a large hat. It was characteristic of her when feeling insecure to want to hide beneath a hat the way some people retire into basements when frightened.

As soon as Laurette arrived at the luncheon Mrs. Campbell, also wearing a large hat, sailed up to her. She had, as Gerald du Maurier put it so aptly, "decided to make a meal of the little American actress."

"I'm so glad to see you, my dear," rolled out the warm enchanting voice. "They tell me you're the greatest actress in the world. Why do you wear such a big hat? You shouldn't. It hides your nice eyes. They also tell me you wear a wig on the stage. Why? Isn't your hair all that it should be?" *

It was the Campbell genius to hit a vulnerable spot: Laurette's physical appearance. Although noted as a beauty and admired as such, Laurette had little or no confidence in her looks. It was her deep-rooted conviction that she was not beautiful and that only by sheerest artifice and the most ingenious dressmaking did she triumph over her many physical defects. Mrs. Campbell had scored a bull's-eye. To make matters worse Laurette counted ten and Mrs. Campbell seeing her victim hesitate pounced again. "Why the wig, my dear?" she persisted, boring her beautiful eyes into Laurette's, as though upon the answer hung all Mrs. Campbell's happiness.

"Well, my husband and I thought Peg, being Irish—she should have bright red hair—sort of carrot-top."

The lameness and flatness of the remark was fatal. Laurette said later, "When I became better acquainted with Stella I knew all she needed was a faltering answer and she was off, romping all over her victim."

The hostess tried to divert Mrs. Pat, as one might call off a too-sportive Newfoundland, but without success.

Samson shorn of his locks was never weaker than Laurette

---

* "Mrs. Pat ad Libitum" by Laurette Taylor. *Town & Country*, December, 1942.

without her quick tongue. But she thought that her husband's manners were perfect and was determined to imitate them as closely as possible.

In the weeks before the opening of "Peg" there were many social affairs and Mrs. Pat seemed to be at them all. Invariably she singled out the young American actress for her unwelcome attentions. Hartley's only advice was, "Avoid her."

"That's easy enough to say, Mr. Manners, but how can I do that when the woman follows me like a cat follows a mouse?" Laurette retorted. "You are making me too timid with your advice," she told him miserably, but gripped by insecurity held her tongue.

It was while sitting between Gerald du Maurier and Sir Herbert Tree at a supper party that Laurette spontaneously revolted. It was in Tree's famous tower room above His Majesty's Theatre in the Haymarket. Du Maurier was then at the height of his popularity on the London stage. He was one of the most charming men that ever lived but like Laurette insisted that life and people amuse him, and if they did not grew as petulant as a child. On this particular night he apparently decided after some general remarks that the little American actress was not going to amuse him, and in that infinitely polite way of the British began to ignore her, addressing his remarks over her head to Tree. Hartley, sitting at the other end of the table next to Lady Tree, began to look worried, and it was plain to Laurette that he was dexterously carrying on a conversation with the hostess to which he was paying not the slightest attention.

"He's worrying about my hasty tongue," thought Laurette, "but I'd like to know where the divil it is after all these weeks of counting ten. There's nothing in my sound box but 'yes' and 'no' and few enough of those."

The conversation between Tree and du Maurier had branched into a discussion of life after death. To Laurette's stupefaction she heard Tree suavely denying the existence of God, and du Maurier, the existence of life after death. "Well!" thought Laurette. "An atheist and an agnostic! And here I sit an Irish Roman Catholic, *dumb,* between the two of them!"

Du Maurier had turned to her. "Don't you agree, Miss Taylor?"

"I certainly do not!" Laurette replied in a voice she had never used before in England.

She heard Hartley's fork drop warningly but took no heed. Vehemently she sprang to the defense of her beliefs. There was a flutter of amusement behind du Maurier's eyes, and Tree bent his gaze upon her with exaggerated seriousness.

"Of what religion are you, my dear Miss Taylor?" asked Tree.

"I'm an Irish Roman Catholic."

"Well, of course, your religion would never *allow* you to be an atheist or an agnostic, would it, Miss Taylor?" du Maurier interpolated solemnly.

Laurette felt they were "spoofing" her but went on. She asked how such intelligent men, gifted by God as they were, could say there was no God? How such men as they, who knew that people only start progression in life at thirty or so, could think it all ended at sixty . . . seventy . . . eighty!

"Do you believe then," questioned du Maurier, "in angels and harps, Miss Taylor?"

"No," Laurette replied haughtily, "I have not believed in them since I was ten. But it is ridiculous to say man has no future beyond the grave; to declare the spirit that keeps him seeking, discovering, inventing on this earth ends completely in the dark ground."

Laurette in a passionate defense of her beliefs had found herself. As she put it, "For the first time I could feel myself creeping cozily back into my skin."

There was no lagging of the conversation from then on. Laurette and du Maurier, in particular, became great friends. She confided her terror of Stella, and he gave her some good advice. "Speak out, as you did tonight. Give Stella a verbal spanking. She despises people who are afraid of her. Perhaps she heckles them to make them brave. Talk back. Get angry. Don't try to slide away from her. Face her and don't let *your* eyes drop first."

Laurette soon learned to handle Mrs. Pat. They never became friends but their verbal fencing usually ended in a draw and they held each other in a wary respect.

Laurette was fascinated by verbal cruelty. It is perhaps one of the keys to her complex nature that she tended to look on a merciless tongue as a superior line of defense rather than a coward's weapon; a virtue rather than a vice. One of the plays which she wrote in the latter years of her life had for a heroine an inexcusably cruel woman who in the warped view of the author appeared as a highly admirable character. It was a logical evaluation for one who increasingly came to use a sharp tongue to hide feeling, brusqueness to ward off emotion.

She was proud of her "honest tongue" as she called it, and never allowed herself to consider the hurt it gave others. That seemed fair enough, for after all she never allowed herself to consider her own hurts. They were something you buried, something you took out in the sacrosanct world of make-believe where vulnerability of the spirit became an asset rather than a liability, and each minute perception of suffering, yearning, aspiration and defeat, a part of the glorious mosaic of creative expression. It probably never occurred to her that many had no such refuge, that kindness was the sanctuary of ordinary mortals.

But Laurette in England did not feel the need of a sharp tongue, only a quick one. Her spirit's armor sat as lightly on her as at any time in her life. She was expanding. The warm sun of success, her love for Hartley, the ease of living that wealth brought, all mitigated any need for defensiveness in the areas of feeling where her insecurities lay.

The English adored her as Peg. "Not in twenty-five years has London taken an actress to its heart as it has Laurette Taylor," stated a London correspondent in his cable to *Variety* in New York. It was a wartime London in which the play opened, and the sunlight and sweetness and rugged optimism of Peg fitted in perfectly with the whistling of "Tipperary," "Keep the Home Fires Burning" and the swing of marching feet as the British Tommy, unassuming and unconquerable as Peg herself, mobilized for war. While other actor-managers were frantically trying to assay the taste of the public, now that the conflict had come, "Peg" boomed happily along as though it had been made to order for the troubled times. During the first year of the London run, the gross receipts were two thousand pounds a week, the largest of any show in that period.

Upon the success of "Peg," Laurette was promptly lionized by London society and easily extended her conquests beyond the footlights. She no longer heeded Hartley's caution and he conceded she no longer needed to. A London society journal burbled: "She is the first American actress to make a complete social conquest of London society. There is no function of importance now given at which she is not one of the most prominent guests. At receptions, dinners, charity matinees she acquits herself with much distinction."

It was in England that Laurette first gained an enviable reputation as an after-dinner speaker. She spoke extemporaneously, asking only the one consideration that she be called upon last. Her wonderful sense of mimicry, her ability to give spontaneous expression to feelings and impressions which most people smother or lose altogether under stiff and formal verbiage, delighted her listeners. It was a style as evanescent as her acting but no less magical. Those who heard her might not remember long what she said, but they went home chuckling and feeling warm and full of good fellowship, even the bad speakers whom she sometimes parodied. She brought an artful originality to what is so often a deadly occupation, and many an after-dinner speaker, assiduously rehearsing before a mirror with carefully prepared notes, envied her achievement.

Laurette came to have an abiding admiration and affection for the British. In 1914–15 she saw them at their best: unprepared for war, suffering enormous casualties during and after the retreat from Mons, their quiet confidence and courage, their ability to take in stride the tragedies daily mounting around them was an inspiration. In her first seven months in England she gave fifteen benefit performances. Lady Bathhurst, Lady Paget, the Marchioness of Townshend, Lady Tichborne, all working selflessly in the war effort, never had to ask twice for her time and talents. Queen Mary personally requested Laurette to appear at a charity benefit she was sponsoring. Stated Her Majesty, who with King George and the Queen Mother Alexandra had attended a performance of "Peg" and several of her benefit shows, "Quite the most delightful actress America has ever sent us."

On a souvenir program given to the audience on the occasion

of the one hundredth London performance of "Peg," Laurette wrote the British a love note. "Dear British Public:" it read. "It has been a great privilege to be in England during this crisis and a great honor to help her smile. England knows the time to smile, and the time to fight. She will never know the time for tears."

It would be hard to exaggerate the affinity between wartime England and Peg, and few made the distinction between Peg and Laurette, so lovingly had Hartley drawn the inner spirit of his bride. Peg, humanizing the home of the haughty Chichesters, was little different from Laurette breaking down the reserve of the English people. As the mass tragedy of modern war hammered the stiff barriers of English society, the individual emerged and was evaluated. The grocer boy standing by his horse requisitioned for war, trying not to cry, was as much a part of the show as the titled Lady diligently organizing her charities. The human qualities of Peg were very much at home in such a world.

Although maintaining a town house at Regents Park West, Hartley and Laurette kept a country place at Maidenhead on the Thames open all year round and spent many week ends there. Longwood was a paradise of gardens and greenhouses, neatly tended gravel paths and wooded walks. There were two grass tennis courts which were the joy of the tennis-playing Manners family. Laurette loved it. The growing pressure to conceal her children as she became more and more identified with the eighteen-year-old Peg was not so great at Longwood as to totally eclipse delightful moments of family life: tea and crumpets by a blazing fire, punting on the Thames, bicycling into the village with "the kids" to the toffee shop, coming back by the cobbled road around Windsor Castle in order to take the terrifying hill which circled its massive walls. Hartley, no cyclist, looked forward to a family game of snooker in the billiard room after tea, and the tennis courts were constantly in use.

At Longwood and the town house there were many visitors and many gay parties during the winter and summer of 1914–15. It was the fine-edged gaiety of wartime that is both heightened and thinned because it covers a universal sense of danger and

death. And there were the wounded soldiers who came to Longwood on Sundays in charabancs from William Waldorf Astor's
nearby Cliveden, which had been converted into a hospital. They
crowded the billiard room and tennis courts, lounged in the sun
with "fags," beer, and sandwiches. Hartley and Laurette visited
the hospital and on rainy Sundays took the soldiers into the village where they arranged to show Charlie Chaplin films.

Summer was a drift of pleasant company. There were the
steadies like Percy Ames, the English Alaric, and his wife, Sybil,
expert bridge players with whom Laurette continued to play her
atrocious game; A. E. Matthews, the English Jerry; the Kemble
Coopers; Sir George and Lady Alexander. Irene and Vernon
Castle, gracefully dancing in "Watch Your Step" at the Empire,
came down of a Sunday to stroll long-leggedly by the river with
two long-legged Russian wolfhounds. Ethel Levey, the dark
kinetic musical-comedy star, brought the war-ace, Claude Graham-
White, whom she later married.

Elsie Janis came with her co-star of "The Passing Show," Basil
Hallam. Wearing black cutaway, pearl gray topper and vest, and
swinging a gold-headed cane, Hallam was devastating the female population of London with his singing of "I'm Gilbert the
Filbert, the Knut with a K." They were the gayest lovers in England, and even the most patriotic thought it a shame when Hallam
removed the warmth of his personality from the Home Front to
man an observation balloon in France. He was killed barely a
year later trying to parachute as his balloon drifted toward enemy
territory, and the man who had been with him and survived, wrote
Elsie, "I never thought it would be Gilbert the Filbert who would
give me the courage to face death."

The audiences at the Globe were crowded nightly with men
in uniform. They came not once but again and again when on
leave from the battlefields of France. They wrote Peg from the
trenches as they would write to their best girl, long, self-revealing
letters, carried her picture into battle as a talisman against the
death and destruction they faced. Laurette was extremely proud
of these letters and kept them when she destroyed all others.
They were in a faded folder among her few papers when she died,
marked in her handwriting: LETTERS TO KEEP; page after closely

written page, echoing the hopes and fears of young men in a war-torn world of over a quarter of a century before.

Among the many attractive young men in uniform who thronged London in 1914–15, Laurette had her full share of beaux. She was thirty years old and at the height of her loveliness. Her face had the open speaking look of a young girl, a look which seemed to ask life to be good to her as she began to live tentatively under the sun of Hartley's devotion in a world that she never quite dared trust before. It was an expression of great sweetness and expectancy behind which still trembled the uncertainty of her approach. It made the masculine heart turn over, and many who might have been awed by her fame were made bold by the warmth of that so ingenuous look.

One of the most persistent and for a while anonymous of her admirers was a young man in uniform whom she first noticed sitting alone at Ciro's where she and Hartley were dining. With surprising regularity thereafter he turned up either alone or with a fellow officer wherever Mr. and Mrs. Manners happened to be. At first Laurette thought it coincidence, but soon realized the occurrence was too frequent to be consistent with the laws of chance. One evening a mutual acquaintance brought him backstage and introduced him as Captain Harold Alexander of the Irish Guards. His best friend and fellow officer, Captain Eric Greer, immediately materialized to be introduced. Thenceforth these two squired Laurette about London at every opportunity: tea at the Carlton, supper at Ciro's, dancing at the Four Hundred or some other popular spot. Occasionally they were joined by other officers of the regiment, Jumbo Reynolds, Sidney Fitzgerald, Charles Moore. The Guard's Boat Club was close to Longwood and Laurette entertained them on week ends with tennis, dinner and dancing to the gramophone. She helped their regimental charities, sent packages of food to France, mouth organs by the gross, accordions and gramophones.

Alexander and Greer were exceptionally handsome and charming, yet strikingly different in looks and temperament. Alex was blond with fair skin, his manner reserved and shy. Greer was olive-complexioned with black hair, dark eyes and a most infectious smile and sense of fun. Both were serious students of military history and ambitious in their military careers, but one would never have guessed it when they were on leave in London. The order of the day was "eat, drink and be merry" and these two were as votive to that cause as they were to chasing the Hun.

They fell quite frankly in love with Laurette, "as everyone must have who saw her in that lovely part," Alexander wrote years later, "and after being introduced to her we were more in love with her than ever."

Laurette never quite knew when they would come; a whoop of joy from Greer outside her dressing-room door, or Alex's quiet whistling of "Valse Mauve," the theme music of "Peg," might be the announcement. One time their swords, skidding together across the floor of the entrance hall and into her living room, was the first Laurette knew that they were home from the wars and ready for fun. With Hartley they were as deferential as children, calling him Mr. Manners long after they were calling his wife Peg. They too wrote to her from the trenches such British-isms as Greer's, "Five o'clock, and all the world apparently at its tea, for a beautiful hush has fallen on everything. I will say *that* for the Hun artillery men—they are very regular with their meals." And such shyly devoted tributes as Alexander's, "My men show the best of musical taste by singing and whistling 'Molly Brannigan.' " (One of Laurette's songs in "Peg.")

When the gramophone and records arrived at the front Alex wrote wistfully, "The gramophone is a great success—but what's so funny is that when I go to a music hall or review now I know all the songs by heart and they remind me of my dugout and people out here. It seems all round the wrong way—the tunes ought to remind me of London."

Alexander went on to fulfill his promise as a brilliant military student, becoming Field Marshall Earl Alexander of Tunis, the great Commander in Chief of the Middle East campaign and Supreme Allied Commander of the Mediterranean theatre in World War II, subsequently Governor General of Canada, and, in 1952, Britain's Minister of Defense. Greer was killed in France in 1917.

There were not many memories more tender in Laurette's heart than that of Greer when he came to Euston Station with Jumbo Reynolds on a gloomy day in December, 1915, to see the Manners family off on their return to America. He was, as always, gay. When the train started he left Reynolds behind and stepped along by the coach door faster and faster until he reached the platform's end. There he teetered in mock peril, circling his cap in a wild, boyish salute, his smile seeming to warm the whole of the cold and dreary station behind him.

Immediately he wrote of his disillusionment in a London of which Laurette was no longer a part: "I wonder when you were a kid did you ever go into a room the morning after a Christmas tree or some kindred beano had been celebrated there? The night before, the place had been a sort of Crystal Palace, infinitely large and gorgeously magnificent. Now—the candles are out (and most of the candle grease on the floor), the holly has fallen from the wall . . . And you looked around and were so surprised to see what a silly, ordinary little room it was, that you nearly cried just out of pity for your disillusioned self. . . . Well— that's the way of the world with Jumbo and me since last Saturday. We've come to the conclusion that we are just surprised to find how very ordinary everything and everybody is, and we think now that it was only natural that you should leave a country that was obviously smudged before it was dry."

Alexander wrote in February, 1917: "You remember your photographs in the case? I have carried them on me out here every day and they have never yet missed a fight—so if you got hit, it would kill me."

And later from Jumbo Reynolds: "Eric and I, and I know Alex, are all determined to make a pilgrimage to New York City when this little affair in Europe is over. So one fine day three much-wearied warriors will present themselves at your portal and demand admittance for old times' sake. Possibly there will be only two or even one warrior—in that case you will understand that the absent ones—owing to their having mislaid their bodies—are unable to step down from Heaven to attend you."

Laurette never forgot the golden young men of England, so many of whom died on the battlefields of France. Unlike the more cynical youth of World War II, they had been children of a world at peace and the bloom and hope of that world was on them. They struck a responsive chord in Laurette that was not touched again by the more sophisticated group of friends which fame later gathered about her. Who can tell of the threads that hold and the ones that break in the human soul? A handful of letters stand as mute evidence that the lessons of comradeship and courage she learned in England went deep, were buried some place, with all the other treasures which she so strangely guarded from corruption.

It began to look as though the British public would be perfectly satisfied to have Laurette play "Peg" forever. On May 31, 1915, the day of the thousandth performance, Laurette awoke to find on her breakfast tray a congratulatory cablegram from America. She immediately cabled back: "Why congratulate me? What I want from someone is sympathy." She moaned that she was in bondage to "this divilish girl of my husband's imagination which people have come to insist is me." But she was really quite content. Her stay in England had been the happiest period of her life, and personal happiness was so new that she was willing for a little while longer at least to keep her ambition in harness.

As she drove in that evening for the performance the glow of a full moon was just beginning to suffuse the horizon. Onstage, near the end of the second act Laurette thought she heard a dull "crumping" sound. But the orchestra was playing "Valse Mauve" and she could not be sure. In the Chichesters' moonlit living room she was begging Mr. Jerry to let her have one more waltz when she realized that an unearthly silence was slowly taking possession of the audience. Laurette's legs began to shake. She could hear plainly now the sound of guns. It was London's first Zeppelin raid. The audience and cast were ordered to the cellar.

After it was over the play continued, but as far as Laurette was concerned "all comedy was dead." That night, back in the quiet of Longwood, she started up constantly from sleep, dreaming the walls of the theatre were collapsing around her. Hartley stayed by her side until dawn.

The second time the Zeps came, in August, Laurette and the call boy were alone backstage after the performance. At the familiar crump of the explosives they grabbed each other by the hand and fled to the cellar. Hartley found them there still holding hands and praying. He tried to make light of the matter, quoting a line from "Peg": "Come out and look at it, Laurie, they're beautiful in this part of the country."

Laurette glared morosely. "You English and your little jokes! I don't think that's either funny or appropriate. Where have you been? Why weren't you here to take me home?"

"Sorry, old dear, I was just finishing a rubber at the Green Room Club. Then my partner insisted we have a look at the thing from the roof. It really was quite beautiful, the lights crisscrossing and all that sort of thing. . . ."

"Finishing a rubber! My God, Hartley! Do you have to finish a rubber even in a Zeppelin raid?"

Speechless, Laurette allowed herself to be led from the cellar and taken home.

Warning sirens wailed throughout August. Laurette's sleep was fitful and broken by nightmares. Finally on doctor's order she took a month's rest at Longwood.

A week after her return London had its worst raid. The bombs fell in the thick of the theatre district and four of London's famous theatres, each playing to capacity, narrowly escaped destruction. Hartley passed the devastation on his way to the Globe; also the bus on which one bomb had made a direct hit. He never forgave the Germans for the sights he witnessed on the streets of his beloved London that night. His rage was expressed in three one-act plays that were his own particular hymn of hate against the Hun: "God of My Fathers," "Day of Wrath," "All Clear." * On his orders Germany was the one country in the world where "Peg O' My Heart" was never produced.

Laurette continued to play until November but the heart was out of her. She was sleepless, nervous and, for the first time in her life, ill. A nagging, persistent pain had developed in her side. On top of this she learned that her mother, who had gone to a sanitarium soon after she left America, had taken a turn for the worse.

Once again, with "Peg" playing to packed houses, Laurette de-

* In his will he bequeathed a substantial sum to the Royal General Theatrical Fund on condition that the two dealing with Zeppelin raids be produced alternately for six years so that "remembrance of the atrocities committed by Germany on the English people might be kept alive for at least that period." Upon his death in 1928, the bequest was considered an embarrassing memento of war hysteria and was declined.

cided to close the show. The children left their schools in Surrey, and on the second of December the family boarded the Dutch ship, the *Nieuw Amsterdam,* and started the cold rough journey home through submarine-infested waters.

The trip was so vilely rough, with mountainous seas tossing the tiny ship like a cork, that even those in the best of health held tremulous thoughts of death, and the constant threat of submarines did not help to ameliorate these feelings. Laurette was so ill that she never left her bed. Once, convinced that death was near, she called Dwight and Marguerite to her side and gave them last instructions.

The wonderful spirit and gaiety of the London days seemed to fade out behind each monstrous slate-gray wave racing eastward. Laurette lay on her bed with a feeling of dread in her heart, some premonition of the sorrow that was ahead.

*

# *Death of Elizabeth*

Even before Laurette left for England, Elizabeth's headaches had become more frequent and she complained of dizzy spells, but her illness had not been diagnosed for the fatal thing it then was: pernicious anemia. Before sailing Laurette had put her own physician, Dr. Oscar Leiser, in charge, told Elizabeth to give up sewing, enjoy herself.

But idleness did not come easily to one who had worked all her life. Elizabeth would buy herself a beer or two, go to a show, shop for a dress or bonnet, but other than that the ample allowance which Laurette provided meant little. Secretly she occupied her days learning to read and write. She bought simple grade-school spellers and blue-lined copy books in which to practice. Elizabeth still held the deep suspicion that the world was divided into those who "did things" and those who fooled around with reading; she was a little surprised to find herself in the latter group, and not a little sheepish about it.

In the autumn of 1914 she returned from a brief trip to the Adirondacks gravely ill. Dr. Leiser ordered her at once to the Austin Sanitarium. Sister Nellie hastened up from Asbury Park with her daughter Mabel in order to be near.

"I ran my legs off for copies of *Variety* and other theatrical papers," Mabel recalled. "She was always wanting news of the theatre and particularly of Laurette." Still not satisfied with her writing, she dictated letters to Mabel or Nellie, and with their aid began a rather unsatisfactory correspondence with her famous daughter across the sea.

Laurette could not understand why Elizabeth was sick and in short hasty notes sent a stream of suggestions. "I think you should go and have your teeth out," read one. "God knows I wouldn't go near a dentist unless I was dying, but teeth can cause a lot of trouble. . . ."

Elizabeth would fret: "What's the matter with that girl! How can I get out of my bed and go to a dentist? Faith, I'm too sick, and besides, my teeth are all false. The crazy loon knows that!"

Laurette's letters began to play on one theme: she would like to come home if her mother was really ill but it was a question of getting out of her contract. Elizabeth consulted with Dr. Leiser: "You know, I think the girl wants to get out of that contract and come home. Maybe it's an excuse she's lookin' for. Do you think it might be that, now?"

Dr. Leiser looked stern. "Now look here," he said. "Your daughter's at the height of her career, she's making good money; you don't want to bring her home just as she's cashing in on all her hard work, do you? She may never have another 'Peg,' remember that. You're just going to get her all upset thinking she should come home."

"It's not that way at all!" Elizabeth retorted indignantly, but there was not the fire there would have been had she been more herself.

But Dr. Leiser had been left in full charge and his word was law. Rightly or wrongly, he withheld from Laurette the gravity of her mother's illness.

The days dragged on. One day Elizabeth said wistfully to her sister, "It's a grand thing to have a daughter that's famous but there's many a heartache goes with it, Nellie."

The letters between mother and daughter grew more frantic. Elizabeth fussed and fussed; she was certain that Laurette wanted to be rid of the contract. As the weeks and months went by and her strength dwindled this became a wistful refrain. Laurette fussed on the other side of the ocean, unable to understand her mother's continued illness: "I pay that doctor enough money to find out what's the matter with you!" she wrote indignantly.

At last a letter arrived from London: "I can't come to you, so you must come to me." Laurette would make all the arrangements on the other side; the doctor and two nurses would travel with Elizabeth; there was nothing for her to do but get on the boat.

Elizabeth was beside herself with joy. She had always wanted to go abroad. She would visit Ireland and Galway Bay where her mother and father were born; it was a long dream she had never hoped to realize. One of the nurses was Irish and she too had people in Ireland; they would go together. They prattled like children as they prepared for the journey. Two pink spots glowed on Elizabeth's cheeks.

The day before the ship was to sail a cable arrived. Six words: "DON'T COME. AM COMING TO YOU."

Elizabeth's heart was broken and gloom hung thick around the sanitarium. The next day the ship sailed without them. It was the Cunard liner *Lusitania* bound on her last fatal voyage to England.

It was six more months before Laurette came home on the *Nieuw Amsterdam*, arriving December eighth. She was taken by ambulance to the Hotel St. Regis. There Dr. Leiser examined her and an operation for hernia was scheduled for December tenth. Not many hours later Elizabeth walked into her daughter's bedroom, fragile as Dresden china, the ash-white of death's approach on her face. As soon as she had learned that Laurette was ill, nothing could keep her from going to her child. Laurette never forgot that figure standing at the foot of her bed, a little sealskin jacket around the shoulders, and a hat incongruously gay with violets on its brim. In no time at all Elizabeth was in the twin bed beside her and the two giggling like schoolgirls, comparing aches and pains.

Elizabeth stayed the two days before the operation. They

amused themselves scanning the papers, catching up on theatrical news. Proudly displaying her new-found ability to read, Elizabeth spelled out the headlines and laughed with Laurette when she made mistakes. The lined copy books were brought out for her daughter's inspection, filled with such simple words as CAT and DOG spelled out over and over again, in a large childish hand. Those copy books, along with the letters from France, remained among Laurette's few treasured possessions until the day she died.

But the lift of having her child back was transitory. Elizabeth faded fast. Laurette was beside herself with grief when told the nature of her mother's illness. She would not accept it. She ordered one blood transfusion after another although the doctors insisted that they were quite useless, that Elizabeth was beyond all help. When Laurette was well enough she and Hartley and Nellie went to St. Patrick's Cathedral, lit candles before the Virgin and prayed. Nellie had lived surrounded by people to whom prayer came almost as instinctively as breathing, but to her daughter Mabel she confided that never had she seen anyone pray as Laurette prayed that day. She knelt at the railing of the Virgin Mary's shrine totally oblivious of her surroundings. She bowed herself low, and that soul of hers that did not know how to do anything by halves, begged for the life of her mother.

Elizabeth died on December 17, 1915, as the doctors poured the last useless transfusion into her veins. She was fifty-one.

Laurette was gravely ill for days, an illness that was in her soul and spirit. Night after night the faithful Hartley sat by her bed as she tried to sleep. She would fall into a fitful slumber only to awake screaming. Repeatedly she dreamed that her mother, lying on a bed of roses, raised an arm and beckoned her to come. She would cry out in terror, "No! No! No!" clinging to Hartley like a child.

In a daze she went through the long typical Irish wake. For three days relatives and friends came from far and near. They used the funeral parlor like a social hall, chatting and gossiping, slipping out for a bite to eat, stepping up now and then to glance at Elizabeth lying in the light gray coffin with its pink satin lining, looking more rested than she ever had in life. Jim came. No one had seen him in years; he was a stranger in their midst. The buzz of talk among the mourners abruptly ceased. One could hear the whispered, "There's Jim!—There's Jim!—There's Jim!" circling the room as he shuffled embarrassedly up to the coffin and looked at his wife. Then he turned and stood irresolute, waiting for someone to speak. Laurette walked up to him.

"What are you doing here?" she demanded, eyes blazing. "If you had been kinder to her in her youth, she might have lived longer!" There was black hate in her eyes. Jim, with a half-smile that was more pathetic than tears, stood a moment, hesitant, facing his daughter, then turned and walked out. Laurette's fury left as quickly as it had come. She shrugged and remarked indifferently to Nellie, "Maybe I should have been nicer to him. After all, if it wasn't for him I wouldn't be here."

Several years later she learned that Jim had been picked up on the street gravely ill. She arranged for his medical care at a hospital. Told that he had not much longer to live, she sent him to a quiet home in the country. When he died, Laurette buried him beside Elizabeth in Woodlawn Cemetery.

Something went out of Laurette after her mother died; a just-beginning trust in life that the climate of success and happiness was establishing in her. She resented her mother's death. She held it against God and found in it the animus that had always lurked in the realities of life for her. She closed up on these realities; she was the little girl who wouldn't play because she couldn't win, the little girl who was going to be somebody else because it was better and safer than being herself. After her mother's death, over which she wept most bitterly, she did not weep again for over twenty years; not even when Hartley died.

Her acts of generosity, which were many, became brusque as though she were afraid of the emotional claims they might evoke. After Elizabeth's funeral she called in her Aunt Nellie and Cousin Mabel Tye who had been so loving and faithful. "I want you to pick out a house in Spring Lake and I will buy it for you. You have never asked me for anything. I want to do this for the affection that was between you and my mother. I will never forget that you were with her at the sanitarium when I could not be."

Nellie finally agreed. As Laurette made out the check and handed it to Mabel, she said, "I never want you or Nellie to mention this again to me or to anyone," and with this she seemed to close the book once and for all on sentiment.

Ever so subtly Laurette's face, which could mirror the most fleeting moods and emotions, lost the open expectant look which had made it so beautiful; as time passed it became a seeking, questioning look with small momentary tremors of fright passing behind the eyes, so incongruous with the brash, relentless tongue, the increasingly cavalier way of handling emotions, her own as well as others'. The closer one was to her the closer one had to look for tenderness. It was there and ever so shyly at times would peer over the threshold of that questing, frightened look, but to woo it further was almost impossible. It made those who loved Laurette ache a little that what was so tender and beautiful in her lurked deeper and deeper in the rooms of her imagination, out of reach . . . will o' the wisp . . . haunting. Those who had the best of it were those who knew her not at all: the audiences she played to. Theirs was the full impact of the duality that grew within her: the lonely princess locked in the tower, symbol of all that tender union can be, the isolation of spirit that gave her art the last nuance of human understanding.

"It must be wonderful to live with such a woman!" many would exclaim as her talent flared higher and higher.

No. You do not live with her; you seek her maybe; but only in the theatre do you find her.

*

# Fame, Money–and Much Love

The world of make-believe was where Elizabeth and her dreaming daughter had experienced their closest companionship. Now that Elizabeth was gone, the theatre was more than ever Laurette's home, and Hartley was her partner in that never-never land where she preferred to live.

Hartley was less troubled than many would have been by what was elusive in Laurette's nature for he too avoided the more turbulent aspects of reality—for different reasons. He was not by nature a violent man. He built a world carefully planed to temperance and controllable emotions. He trained Laurette to live in that world. He disciplined her in the theatre as well. In his plays she was confined to certain areas of conduct and emotion; she never played a passionate love scene, never had close physical contact with a man, never played a mistress in any of the roles he created for her. If asked why, he would have given a moralistic reason, but he must have known all too well that there were tides in her better left undisturbed if one was to live temperately, as his whole nature commissioned him to live. The primary force of his influence on Laurette was toward temperateness in both her personal and artistic life. In its superficial evidences her art required and was improved by this, but in its depth was to be dangerously confined. Because Laurette sought emotional balance which she knew that she woefully lacked, and because in the past she had been hurt by emotional excesses, she was grateful for his calm and quiet guidance, for his God-given gentleness which was "as the dew of Heaven" falling upon her life after all the turbulence she had known. They were supremely in love, supremely happy together. Neither of them guessed at the danger that threatened them, the pressures that were building up to destroy their happiness.

For the next nine years Laurette lived in the land-locked harbor of Hartley's love, appeared mostly in his plays. Some were strongly emotional in theme, "The Harp of Life," "Out There," "The National Anthem"; but none had the simple, direct animal passion of Luana which Laurette had found so satisfying. Hartley's passion when aroused was a moral one; otherwise his nature was pure of violence of any kind.

Their immediate problem was to get away from "Peg."

"I don't want to hear about her again until I'm eighty," said Laurette; "then I'll revive her."

Hartley had a little nugget called "Happiness" in his kitty, a very successful one-act play which they had done in London as well as New York, and which subsequently he had roughed out to three acts. But Laurette thought the character of Jenny so much like Peg that the play would have the same success and imprison her in the one part for three or four years. So Hartley obligingly buried "Happiness" in a bottom drawer.

Their partner in this odd search for a not-too-successful play was George C. Tyler, who had journeyed to London in the spring of 1915 to get Laurette's signature on a contract. In a day when managers were being excoriated for their rank commercialism, Tyler was of that rare breed who considered the worth of a play first, box office second. Throughout a long career he gave expression to a native venturesomeness by launching many an unknown on the road to stardom: Helen Hayes, Alfred Lunt, Lynn Fontanne, Glenn Hunter were some. He brought the great Italian actress Eleanora Duse to this country and was the first to introduce the Irish Players. Through Laurette his gambler's spirit was given fresh impetus for she was constantly seeking to test herself along fresh and untried paths. Her prismatic moods, boisterous enthusiasms and driving ambition held him enthralled. In the six years of their association Laurette and Hartley threw ideas at him like punches and after the first grumbling gasps Tyler was always game. "God A'mighty!" he would catapult from his considerable middle; or, "Girl, you're crazy! How the hell are you going to do that?" But even as he rocked with the punch, the light of battle would flare in his eye. Hartley and Laurette loved him for his enthusiasm, his willingness to take a gambler's chance.

After Elizabeth's death the Manners family had moved from

the St. Regis into a sunny top-floor apartment of a new building on West End Avenue. Tyler, a bachelor, lived just around the corner with his sister. He loved to drop in for an hour or so to see "what was up." His attitude was that of a kid who can't resist watching the circus unload. He would return from these visits to regale his sister with stories of Laurette's mood of the moment, her wit, her latest ambition. "Greatest of them all!" was his term for her. In 1945 when friends brought to the nursing home where he was dying news that Laurette had triumphed once again on Broadway, that was what he murmured, "Greatest of them all!"—and the phrase held his lifelong wonderment at her artistry.

After one false start with a try-out in Philadelphia of Hartley's sophisticated comedy called "The Wooing of Eve," the triumvirate decided on "The Harp of Life" as the play in which to bring Laurette back to Broadway. In every aspect it was about as different from "Peg" as could be imagined. In it Laurette played the thirty-six-year-old mother of a nineteen-year-old son. The story dealt with the teaching to the young of what was then referred to rather antiseptically as "sex hygiene." But in spite of this somewhat daring theme Hartley's treatment of it was essentially Victorian, and critics, like Heywood Broun, bumbling untidily into a more perplexed but far more honest era, scoffed at the old-fashioned manner in which it was handled. As proselytizer for a balder honesty, he trampled over the many subtleties of the play and of Laurette's interpretation. These were not, however, lost on others. "BEAUTY AND TRUTH IN THE HARP OF LIFE" the *New York Times* headlined its review, "A Delicate, Tender and Searching Comedy. . . ."

Burns Mantle welcomed Laurette back to Broadway in these words:

> Her acting is as elusively beautiful as the color of a flower and as impossible to describe. She is the mistress of a thousand tricks, but so perfect is her sense of the theatre and so absolute her command of her art that trickery is the last charge her devoted audience will make against her. How glad we are that she is home again.

On the whole Laurette and Hartley were well pleased with their welcome. In the majority of the reviews the play shared honors with the star. What's more the audience accepted with good grace the fact that Peg had grown up, and that, alone, Laurette considered a triumph.

"I vowed I'd make my audience grow old and interesting with Peg," she said, "and I've done it."

The part of Sylvia gave her a chance to wear smart clothes, to be gently feminine, and to play with a mature emotional power which her hoyden roles had not required.

So carried away was Burns Mantle by Laurette's technical resources that he suggested an interesting experiment. Why not have the stars currently on Broadway swap roles for one performance? Would they be game? His list:

Maude Adams    —"A Kiss for Cinderella"
Francis Starr    —"Little Lady in Blue"
Emma Dunn      —"Old Lady 31"
Elsie Ferguson   —"Shirley Kaye"
Ruth Chatterton—"Come Out of the Kitchen"
Laurette Taylor—"The Harp of Life"

Only Laurette and Emma Dunn responded enthusiastically to the challenge. "Let's draw the roles out of a hat," wrote Laurette to the critic. But nothing came of the idea.

"Isn't it a pity that we aren't more enterprising?" commented Laurette.

A notable event on the first night of "The Harp of Life" was the debut of a young English actress, Miss Lynn Fontanne, whom Laurette had brought to America to play with her. They had met at a society tea given in Laurette's honor in London. Shy, awkward, and virtually unknown, Lynn was, in her own words, "terrified at the posh doings." When her companion suggested she join the queue waiting to meet the visiting American actress, she exclaimed, "She doesn't want to meet me. I'm much too unimportant." Looking extremely prim in a little hat with two long velvet streamers down the back, she took a seat across the room and sipped a cup of tea. Suddenly the group around Laurette melted away, and the two women found themselves staring at each other. At that moment it dawned upon Lynn that the guest of honor was quite as terrified as she, and this gave her the courage to cross the room and slip into the chair beside her.

"I'm an actress," she explained breathlessly, "just a little actress!"

"You are!" There was enormous relief in Laurette's voice. "What have you played in?"

" 'Milestones.' "

"I saw that! What part did you play?"

"Gertrude."

"You were wonderful! What else have you done?"

" 'My Lady's Dress.' " . . . "What part?" . . . "You were wonderful!" They beamed at each other like two kids who had discovered they lived on the same block. Lynn's hand, clutching her teacup, was still shaking.

"Will you come and play with me in America?" Laurette shot at her.

"Boom! Just like that she asked me!" was the way Lynn later described the invitation. "I said, yes, of course, but I didn't take her seriously. Later, while slipping into a luxurious summer ermine, she asked me to a party she was giving the next night at the Grafton Club. I had only three pounds to my name but the next day I went all over London looking for an evening dress for three pounds. Finally I found one at a place where they sold old rented theatre costumes. I went to the party and had a glorious time. Frequently after that Laurette asked me to her dressing room and we talked parts and plays. She was very, very kind to me in every way. But when she returned to America, I never expected to hear from her again. I was driving a canteen down in Devonshire a few months later when I received a cable from her offering me a part in her next play at one hundred dollars a week. It was an unheard of sum of money. A manager friend of mine looked at me with new eyes. 'Are you worth twenty pounds a week?' he asked incredulously. I didn't know that I was, but I sailed ten days after I got the cable."

Klaw and Erlanger, under whose banner "The Harp" was produced, refused to pay Lynn's passage so Hartley cabled the money. Manager Tyler, apprised of her arrival, was indignant.

"God A'mighty!" he growled. "We have hundreds of girls in America who can play that part!"

"Not the way this one can," Laurette replied. "Hartley wrote it with her in mind."

When Tyler saw the English import at the first rehearsal he let

out another "God A'mighty!" Lynn, arriving in the midst of New
York's midwinter cold, had draped a large boy's sweater over
her scrawny frame and looked, according to Laurette, the epitome of Kipling's "rag and a bone and a hank of hair."

On the opening night of "The Harp" however, Lynn triumphantly vindicated Hartley's and Laurette's faith. As the nineteen-
year-old son's shy fiancée "arrived at the age where she is all
bones and blushes" she was an instantaneous success with the
American public. Lynn was in the next four plays that Hartley
wrote and won new distinction with each role. "She was sometimes gauche, but so true," Laurette said of her. "While acting
with her I forgot we were actresses." And added enviously, "She's
the only woman I know that twenty pounds turned into a beauty."

The box office at the Globe was still healthy in the spring of
1917 after a three-month run but world events of that year were
boring deep under superficialities, turning people's thoughts to
basic concepts of right and wrong, courage and honor. The Germans had used poison gas; Americans had died on the high seas.
A large segment of America was behind its pacifist President who
wanted to keep the country out of war, but it was impossible for
those like Hartley and Laurette who had seen war firsthand in
Europe to remain neutral in feeling. Hartley, as a patriotic Englishman, had been deeply affected by the indiscriminate slaughter
during the Zeppelin raids, deeply touched by the courage and
cheerful sacrifices of his countrymen. His moralistic fury at the
atrocities of the Hun had already brimmed over in the three one-
act plays he had written while still in London. Now he felt the
need to uncork his patriotism.

"He's plumping out with a good idea," Laurette told Tyler, and
at once they were both all solicitude and enthusiasm.

It was in March of the fateful year of 1917 that Hartley closeted
himself in his study and commenced to write at fever pitch. Laurette and Tyler hovered outside the door like relatives awaiting a
birth. Tyler, on the rough outline Hartley had given him and
before seeing a word on paper, hurled all caution to the winds,
procured a theatre in Atlantic City, began to assemble a cast and
make sets.

After the first few days of constant writing Laurette sent Tyler a telegram, "I think I should tell you I haven't allowed Hartley out of the apartment for two days except for air."

Tyler wired back, "Is air absolutely necessary?"

In ten days the first act was completed and rehearsals began. By the time the second and last act was finished, the first was out of the way. Tyler rushed around trying to find a one-act curtain raiser, but Hartley plunged on, writing an epilogue on the train to Atlantic City.

Four weeks to the day after he began, his war play, "Out There," opened in Atlantic City and two days later had its première in New York. It was generally conceded by the critics to be not only his best play but also the best produced by the conflict. It was a work of great tenderness and surprising simplicity, all the more notable in that it was written in the midst of the mounting passions of war by a man who possessed a remarkable ability to hate.

For the first time Laurette's performance, brilliant as it was as Annie, the little Cockney scrub who longs to do her "bit" for her country, took second place to Hartley's work. One critic began his review: "For once Laurette Taylor must bow low to her husband . . ."

No one was more delighted to do so than Laurette. She'd always known that he was a good dramatist; now at last he was achieving the recognition he deserved. Alexander Woollcott was "dancing in the streets" both about the play and "this delightful partnership of the theatre which seems destined to find a place in its history as honorable as that won by the partnership of Gilbert and Sullivan, or Barrie and Maude Adams." She liked what he said of her performance of 'Aunted Annie who becomes 'Appy Annie, when she at last wins the coveted uniform of a Red Cross nurse: "You could ask nothing better than the girlishness, the jaunty humor and the fine fervor—the uplifting fervor of her performance. You can imagine nothing more inspiring in the theatre just now than the sight of her standing with hands clasped, cheeks flushed, her eyes as big as saucers while she whispers again and again, 'We're goin' t' win, ain't we, doctor? We gotta win! Bli'me!' "

It was a delicious triumph for husband and wife. There was an air of satisfaction and fulfillment both in the theatre and at home. In fact home and theatre were almost interchangeable. Most of the company members were close friends. Hartley spent almost as much time backstage at the Globe as Laurette, and it was not unusual for them to have dinner together in her dressing room between matinee and night. Beside the satisfaction of a joint success, of perfect teamwork between star, company, author and producer, all of whom had worked under pressure to bring the play to Broadway at the psychological moment, "Out There" expressed certain fundamental concepts of humanity and service and, while in the theatre, Hartley and Laurette felt close to those who were fighting and dying for those concepts in Europe.

Tyler clucked over the pair of them like a contented mother hen. Often he found himself pinch-hitting with the press for the chronically unpunctual Manners team. "You wait and see," he would tell some reporter waiting for an interview. "She'll stroll in here five minutes before the curtain goes up and think she can give an interview. But I'll say one thing for her, she's the only actress I know who can arrive at eight twenty-five and make an eight-thirty curtain!"

Laurette makes him eat his words by arriving fifteen minutes ahead of time, beaming and dipping a little as she walks which is characteristic of her in a happy mood and when she is about to charm the press. This was to be a double interview but she explains that she has been unable to locate Hartley all day so they will proceed without him.

Tyler takes up a stand at the dressing-room door and peers down the corridor from under the visor of his cap, which seems glued to his head as the inevitable cigar is glued to his lips. He waits to shepherd Hartley along as soon as he arrives at the stage door. "If there is one person more unpunctual than Laurette, it's Hartley," he explains to the interviewer.

Laurette begins to talk, throwing off her hat and coat, kicking off her shoes. She starts in by telling the reporter she doesn't like interviews. She thinks they are silly. She hates to be misquoted. When she was brash and young and an interviewer asked her if she had a hobby she said, "Yes, collecting ten-dollar bills." But she has learned tact since then, thanks to Hartley—well, at least, some. She is asked how it happens she has had a song to sing in each of her plays so far, "Peg," "The Harp," "Out There." That's easy, she likes to sing, she'd rather sing than anything else in the world so she has Hartley put a song in each play.

"My voice isn't so good, but I work hard on my songs. It's good training, and I like it. As Hartley says of my voice, 'A poor thing but mine own.'" She explains that Annie's rendering of a whole repertoire of Cockney songs in the second act, which takes place in a hospital ward, came about purely by happenstance. . . . "No, really, I didn't say to Hartley, now everybody is to wait while I sing my songs. The scene required that I make up several hospital beds. I did so hurriedly, humming snatches of tunes. A friend of mine who had worked in the French hospitals told me I couldn't do it that way—that there was a special technique to making up a hospital bed. I had her teach me each detail. To my dismay I found the scene running six minutes instead of two or three, so I began singing songs I had picked up in London—'We Live in Trafalgar Square,' 'Please Don't Steal My Prayer Book, Mr. Burglar,' 'They're Afraid He'll Set the Waterworks on Fire.' The songs made a hit besides giving me time to make up the beds properly."

Tyler from the door: "We're going to put you on as an Irish singing comedienne."

Laurette registers extreme pleasure.

The interview progresses with more joshing between Tyler and Laurette. Hartley at last bustles in with many murmured apologies; he has lost an hour somewhere in the morning and has been in mad pursuit of it all day. Laurette turns the interview over to him and retires with the colored maid to dress for the performance.

Hartley exchanges a few words with Tyler about the "house" for the afternoon, then turns to the reporter. He becomes extremely sober, somewhat didactic. His "cause" of the moment is the mounting difficulties between managers, actors and authors; he considers it of vital importance to reconcile the conflict of interests between the three elements if the theatre is to survive. Tyler, still at the door listening for the final "five minutes to curtain" call, tries to speed up his scholarly discourse. "In one sentence, here it is: They must all get together." Hartley nods in grave acknowledgement of this typical Tyler summary. Only one who knows him very well will catch the twinkle of amusement behind his large, rather sombre eyes.

The United States declared war on Germany two days after the opening of "Out There." Neutrality was gone overnight. Active participants at last, the American people found that the play struck innumerable chords drawn taut within them. The timing of its arrival on Broadway was, as Woollcott shrewdly stated, "the envy of every counting house on the Rialto." New York's Mayor John Purroy Mitchell asked for a picture of 'Aunted Annie to be used as an enlistment poster. Annie's ardent, oft-repeated phrase to those who seemed hesitant to serve their country, "If I go, will you go?" was used at many a recruiting rally. Thus did the little Cockney scrub of Camden Ta'an slip into American history.

At this period in her career, Laurette found herself in the enviable position for an actress of being able to do just about anything she wanted in the theatre. She had both a playwright and a manager willing to give free rein to her ambition and follow almost any course she cared to dictate. On her return to America, Hartley had gathered together the nucleus of an excellent company, members who had played with Laurette in three productions, notably Lynn Fontanne, Frank Kemble Cooper and Philip Merivale. In "Out There," they had been joined by that superlative actor, J. M. Kerrigan, product of Dublin's Abbey Theatre. Laurette was never afraid of competition. Hartley invariably surrounded her with top supporting actors, and as one critic put it, she was noted for her "heroic gifts of excellent roles to the members of her company." The next step in her career was obvious, and one that had been in her mind since she got her first toehold on Broadway: a repertory theatre.

In 1915, Grace George had launched herself as actress-manager at her husband's beautiful Playhouse Theatre on Forty-eighth Street. Like most attempts at repertory, it had not been a financial success, but Miss George had added immeasurably to the luster of her name with performances in Shaw's "Major Barbara" and a revival of "Captain Brassbound's Conversion." At the time, Laurette was more envious of Grace than any other actress on Broadway.

Repertory's appeal for Laurette was in the opportunity to play a wide variety of parts and play them exclusively, and for a limited time only, in New York. She was emphatic in her contention that once a struggling actress made the Great White Way she should stay there. "Failures don't hurt you," she told young actresses seeking advice; "they help you, if you're strong enough to stand up under them. In my first four years in New York I played seven parts. I was in three failures, one after another, but the important thing was I stayed in New York."

It was in the great metropolis, fickle and pleasure-loving, that Laurette found the new challenge she wanted to meet. Hardship, failure, stardom and overwhelming success were hurdles she had taken; now versatility and growth were her aim, and she considered a New York audience the perfect yardstick for taking her measure as an artist. "To hold your place on the New York stage takes skill and foresight as well as talent," she said at this time. "It is easy enough to be a successful ingénue. You have really to know nothing. You have only to be charming and young, and since New York is the most voluptuous city in the world, there are great rewards for charm and youth. But to hold your place in turn against the constantly rising tide of competing youth you must have something more lasting. Consider the superannuated ingénue. Is there anything more tragic?

"New York is not a city of fixed and settled theatregoers like London and Paris. There a favorite grows old among people who see her so often, and are so faithful to her that they are scarcely aware of the ravages that time is making on her. But New York is a place of shifting crowds, the majority of its theatregoers are irreverent strangers. And the man from Colorado seeing the smile and hair and eyes of the famous beauty for the first time, is unabashed and merely says, 'Oh, is that she? Why, she is older than I thought.' "

She encouraged promising young actresses to do character parts while still young. When the lovely Carroll McComas hid her youth and beauty in the slatternly "Miss Lulu Bett," Laurette congratulated her warmly. "You are so right. Play character parts when you're young and you'll never grow old in the theatre."

That evil day Laurette vowed would never come to her. "I have the old-fashioned theory that acting means applying creative intelligence to a broad variety of characters. I mean to act until I am sixty and out of an instinct for self-preservation I shall not let myself be tagged. Indeed I am so forehanded that I have picked out for myself the play I mean to do when I am fifty. I shall play then Margaret Deland's 'Iron Woman,' which I think one of the greatest characterizations I know."

She did not play the "Iron Woman" at fifty. At fifty she was generally considered a "has-been," and a younger generation of theatregoers had never even heard of her, or if they had, thought that she was dead. But Laurette was not underestimating the strength of her instinct for survival as an artist. It would operate long after personal survival had lost all meaning. Not at fifty, but at sixty she would be back on Broadway at the top.

But this is ahead of the story. Repertory, Laurette decided, was to be her next step. "Out There" had served the psychological moment magnificently. Laurette wanted to get on to other things and Hartley and Tyler followed obediently in her wake. Hartley had revised "The Wooing of Eve" and, on the theory that America's wartime audiences wished to be distracted and amused, the frothy inconsequential little comedy followed "Out There" into the Liberty Theatre in November, 1917. Hartley had four other plays either completed or outlined which were to follow. "The Wooing of Eve" was Laurette's third play within a year, and the first failure for the partnership. It brought a crescendo of moans over Laurette's refusal to change playwrights. In the role of Miss Alverstone, a witty, sophisticated, self-reliant American girl in England, the notices were again all hers; author and play were excoriated by the critics.

"To play 'The Wooing of Eve' for four straight weeks would not completely destroy Laurette Taylor's following, but I am sure would reduce it to a minimum," said Burns Mantle. "A few hundred of us would still hang on believing in her as the most

gifted American comedienne. The play was 90% silly and unin-
teresting and only 10% Taylor, which is its only charm."

Critic Ralph Block soberly pondered this quality in Laurette
that "lifts bad material out of its depths . . . a quality outside
the trickery of acting, some fever that is entirely a possession of
the human spirit and sweeps over the edges of the stage to catch
the audience and draw its members near . . . some impetuosity,
some recklessness, that can sweep a good deal of opposition before it."

Because of the bad notices and a sharp theatrical depression
then running its course, it seemed advisable to abandon the idea
of repertory for the time being. The next search—and a quick
one, for "Eve" was dying of inanition—was for sure-fire box
office.

"I can be ambitious some other season," Laurette said philosophically.

They did not have to look very far. Reposing in the bottom
drawer of Hartley's desk lay "Happiness" waiting to speak its
little piece which, like "Peg," was quite unpretentious: just to
warm the human heart with laughter and understanding, and give
it hope.

While "Eve" limped along, Hartley worked at top speed to
bring the rough three-act draft to completion. Rehearsals of the
first act began while "Eve" was in its third week. It was hoped
the new piece could be brought into the Liberty without the
necessity of an intermission. But once on a downhill path, Laurette
gave a play short shrift. She refused categorically to allow cut-
rate merchants to purchase blocks of tickets for any reason, so
as soon as patronage fell off at the box office, "The Wooing of
Eve" was unceremoniously carted away to Cain's warehouse, just
short of a week before "Happiness" was ready.

"Happiness" was just what Laurette had feared, a box-office
success. Again rose the peans of praise coupled with the howls
over the waste of her talents.

Critics supposedly wield a deadly weapon on plays they do not
like, but "Happiness," like "Peg," they failed to assassinate. The
story of Jenny, a Brooklyn errand girl, who delivers a dress to a

rich and bored young woman and stays on to teach her the meaning of happiness—Jenny's definition, "lookin' forward"—was a
heart-warming one with universal appeal. It drew thousands of
letters, extraordinary letters which contained stories of near sui-
cides, of confused adolescents finding themselves, of those who
had lost courage regaining it, all through the simple message of
the play.

Again Hartley had drawn on certain basic qualities in Laurette's nature which he found so endearing and admirable. Anyone
who ever saw Jenny rocking back and forth in Mrs. Crystal-
Pole's plush Park Avenue living room, supposedly enjoying the
benefactions of leisure which have been thrust upon her, and muttering, "I'm sick of the sight of my Sunday suit!" will never forget the picture.

And again Hartley confounds the critics of his talents by writing a love scene between Jenny and a young Irish electrician,
played by J. M. Kerrigan, so natural, so fresh and delightful, that
it seemed not theatre at all but a transposition of life itself across
the footlights.

The mounting groans over the waste of her talents annoyed
Laurette without in the least upsetting her artistic peace of mind.
She simply did not agree with the critics. Hartley was a magnificent playwright. It was ridiculous to say he created roles to
suit her. After "Peg" he had written about a thirty-six-year-old
mother of an adolescent son and left it up to her to make her
own adjustments. "Out There" was a child of his brain fever
about the war, and the fact that her knowledge of the English
Cockney and the Cockney accent was limited had not stopped
him from creating 'Aunted Annie.

As for the sketchiness of his plays—how about Barrie whose
plays were called formless at first and now are called whimsical?
"The Taylor-Manners combination is here to stay," Laurette announced with finality. "Why, thanks to Hartley, I have scored a
record no other actress can match. Only one failure in five plays."

You would expect Laurette to be belligerent with anyone who
disagreed with her. She enjoyed belligerency. She took on the
critics singlehanded. Hartley did not participate. He was modest
in the assessment of his own talents; he was also invulnerable in

the joy that the exercise of these talents gave him; he lived with
his characters, he loved them, and he was true to them. To see
them touched into life by the genius of his wife was a joy that
superseded any disappointments he might feel at the lack of
recognition he received as an author. There is little question that
he was the more rounded and satisfied of the partners. It is equally
true that the complaints of those who observed Laurette's talents
confined in the Manners mold were legitimate, in that they recognized intimations of a far more powerful instrument of expression. John Corbin makes a penetrating analysis of the debits and
credits of Hartley's playwriting, and sounds an oddly ominous
warning as to the strictures upon Laurette's genius:

> Mr. Manners has stuff in him that is worthy of the finest shap-
> ing, the most diligent process of perfection. The theme of "The
> Harp of Life" appealed to the finest sensibilities, the deepest intel-
> ligence, and Miss Taylor's character of the mother was for two
> acts a thing of subtle and consummate beauty. 'Aunted Annie was
> both as a character and as an inspiration quite equal to anything
> in the war plays of Barrie; and the scene in the hospital was the most
> genuine and moving episode from the front that has been seen on
> our stage. Even Jenny in "Happiness" is, in her qualities of heart
> and humor, own sister to Peg. But all that is good in them exists in
> spite of Mr. Manners' impressionistic technique, and is diminished
> because of it. . . . A word in behalf of Miss Taylor, or rather in
> behalf of what she might be, but is not. She also needs the inspira-
> tion and sustaining force of the better-made play. Those who re-
> member her little Kanaka girl in "The Bird of Paradise," know that
> *she has resources in feminine allure, in poetic passion and in exalted
> tragedy, which since then have remained dormant. . . . is it pos-
> sible that a great talent and a high spirit is being subdued to the
> level of these theatric improvisations—probably the greatest talent,
> the highest spirit of our times?* (Author's italics)

Art and personal happiness are rarely good bedfellows. Years
before meeting Hartley and again when their partnership was
breaking up, Laurette made this stark statement: "Artists to give
their best to their creations should be born without a sense of self-
preservation."

In trying to objectify her feelings for Hartley and what he
meant to her, Laurette had some curious things to say. "I had one

tempestuous childhood and was hardly out of that when nature built another for me."

This is an obscure statement unless one understands that "nature" to Laurette was an all-inclusive word for sex, passion and the desire to have babies. "Nature" had become suspect, first under the lash of her father's whip, and later in her marriage to Charlie Taylor, which had been a disastrous emotional experience primarily because of these undisciplined forces. With that odd mind of hers, which could be so arbitrary about what to accept and what to reject, she repudiated and feared "nature" as something that almost destroyed her. It is extremely doubtful that Laurette would ever have married a second time had she not met a man as gentle in aspect and disciplined in his emotions as Hartley.

She states these things in her own oblique way. "When I met Hartley I had experience without discipline; confusion without understanding; nerves without balance." Hartley supplies discipline, understanding, balance. She is grateful to him for bounding her world, for stilling the floods of her emotional confusion. The powerful drives are now nicely contained and buoy the many cargoes of her rich nature: love, happiness, pleasure, and the work of her imagination in the theatre. This full and quiet tide which she rode with Hartley was perhaps more than sufficient for her personal happiness. But the potential tragedy in that happiness was that the artist in her demanded flood tide too, and would take no less.

But in those days there were no shadows; everything was fun. It was fun to walk into your playwright's study when he was struggling for an innocuous opening scene for "The Harp"; to rumple his hair so that the dark curls fell over his brow, and say: "Let me be on the stage while the audience is still banging down the seats—oh, come on, Hartley, let me!" and have him obligingly write such a scene, and the two of you enjoy the astonishment of the audience when the curtain rises to discover, not a maid arranging flowers or answering a doorbell, but the star herself, Laurette Taylor! It was fun to make a peephole in the scenery and stand head touching head while a performance was in progress, watching for wandering looks or idle fanning through programs, signs that a scene must be cut, a speech speeded up. Your indignation when he says, "You have no high harmonics in your voice, darling. You must take singing lessons to develop them." Then you promptly fall in love with singing and announce you would rather sing than speak. "That's becoming obvious, old dear, you're beginning to sing everything you should speak. I suggest you stop the singing lessons now." There is no use being indignant; his eyes are luminous with devotion, every element of your life and career are his concern, and he knows so well how to order these things that life flows in a smooth pattern of love and work.

"All right, Hartley, but please write me one song in the next play. After all, I've spent a lot of money on this singing voice of mine."

Exciting beyond anything is the moment when Hartley emerges from his study with a finished script and reads it to his Laurie. This is the moment when creator and interpreter fuse and there is a whole new projection of experience where the two of you begin to breathe and have your being together. This way life can never crowd you, face you up to its drabness, the horrible boredom of its daily importunities, the boring sameness of yourself and others. . . . How large and full of light are Laurette's eyes as she announces to her children, "Hartley has written a wonderful play! Really wonderful!" and the curling mouth seems to be savoring the taste of rich food as she says it.

Rehearsals were becoming family affairs with fellow players like Violet, and Frank Cooper, Philip Merivale and Lynn Fontanne, all of whom were close friends. There was an easy camaraderie, a sharing of little hierarchical jokes, the gentle spoofing of friends well met. "The Terrible-Tempered Mr. Bangs" Laurette called Merivale for his wild moodiness which became the most sensitive barometer of feeling when on the stage. He could slam his dressing-room door and swear like a pirate over a broken shoelace or a domestic upheaval, and Laurette would forgive him—or not even have to think of forgiving him—because he played with such sensitivity. Violet fascinated Laurette with her tart humor and utter regality of manner. Lynn was like her own flesh and blood, warm, eager, receptive, living for the theatre. . . . It

was Lynn wrinkling her nose and giggling over some new beau
they had shared at a party the night before . . . Lynn up to supper, obligingly eating all the fattening foods Laurette dare not
touch and not gaining an ounce—"darn her" . . . Lynn at the
dressmaker's, with Laurette loudly envious of her "elegant bones."
"In me they lose the pins, on Lynn they bend 'em." . . . Lynn at
rehearsals, one long forefinger pressed to her lower lip, toes pigeon-
ing in. " 'Ere now, me girl," Laurette would say. "Mind abaht
the toes now." Or, in a scene together, " 'Alf a mo', dearie—you've
'opped my line." They had taken to prattling together like two
Cockney fishmongers since the days of "Out There." There was
nothing but affection between them and Laurette took a terrific
pride in Lynn's success. Fluid, adaptive, the girl blossomed under
Hartley's tutelage. She lost her gauche ways and pigeon toes and
went on to become one of the finest actresses in America. "In later
years I admired her technique," Laurette said, "but she never again
touched me as deeply as she did under Hartley's direction."

No closer bond existed for Laurette than devotion to the theatre shared with another.

Indeed it would be hard for Laurette to distinguish in her mind
between favorite actors and favorite friends. Good actors she was
always half in love with, bad actors she could not abide. On the
rare occasion that she found herself sincerely fond of someone
who was not a good actor, it pained her greatly.

"Poor So-and-So," she would sigh, "such a nice person but no
talent."

Once playing a summer-stock engagement, a young man who
was extremely handy around the theatre was given a small part,
and played it very badly. Laurette insisted that he be got rid of.

"But Miss Taylor," pleaded the stage manager, "he's been with
us for years. He's so willing—such a good trouper."

Laurette leaned forward and spoke with great distinctness so
her meaning could not be lost: "Elephants are good troupers, Mr.
Smith. But I don't want them in my company."

She shunned a poor actor in her company with all the finesse
of one trying to avoid leprosy. If urged by Hartley to invite such
an actor to her home, Laurette would burst out, "My God, I have
to suffer with him for three hours on the stage, isn't that enough?"

Before Hartley took her in hand, Laurette's direct and swooping attacks on another player's conception of a part, "piece of business" or manner of speech could be unsettling in the extreme. Bad actors could not take it at all, and even the good ones quailed. She blamed this explosive impatience on her "quick theatrical brain" which her early training had given her.

"Until I met Hartley," she explained, "I had no patience with the actor who sort of crochets his part into the proper squares first then knits these into what develops to be the entire pattern, because I could always see the character spread out as a whole first, and then go about the tedious business of the small accents that make perfection."

During the first rehearsals of "Peg" Laurette sat watching one of the players doing an entrance over and over until she could stand it no longer. "Oh, it's so easy!" she burst out. "Why do you make such a bother?" For the next half hour the unhappy man moved as though congealed in ice.

After rehearsal Hartley told her she was never to do such a thing again, whatever her opinion of the methods of the other members of the company, she could keep it to herself. He quite appreciated her unerring sense of the theatre, but actors were also people and had to be handled in different ways to get the best out of them.

"That's my job, Laurie," he told her, "not yours."

She promised to do better.

A few days later, Hartley suggested to another member of the cast a piece of business which to Laurette seemed simple, but the actor kept protesting its difficulties. The next thing he knew Laurette had grabbed the props from his hands and was showing him, "That's the way to do it, see?"

That night Hartley was stern. "Laurette, whenever you do anything like that again, I am going to dismiss you from rehearsal. Go shopping or go home. I'll straighten these problems out myself. Without your help."

"Suppose I don't go?" said Laurette, belligerently sticking out her under lip.

"Then I shall dismiss the rehearsal," said Hartley quietly.

"It was rather like teaching a puppy where his duty lay," Lau-

rette recalled wistfully. "After a while at a certain tone in Hartley's voice, I either went shopping, went home—or shut up."

She learned to control her tongue to a certain extent, but was
always happiest with fanatics like herself for whom nothing existed but the correct projection of a part. Under her frankness they
blossomed like plants exposed to direct sunlight. There was never
a good actor who was not at his best when playing with Laurette.

Laurette came to have the deepest respect for Hartley's knowledge of the theatre. In denouncing him as a playwright, it was
often forgotten how superbly his plays were staged and directed.
As a director he could unerringly indicate what it was he wanted
—a mincing fop, a blushing girl, a brazen harlot—all with a minimum of gesture and speech, as an artist roughs out a sketch, leaving the actor to fill in the light and shade of his own interpretation.
His patience was infinite. It had to be with Laurette. She never
did learn to concede gracefully. If she liked a piece of business,
she would stick to it and argue *ad nauseam* before relinquishing
it. It was usually too broad, too slapstick a gesture over which
they clashed. "It's too much of a muchness, darling," Hartley
would remonstrate. The mild phrase would only infuriate her. No,
the business was good; she would do it that way. Nine times out
of ten, if she persisted, audience reaction proved her wrong. Then
she'd be madder than ever. But she'd drop the business no matter
how dearly she loved it, because in the theatre she was never the
little girl who had to be the winner as she was so often in life.
It was not *who* was right but *what* was right in the theatre with
Laurette, always. Under Hartley's tutelage her performances became translucent, flawless, serving to perfection the "right life"
of her imagination.

With all this disciplining both in and out of the theatre, she
nevertheless considered herself thoroughly spoiled. No business
or managerial detail was allowed to intrude upon her; no money
concerns—either where it came from or where it went—ruffled
her pleasure in spending it; squabbles with actors or stage crew,
travel schedules, publicity, billing arrangements, every mechanical detail of production cleared through Hartley, with his prime
consideration an untroubled path for his Laurie. Her one function
was to project . . shine . . live without molestation in her enor-

mous fancy. He would do the rest. They ate, slept, dreamed theatre and their teamwork was flawless. "When Hartley was alive,"
she said wistfully in her later years, "I was kept like a very fine
racehorse."

\*

# *Laurette and Her Children*

Laurette's children were satellite to these engrossing activities
and this partnership. Possibly by mutual agreement or perhaps
because it may never have occurred to Laurette to make them part
of his life, Hartley never assumed the role of father to Dwight and
Marguerite. He would have been acutely embarrassed by having
so intimate a relationship thrust upon him. Like an animal mother,
Laurette reserved the raising of her pups to herself. She loved
them in much the same way and what training she gave them
had some of the same ferocity and unreasoning directness. In
that faraway night when she had stood over them while they
slept and wondered if Hartley could accept that part of her to
which they belonged, she may have made one of her arbitrary
decisions that he could not, and closed her mind upon the possibility once and for all. However it came about, Hartley took no
part whatsoever in the children's upbringing. Laurette disciplined
them, looked after their health and general welfare, made all decisions upon their amusements, clothes and education.

Her interest in these matters went on and off like an electric
light. At times they found themselves without even the basic
necessities of clothing and other creature comforts . . . Marguerite's skirts climb up her coltlike legs as she grows, month by
month until even Hartley is jogged out of his Sybaritic preoccupations and diffidently suggests to Laurette that they be lowered
for decency's sake . . . Dwight's teeth, blissfully unacquainted
with a tooth brush for an entire vacation, gather such a mossy

plaque that one day while beaming at his mother, he is pounced upon for his shameful neglect and retorts with spirited self-righteousness, "But I haven't got a tooth brush."

A pain or childish indisposition coming at the wrong time is simply a nuisance, and all mention is to be suppressed until Laurette can get around to doing something about it. She has little or no understanding of pain, never having had any except for the hernia on returning from England. She hates illness, again as an animal hates and lashes out at weakness or physical disability. She tends to take it as a personal affront if a child vomits or breaks out in a rash; an underlying antagonism is quite manifest until the child grows well again.

Family life even in the rudimentary form in which it existed was never settled. It seemed to consist, except for the calm figure of Hartley, of a series of explosions of either animosity or affection emanating from a base that could not be logically explored and therefore anticipated. Flagrant breaches of discipline went entirely unnoticed, while minor or even imagined infractions brought the abrupt impact of Laurette's fury like a bolt from the blue. With her penchant for emotional extremes, which she could not indulge with Hartley, she tended to believe the outlandish and ignore the obvious in any misunderstanding with her offspring. A scene, as stated before, was considered by Laurette as wholly salutary and indicative of having discharged in full her parental duties.

She was childishly defensive about these duties. Once she burst out to Zoe Akins, the playwright, "I'm a good mother. All during the war I saw to it that Marguerite washed her hair in eggs." It was quite true. At intervals she would dispatch a telegram to the Mother Superior of the convent where Marguerite boarded: "PLEASE WASH MARGUERITE'S HAIR IN EGGS." This type of dramatic attention was in certain respects quite as harrowing as her neglect.

As her popularity with the public grew and she continued to depict the very essence of youth in the theatre, these unusually tall and rangy children became an increasing embarrassment. Laurette tackled this problem in characteristically heroic style.

On the eve of his tenth birthday Dwight's heart was almost broken by the parental announcement that, contrary to his high expectations, he would not advance to the treasured age of two numerals but would remain nine. His despairing protests were of no avail. From then on this secret was buried in the family archives, lost to family memory, and was never again exhumed even to boost the faltering confidence of Marguerite who, without the cut in the age differential, was suffering by the comparisons to her talented brother. It is indicative of the strong hold Laurette's fantasy life had upon the members of her family that despite striking evidence to the contrary, such as photographs of Dwight towering above his baby sister, their classes at school, and later, a natural gravitation to their proper age groups, this fraud became fact, and only the digging up of records upon Laurette's death re-established the truth.

It was in England that Laurette began the capricious program of concealing her children entirely or exhibiting them with pride, depending upon the place, the people, and her mood of the moment. In this she was to some extent a victim of the mores of the day which required an actress to remain eternally young and eternally infertile to maintain her popularity. But Laurette improved upon the mores by indulging without thought both an intense pride in her children and an equally cavalier disregard for them when they interfered with her career.

Because of this violently shifting behavior Marguerite and Dwight learned at an early age to improvise on their conduct at a moment's notice as the need arose. Sensing that they were to be exhibited as prize pieces, they immediately galvanized themselves into what they considered to be their most winning behavior, or realizing they were *personae non gratae*, they attempted to dissolve like the Cheshire Cat, taking even their smiles along.

The crowded streets and shops of London were fraught with hazard when in the company of their mother. It is so easy for a child to forget everything about its parents, no matter how famous and brilliant, except their parenthood. It took many a sharp command or low growl in the throat to warn them that it was Laurette Taylor the actress, not their mother who for the moment was holding the center of the stage. The cry of "Mother" is still almost an umbilical attachment in the very young, and the scowling, angry figure that bears down upon one because of that cry has no relation whatsoever to the being who has been evoked. The sun blacks out. Fear takes the place of pleasure. There is a cataclysmic sense of loss, both of the wonder world discovered a moment before and of the beloved parent to whom one has called to share the wonder. It seems an eternity later that a sales-girl's titter, or a Cockney voice saying, "Oh, Miss T'yler, you were just lovely! I must 'ave been 'alf a dozen times to the show!" gives the cue that has been woefully missed; that it is "Miss T'yler," not Mother with whom the child walks.

Summers were not so bad, particularly when the family returned to America to spend most of them by the seashore; there was a wonderfully rich companionship of swimming, tennis, loving the sun and the sights and smells of the seashore together. Forced by increasing weight to devote her summers to reducing, Laurette withdrew from the public eye and saw only intimate friends most of whom were in on the secret of her motherhood. Thus the rude shock of being disowned came less frequently. But the prospect of winter holidays developed something close to an anxiety neurosis both in Marguerite and Dwight. Christmas and Easter were auspicious times for the brilliant opening nights which Laurette and Hartley commanded. Freshly and triumphantly before the public, Mr. and Mrs. Manners were in great demand socially. Vacation days were a whirl of events, but for the children, abruptly transferred from the austerity of Catholic schools to the glittering, fast-moving life of a reigning Broadway star, they were days etched with sharp uncertainties and grueling misapprehensions. Dizzily they swung from the spotlight to oblivion.

Even the glamour of witnessing their mother's performance in her latest success was tinged with a certain melancholic sense of loss, an instinctive search under the grease paint, the aura of the make-believe personality, for what was familiar and reassuring. Children seem to long for the commonplace in a parent; a perversity rarely appreciated, and certainly not at all by Laurette, who loathed the commonplace.

The association of stage and parent adds to the confusion of young souls already struggling to distinguish the real from the false. Marguerite never forgot the terror that seized her when, in "The Bird of Paradise," the curtain fell on the vision of her mother poised on a rocky ledge above the volcano's seething crater, and rose a second later to reveal only Luana's native lover peering into the fiery depth. Make-believe and reality merged with shattering finality and the piercing scream "Mother!" rang through the theatre. Long after she was jerked from her seat in the balcony, rushed to Laurette's dressing room to be shown her mother alive and unharmed, Marguerite's wild sobbing continued unabated. As for Dwight, it took years of adolescent research to discover that beautiful but stupid women were not wearing elaborate masks and disguises over sleeping intellects and unawakened souls, but were—simply stupid.

Ship travel turned out to be the worst of it. The children while still small made several crossings between London and New York with their famous mother. In the limited confines of a ship the hazards of concealment were greatly intensified. There were the reporters and photographers to be rigorously avoided, and what with the normal confusion of arrival and departure, farewells in the cabin, statements to the press, the children were in a fever of uncertainty about whom to greet and from whom to hide. It was a nightmare of dodging behind trunks, being shoved into bathrooms for indefinite stays and abruptly released into the arms of family friends cognizant of their existence. Marguerite for such occasions was dressed in the most babyish outfit Laurette could find, usually pink ruffles. Dwight took advantage of the situation to stroll about in a manful attempt to appear to be traveling alone.

The days at sea were not much better. Playing on deck, the children would spy Laurette out for a brisk walk with some unknown companion. A lift of the eyebrow, or shoulders exaggeratedly turned, meant they were to pass each other as total strangers. If the children were so unfortunate as to lunge forward in spontaneous greeting, there would be a glared warning to retreat, causing in their small bosoms a pell-mell reversal of responses which reduced them to something close to gibbering idiocy.

Occasionally, shipboard departure was planned as a game so that they could at least feel like participants in the event. The press would be ushered into one room of Laurette's suite while

Marguerite and Dwight hid in an adjoining bedroom. The conspiratorial silence, the signaling back and forth, the suppressed giggle as they listened to the gay and animated talk on the other side of the door, inflated their egos with a dim but definite sense of accomplishment. And when the conference was over and Laurette flung open the door, they would run laughing to her arms, fairly bursting with pride. But it was never really quite clear to them why they were so unacceptable at certain times and so desirable at others. Their joyous return to the bosom of their parent was tinged with the hysteria of the outcast whose numerous exiles begin to overshadow his reclamations.

Laurette was entirely obtuse in such matters and never understood why the children could not take this on-again-off-again relationship as a game. Her own childhood had consisted of being first this one and that one, French or Spanish, soulful adventuress, prankster, siren; all these masks were more entertaining than the real, the everyday personality. Then why should her children object to assuming different roles for different occasions? One moment they were glorious extensions of herself; the most beautiful, the most talented children in the world. The next, this beauty and talent with which she invested them was competing with her, embarrassing her career; immediately they became strangers, interlopers, and she would have none of them.

This was the flux in her so difficult to understand and to live with unless it was comprehended at its source as that mysterious genius force which, like the tide setting in for the shore, carries before it or overruns willy-nilly everything in its path.

It was difficult not to fall into chronically furtive behavior. As the children grew older and acquired sophistication, they attempted to counteract this tendency by a studied attitude. Dwight, who was an exceptionally gifted and beautiful boy, walked into every situation determined to overcome its difficulties with an irresistible show of charm. Marguerite hid terror and the urge to skulk under a haughty, at times almost glacial, composure. Her charm being a lesser potent, she did not rely on it in any key situation of uncertainty. It was an attitude which Laurette, with no small degree of asperity, dubbed a "princess-complex." In any tense situation between them—and there were many—this "princess-complex" was usually the final defense of the daughter and the last straw for the mother.

There is a question as to who was most puzzled by the relationship, parent or children. As Laurette lost touch with the primitive impulses which had made her fiercely guard and protect them when they were small, there was a mutual bafflement. It was a relationship which did not lack love but did lack, almost totally, any form of adequate expression. It is a fact that more and more these primitive impulses which had guided Laurette as a mother went into the theatre. And it is a fact that in the theatre the children were forced to find what was lost to them in life, the tenderness and understanding that lit Laurette's performances like a lantern. For, it was in the portrayal of mother love, of a mother's fierce devotion for her child in such plays as "Humoresque," "Alice-Sit-by-the-Fire," "Outward Bound," and "The Glass Menagerie" that Laurette reached the height of her art in her mature years.

Here again is the magic and mystery and the heartbreak of the creative artist.

At Christmas time Laurette expiated all her sins of omission in regard to family. Christmas was a day dedicated to family and, unless there was a first night, it was pursued with exhausting concentration. On Laurette's order no one stirred from the house all day. Even when the children were grown, any suggestion that they accept an outside invitation brought grievous cries of family betrayal mingled with rage. Relatives who might have been dead and buried for all anyone knew at any other time of the year, arrived for Christmas dinner and were showered with gifts. Sister Bessie usually turned up with her brood of five, Laurette's brother Edward, and his fiancée, various Cooney and Dorsey cousins, nieces and nephews. Loretta Cooney, who had got herself in many a difficulty as a child opening every package under the tree whether hers or not, was now undisputedly in charge of the show. She had bought the presents, wrapped the presents, put them under the tree which she had decorated herself, so why shouldn't she open them and enjoy them to her heart's content? Christmas was finally and magnificently hers! Mechanical jump-

ing tigers, a crawling cat with eyes that light up at each turn of
the head, jewel-like feathered birds that sing in golden cages,
dolls of staggering originality wearing fabulous clothes, clowns
that somersault on high wires; anything and everything that ex-
cites, astounds, amuses, until you clap your hands, rock with
laughter, and pull your knees up just as you did as a child from
the exquisite astonishment and delight that such things bring.
"What is it, Marguerite? You wanted a rocking horse! . . . Oh,
good Lord! Anybody can have a rocking horse—that's just damn
dull! Don't you like that cat, that wonderful cat? Why, he might
be alive! I never saw anything like it! It's positively *creepy*.
. . . What is it, Bessie? You could have used some money? Oh,
my God! On Christmas do you have to be so practical? The kids
are enjoying their presents if you're not. Go back and sit down!"
And so it goes, Laurette having the time of her life with everybody's presents. Woe betide the one who gives *her* an even faintly
practical or conventional gift. "What's this, an antimacassar? Oh,
a shawl. Well, dearie, I'm not that old. I'll give it to the cook—
she's an escaped slave and once shook hands with Lincoln. . . .
*Darling*, gloves. . . . How nice. But I don't wear gloves except
to funerals. Perfume!—M-m-m. But why should I use perfume?
I have a nice smell of my own. Come on, everyone, let's have
turkey. . . ."

Only Hartley escapes. Whatever unbearable conventionality
there is attached to a gift of jewelry, he covers over by seeing
that each piece is specially designed for her by Marcus & Co.
under his supervision. Gloriously romantic pieces. Matching sets
of necklace, bracelet, pin, ring, given piece by piece at Christmas,
Easter, opening nights, anniversaries; one year in sapphires, the
next in rubies, the next in emeralds. Never in the subduedly elegant velvet case, but in an old cigar box, buried in excelsior, boxed
and boxed again and finally crated until it is the size of a suitcase.
Or in a flowerpot with a single lily growing in it, and only because he has never sent her a potted flower, and she knows his
tricks, Laurette begins to dig until she hits a small tissue-wrapped
object; a pigeon-blood ruby, perfect, flawless, set in a platinum
ring. If she is not astounded by its originality, which she generally
is, she is delighted by the manner in which it is presented. Once
he gave her a diamond necklace, not specially designed for her

but replete with fabulous stones. Laurette labeled it "character-less." It might have been bought for anyone, she told him; besides, she did not like diamonds. She never wore it, and eventually it was returned for something more alluring.

Hartley escapes in other ways, too. He is the only one allowed from the house on Christmas day. Laurette knows that it is useless to try to keep him for family get-togethers. As surely as sea gulls flying inland presage a storm, the sight of Hartley, hat on head, cane crooked over arm and drawing on his gloves as he passes from study to front door, is an infallible harbinger of a family conclave. To members already arrived he explains with the most charming and diffident smile that he is "just off to the club." There is gracious handshaking all round, of the hail-and-farewell variety, and he is gone leaving all suffused with good will and feeling a bit as though they have taken part in some historical event.

Hartley's orbit could be charted as exactly as that of a planetary body. No bachelor ever changed his habits less upon entering the state of matrimony. Wherever the family resided, his quarters—bedroom, study, dressing room and bath—were separate from the rest of the house, and these quarters were sacrosanct. The children never came there except by special invitation, and Laurette claimed that she herself did not invade them, "unless a thunderstorm was brewing or I couldn't balance my checkbook." He was referred to by the family as "the bachelor in our home," and treated as such. His stacks of shirts, socks, gloves, dozens of handmade shoes and meticulously tailored suits, all in their exactly designated places, were the wonder of an otherwise haphazard household. Row on row of mysterious nostrums, unheard of hair tonics and mouthwashes lined the shelves of his bathroom, and cigars, pipes and smoking tobacco were "props" in any room where he functioned. The one unruly element in his life was his smoking. He was rarely without a cigarette or cigar between his lips and the disposition of the ash was of perilously small concern to one who had for so long inhabited club rooms and hotels; he left a trail of it about the house, and after an evening's session of bridge or storytelling there was apt to be a fine white sift around him as around a spent volcano.

His relationship with the children remained on exactly the

same basis that it had been when his was the status of honored
guest evening after evening in the bungalow in California. They
coined the nickname "Jartley" by using his first initial and eliding
the H of Hartley. They remained on their best behavior with him
and he on the most formal terms with them. If they missed anything by his not assuming the role of father, they were entirely
unconscious of the fact. This oddly Victorian relationship held
for them a unique charm. Both children came to adore him in a
shy, uncommunicative way, and he returned their feeling in the
same manner. As they grew into adolescence, his influence on
them was considerable for all that he never presumed to offer
them a word of advice or correct them, except by inference. The
very rigidity of his code of behavior stood out for them in a
world of fluctuating values. Criticism of such rigidity never occurred to them. It *was*. Over the years, imperceptibly, they an-
chored in its lee, came to depend on it, as Laurette did; let it
bound a world that otherwise tended to explode into emotional
instability.

# *Tokeneke*

During the summer of 1916 at Tokeneke, Connecticut, Laurette
discovered Hartley's one failing—if such it could be called. He
was an intermittent drinker. It was a form of drinking which,
other than in its unbroken continuity once begun, seemed to be
not in the least compulsive or given to any of the uglier aspects
of alcoholism. If anything, drinking improved him; it extended
his characteristic urbanity, brought the Irish leprechaun out from
under the British Lion. At times and for periods he would even
drink too much but the only sign would be an increase of Puckish
humor, the capsule capering of a free spirit which, when sober,
he lacked.

Laurette at first looked on his drinking as one more fact of Hartley's superior sophistication, his knowledgeableness in a world that was quite new to her. He knew how to drink, obviously, and it was quite *comme il faut* in the circles in which he moved. She became his pupil in this as well as the other amenities of the good life.

It was after they returned from England that she noticed how methodical his drinking had become. There were no parties at the time because of Elizabeth's death and Laurette was recovering from her illness, but during the course of an afternoon and evening Hartley would down a considerable number of highballs and the next day begin all over again. There were no Bromo Seltzers, no depressions, just a steady genial glow, a willingness to pass endless time in storytelling, late hours and badinage: "Come on, old dear, sit up with me while I have one more for the road," sort of thing.

That spring he began to grow a beard, an adornment of such dashing contour that it made him look like a character out of the novels of de Musset. By the time they moved to Tokeneke for the summer, the beard was flourishing and so was Hartley.

Oftentimes that summer Laurette could be found studying her spouse with an amused grin on her face as though she were appraising a partial stranger. Here was a Hartley with more elasticity than she had ever known. The curls over the widow's peak were just a trifle more unruly and occasionally a flush on the cheeks made the dark brown eyes more lustrous than ever. But that was all. Control of his drinking seemed to be as constant as the drinking itself. This was to Laurette indeed a marvelous thing, and when she realized there was to be no "spilling over," she began to enjoy this new and wondrous Hartley.

It was a long lazy summer with many congenial friends as neighbors. For almost the last time Laurette could enjoy her vacation days rather than spend them grimly battling her lifelong enemy, fat. The John McCormacks were next-door neighbors on the rocky promontory where both families had homes overlooking Long Island Sound. Little footpaths were quickly worn in and out the rocks between the two houses; tennis, picnics, swimming from the McCormack yacht the *Macushla*, or sailing out

on the Sound in the bevy of canoes were everyday affairs. In
August, Grace George and her husband, William Brady, took the
third house on the promontory and the little footpaths extended
in that direction too.

Drinking made Hartley extremely sociable. All his rather tight
prejudices dissolved in a glow of good fellowship which nothing
could disturb.

McCormack was a fanatic about his tennis and kept himself in
a constant state of aggravation over his game by importing such
opponents as Maury McLoughlin, then champion of the United
States. Like a child he had a tempestuous dislike of losing and
made little attempt to dissemble the fact. When sober, this nettled
the urbane Hartley; a methodical, uninspired player, he could
win or lose with equanimity. But one day, with dark curls blissfully awry and cheeks flushed, he teamed up with John for a
game of doubles. They were roundly beaten. Disgustedly, John
hurled his racquet over the backstop into the Sound. Promptly
Hartley's sailed after it. John turned, lowered his big, handsome
head and stared at Hartley unbelievingly.

"Now what in the name of God made you do that, Hartley
Manners?" he asked.

Hartley beamed. "Serves 'em right," he chirped happily. "Bally
old things lost the game for us!"

John and Peg—McCormack never called Laurette anything
else—constantly argued, but with them it was a form of mutual
admiration; they tried out each other's sharp tongues for the sheer
devil of it. John had been singing at Covent Garden when Laurette brought "Peg" to England. He and his wife, Lily, went
down to Eastbourne for the out-of-town opening. Afterwards,
he stood in the dressing-room door and his tribute came out this
way:

"Hello, Miss Taylor. I think you are magnificent, but whatever
salary they're paying you, it's too much. There are hundreds of
girls in Ireland, kneeling in her churches and walkin' her streets,
just like the one you play—and, faith, they'd do it for the price of
a day's washing."

John even put up with Laurette's tennis although more than

once he was driven to exclaim, "For the love of God, Peg! Is it eggs ye are frying on that racquet, or are ye serving the ball?"

On an occasional Sunday Laurette went to church with Grace George and Bill Brady, but she was on somewhat strained terms with the Catholic Church because it had not recognized her marriage to Hartley. When chided by Grace for her backsliding, Laurette answered with considerable spirit, "Well—ll"—and the word would be slurred with a high childish indignation—"the Church doesn't recognize my marriage to Hartley, so I don't recognize the Church."

Religion, as everything, was a highly personal matter to her.

One day toward the end of summer Laurette was in the middle of a story at luncheon when Hartley excused himself for a moment and went to his room. In a short time he was back, slipping quickly into his chair as though eager not to miss a word of what his wife was saying. Glancing up, Laurette broke off in astonishment. "My God, Hartley! You can't do that to me! I didn't know who you were!" For there he sits, beard gone, the beautiful skin (that has been buried for months under a black mat) now smooth as a baby's, the brown eyes looking more enormous than ever. He is another man entirely. He is, Laurette soon discovers, by the stroke of a razor a non-drinking man for the next six months, maybe a year, maybe two. Sometime, somewhere in the future he will arrive home in the evening from a dinner, or from the club, and she will know that he is "off the wagon." There will be the unmistakable aura of that other man again—the monk who has munched on the lotus—leprechaun with a load of liquor —but until that time not a drop will pass his lips. This is the man she learned to live with and years later learned to envy for a control of—and seeming imperviousness to—alcohol, which she was to fail for so long and so heartbreakingly to master.

# Shakespeare–"My Hair Shirt"

"Happiness," settling down to a steady canter at the box office, brought out the usual reaction in Laurette. She grew restless. She wanted to try herself in some new field, set up new hurdles to surmount. She chose the biggest and toughest of them all: Shakespeare.

"Critics keep telling me I have the voice for it, the face for it, the ability for it," she said to Hartley and Tyler, "so . . . why don't I do it?"

There was nothing tentative about her plan. While continuing as Brooklyn Jenny, she would give special matinees consisting of a condensed version of "The Taming of the Shrew," two scenes from "The Merchant of Venice" and the balcony scene from "Romeo and Juliet."

"I'm bound to be good in one of them," was her theory.

Hartley and George Tyler were aghast. "But, my dear!" Hartley remonstrated, "that is a defiant approach to the difficulties of Shakespeare. A short scene at a benefit where you can't be criticized, perhaps; find out your faults, then tackle him before professional critics. But this . . . !" Laurette would not listen. Tyler, after a first solar-plexus grunt, began to take a fancy to the idea.

"Who knows, Hartley? . . . All her ideas are revolutionary. . . . This has never been done. Might mean a revival of Shakespeare's popularity. In one sentence: Let's do it!"

Laurette swept the two along with her enthusiasm. The approach was to be modern, the lines to be read colloquially; the meaning of the speech to come first, the rhythm to take care of itself. No heavy cloak of reverence for tradition was to hang over the performance nor was there to be slavish imitation of famous predecessors. It was to be essentially Laurette's conception of Shakespeare. A prerequisite of casting was that none of the actors was to have played Shakespeare before.

"I think she will be severely punished," was Hartley's final word. "She should wait a year or two at least."

"Nonsense!" exploded George. "It takes young courage to do this sort of thing."

At rehearsals Laurette had a field day; for the first time Hartley as director was overruled on many of his cautious and conservative suggestions. "The Taming of the Shrew," with Shelley Hull as Petruchio, was to be a roughhouse, a regular Hellzapoppin'. A French actor was chosen for Romeo because, Laurette averred, even his "good morning" had a natural passion.

Hartley protested. The actor had a distinct accent. "The scene is a duet, Laurie, a violin and a cello. If he has an accent you must have an accent." He was overruled: the actor's accent was so mild as to be discounted entirely, Laurette insisted. To emphasize the sense of physical separation between the lovers in the balcony scene, Laurette was to wear a long Mélisande wig, the tresses of which would hang far over the balcony so that Romeo could touch them with his hand.

The company was carried along by this spirit of innovation. O. P. Heggie, who was to play Shylock, spent hours of research until he discovered the exact cap that Shylock should wear— small, high, absolutely square and of a hideous yellow. Perched above his gentle face and pale blue eyes, it gave him, according to Laurette, the look of an organ-grinder's monkey. She told him, rather tactfully she thought, that the cap was "too authentic," persuaded him to make it less tall, less square, and less yellow.

On that fatal afternoon the "Shrew" came first and was played to the hilt as Laurette had conceived it. Shelley Hull threw Laurette all over the stage, stepped on her toes, and finally tossed her on a divan with a force that, according to one critic, "probably would have knocked a Shakespearean actress into insensibility."

The applause at the end of these spirited scenes was terrific. Happy, nervous, triumphant, Laurette dressed for Juliet. There was a murmur from the audience as the moonlit garden of the Capulets was revealed, Juliet's tresses trailing over the balcony with the vines. Then Romeo commenced his soliloquy from the shadows. The accent, successfully muted at rehearsals, fairly swamped his speech. "R-r-r's began to roll all over the stage like

hoops," Laurette recalled. He raced along with Gallic impetuosity and finally in a tempest of feeling leaped upon a bench to
capture the golden strands of Juliet's hair. "The whole balcony
began to sway like a ship in a storm," Laurette continued. "By
the time Romeo came to the speech, 'Wer-r-r-t thou as far-r-r as
that vast shor-r-e washed by the fur-r-r-thest sea I would adven-
tur-r-r-e for such mer-r-r-chandise,' I knew panic. Hardly daring
to breathe, I finished the scene with only one thought in mind:
to get the curtain down before the balcony came down."

To continue in Laurette's words: "Portia did not turn out the
way I intended her to be. The laughing audience at the end of
the balcony scene had left me a little uncertain. We made the
wait longer than usual until the swaying balcony could exhaust
its laughs. By the time I was in Portia's golden dress, I was again,
more or less, my cocky self."

The first scene between Nerissa (Lynn Fontanne) and Portia
went well. For the trial scene Laurette stained her face, covered
her gold locks with a black wig and donned the doublet and hose
of an Italian lawyer. This was another innovation of hers because
she felt Bassanio's failure to recognize Portia was ridiculous, unless she wore an adequate disguise.

Hartley had protested the tights. But Laurette had been adamant; they were the prescribed costume for an Italian gentleman and she would wear them. "You don't want a criticism hung
on your legs," he told her miserably. She conceded a few inches
—a few inches more of robe to hide the tights.

Now dressed and gazing into her dressing room mirror, Laurette was sure that she was going to be at her best as Portia.

"First-night nervousness is engendered because, no matter how
careful your preparation, you cannot tell what freak turn in
your mind is going to trip you up. It wasn't the tights or the
more voluminous robe. The quality-of-mercy speech I felt certain would be read as never before for its appeal, its reasoning, its
rightness. But when I came to it and uttered the first words, 'The
quality of mercy is not strained,' something came into my mind
that had never been there before. Why, I thought, it's like the
beginning of a popular song!

"Perhaps it was because I heard that speech most often quoted

—and most often *sung*—sung by both amateurs and professionals. Whatever the reason, I distinctly heard a tune and could not release myself from its lilt:

"The quality of mercy
Is not strain'd
It droppeth
As the gentle rain
From heaven
Upon the place beneath."

Laurette was not deceived by the great volume of applause at the final curtain. It was for the effort. Just as in "The Girl in Waiting" when sudden stardom had almost knocked the artistry out of her, she anticipated the criticism that was to follow. In a speech to her faithful after the final curtain she said the afternoon had signalized her crucifixion. She knew that she was not a great actress but she hoped someday she might be, and Shakespeare was a part of her training. However, she defended her right to interpret the classic roles as she felt them; she reasoned that archeological research in what others had done would profit her nothing and her audience little; that she hoped to continue to play the parts until she acted them as they should be acted.

The critics were on the whole generous. Said Burns Mantle:

. . . In the matinee she gave yesterday there was nothing we could single out for praise save the superb courage which prompted her to attempt it . . . she boldly staked her artistic reputation on her own conception of the classic roles that the greatest actresses of all generations have either fearsomely avoided or rankly played in studious imitation of their famous predecessors.

By all the Shakespearean standards we know anything about, she failed. . . .

Yet . . . there is a prompt reaction to the courage that prompted the test. How many of our allegedly fine actresses would have dared so much? Or, having no need of either the money or the fame such an experiment might bring, would have worked so hard and risked so much for the mere satisfaction of doing something worthwhile?

The company was deeply depressed by the notices, but when her co-workers found that Laurette could laugh, they laughed.

They rehearsed the bad spots, and played eight matinees instead of the two planned.

The only one of that brave company who ever had the courage to tackle Shakespeare again was Lynn Fontanne. Her extremely successful "The Taming of the Shrew" some seventeen years later was given much the same rough-and-tumble interpretation Laurette had tried. From a later vantage point it is a question whether the critics were not suffering a slight case of Charley horse themselves in their approach to Shakespeare. Since those days the Bard has been given entirely modern treatment and colloquialized to a degree. Had Laurette brought her ideas to a group such as the Old Vic Players, her bold plunge into Shakespeare might have ended quite differently.

However, Laurette made no attempt to shift the blame but took it all on her own shoulders. Later, in an article defending what she had done, her healthy belligerency was back. "If you are to make a family bible of Shakespeare, do so by all means. But put him on the parlor table and don't put him on the stage." And she ended, "However, if my public doesn't like me in these roles, I can only say with wifely devotion, 'Shakespeare is dead, long live Manners.' "

*

# Red Cross Tour

After the Shakespeare matinees Laurette was more restless than ever and soon began plaguing Tyler and Hartley with another idea. "I want to do something for the Red Cross," she told them, "something really big. Can't you two think of something?"

"Happiness" would close for the summer and the road tour would not begin until autumn; in the meantime, what could they do?

Tyler came up with a chronic enthusiasm: an all-star cast.

They could make a tour of the big cities with "Out There." Hartley enthusiastically concurred. In lightning time fifteen other top-ranking stars were lined up:

George Arliss

Julia Arthur

George M. Cohan

Eleanora de Cisneros

Mrs. Fiske

James K. Hackett

O. P. Heggie

De Wolf Hopper

George MacFarlane

Burr McIntosh

Beryl Mercer

Chauncey Olcott

James T. Powers

Helen Ware

H. B. Warner

All-star benefits were an integral part of England's war effort, but in America it was a new idea. Individual performers like Elsie Janis, Mary Pickford, Douglas Fairbanks, Sr., Charles Chaplin gave unstintingly of their time to the various bond rallies, but this was the first time that a whole production and company of players took to the road on a fund-raising tour.

What followed was an exciting study of chain reaction in patriotism. The carload of scenery and sixteen players traveled on a tight schedule. In three weeks they gave twenty-three performances in seventeen cities, journeying as far west as St. Louis. Every penny of the tour went to the Red Cross. Each player gave his services and paid his own travel expenses as well as those of his personal staff. In the majority of the cities, vying with the patriotism of the troupe, theatre managers took no rent, hotels made no charge. Citizens turned out to feed, transport and entertain the stars. Single seats sold for two hundred to five hundred dollars, boxes for two to five thousand dollars. An autographed program was auctioned off before each performance and drew sums ranging from a low of eighty-five hundred dollars in Providence, the smallest city, to a staggering twenty thousand five hundred in Pittsburgh. This last city, as generous as it was rich, went "over the top" for the whole tour, with an advance sale of $114,884. At the end of the Pittsburgh performance the curtain was raised and the stars applauded the audience. In three weeks the tour raised $685,632. It was by far the most remunerative of any of the benefits given for the Red Cross in World War I.

Laurette had a grand time. Some of the gamin of her trouping days revived. She was by her own admission the "Peck's Bad Boy of the outfit."

When the tour was planned Hartley felt it advisable to warn her of certain hazards. "Some of these people know much more about the theatre than you will ever learn, darling," he told her. "They are *disciplined* as well as inspired. Have respect . . . learn from them . . . *and* curb your sense of humor."

"Curb my humor?" Laurette asked. "What does that mean?"

"Remember millions of people in the world haven't any. Otherwise Mrs. Leslie Carter could never have made a living as an actress."

If Laurette had thought to take offense at his warning, she forgot everything in explosive laughter.

But almost at once she was in hot water. At the conclusion of the second performance the stars were gathered in the wings for a company call. When the curtain rose each modestly hesitated to be the first to walk onstage. On the fourth curtain Laurette could stand it no longer—the center of the stage she claimed was positively shrieking, "I've been a good friend to all of you. Why desert me in front of a twenty-eight-thousand-dollar audience?" *—so impulsively she leapt into the middle of it and took a bow. "I explained it for the next three towns," she said woefully.

This was a minor occurrence and was passed off with good humor on all sides. But one criticism did sting and she reacted with characteristic vigor.

While making a collection in the aisles in New York Laurette was offered five hundred dollars for an imitation of Cohan. She promptly gave out with "I'm a Yankee Doodle Dandy." The man offered another five hundred for an imitation of Chauncey Olcott. Shamelessly Laurette launched into that great ballad singer's "Inniskillen." Next he offered five thousand dollars for five short songs. "Proving," remarked Laurette, "he was one man who held the same opinion I do of my singing."

The next day Laurette learned that her "cabaret stunt" had been considered undignified by certain members of the company. She gave her answer in her diary of the tour.**

* "The Greatest of These—" by Laurette Taylor. George H. Doran & Co.
** Ibid.

I doubt very much whether the men who are fighting for us appear dignified as they fall in the mud, shot through, having made of themselves a human wall between the Hun and us. It's the cause they think of, not how they look.

It was also suggested that it was not consistent with the dignified future I hoped to make for myself on the American stage. There will be *no* future for *anybody, on any stage,* unless we forget "our very own selfish selves" for at least "the duration of the war."

A minister who preaches the word of God has a dignity, no matter how poorly he may speak, because of his subject. So I feel about one's country. Dignity! It's a funny word to look at—all points and arrows, like a porcupine's quills, and was meant to be used in the same manner, as a protection. . . . I will sell whatever dignity I have to help bind up a soldier's wounds—and trust to luck, and Hartley Manners, for my future on the stage.

Hartley could be very tender when defeats came to her. She knew nothing of half-measures, or half-devotions to causes or people. It was all or nothing with Laurette. As he made rules to guard her, so from his great tenderness he surrounded her with understanding when the rules were broken.

In the beginning of Laurette's diary is the entry: "I keep wondering what Mrs. Fiske is like. At a distance I adore her but one feels one must go carefully with her. Some friends you achieve, some you thrust yourself upon." While Mrs. Fiske sat out the performances night after night, waiting to make her appeal for the Red Cross, Laurette noted how curiously quiet she was, "yet violently alive, nothing moving but her foot which keeps up a soft incessant tapping . . . a still personality that chugs underneath like a Pierce Arrow. Being a Ford myself—all noise and rattle—I admire tremendously the other thing." And another entry: "Why are people afraid of others? I want most frightfully to talk to Mrs. Fiske, but one rarely sees her, and the only opening speech I can think of is, 'Do you play bridge?' If she should say 'No,' where do I go from there?"

At the end of three weeks Laurette had made no progress toward a closer acquaintance. Her pursuit had been guilelessly eager and no doubt had affrighted the notoriously reserved lady. One torrid night, in Pittsburgh, Mrs. Fiske could not be located backstage and a harried stage manager finally found her dressing on the roof. A company wag was unkind enough to suggest she had gone there to get away from Laurette.

When Laurette bemoaned Mrs. Fiske's gentle but determined flight from her overtures, Hartley, grave-faced but with an impish twinkle in his eye, rummaged through his mind as one might go through a toy box when a child is verging on tears and came out with a little jingle, authored by heaven knows whom, and from heaven knows where:

> Heighho!
> That's the way!
> The peaches go.
> Only the lemons stay.

He could always bring a smile to Laurette's lips and knew the panacea for childlike hurts.

The exhausted couple were home on Sunday the second of June. Laurette had had her fill of heat, coal dust, washing in metal basins, sleeping over rumbling trucks, which pertained to even the best of train travel in those days. "Heat and noise as eternal punishments," she wrote, "are not possible. There must be some gentler chastisement like being trampled by wild horses."

They went immediately to Easthampton, Long Island, where they had taken a house on the dunes, and Laurette began to heal her soul of noise and dust and heat by daily swims in the Atlantic.

*

# Easthampton

Laurette and the Atlantic Ocean had a very special relationship. Like the little girl who never found anything completely satisfying until she saw her first elephant, the ocean fully lived up to expectations for Laurette. Its heroic proportions satisfied her soul; its inexorable will and intent were brother to her own. She treated

it with the combination of wary respect and familiarity that a
puppy has for its mother.

To see her walk into the ocean, hear her sharp cries of pleasure
as she was shoved off balance or smartly slapped by a wave, was
very much like watching an animal baby walk into the circle of
its mother's rough but therapeutic attentions. She was acutely
aware of the ocean's strength; she never attempted the conquering
attitude of a strong swimmer, which she was not, but preferred to
let it tumble her around, seethe over her, move her back and forth
in the shallows while she lay face down and quiescent as the waves
broke and withdrew. It was a very special Atlantic that Laurette
came to know on the shores of Easthampton, because there it rides
free for three thousand miles from the ledges of the European
Continent and seems to cast itself upon the land with pristine joy.
Laurette, no matter where she was or what she was doing, would
feel an overpowering need to come back from time to time to re-
vitalize herself in those waters.

She loved the village of Easthampton itself with its stately elms
arching over the main street, and the graveyard directly in the
center of things as though the villagers had truly said to their dead,
"Don't leave us." There were the old gaffers who sunned on the
curbing and watched the summer visitors with rheumy eyes; who
had in the attics of their homes Pilgrim Hats with shiny buckles
come down from their forefathers, and blunderbusses that almost
made you see the wild turkey and the stalking Indian. For Easthampton was old in terms of the New World, and the names on
the fishing boxes out on Montauk were the names in the earliest
history of the village when it lived by whaling: Edwards, Parsons,
Miller, Baker. Lion Gardiner, the first, who purchased Gardiner's
Island from the Indians in 1639 for "ten coates of trading cloath,"
is buried in the village graveyard and his descendants, who still
own the island, lived for many years in two of Easthampton's
oldest cottages, a stone's throw from his resplendent effigy lying in
full armor atop his tomb. Close by stands the wisteria-covered cottage where John Howard Payne wrote "Home Sweet Home."

There was magic in the ground of Easthampton in those days
and perhaps still is. One walked the quiet lanes breathing the
fragrance of honeysuckle twisted on weathered post and rail and

the scent of lilac mingled with the sharp salt smell of the ocean, and you knew that many had walked there and loved the ground and called it home. From it came a sustaining force palpably alive and responsive, and Laurette, the primitive, so often battered and so blindly hungry, threw herself upon the earth there and cast herself into the waves thundering on the shore, and was renewed.

It was in the quiet byways of Easthampton that Laurette began in earnest her lifelong tussle with fat. Only five feet five—a good height for the theatre, she maintained, because you could make yourself look tall or short as a part required—it was a height which could not bear with grace one extra pound of flesh. Each summer for the next nine years she set about licking the excess weight that gathered on her bones through the winter. The word *licking* is used advisedly for Laurette looked on fat as an actual adversary of extreme cunning with no respect whatsoever for the Queensberry rules. It was in a mood of dull fury that she squared off to battle her enemy for three months of every year. Her methods were heroic and uniquely her own.

Each morning at ten Laurette slams out the screen door of the house caparisoned as though heading an expedition into Antarctica. Over a suit of solid rubber, reaching from neck to knees, she wears a blouse, two wool sweaters, a wool skirt, heavy stockings, and a scarf tied high under the chin. A round felt hat with wide brim pulled low obscures all but a view of the path directly at her feet. For two hours thereafter, with head lowered, shoulders hunched and looking neither left nor right, she plods straight ahead in the manner of an aggravated and not too active beetle. Anyone who dares accost her is damned eternally. No one is supposed to know who she is, although it would have to be a most uninquiring mind that failed to wonder at the identity of so fantastic a figure puffing along in the summer sun. She became, unbeknownst to herself, one of the sights of Easthampton, along with John Drew on his courtly saunters around the environs of the Drew home on Lily Pond Lane, and is remembered by many with something of the same affection. There was a winning naïveté in the dogged, straight-legged walking, the angry warding off of all recognition as Laurette forced her body back to an ideal of beauty that was in her mind and which, more importantly, she had left in the mind

of her public. This was Laurette Taylor in hiding; this was work
behind the scenes and there was to be no memory of it, along
with no sign of fat when she came before her public once again.

Upon her return, soaked with perspiration and almost apoplec-
tic with heat, she dresses for a swim in the ocean. For this she
covers up again, not as warmly but almost as completely as for
her walk. A loose-fitting blouse with sleeves is buttoned up to
the neck over a skirted swimming suit, a bandanna is tied over
bathing cap, sometimes one over her shoulders.

"Lockdune," the home the family finally purchased in Easthampton, was situated on one of the many fresh-water ponds
which lie along the inner side of the dunes. To swim, Laurette
ferries across the pond in one of the two canoes moored at the
dock at the foot of the lawn. Usually her daughter, the only other
swimming enthusiast in the family, accompanies her. Manning
the front paddle, Laurette, with voluminous blouse and bright-
colored scarves blowing in the breeze, looks more like a gypsy
than a swimmer. The purpose of these is partly to avoid sunburn,
but only partly. Laurette loathes fat; she does not expose it even
on the deserted beach to which she is going, she does not wish to
look at it herself except to find it gone.

After an hour's swim during which there is much pseudosci-
entific battering of the fat by the waves, it is time for lunch. The
meal, for Laurette, consists of revolving round and round a table
laden with all the fattening foods she could think to order from
her superb Southern cook and which she cannot touch; macaroni
and cheese, stuffed baked potatoes, hot biscuits, popovers, fish in
a heavy cream sauce which she often makes herself. Round and
round she goes, urging upon each member of the family another
spoonful of this, another bite of that. To a crescendo of lip-
smacking, agonized groans, and a flurry of insults they strive man-
fully to eat for her, but their efforts invariably fall far short of
the performance her hunger demands. "Oh, you long, tall glass of
water!" she cries out to one or the other of her skinny offspring.
"Are you going to leave that delicious macaroni?" or "Do you
mean to tell me you're not going to have another popover?"—
picking one from the plate, lathering it with butter and reluctantly
passing it to the object of her scorn—"There's nothing against

*you* gaining an ounce, you know!" If she cannot eat food or make anyone else eat it to her satisfaction, she can at least talk about it. She discourses at length on how wonderful it is going to be when she is old, no longer in the theatre, and can eat anything she likes. Wearying of the polemics, Marguerite comments dryly, "You probably will have lost your appetite by then."

"O-o-oh—you!" shrieks Laurette in positive agony. "You would say that! You're a sadist, that's what you are, a sadist, to even think of such a thing!" Finally, down she plumps to a tomato, a bit of lettuce and a hard-boiled egg, and picks an argument with Hartley who is leaning back in his chair watching her through a drift of cigarette smoke with that quiet smile he always has for his Laurie, whether her mood is belligerent or sweet.

Halfheartedly she wrestles with the growing social demands of her now-adolescent children. It was so much easier when they were two quiescent units that could be fitted in where it was most convenient. Now they impinge on her own program; the social activities of teen-agers simply have no place in a routine which approximates the strict regimen of a pugilist's camp. It is extremely annoying to have slat-sided flappers driving up in open roadsters inquiring for your son just as you return hot and perspiring from a walk. You brusquely suggest they follow the mournful notes of the saxophone emanating from the garage, where Dwight has set up a studio to draw and paint and blow and bang on various musical instruments. Then you turn away quickly, keeping your head down; you know very well that their sharp little eyes have bored under the brim of your hat, and that they will rush home to tell their parents how "perfectly hideous" Laurette Taylor looks offstage, "all red and blotched."

And those depressing little girls who come to visit Marguerite, who don't seem to have anything to do but sit around eating jam sandwiches, whispering and staring. The extent of *their* social life seems to be wanting to spend the night and eat more jam sandwiches in bed; but of course you can't have that.

"Haven't they got beds at home?" you ask crossly.

No one is allowed to see you in the morning, not even these troll-like little creatures, for fear they will also report back to your "public" that you are not as young as you look on the stage. With few exceptions, parents who try to pay a formal call or leave cards create a veritable crisis in the household. You insist they be shooed away like stray dogs which have trespassed on the porch. Of course you won't see them! Of course you won't meet them! They are trying to pry into your private life and are bound to be damn dull having such damn dull children!

You do your duty as a mother. There is no question about that. You've talked to your society friends and arranged for your daughter to attend a highly recommended finishing school for young ladies in the autumn. And you have discussed at length with the mercurial John Barrymore the advisability of Dwight going to Harvard, because John, like your son, wanted to be an artist in his youth; *ergo,* John is eminently fitted to say whether college helps or hinders an artist.

No one can say you are not watchful. The day, for instance, Marguerite curled up on the beach in front of the house and lay inert for hours. You glanced from your bedroom window from time to time with growing alarm. All sorts of suspicions gathered in your mind. Characteristically, you chose the most outlandish and girded yourself to act. No child of yours was going to suffer for lack of a confidante no matter how grave the secret. The suffering caused by your own abysmal ignorance in sexual matters during adolescence is still vivid. Stomping down the stairs and along the weathered boards to the dune's edge, you take up a stand above your daughter's prostrate form. One finger tamps nervously on a cigarette as you brace yourself for the worst.

"Marguerite!" Voice is carefully pitched to carry over the sound of the waves, and you are rather pleased with the nice mixture of matter-of-factness and imperious command that is conveyed. "You must tell me at once! Are you going to have a baby?"

How could you possibly know that this long inertia is the result of the highly unremarkable occurrence of an older boy whom Marguerite secretly admires bumping into her on his bike the day before, and the resultant callow and sentimental speculations as to whether he bumped her accidentally or on purpose? It is entirely unfair of the child to raise her head in so weary and disdainful a manner and retort, "Mother! Please! I am *only thirteen years old!*" You were only trying to help, and you'll be damned if you can understand kids nowadays, they're so blasé. And back you go into the house puffing on your cigarette and feeling quite sat upon.

Hartley's course remains tangential to the rest of the family. In a deep well of a room with a skylight, separate from the rest of the house, he is evolving the character of L'Enigme, a sultry Italian lady, fortuneteller *de luxe* to Roman society, with a mystery in her past. Dark theatric characters fill his brain, keep him company through the long hours of the night while others sleep. As usual, he retires a few hours before the rest of the household rises. He is at breakfast when the family return from walks, tennis, morning swims. Hair rumpled and curly, wearing an immaculate lightweight robe initialed J.H.M., the inevitable cigarette hanging from his lips, he invites you to visit. . . . His night has been bally awful . . . that old fellow with the beard was back again . . . "I give you my word I don't know what to do with him—but there he is, sitting about, messing up my scenes. I have to put him in the play someplace, I suppose. He's ha'nting me, positively ha'nting me . . . !"

He smiles, a shy, boyish smile, and maybe taps the hand of his visitor, a quick playful tap, which is as sentimental a gesture as his repertoire affords.

He barely glances at the ocean from summer to summer and almost never goes on the beach. When he does he resembles a cat walking through wet grass, raising a foot high after each step and shaking it free of sand with obvious distaste for the whole adventure. His concession to summer activities is a politely dogged game of golf at the Maidstone Club, a game that sticks in the nineties despite unremitting efforts to improve it, and a methodical game of tennis, reliable but uninspired. Occasionally he consents to be motored around the countryside although he loathes cars and never learns to drive one. Persuaded to walk out on some scenic promontory for the view, he will like as not take up an oratorical stand, declaim some histrionic passage nobody has ever heard of from some dusty classic nobody reads, and having used the whole of nature as a backdrop for this antique and creaking performance, return to the car, place his cap on his head and wait to be motored home. You must look in his eyes to see the smile, secret, self-amused.

Laurette is grumpy, difficult to live with during the first few weeks of her arduous program, but as she begins to lose weight, "feel her jawbone come through again," perks up, starts to live with zest, talks parts and plays, reads omnivorously with a wide taste, enjoys tennis in the afternoon with a few friends, bridge at night—her chronically bad bridge, played with alternate cries of dismay and triumph and many a bitter accusation that the rules have been changed on her.

She loves the purely social side of this expanding world of hers, the world of the "swells" that as a child she watched standing by the canopy of Pabst Restaurant. But she takes it with a grain of salt. To have conquered it is enough and boredom begins just the other side of conquest. Her rigid standard of the acceptability of others is still, as always, that they entertain and distract her. Occasionally, very occasionally, in a fit of some deep-seated self-doubt, or because she decides it is a more captivating way to meet the strictly social occasion, she lapses into an imitation of a lady; what is worse, a gentle, rather mindless lady. The impersonation is surprisingly bad. Those who know her well are startled to hear a lisping hesitant sentence fall from her lips, a mindless "ha-ha," generally delivered into the ear of one of those dull but overpowering monuments to social probity who are found embalmed upright in the drawing rooms of the haut monde. Fortunately the fanciful seizure does not last—possibly because it is so bad. She is soon back "in her own skin," needling the inelastic, bedeviling the dull, insisting she be amused, distracted, astonished. Those who can do any one or all of these things constitute her aristocracy no matter what their blood, position, or success in life; the others are summarily cast into outer darkness.

However, she did draw an arbitrary distinction between her purely social and her purely theatre friends—the "glorified bums" as she affectionately called the latter. An example of this—to leap ahead a few years—was the occasion of showing the movie "Happiness" at home on two consecutive nights. Her professional friends were to come the first night, her society friends the following evening. By some misunderstanding, Mrs. Douglas Robinson, sister of Teddy Roosevelt, showed up the first instead of the second night. One might have thought the dropping of this social plum on one's doorstep on any night would have been acceptable; but not to Laurette. She greeted Mrs. Robinson with an indignant, "What are *you* doing here? You're supposed to come tomorrow night!" Mrs. Robinson loved it, stayed, and enjoyed her evening with the "bums" enormously.

One type of society woman alone baffles and awes Laurette: the hard, brittle creatures who devote themselves almost exclusively to the care of their physical being. Like a child she takes their shining surfaces—their lacquered nails, gleaming coiffures, scientifically pummeled bodies and pomaded skins—as manifestation of a supreme confidence in their physical charms. She has none of this at all; indeed she is entirely vulnerable on this score. In the theatre, it is true, she has absolute assurance and can project whatever may be demanded in a part: beauty, seductiveness, great physical allure. But there the primary consideration in creating the illusion is to obliterate herself. In everyday life this cannot be done, and as a result the uncertainties and doubts entertained as to her personal attractiveness are at times profound. She is convinced that primarily by trickery, make-up, lighting, hours of arranging, pinning, draping, she gives the illusion of beauty. When she prepares for a party she may change her costume three or four times; cut it, pin it, put flowers on it, take them off again, start all over with another gown. Long after the appointed dinner hour she will display the final effect to the family, "Well-ll-ll," she will roll out with a high childish intonation, "not so good, eh?" or, if at last pleased with the effect, "Pretty good for a sow's ear, what?" She has done it all herself—managed to disguise some physical unacceptability that seems to haunt her. Undoubtedly, this was a major reason for Laurette's preference for character parts even while young, parts which called for wigs, costumes, special make-up. Physically, these left very little of herself showing, and mentally, of course, she had consummate ability to become the character she was playing.

Her greatest difficulty was with straight roles, and much of this was because the clothes she wore were supposed to become her rather than conceal her. This uncertainty about clothes reached fantastic proportions at times, but being an indomitable woman she conquered her uncertainty by equally fantastic measures. Just before the opening of "The National Anthem" in which she played a smart, fast-living young woman of the jazz age this lack of confidence gripped her with shattering finality. Bergdorf Goodman had designed her clothes, among them a five-hundred-dollar cloth-of-gold evening gown. This gown in particular, probably because of its décolletage, became the focal point of Laurette's last-minute self-doubt. In a state of heroic despair she took up shears the day before the opening and cut every seam and tuck of the sculptured lines, resewing the dress closer to her modest heart's desire. Legend has it that upon Laurette's entrance on the opening night, a dull thud was heard in the audience as Mr. Goodman toppled from his seat in a dead faint.

Loss of youth and ugliness were curiously synonymous in her mind. She began laying the groundwork for surviving the horrid condition of youthlessness almost from the time youth's first bloom touched her. Her damning of the "personality" actress was an adjunct of this ever-present horror, her career, in large part, motivated by flight from this pit where, with the first wrinkle, she will be buried. She has no mercy on ugliness in herself or in others. Her comments are never sharper at a play or moving picture than when she sees someone exhibiting ugliness unintentionally, or as a *forte* in grotesquerie. "Isn't that terrible?" she will exclaim, "Oh, isn't that terrible!"—not in a mature and considered manner, but putting her hands across her stomach and laughing involuntarily like a child who assimilates horror but has, as yet, no capacity for pity. Watching a politician or businessman speaking from a movie screen, she will mutter, "He has no right to be so ugly! Look at that wooden face, that stomach—that paunch—that awful puss!" It makes no difference who he is or how noble his statement, "He has no *right* to be so ugly!"

Only the greatest charm, the greatest talent mitigates ugliness for Laurette, makes her forgive and forget the ravages of time. She battles ugliness in herself, fat, age; she gives these hideous aspects of life no quarter. Her pitilessness for others may be forgiven in that she is pitiless with herself. During the years of her supremacy she engaged these enemies without letup, fought tenaciously to keep them from marring the ideal she wished to project across the footlights, from breaking down her lines of communication with her audience. "The audience receives first a visual impression before you have time to weave the mental picture." She was more than willing to perform this penance for the communion it made possible for her spirit in the theatre.

By autumn after three months of routine exercise and rigid self-discipline, Laurette is beautifully slim, skin toned and firm, and she is eager for work. If rehearsals for a new play do not call them immediately to town, there comes a day when Hartley grows restless. "The autumnal spirits are abroad," he will announce in oracular tones some morning, and from then on the days of their stay in Easthampton are numbered. His quiet but merry course through the full summer months is over. The first snap of autumn brings out the melancholy Irish in him: he is depressed; he listens and swears that he hears sounds that are astral and unhappy; he longs for the city. Looking into his enormous and always slightly brooding eyes, one can believe almost anything. Laurette does. . . .

It is time to go.

This first summer in Easthampton is the beginning of a pattern of life for Laurette and Hartley that will hold for the next nine years and be looked back on as the high plateau of their happiness and success together. Then the pattern begins to break, a thread here and a thread there. The life at Easthampton, the strong warp upon which the bright design was woven, is the last to go; that lovely place to which Laurette responded so deeply and which in turn seemed to respond to her, succoring and renewing her spirit, solacing areas of her being that knew so little refreshment.

*

# One Night in Rome

Hartley did not feel adventurous in the shifting values of the postwar era. His burning causes were for the moment behind him, and no inspirational message plagued his mind. After the lightning speed of his preparation of "Out There" and "Happiness" he reverted comfortably to the methodical techniques of playwriting which were characteristic of him. He was no bloomin' George M. Cohan he said, and four drafts of a play with him were standard.

"One Night in Rome" which he had first drafted in 1917 and worked on the following summer was not finished until the fall of 1919. Laurette was quite familiar with Madame L'Enigme by that time. She had worked on the part for a full year. While playing Brooklyn Jenny every night she was studying Italian every day, and perfecting the accent and the quick fluid gestures of an Italian noblewoman.

"Hartley insisted L'Enigme be Roman," said Laurette, "so I went searching for Romans as well as Italians." There was an added fillip to any party where a model could be studied firsthand. "We go about like a couple of ragpickers," Laurette declared, "a little bit here and a little bit there for our plays."

"One Night in Rome" was an excellent play to bring to Broadway in December, 1919. There were over one hundred and fifty productions that season, ranging all the way from John Drinkwater's inspiring "Abraham Lincoln" to the gaudy and tasteless spectacle "Aphrodite" at the Century. Almost anything went. Money was easy in everybody's pockets. Thousands of returning veterans of the AEF wandered the streets looking for a last bit of excitement between Paree and home. "Rome" had a little bit of everything for these uprooted and restless customers of the Great White Way—mystery, suspense, romance, decorative appeal, while managing withal to achieve considerable distinction.

As L'Enigme, a woman of noble birth, turned fortuneteller to
earn a living, Laurette wore a black wig and long clinging robes.
For the first time since Luana she boldly departed from her
Anglo-Saxon characterizations, the boisterous, the lusty, the droll.
L'Enigme was old Europe, mellow, tolerant, racially sophisticated,
a little weary and terribly glamorous. A hazard for the Harlem
hoyden, ex-Mici, ex-Peg, ex-Jenny? Not at all.

> Reported Broun: Last night she displayed qualities that we have
> never seen in her before. There was a lofty dignity that was new
> and effective. There was great allure and romantic suggestion.

> *The Sun:* She did not look in the least her roguish self. The sud-
> den smile, the infectious twinkle of her speaking eyes, the gamin
> devil-may-care humor—none of these familiar traits of her per-
> sonality were to be seen. But the irresistible charm that attaches to
> every word she speaks and every movement she makes was as po-
> tent as ever. . . .

And of the play? Well, Burns Mantle, who thought that Laurette gave "what was by long odds the most fascinating and the
finest performance of her career," considered "One Night in
Rome" "immeasurably the best play Hartley Manners has written."But he was almost alone in his good opinion. "A poor uncertain little comedy so anemic and so troubled at its joints," said
Woollcott. Alan Dale: "All the merit it contains is that it is a good
vehicle for Miss Taylor and a bad play for anybody else." And
the *Times*—and this one really hurt—"You can almost see dressmaker Manners with his head on one side and his mouth full of
pins."

"Alas, poor Hartley!" Ethel Barrymore once remarked. "Only
the audiences liked his plays."

In a curtain speech Laurette told the audience that the play
was intended only to entertain and apparently from their reception it had fulfilled that purpose. Referring to the last act's surprise denouement when L'Enigme sweeps off her black wig to
reveal tawny tresses, Laurette quipped, "Competition is very keen
this season. When I heard that Aphrodite had taken off her clothes,
I knew that to keep up with her I would have to take off something. So I decided to take off my wig."

She stood close down by the footlights, holding out the black peruke, shaking back her own long golden hair, laughing with them, enjoying the little joke she had made. This easy, warm relationship with her audience was one of the phenomena of Laurette's career. It was as though in the course of the evening each had fallen a little bit in love with the other. Laurette had a favorite passage in a novel by Paul Bourget which spoke of a man and woman in love as being "transparent" to each other, and this she paraphrased when speaking of a particularly receptive audience as, "we stood transparent to each other." Laurette and her audiences were often like that. The little talk she gave at the final curtain was like the intimate exchange of two people who have shared a few hours during which neither has held back in spirit, mind or heart, and these last smiling, inconsequential words are the light measure of the total investment each has made in the other.

The glow did not rub off when Laurette got home. She prattled and was gay. She enjoyed her good performance as much as anybody. "I was good, wasn't I?" she would say with no conceit whatsoever. Nor was there any false modesty. She could never be guilty of so brackish an insincerity as, "I wasn't too awful, was I?" What nonsense. Either you were good or you were not good. Laurette was concerned not with herself but with an inner vision of truth, and there is no compromising with truth. Either you project it or you fail to project it, and that is all there is to it.*

This radiant Laurette is grateful to Hartley for the opportunity to interpret a full and well-rounded character, and her wholly alive and animated being tells him so. Her respect for the playwright is profound. "You have to have the play, you have to have the character, and you have to have the lines or you cannot give a great performance. I don't consider the interpreter has such a divine gift as the creator. One creates where nothing existed. The other takes that young birth and nurtures it into perfection." L'Enigme was "a wonderful woman." Hartley had written her that way and his wife had interpreted what he had written.

After the first-night reception in the Criterion's Green Room, Hartley and Laurette had gone home together alone. This was

---

* cf. Norris Houghton, "Laurette Taylor," *Theatre Arts*, Dec. 1945.

generally their practice following an opening. Their "child" was never quite born until they read the early editions of the morning papers and, like most parents at such a time, they preferred to be alone. Scrambled eggs and bacon; Laurette in a loose robe, "mules" dangling from her toes, shaking her long hair free over the back of her chair, lighting a cigarette; keyed up, terribly gay from that "lovers meeting" between herself and her first-night audience.

"Didn't they laugh at my speech, though? . . . Did you hear that gasp when my wig came off? . . . The first act held up beautifully. I was a little afraid of that first act, Hartley—there's an awful lot of me in it. . . . I must tell Greta not to fidget (another Cooper girl making her acting debut); she must learn to stand still. 'But, Laurette, I could see you talking in the wings,' she said to me, 'I thought you'd never come on.'

"Listen, my girl, I told her, I'm just going to leave you there some night and tell a long, long story to the electrician until you learn not to fidget.

" 'All right, Laurette—but if you do I'll start to whistle—I know I shall—break right into an arpeggio, you wait and see. It's bound to look a little peculiar, darling, with me in the Oriental robes of L'Enigme's servant!' The fool! I bet she would too— even fish out that monocle of hers from under her blouse and squint at me offstage."

Hartley says little, chuckles, watches Laurette, reflecting her happiness. Yes, this is the best time for him, with Laurette alone, in the rich fulfillment of their work together.

At dawn he taxis out to the nearest newsstand for the morning papers. He is quite prepared for the worst. He has in his nature a broad streak of pessimism. He is also a man of wisdom and love, and the evening has already heaped his rewards upon him, rewards not vulnerable to the worms of jealousy or discontent; for has not Laurette possessed the character he created; breathed life into it, held spellbound an audience, and does she not glow now like the sun, moon and all the stars together with the satisfaction of their mutual creation?

The critics? Tut! Tut! My dear! What pleases Tweedledum displeases Tweedledee. Why worry. He smiles at her indignation. . . . They are unkind, unfair . . . the remark about "dressmaker

*5 years old*

At the age of five Laurette was already prone to fits of melancholy.

Elizabeth Cooney, Laurette's mother, as a young woman in the 125th Street home.

Truly—Foolish
Laurette

Two pictures of Laurette in the 1903 production of "Rags to Riches."

The "incomparable" Laurette in 1903.

Laurette with her young son, Dwight. This picture was used by Charles Taylor as a theatre poster for "Yosemite."

Charles A. Taylor as a young man in California.

As *Mercedes* in "Yosemite."

A music sheet from Laurette's greatest success, "Peg O' My Heart."

J. Hartley Manners and Laurette in 1924.

"Pierrot the Prodigal," 1925.

Laurette in the 1932 production of "Alice-Sit-by-the-Fire."

"The Glass Menagerie," 1945.

Manners" rips her up pretty badly. . . . He gives a little shrug, brushes the cigarette ash from his lapel, rests his eyes again on his wife's face, shy, pleased that she will fight for him; his Laurie.

This is the full summer of their love. There are no autumnal ghosts to haunt him. If his eyes brood a little, it is the shadow of that inner separateness, never quite broken down even with the one he loves the most.

*

# Riot in London

After a run of five and a half months, "One Night in Rome" was taken to London under an arrangement with Charles B. Cochran. On April 29, 1920, a brilliant assemblage, gathered at the Garrick Theatre to welcome Peg back to England, was to witness instead one of the most incredible and shocking experiences of Laurette's career.

Soon after the curtain rose a mild commotion started in the gallery and there were good-natured shouts, "We can't see." This was understandable because of the Garrick's high old-fashioned gallery and the fact that the first scene, a small interior, had a low ceiling. The stage manager whispered to the company to play down by the footlights and the noise stopped momentarily. Presently pennies began dropping on the stage and Cochran rushed back determined to stop the show and demand order. But Laurette, about to make her first entrance, persuaded him to wait. She received a tremendous ovation. With the help of Chiara (Greta Cooper) Laurette began to move chairs and tables downstage and immediately there were encouraging cries from the always vocal gallery gods, such as "That's the ticket!" "Thanks, Miss T'yler." "We can see all right." The scene continued without further interruption.

Cochran, still uneasy, wanted to speak to the audience before the second act but Laurette persuaded him to let her do it. She apologized for the poor sight line and said the ceiling would be pulled up into the flies for the remainder of the performance so as to give an unobstructed view from the gallery. "You see the scenery was planned for America where we do everything on a small scale," Laurette joshed, and got a good laugh and some hearty cheers.

Everything seemed to be all right.

When the curtain rose on the second act, however, there were immediate cries and catcalls of "Go back to America!" and "We don't want you here!" The rioters were obviously organized and well distributed in small groups throughout the gallery. Other shouting could be heard: "We can see! It's an organized gang." And so on. Pennies, pieces of tiling began to rain down on the stage, and finally sneezing powder and "stink bombs."

The actors tried valiantly to carry on but the mounting pandemonium made it impossible. The stalls and pit rose in wrathful indignation. Elegantly dressed men and women shouted up at the gallery, booing, shaking their fists, calling for a show of English sportsmanship. Seymour Hicks made an impassioned plea from his box for fair play. "This is not like England!" he protested. Other idols of the English stage begged for order to no avail. The American Ambassador, John W. Davis, and his party quietly left the theatre by a side door.

Laurette, waiting to make her second-act entrance, was standing in the wings listening incredulously to the uproar. Cochran took her hand and led her onto the stage.

"I have not brought this great artist two thousand miles to be subjected to such treatment——" he began.

"Artist! What does that matter—artist?" Laurette interrupted. Then she shouted up at the gallery, "You shouldn't treat a scrubwoman this way!" and sobbing hysterically fled from the stage.

House lights were turned up and the curtain rung down. Milling first-nighters continued to exchange insults. Finally a loyal faction in the pit gave three resounding cheers for the star. After a while the audience began drifting out into the street there to resume their wrangling or stand in stunned silent groups.

Mrs. Pat Campbell and David Belasco were the first to reach

Laurette's dressing room. Belasco dropped to his knees and covered Laurette's hands with kisses.

"Such pluck! Such gameness!" he murmured, turning the white crown of his head to see if the reporters had arrived.

"Why did this happen to me?" Laurette moaned.

"It's wonderful! Wonderful!" Belasco whispered, still kissing her hands. "I wish to God it had happened to one of my little girls!"

Mrs. Campbell lifted her voice in throbbing sympathy. "It's a shame. They just don't like you this time."

The room filled with people. Everybody had a different theory as to the reason for the riot. Cochran came to say that the galleryites were crowding into the alley demanding to see Laurette. She must speak to them.

"Never. Not for anything in the world will I face them."

"But you must. They are there to assure you of their affection and loyalty. The riot was not against you, or the play. . . ."

Laurette sat frozen in her chair. *Her* audience that she had always played with as you play with a baby, evoking smiles, frowns, tears, had risen against her, a hydra-headed monster, uncontrolled, alien, hostile. . . . No! No! No! She would not see them.

Stella Campbell said she would speak to them, they knew her; but Laurette must stand beside her. Scarcely aware of moving Laurette rose and trailed after the English actress like a leaf in the wind. She found herself at the stage door looking over Mrs. Campbell's shoulder at a sea of upturned faces.

"Eh, there! Stella!" came the friendly greeting. "Yew in this pliy? We didn't see yew." Then, "We want Miss T'yler. We want Miss T'yler," a sing-song chant, louder and louder down the length of the alley and finally out in the street.

"You can't have her," said Mrs. Pat. "You've treated her very badly."

"Please, Ma'am, we did not."

"Who did then?" pounced back Stella.

At that moment her eye fastened on a poor unfortunate fellow standing in the front of the crowd. An enormous goitre deformed his neck hanging down over his collar. Pointing to him, Stella cried, "You did it, you naughty boy!" She leveled a finger directly at the hideous lump. "Naughty! Carrying concealed bombs into the theatre."

The man, livid with fury, jumped up on the steps. The crowd surged forward. Someone pulled Laurette back. Someone else grabbed Stella and the stage door was slammed shut.

Near panic gripped those within. Stella was pale and silent, and for the first time in her life seemed to realize what her cruel, unbridled tongue had done. Outside the commotion was terrific. People were pressing forward to see what had happened, crushing others against the steps. There were Cockney oaths, fists beat on the door. And above it all, the insistent chant, "We want Miss T'yler. We want Miss T'yler."

The shock that had held Laurette spellbound broke under Stella's awful demonstration of cruelty. She pulled the door open and walked out on the steps. Cochran followed and stood beside her. Those who had milled against the door backed down and gave them room.

"I want to know who did this dreadful thing!" she demanded. "You must have seen."

"We didn't do it, Peg. Not us. H'it's a shime, so h'it is."

"I know it wasn't against me personally. But whatever the reason, it has doomed the play. The English are the last people in the world to create a disturbance. It is such un-English behavior—especially in the theatre. You not only admire the actors but have affection for them besides——"

"We 'ave for you, Peg! That's certain!" someone piped up.

"You can't throw pennies any distance without pitching them," Laurette went on. "Some of you must have been sitting by the rowdies, seen an arm go up. Write me, tell me where they sat, what they looked like. Mr. Cochran has offered five hundred pounds reward for the arrest of these people. He says we'll open in a week or two. . . . Perhaps. . . . But I don't think the play will survive this."

"Y're wrong there, Peg. We'll be back. Yew wait and see . . . ," the crowd called.

Later at the Berkeley Hotel the gloomy post-mortem went on. As theatres let out all over London one stage celebrity after another arrived at the Manners' suite, each making a more dramatic entrance than the one before: Cyril Maude, Haddon Chambers, Dennis Eadie, Johnston Forbes-Robertson, Sir Gerald du Maurier, Robert Loraine.

"Who has done this foul thing?" cried Loraine hurrying in.

The atmosphere throbbed with the highest-paid emoting talents of the British Empire. Hartley, as deeply stunned as Laurette, had taken to whiskey sodas and like his wife had little or nothing to say.

"We shall none of us play tomorrow," said du Maurier. "We will close the theatres in protest."

"No, we will keep them open," said Loraine. "Miss Taylor will play at my theatre one night, Wyndham's the next, and we will play the Garrick when she plays at ours."

Ultimately it was decided to compose a letter of protest to the *Times*. Walter Creighton, Cochran's confidential representative, was chosen to telephone it to the editorial offices then and there. He did so, according to Cochran, while "practically all the actor-managers of London stood around prompting, altering the wording, interspersing his sentences with 'Bravo!' and other expressions of approval." *

So came to an end an exhausting and harrowing evening. The Garrick was closed for almost a week while Laurette and Hartley went away to the country to rest.

The reason for the riot never came to light. Various explanations were brought forward at the time, none of them entirely satisfactory. It was rumored that Cochran had made enemies as a promoter in the prize-fight world. Some papers played it up as an anti-American demonstration because of the flood of American plays and players then invading the English stage, but this did not seem likely as Laurette was a great favorite with the English, married to an Englishman, playing in his play, and entirely surrounded by an English company. In farfetched statements it was suggested that there was resentment because Laurette had left London during the air raids; because she had not performed on shipboard for the Seamen's Benefit when returning to America in 1915. A story of the riot, printed in some American papers be-

* "The Secrets of a Showman," Charles B. Cochran. Henry Holt and Co.

side an account of the British breaking up a Sein Fein parade on the same day, gave rise to the rumor that the Irish had started the riot to alienate American sympathy from the British. And just to make the international confusion complete, Cochran announced that in his opinion the riot had been organized by pro-Germans who did not like his attitude toward German plays.

Many years later showman William A. Brady emphatically stated to Laurette's daughter that none of these conjectures was correct.

"Fact of the matter is," said Mr. Brady with his customary vigor, "it was started by Peggy O'Neill's boy-friend. Peggy had played 'Paddy, the Next Best Thing' in London that season. She had never forgiven Laurette for snatching Chicago from her when she was the number one road-company Peg. O'Neill's tough boy-friend decided to avenge the wrong and organized a gang to break up Laurette's first night. That's not speculation. I happen to know that's true."

This belated explanation would seem to be the most logical of any advanced.

It is not surprising that a thick cloud of rumor and speculation hung over the event and it almost became a *cause célèbre* between England and America. The last time that a hostile claque had appeared in a London theatre was in the year 1809.

When things went terribly wrong, Laurette always wanted her family close. After the first night debacle she cabled her children to come immediately, and they were catapulted from their respective schools and onto the first boat sailing for England.

The same glittering audience attended the second opening, the gallery packed with those who had tried so loyally to express their affection for Laurette that first night. It was hoped that the organized rioters were not there, but no one could be sure. Bobbies were on hand to keep the crowds moving into the theatre and watch for suspicious characters. Ambassador Davis was in his box, heavily guarded. The performance took place amidst funereal quiet, interspersed with loud, nervous handclapping. Each entrance and exit was vociferously applauded; every other sound, including laughs, was heavily "shushed" by an audience determined to have no trouble.

After it was over, Laurette came forward, sat herself down cross-legged in front of the curtain and described just what it was like to play under such circumstances. Soon the audience was laughing as they had not laughed throughout the performance.

"Such charm as I have never seen in my entire life!" said actor-director, John Cromwell, who was among the first-nighters on both occasions. "She had that audience eating out of her hand!"

But nothing could pull the play back from the blow it had received.

In a strange malaise of spirit quite unlike them, Laurette and family wandered about the large house near Regent Park rented by Hartley in an effort to bring cheer. It was unusually muggy and hot in London that summer and the doors of the dark and gloomy rooms, left open for ventilation, seemed instead to communicate only the general family depression. Marguerite had contracted a foul malady with the medieval sounding name of seven-year itch, and spent most of the days and nights scratching her tortured flesh. The miserable, itching child became a symbol to Laurette of the life that had suddenly collapsed like the slats of a bed that has been jumped on too hard.

"Stop that scratching this instant!" she would call, her voice vibrating with anger; or, "If you must scratch, close your door so we can't hear you. Do you realize you are keeping everybody awake with that clawing?" Scratch. Scratch. A horrid leitmotif to the treacherous blow that had been struck at her without warning out of nowhere.

Laurette and Mrs. Campbell met again. Lord Lathom, a wealthy young bachelor and patron of the theatre, had backed Mrs. Campbell in a production of "Madame Sand." After a brilliant opening for which Lathom had bought the house, there was a party in his home at Great Cumberland Place. The invitations read: "To meet George Sand and her Lovers."

Lester Donahue, noted pianist, described what happened. "Mrs. Pat, in pink velvet with a pink velvet crown on her head, was talking to me in the dining room when Laurette and Hartley arrived. Laurette saw me, but not Mrs. Pat, and sang out, 'Hello, Lester. The invitation read to meet Mrs. Pat and her lovers, and I couldn't resist that!' Then she swept on upstairs where most of the guests were assembled in the main concert room. Later, Ned Lathom, myself, Laurette and several others were sitting on cushions on the floor. As usual Laurette was being vastly amusing, and we were laughing uproariously when Mrs. Pat came up the stairs. Spying her, Laurette broke off to remark, 'Ah, here's Mrs. Pat. Just like the rain, we know she's good for the crops, but we hate to see her coming.' There was a quick explosion of laughter. Mrs. Pat, ignoring everyone else, bore directly down on the group.

" 'What is that horrible woman saying about me now?" she demanded.

"Ned, the tactful host, immediately made up a story out of whole cloth. But Laurette would have none of it. 'He's just trying to be polite,' she announced. 'I said no such thing. What I did say was—' and while the rest of us gaped, she repeated her exact words to Mrs. Campbell."

"I believe," concluded Donahue, "it was the only time anyone ever saw Stella Campbell bereft of speech. But she was—just that."

"One Night in Rome" never fully recovered from the body blow of the first night, and played to declining business until it finally closed at the end of July after 104 performances. During that month Laurette gave three charity matinees of "Peg" which brought back far happier memories of London, and were notable for the fact that A. E. Matthews played Jerry for the thousandth time, while the faithful Michael was on hand to play himself for the 1,107th time.

Laurette and Hartley vacillated on their next move. There had been talk of taking a place on the Thames and reviving "Peg" in the autumn, but they could not make up their minds.

After several weeks there had still been no decision on what to do. The semiparalysis of the family spirit continued. One Sunday in August, Laurette and the children trailed down the long staircase of the gloomy house to face with little enthusiasm the many and varied dishes of an English breakfast simmering over alcohol flames on the sideboard. Hartley had preceded them, an unusual event. He was studying the morning paper, one eye closed against the column of smoke rising from the cigarette between his lips. He seemed to be in a quietly jocular mood, the source of which he did not immediately disclose. He discoursed on the weather, the shameful profiteering by theatre owners, the unhappy position of the British dramatist who could not get his plays produced in the West End. His audience on the whole was apathetic but of this he seemed oblivious. Slowly he turned the page of the paper.

"I see," he said, clearing his throat, "that the *Aquitania* sails for America tomorrow."

The one open eye surveyed the faces around the table somewhat balefully, awaiting a reaction. Slowly a longing that had not been spoken or even admitted before took possession of the others. After a suitably dramatic pause Hartley voiced it for all. "What do you say we hop it, old dears, eh?"

Laurette gave a cry of delight that came straight from her diaphragm. The children stampeded for their rooms to pack. The spell was broken. Hartley had wrung the neck of gloom, strung out the bells of joy, and Laurette's world was right side up once more.

\*

# *The National Anthem*

"Peg" had earned the Manners family over a million dollars by 1919. For two years after the London opening ten companies played it nightly across the world. France, Italy, Hungary, Holland, South Africa, Australia, New Zealand, the Far East, all had their Pegs and Michaels; only Germany had none. As the major depression of 1921 got under way, it seemed an eminently safe bet to revive the durable colleen. Also it would stir up interest in the motion picture which was being negotiated. Following a New York run of three months at its old home the Cort, Laurette took the play to Chicago, the city Hartley had fought tooth and nail to save for her. After four successful but torrid weeks they were glad to be back in Easthampton.

Wrapped in her own exhaustion Laurette took no notice of the fact that Hartley was unusually moody and depressed. He is subject to such moods, and when he is not writing they tend to draw out. It has been over two years since "One Night in Rome" was completed and as the summer of 1921 advances, he is still without inspiration. He retires to his study only to lie on the couch for hours, or putters about his sacrosanct quarters through the long watches of the night, but the writing paper neatly set out on his desk remains blank. He tries a shift of scene, moves to town for a week or two and from there writes to Marguerite: "Life moves grayly and uncertainly. I sigh for Easthampton and the silences." The change does no good and back he comes.

As Hartley's indecisiveness continues, Laurette's urge to make her bid for the heights waxes strong within her. She was bound for the ultimate limits of her gifts wherever those limits might be, and was convinced she could reach them with Hartley.

It is doubtful whether Laurette ever seriously considered winning immortality by playing the great classic roles, and testing herself in them against the great performances of the past. She was too much an individual for that, her reactions too intensely personal and intuitive. Her standard was invariably an inner concept of what she perceived to be the truth; an arbitrary standard set up by tradition or another's concept might be good, but it was not hers.

This squaring with an inner concept of truth was so powerful and personal a procedure that it was quite impossible for Laurette to do anything that she could not first believe in. Urged many times to play Nora in "The Doll's House" her vehement answer was: "I wouldn't be found dead in the part! That woman should never have walked out on her children!" Ibsen's "Ghosts" deeply offended her. The subject of venereal disease was so repugnant and shocking that it was impossible for her to evaluate "Ghosts" as drama. "Candida" was a role that intrigued her, but she considered that it had been done exceptionally well by several actresses and that she would bring nothing new to the part. "If another actress plants her flag first on a goal you have set yourself, you must turn back, and start toward another." This was her stated philosophy. She believed firmly that Hartley would someday write the great American play and she would play in it. They would establish their own theatre and, with half a dozen of the best actors and actresses in America, they would, under Hartley's supervision, produce plays—Hartley's and others—in the highest traditions of the drama. "I want to do it on a fine and worth-while scale or not at all," she told him. This was still their dream.

As the months go by and there is no new script in her hand, Laurette feels the pressure of time. She is thirty-seven years old. The "theatre piece," "One Night in Rome," she thoroughly enjoyed; the revival of "Peg" was a pleasanter romp than she had imagined it would be, and a firm offer to immortalize her classic role in the moving pictures is an exciting and new challenge. But uppermost is a desire for a play and a part which will take her full measure as an actress. Once and for all she wants to shake the ingénue from her repertoire and plant her standard on new and higher ground. This has become an imperative.

While in Chicago she had read Ashton Stevens her own dramatic abridgement of "Humoresque," Fannie Hurst's best-selling wartime novel. Laurette had fallen in love with the old Jewish mother, Sarah Kantor, and wanted to bring her to the stage.

When Stevens asked, "Why do you want to do it—just a feat of versatility?" her reply was "No, hardly that at all. I want to play an oldish woman while I'm still young enough to play girls; before older parts are forced on me. But it's not that either. The real reason is the sense of beauty that I find in the character and in the play. In that woman there is something of the beauty that Rembrandt saw among the lowly, and I want to try to realize it on the stage." *

But any final decision was held in abeyance, waiting on Hartley's next inspiration.

It was painfully long in coming.

Hartley was moving counter to the tempo of the time, which was growing progressively more frenzied. The old values had been swept away and no new ones were discernible. Speak-easies were mushrooming behind the old brownstone fronts of mid-

* *Actorviews* by Ashton Stevens, 1923. Covici-McGee.

town New York. Homemade gin and scotch were swilled from heavy china teacups. A young man on a date carried his hip flask as a matter of protocol. Sex was an evening's entertainment, brewed with the drink and forgotten with the hangover. Everybody danced. The toddle was out, but old men still toddled, making it an excuse to hold the girl a little closer, wiggle a little more. "Jogging their memories," some irreverent whispered to Laurette and her astonished, shocked laugh rang out across the dance floor. Young men used their partners like staves to remain upright long after bad gin would have had them stretched on the floor. Girls in knee-length shifts from Paris danced on and on, achieving the smooth hard surfaces of stones incessantly polished, or sank in a soft and meaningless surrender to alcohol and the immediate importunities of sex. Jazz was the beat of the time, insistent, merciless on the nerves, setting a pace for a generation which was going no place at terrific speed and which was to win its niche in history as "lost."

To Hartley every aspect of this rude, irreverent time was alien and offensive. He recoiled from its noisy vulgarity. To Laurette, essentially a bird of passage, it was simply a new panorama upon which to turn a bright and curious eye. In the vastness of her innocence she skimmed through its dizzy distractions, an incorruptible in a corrupted age. She did not withdraw from it nor was she impervious to its meaning. Her meeting with F. Scott Fitzgerald, who became the symbol of that hectic age, illustrates the perceptiveness of the artist who stands aside but never apart from life. She had gone to Fitzgerald's Great Neck house with her friends the Herbert Bayard Swopes and playwright Laurence Stallings. As Stallings tells the story, the usual Saturday night drunken bout was in progress. When Fitzgerald saw Laurette he dropped to his knees, took her hands in his, and began to chant: "My God, you beautiful egg. You beautiful, beautiful egg." Then, still holding her hands, he led her to a divan through a scrawl of people, again dropped to his knees and began to repeat, "You beautiful, beautiful egg." By Dada short cut, according to Stallings, he was saying she was all fertility and beauty and symmetry.

When Laurette returned to the Swopes' country house where they were staying, she called Hartley from his card game. "Oh,

Hartley," she began to cry, "I've just seen the doom of youth. Understand? The doom of youth itself. A walking doom!" *

In the cacographic notes of an era as yet barely committed to history, Laurette had read its epitaph.

One other time she saw Fitzgerald. He and his wife Zelda arrived unannounced at the Manners' door on Christmas night, both dead drunk. Wordlessly they staggered to the living room. Zelda fell on one couch and presently vomited. Scott "passed out" on the other.

Under layers of alcohol they had undoubtedly come to worship again the "beautiful egg."

This was Laurette's brush with the jazz age. It never came any closer. She was amazed without becoming in the least belligerent. It was only when the moralist in Hartley took fire and flamed into action, that she took fire with him.

One night as they sat in a restaurant, an inebriated girl made her way uncertainly to a telephone booth close by. She called a number and to an apparently sympathetic listener tried to convey through a haze of drunkenness some mournful circumstance of her life. As she sobbed out her story, one satin shod foot kept time to the jazz band playing in the next room. The tears coursing down her cheeks, the broken voice, and that happy foot beating out the rhythm of the music struck both Hartley and Laurette as compelling drama. How did one say what had happened to that young woman? To a million young women reeling through speak-easies and oceans of alcohol, each with her new freedom tied like a stone around her neck?

Hartley at last had his inspiration.

"The National Anthem" opened on New Year's Eve, 1922. A list of the names in the audience that night reads like a "Who's Who," not only of society, but of the champagne set busy establishing new records in the high life of New York.

Alexander Woollcott voiced the predominant reaction to Hartley's diatribe on jazz: "It is an acrid sermon in four acts, aimed like a rudely pointed forefinger at the dizzy mob of toddling, gin-swilling addlepates who are making a good deal of disturbance these days in the American midst." He found the play "vigorous

---

* *Esquire,* October, 1951. "Youth in the Abyss." Laurence Stallings.

and direct" but ". . . it is a preachment, and it so happens that in writing it, the Reverend J. Hartley Manners became so absorbed in his text that he could think of no speech and invent no incident that did not bear directly on it."

There was no doubt that the first-night audience was deeply impressed—at times quite unhappily so. They were like a bunch of party-minded kids, with paper hats and noisemakers, who had wandered by mistake into a Billy Sunday rally against evils of jazz and drink. A well-known sculptress of the day, standing in the lobby during the entr'acte, was heard to remark indignantly, "I never felt so scolded in all my life!" Others commented with equal audibility that they wished they had gone someplace where it was "more fun."

Hartley had aimed his punches straight. His story concerned the smart set of New York and Paris and moved against a background of swank country clubs and fashionable hotels, to the incessant obbligato of jazz bands. "The Sheik of Araby" was the theme music played over and over backstage with a fast insistent beat that pounded the nerves.

The main character, Marian Hale, is a healthy, well-brought-up young woman whose life by successive steps comes to utter degradation as she tries to keep up with her hard-drinking playboy husband.

The theme was starkly and uncompromisingly developed. Louis De Foe writing in the *World* commented that certain scenes were "none too palatable" and that it was to Laurette's vast credit that in the final drunken episodes the emotion she stirred was one of profound pity. "It is a human, moving, deep and persuasive performance . . . and one that reveals how firm is her grip upon some of the sturdier phases of human character."

Laurette considered "The National Anthem" Hartley's finest play—in fact the *great* play that she had waited for. And Marian Hale she considered her greatest role.

Standing before the curtain after the usual first-night ovation, which on this particular night was charged with a mixture of guilt and defiance of people who had been hammered unmercifully, Laurette said, "I hope this is for the play as well as myself."

If a dramatic success could be rated by the amount of comment stirred up, "The National Anthem" was unquestionably a success. Ministers used its message as a text for their Sunday sermons. Reformers and prohibitionists hailed it, urged everybody to see it. But as Woollcott had predicted, many a lily-livered playgoer took fright at the prospect of being "reformed" by a dramatist, and stayed away. Those who did, according to Mr. Woollcott, cheated themselves out of a "rare experience in the theatre —a superb performance by a great actress. Laurette Taylor is that if anyone in our time, in our country, is. And she never gave more and better evidence of the fact than she does in the shifting moods and circumstances of this new woman Mr. Manners has imagined for her."

Speculation as to why the play failed to draw the public was divided between one faction which considered Hartley "ahead of his time," and another which found him "old-fashioned." Burns Mantle in his *Best Plays* attributes the lukewarm reception to the fact it was belated in theme. Yet when "The National Anthem" was written, F. Scott Fitzgerald's "This Side of Paradise" was only a year out, and "Tales of the Jazz Age" had not yet been published.

. . . And what does Hartley have to say when Laurette inveighs against those who do not recognize his work for the great play it is, and when the public refuses to support it? He smiles— that quizzical smile that comes after he has poured his creative power into his work where no man may molest his triumph—and recites one of his little jingles:

> Did you ever strive to reach the heights,
> And sunning in your own delights, preen your plumes
> And crow, "All right?"
> And did something knock you out of sight?
> It did.

After a run of three months to only modest business, Laurette wrote to Stevens:

> The play received a lot of attention from ministers and reformers, but it is not doing anything remarkable in the way of drawing the public. It is a most exciting drama, really, and I think *the*

American play, but I almost knew what was going to happen when the ministers started to tell their congregations, and the reformers informed the young people in their churches that it was good for their future salvation.

However, I am frightfully proud of the fact that Hartley wrote it and that I play my present part.

Hartley and I are thinking of separating (now, Ashton, hold on, because I do not mean that) professionally. I shall do "Humoresque. . . ."

Hartley is going to write a play after this without anything in mind except fun, frolic and laughter. Believe me, Ashton, there is no profit in being a prophet. Then we shall come together in the next play.

I am forcing Hartley to do this because I am sick of getting so much credit for interpreting something, whereas he creates that something out of nothing. Hartley will present me in 'Humoresque' and I shall pick the actress to play in his play.

P/S. Hartley thinks I am frightfully wrong to cry "Wolf" about the play—so I must correct any impression of failure, Amico. We've just finished our third month to quite all right business—but —we expected more!

The lack of recognition for "The National Anthem" as a great play has been a severe blow to Laurette, and the part so taxes her physically that she is soon close to a nervous collapse. Particularly harrowing is the telephone scene where Marian tries to get help after taking poison. In this scene Laurette was two women, one sodden, almost totally helpless with drink; the other, with mind stark sober and in panic trying to gain control of limbs and speech to summon help. It was a long scene played alone on the stage and it literally tore her apart. Lily Cooper as Madeline Trent, the first to reach Marian's side, wept nightly as the semi-prostrate Laurette clung to her begging to be saved.

On the curtain calls those standing beside Laurette could feel her trembling from head to foot. "If I wasn't strong as a horse, I couldn't get through this act!" she would comment indignantly as she walked from stage to dressing room. Hartley is there as he is through most performances. He greets his wife with "Bright little play, isn't it?" The smile is almost apologetic.

Quite unconsciously Laurette is wringing her hands, nerves

strung out under the nightly hammering of the band which stops only for the entr'acte. Lily has followed Laurette into the dressing room, tears still on her cheeks.

Hartley tries to make them smile. "Ta-a-a TA, ta-*TA*, ta-*TA!*" he sings to the tune of "The Sheik."

"Oh for God's sake, shut up, Hartley!" Laurette cries and barely musters a smile. "I never want to hear that piece again as long as I live!"

It is not like Laurette to carry her part offstage. Usually she drops it and picks it up in the wings with an everyday casualness that is astonishing. But she cannot shake the nerves of Marian Hale, and this troubles Hartley.

For the last ten days of the run a doctor is in the dressing room, and Laurette is under sedatives. Then her nerves, like those of the character she plays, break completely. Business is still fair at the Henry Miller when "The National Anthem" closes.

Laurette's next letter to Ashton is altogether despondent. Always a healthy animal, she is now worried by the inability to get hold of herself.

One must learn to take life slowly and calmly or it will take you quickly. I've always had a *mental* reservation about the value of Life. But never before have I looked at it, tried to take it by the throat, and ask it what the H—— it meant! Perhaps having *all* the reasons for living (Love, money, (certain) fame, etc.) I'm wondering about and overestimating the value of the thing I don't know— Death! . . . During the run of "Anthem" I lost my gaiety. That it wasn't hailed as the great play on American life made me furious. It made me bitter, and "gaiety" said "Oh! prunes. I'll leave her flat. She's losing her sense of proportion."

It was the *very best acting* I have ever done! No wig, no accent, no "conscious" fascination. For it I received less praise than ever before and altogether my values became confused. All these things made me ill, but it's been a good thing. I can *never* be so disappointed again because I will never *expect* so much. Funny things— artists—Ashton. I don't think they would ask to be born one if they knew the half of it. . . .

With my love, Ashton

Lauretta

*

# Hollywood and Peg

After two months of recuperation by her beloved ocean at East-hampton Laurette again wrote to her friend:

> Really, Ashton, I am expert now at sponging all thoughts out of my brain and face. I go to Los Angeles in July to do "Peg" in pictures, so I have nothing to wrinkle my brow for months.
> I keep looking wide looks and smiling engagingly to myself at nothing, and considering my short nose. The only time my face doesn't come up to movie standards is when it thinks. . . .

She is rested. She is divinely slim. Her zest for life has returned with the new challenge facing her, and the fact that meeting it brings her a step closer to possessing her own theatre.

It was a very gloomy young man who waited at the station to greet the famous Broadway actress upon her arrival in Hollywood. His name was King Vidor and he was just twenty-two. "Peg" was to be his first big picture with a big studio and a big star, but he did not look like a young man about to grasp a golden opportunity.

He had seen the tests sent out from the East. They had been made under the supervision of David Wark Griffith and with that illustrious name attached to them, Vidor had no cause to think that they were other than the best possible. But in frowsy wig and dead-white make-up the famous star looked closer to forty than eighteen. Vidor wanted desperately to get out of the assignment, but his bosses had sent him down to the station with a be-a-man-my-son pat on the back, and there he was, looking about as cheerful as a prisoner attending his own execution.

At the first sight of Laurette, he experienced acute relief. She came toward him smiling, and his camera-minded eye saw at once a face all round and animated, essentially youthful. Beneath her hat red-gold hair peeked out in soft coils.

Pumping her hand he burst out impulsively, "For Heaven's sake, let's make a test with your own lovely hair!"

They did. They made numerous tests with different make-up. When Laurette saw the final results she was enraptured. So was Vidor.

Laurette felt like Alice-Through-the-Looking Glass in this new topsy-turvy world of Hollywood. She wrote her children:

> Darlings! The first tests were marvelous profiles and ¾'s—the full face not so good. Next day I had five hours of tests with my own hair curled, and Jartley and I are off in a few minutes to see those.
>
> Never have I been so nervous. They are trying to get Reginald Denny, Maggie! Conway Tearle was partly engaged, but he wanted to be featured, and Hartley won't agree. So!
>
> Last night we went to the Hollywood Bowl, an enormous place built in a natural hollow surrounded by high hills. A symphony orchestra, led by Alfred Hertz, poured out most delicious music. The other side of the hill is the Hollywood Passion Play (really). Henry Herbert is playing Christus—and from a drinking (moderately), smoking Lambs Club actor, he has turned ascetic. He lives in one room, but on the mountainside, never comes into town, etc. Imagine! Hollywood with its Fatty Arbuckle, Christus and symphony orchestras!
>
> We visited Mary and Doug. "Robin Hood" has just been finished—and Mary is working on "Tess of the Storm Country." She has been very sweet. I use the same make-up she does. They were taking a snowstorm and the temperature was eighty degrees! They had built a hut half floating on an artificial pond with artificial ice blocks. Mary and her lover were packed in cotton wool up to their waists, and pounds of paraffin over that—standing half done up in cotton with fur caps and coats on and the thermometer 80! The powder puff had to be used every second between short shots to keep the perspiration from melting the paraffin. Douglas's castles are still standing across from Tess's hut, and he was wrestling with Abdullah, the Turk, who keeps him fit. Imagine wrestling *voluntarily* at 80 degrees in the shade!
>
> Well, so long, my sweeties. More when I return.
>
> Mommer

Before the "shooting" of "Peg" started, there were other difficulties to iron out. Hartley with acid politeness insisted on the "little matter" of putting the play back into the script. The cameras waited while he revised the manuscript himself. Then came the question of Michael who had made the trip to perform his veteran duties on the screen. Metro was not impressed by his talents. A trick dog was engaged for the role.

"We can't possibly have that," said Laurette. "We must have Michael. After all, he almost died in that desert heat to get here —it's only fair!"

"Does he do any tricks?" asked a worried functionary.

"Yes, he has some wonderful tricks. He loves me so much he never leaves me, and that's the greatest trick in the world."

"But people like trick dogs on the screen. What tricks does he do?"

Laurette answered, "He won't do a darn thing, but he will not go off the screen while I am on it. Let him be around."

So Michael got the part. Just as Laurette predicted, wherever she was on the set, there was Michael looking roguish or bored, yawning or napping, but always close to his mistress's side. When she moved, Michael moved; when she talked to him he wagged his tail, when she talked to someone else he went to sleep. Nothing bothered him.

Once, during a scene in the Chichester kitchen with Hawkes, the butler, Laurette absent-mindedly filled a large bowl with milk, broke crackers into it and fed Michael. Catching sight of the worried functionary watching from the side lines she broke off the scene with a triumphant, "What did I tell you! Michael's hungry as no trick dog in the world has ever been hungry before!"

There was a reason for Michael's spectacular hunger; he was about to produce puppies for the fourth time. To conceal the vernal bulge so out of keeping with his male characterization, he had to be lit more carefully than the star.

Few experiences are more shattering to dyed-in-the-wool theatre people than the initial brush with movie-making. Laurette certainly found it so. Location the first day of shooting was atop a high hill at Lake Sherwood some thirty miles west of Hollywood. The scene represented Peg's home in Ireland. There was a white, thatched cottage inside which the pigs, chickens and geese were housed when not being used for bucolic atmosphere on the set. Just after dawn, Laurette, in costume, Hartley in white flannels, white shoes, cane and linen cap, the colored maid and Michael plodded slowly up the hill. The day promised to be a scorcher.

Soon after they reached the hilltop cameras began to grind. Russell Simpson, who played Peg's father, mouthed some meaningless words at Laurette. When she moved the cameraman yelled, "Stay in the chalk marks!" The reflectors blinded her. Her make-up began to run. A dresser dashed out and beat a huge powder puff all over her face while Vidor explained in a drawling voice just what she was supposed to feel. Laurette broke up almost immediately.

"I can't play Peg on a dollar bill!" she shouted defiantly, "and I *can't*"—glaring at Vidor—"turn on the hot and cold water just because you tell me to——" and promptly fainted.

When she revived she was lying on the floor of the cottage with pigs, ducks, chickens and geese milling around, and the stench of the barnyard choking her nostrils. Staggering up she called to Hartley and the maid, "Come on! Let's go back to New York!" And without another word, the three of them, Michael close at heel, trooped down the hill.

That was the end of the first day's shooting.

Laurette wanted to quit. Vidor wanted to quit. Various studio emissaries appeared, smoothed ruffled feelings and everybody agreed to try again. After that first nervous day, young Vidor handled his star more skillfully. He gave her free rein with stage techniques, then showed her in the "rushes" why they would not work.

"They turned out all character and grimaces," Laurette admitted. "And that way he finally convinced me he knew more about making movies than I did, which was fortunate for us all."

Vidor quickly realized that it was in an atmosphere of spontaneity that Laurette did her best work, so that "Peg," even though one of Metro's most important pictures, was filmed with the informality and on-the-spot improvisation that characterized the making of "independents" in those days. Douglas Fairbanks dropped in and contributed a whole comedy sequence of Peg finding a flea on Michael, which was incorporated then and there. Nazimova, working on the same lot, advised Laurette against using "mood music" to bring forth tears.

"That is no good, Laurette," Nazimova said in her deep, brooding voice. "Just sit down, and feel terr-rr-ibly sorry for yourself, and you'll cry—after a while."

Some of the hardest scenes were done at night when Laurette was at her liveliest; laughing, talking and telling stories right up to the moment of shooting, she would step before the camera relaxed and animated. Viewing the day's rushes Laurette would squeeze Vidor's arm, chortling with delight as she watched her shadowy self upon the screen.

One morning the call was for eight o'clock on location in the San Fernando Valley. With a punctuality quite unlike her, Laurette arrived on the stroke of eight. No director was in sight. No cameraman. She searched the set, growing more and more furious. Here she was, ready to work at this ungodly hour, and no Vidor to applaud her virtue! Finally, behind a hedge she came on director and cameraman, crouched on the ground engrossed in filming the activities of an ant hill.

"There was King," she would recall with the greatest relish, "down on his knees, and not one damn thing in the world existed for him but that ant hill!"

From that day forward she had no reservations about King Vidor, either as a craftsman or a person. She frankly adored him. And he adored her. They worked hard together and played hard together. The making of "Peg" was fun from then on.

Laurette never quite got over her astonishment at the ways of movie-making. Many a time something would tickle her funny bone right in the middle of a scene and her sudden laugh would ring out through the studio. To make an elegant end to the picture, a finale was added in which Peg, after marrying Sir Gerald (*Jerry*) Adair, was presented at the Court of St. James's. In a pearl-embroidered presentation gown with long train and a saucy ostrich plume in her hair, Peg was to walk the length of the polished court room floor toward the King and Queen. It was a typical Metro "big production" scene with hundreds of dress extras lined up along the wall. At the shout of "Camera! Lights!" Laurette stepped forward. Immediately the camera began to roll backward on its wheeled platform carrying director, cameraman, and assistants; a squad of men wielding mops backed slowly with the camera, erasing tracks and footprints as they went, while on both sides electricians holding aloft lights and reflectors joined the general retreat.

"My God!" shouted Laurette, coming to a dead stop. "I take one step forward and the whole studio moves away from me!"

She can hardly wait for the end of the day to tell these stories to Mary and Doug and her other Hollywood friends. She is having a glorious time. She has gathered a fun-loving group around her so that life on and off the set is one big party. There is swimming at the Pickfair pool, tennis at the Beverly Hills Hotel where Laurette and Hartley live, dancing, and games that last far into the night.

Laurette discovers games in Hollywood, and they become a dominating passion. "In-the-manner-of-the-word" game; the "one-minute-speech" game, and several others. Most of them require a good deal of acting ability. Laurette gives no quarter in these games, plays them very much according to her own rules, and is loud and self-constituted arbiter of who is good and who is bad. Several women in the group quickly become allergic to this form of entertainment. Laurette is quite unmerciful with her own sex. If they are hesitant, unwilling, shy or slow, she will accuse them of being either dumb or coy, both of which she loathes. It takes a hardy female to stand up to her. With the men, however, she is extremely indulgent. They can take all the time they want; when they fumble they are charming; some of them, she will even concede, are almost as good as she is.

"After a while," Vidor recalled, "we had a hard time getting the girls to come at all if they thought it was going to be an evening of games. It put the men on a spot, because we knew we had to show up or Laurette would never forgive us."

Laurette's energy was inexhaustible. She could work all day and stay up most of the night. One Saturday the group began playing games at three thirty in the afternoon and stopped—with Laurette protesting—at three thirty the next morning.

Through it all Hartley remained urbane, gently alcoholic, rather aloof. He came on the set only occasionally to take Laurette to lunch. Having ironed out all the business details and rewritten the script, he spent long hours alone in their hotel bungalow while she was working. Underneath, he loathed Hollywood. Its sham, its commercialism, its bad manners, its shoddiness corroded his spirit. These were windmills on which he had broken many a lance, and they were everywhere in Hollywood. He held his feeling of repugnance on a thin leash of sarcasm. He considered the venture primarily one of expediency; it would help build that "nucleus" they needed for their own theatre. Laurette, taking Hollywood in stride, laughed at him and his gloomy pre-occupations with the venality and vulgarity of the movie moguls. "Really, Hartley," she would say, "for a *gentle* man, you certainly can hate!"

Wrote Hartley to his stepdaughter, in his best sarcastic vein:

> Just a line to welcome you home to 50 Riverside Drive. It will be nice having you there. We must hear some good music next winter and see some excellent, non-soporific, plays.
>
> For real beauty and art, you have to travel here. All that the Greeks made so perfect seems as nothing compared to the wizardry of the residents of this favored spot. I will tell you of it ever and anon. . . . If you can spare the time, write me of all you thought, and all you did, and all you planned during your long Easthampton summer. How we would have missed Lockdune had not Beverly Hills proved so superb and so soul-inspiring!
>
> With enclosed, procure some sweet-scented flowers. Here they are scent-less. But *so* artistic!
>
> Your mother would send her love, but that she is resting in sweet slumber after another delightful day in her new vocation.
>
> It is as though a new Athens had arisen amid the hills of Beverly and the hollows of Hollywood.
>
> > My love to you,
> > Hartley

Once again it is a gloomy young man who stands in the station, bidding Laurette good-by as she embarks for the East—this time because his Broadway star is leaving him. They have had a wonderful time together both working and playing. It has been "a real crush" as Laurette calls it. It is virtually impossible for Laurette to work with anyone who knows his craft and is selflessly devoted to it without falling half in love with him. Hartley is altogether indulgent of these "crushes." It is the way a child falls in love—"overboard"—completely ingenuous and with great innocence; as Peg would. When Laurette flings off her hat in the train drawing room, presses a thoughtful forefinger to her underlip, gives a sigh that is half content, half discontent, she seems to Hartley to be Peg wanting one more waltz in the moonlight; Peg of the love scene with Jerry, when they return from the dance to which Peg's aunt has forbidden her to go. . . . The strains of "Valse Mauve" drift across the lawn as the two culprits tiptoe into the moonlit living room. . . .

PEG:    Oh I'm so happy! So happy! The whole world's goin' round in one grand waltz, and it's all been through you, Mr. Jerry.

JERRY:  I'm glad it's been through me, Peg.

PEG:    I don't see why it can't all be like this. Why can't we laugh and dance our way through it all?

JERRY:  I wish I could make the world one great ballroom for you.

PEG:    And no creepin' back like a thief in the night!

JERRY:  No—your own mistress, free to do whatever you wish.

PEG:    (Suddenly, with a little elfish laugh) Yet you know, half the fun tonight has been that while I'm supposed to be sleepin' upstairs, I've been at the dance stealin' time. Do ye know "the best of all ways to lengthen your days"?

JERRY:  No.

PEG:    "Is to steal a few hours from the night, my dear."

JERRY:  Well, you've stolen them.

PEG:    I'm a thief, I am.

JERRY:  No. You're the sweetest, dearest—

". . . Laurie?"

"Yes, Hartley?"

"Do you imagine we will return?"

"Oh, yes! It's been fun, really. Fantastic, but lots of fun. Of course we'll come back—if they ask us. Remember the 'nucleus'!"

Hartley looked out the window. Already the Citadel of the Silents had disappeared. Scrub-brush and dust-dry hills stretched to the horizon. They might have been a million miles from civilization. "A new Athens has arisen . . ."

"What you say, Hartley?"

"Nothing . . . nothing, old dear."

*

# *Humoresque*

The chairman of many a benefit dinner during the winter of 1921 was surprised to have Laurette arrive with her twenty-five minute dramatic adaptation of Fannie Hurst's wartime novel "Humoresque" as her part of the entertainment. Because she was currently bounding about the stage as the high-spirited Peg, the last thing anyone expected was an impersonation of an old Jewish childbearer. Laurette had already read it at a dozen dinners when Miss Hurst announced that she had turned her book into a play.

Laurette telephoned at once. Could she come and read her abridgement of the novel to Miss Hurst? No one must play Sarah Kantor but Laurette.

Miss Hurst was skeptical. "I've seen you do a lot of things and you're good," she said. "But I'll be frank with you—I've yet to see the Christian who can properly counterfeit the Jewish accent."

"Maybe there's something in that," replied Laurette. "But what do you say I come over and read Mrs. Kantor to you?"

On Miss Hurst's desk was a manager's check and a contract lacking only a signature. "Don't sign, Fannie, until I speak my piece," Laurette pleaded. When she had finished reading, Fannie Hurst's answer was to enclose the contract and check in a return envelope.

"Humoresque" was Laurette's.

When the news got out, no one seemed pleased. The Jews wrote, "How dare you think you can play *Sarah Kantor!*" And the Irish wrote just as indignantly, "What makes you want to play a Jew?"

What discussions there were between Hartley and Laurette about her decision to do "Humoresque" must remain largely conjectural. It was her decision and he abided by it. He selected the cast for "Humoresque" and personally staged and directed it so magnificently that to him went much of the credit for sustaining its mood and meaning.

He could have had few qualms that "Humoresque" would be hailed as the vehicle worthy of his wife's best talents. His theatre sense was far too acute for that. Miss Hurst's play was a series of emotional climaxes taken from the book, rather loosely and inexpertly strung together. But Laurette saw none of its faults—or if she did thought they could be corrected. She found in the lowly ghetto mother a role of such heroic proportion and such universal appeal that she believed if she made Sarah Kantor live, the play would live.

The theme was one that never failed to stir her deeply: a mother's devotion to her child—this time a poor, tired Jewish mother whose dream has been to find a musical genius among her children. When her little son Leon begs for "a fiddle" she spends her savings to get one. With fierce devotion she nurtures his talent until he becomes a great concert violinist, only to have her heart broken when he goes off to war.

This was Laurette's second try for "the heights." It is doubtful whether she remembered her statement to Stevens after "The National Anthem," that she could never be so disappointed again because she would never expect so much. Once, she said by way of explanation of her vast ambition, "You are either born eager or meager. A little satisfies the latter and nothing the former." And Laurette, whatever else she was, was not born meager.

The role of Mama Kantor was, according to Laurette, the most difficult job of acting she ever attempted. It might, therefore, be well to state here Laurette's basic concept of acting. For one often called an instinctive actress, she was quite definite in her views. She liked best David Warfield's definition: "Acting at its best is a physical representation of a mental picture"—to which Laurette added the phrase—"and the projection of an emotional concept."

"It isn't beauty or personality or magnetism that makes a really great actress," she said at another time. "It is imagination. The imaginative actress builds a picture using all her heart and soul and brain. She believes in it and she makes people across the footlights believe in it. Unless she has done this, she has failed." She goes on to say—and this Hartley taught her—"She must stimulate the imagination of the audience as well. How often does an actress play a part so as to leave you with the feeling that you have so intimate a knowledge of the character that you could imagine its conduct in any situation aside from that involved in the action of the play. Unless this happens, you have seen a limited portrayal." *

But best of all she preferred her own carefree syllogism, "The one great hocus-pocus is putting on the pants of the part. When I play a queen I not only sit on the throne of the queen, but I sit in the pants of the queen."

As Fannie Hurst predicted, the dialect proved a major stumbling block. It not only had to be Jewish but it had to be located geographically: Mrs. Kantor was from Russia. In preparation for rehearsals, Laurette spent part of every afternoon in a little tailor shop on the edge of the Bronx. The tailor and his wife, Russian Jews, obligingly told her stories over coffee and cake, and Laurette told them stories until her dialect approximated theirs. Strolling the streets, she watched the tired, shapeless childbearers of the Jewish race leaning from windows with arms folded across their stomachs, sitting on stoops, or walking, their masses of flesh bunched under cheap corsets which seemed to confine without supporting. She observed the contrast between their quick, vital gestures and their stolid, massive frames. By the time rehearsals began, she felt reasonably comfortable with her accent and movements of body and hands.

The company of eighteen were all Jews with the exception of Laurette and a few minor roles. There were the moppets who played the young Kantor children in the first act, and their grown-up counterparts for the second and third acts; the neighbors and friends of the Kantor family on Allen Street, and Mr. Kantor, played by the extremely able actor, Sam Sidman. It was going to take "a bit of doing," as Laurette said, to be a Jew among so many Jews.

Time and time again she dove into the heart and brain of Sarah Kantor and came up without the soul. The dialect was partly the

* Norris Houghton, *Theatre Arts*, Dec., 1945.

trouble, but there was a further problem. Jewishness, Laurette found, was located deeper than the blood and bone. When Sarah Kantor moved and spoke a whole race must move and speak through her. Beyond the individual was the racial memory of woe and persecution, and this was as much a part of Sarah Kantor as her tolerance and patient humor.

Jacob Adler, the great Jewish actor, whose son, Lutha, played Leon Kantor, the boy violinist, worked on Laurette's make-up. The nose was straightened, lengthened, and nostrils ever so slightly flared. "But," he told her, "it is the eyes that are more character-istically Jewish than the nose." The experimentation went on for hours. To achieve the final effect, he used forty-odd shadings of grease paint around the eyes.

As rehearsal progressed Mama Kantor began to emerge as a rounded and exquisitely beautiful character. But Laurette was not content. In the middle of a scene she would deliberately slip from seriousness into a stunning caricature of her own acting. In the same way that she would often take off another actress's per-formance, heightening just the least bit the falsities to show just where the performance missed, now, she took off her own, and in a storm of disapproval would end, "My God, I sound like Weber and Fields rolled into one!" Or, "Here I am the only Christian and I sound more Jewish than any of you!"

The opening night was on Christmas, 1922, in Atlantic City. Dwight and Marguerite had stayed in New York at their mother's request, for her anxieties over the part precluded any family celebration of her holiday. But at midnight, a frantic telephone call came through to them at home. Laurette was miserable; she had failed to get into Mrs. Kantor's "pants" at that opening per-formance and no one knew it better than she. Her children must come immediately, at once. This was invariably a sign of utter spiritual desolation.

One could never have told from the notices how dismally Lau-rette considered she had failed. They were on the whole excellent. But the knell rang for her in such phrases as "unable to overcome the age handicap" . . . "a too girlish gesture" . . . and even,

"She is too slender for the role"—how deliciously that would have fallen on her ear at any other time! Larded as these phrases were between encomiums, they meant only one thing to Laurette: she had failed to realize Mama Kantor.

"When you are a queen it is impossible to make an unqueenly gesture." And: "If the audience finds me the wrong size, I'm no good as an actress."

Dwight and Marguerite arrived by an early train. With them was Geoffrey Kerr, who, along with Leslie Howard, had practically been adopted by the Manners family upon their arrival in America two winters before in "Just Suppose." Tuesday night they watched the performance. Then back at the hotel the "wake" began. Until five o'clock in the morning every angle of the character, every scene in the play was hashed and rehashed. Through what loophole had the old Jewish woman escaped? Laurette did most of the talking, reading this line and that, analyzing Mama Kantor's emotions down to the last drop of her Jewish blood. But it was no good. It was that dialect! "As Hartley says, instead of forgetting it, I'm practicing my improvements on the stage like a clever child and it's ruining the whole thing."

Hartley tries to console her. "It will come, Laurie. It takes time—that's why we're on the road, and we'll stay out of New York until you are satisfied."

But Laurette is inconsolable.

That forenoon the gloom is still thick. The visitors have arrived late for breakfast. Laurette scolds them. Hartley has already gone to the bedroom to dress for the theatre. Laurette, wearing a rose-colored velvet robe, is pacing up and down the room, a large glass of orange juice in her hand. The gold hair softly coiled over her ears perversely catches the orange tone of the drink, her lips are brightly and carelessly incarnadined; hair, robe, lipstick and drink meet in jarring disagreement and heighten the unnatural pallor of her face brought on by nerves and lack of sleep. The whole effect is that of a Lautrec poster, garish and gaslit, completely theatre. It is hard to believe that this is the same woman one watched on the stage the night before; the Hebraic droop of shoulder, the mask of patient tolerance, the monumental sitting of the tired mother as she holds her sleeping boy and the cheap

violin bought with her savings, and hears in her heart the music
of her dream. Or maybe it is easy to believe; for these are the bold
plastic surfaces of the actress from which a thousand characters
are molded, the fluid careless outline of the interpreter who at any
moment can allow herself to be invested with the stature, size and
mind of another, and for whom the smallest breath of fancy may
become in an instant as solid as flesh and blood.

Now on her face is a small belligerency, a compelling *fixe* on
the problem of this particular character. One feels that the world
can be wiped out around her and she will stand on the ruins trying
to wrest from Sarah Kantor the final secret of her inner life.
. . . Absent-mindedly Laurette puts down the orange juice, and
picks up a cup of tea. She moves across the room and pauses by
a vase of American Beauties sent by an admirer the night before.
There is a sudden blending, robe, hands, face, and the perfect
globes of the roses. Rain streams against the windows in solid
blinding sheets. Laurette stands quietly beside the roses as though
she feels subconsciously that a more harmonious setting has been
achieved. . . . "You'll come to the matinee of course?"

"Of course."

"I want you to tell me *absolutely* what you think."

"Of course."

"Hartley!" she calls, gulps her tea and starts for the bedroom.
"That man is always bathing! See you after the matinee. And
don't be late!" Then she is gone.

There is a sense of vacancy in the room. The imported mourners
tackle dishes that have grown cold under their silver domes. In
a little more than an hour they will be in the audience at the
Apollo Theatre, the curtain will rise, and Mama Kantor will be
shuffling around her crowded Allen Street home, stirring a pot
on the stove, lunging at one of her children with a back-handed
*patsch*, listening to her husband with a kindly, tired smile. She
will completely fill the imaginations of the visitors and they will
forget that they are there to criticize. They will forget the bright
discontented lady of the hotel; or, if they remember at all, it will
appear in memory's eye as an image, shallow and shining as a
playposter compared to the depth and warmth of the portrait un-
folding before them. . . .

The following scene takes place in Laurette's dressing room after the performance:

"You could at least be on time for the matinee! After all, this is very important to me."

"But it was raining and there were no taxis. As it was, we walked all the way, and got soaked."

"And now you have nothing to say?"

"Well—it was pretty wonderful. *You* are conscious of things being wrong, of course, but the audience——"

"*You're* conscious of things being wrong. I wasn't good, was I?"

"Only magnificent, perhaps."

"My God, even some of the Jews are bad! If I played like them, they'd call it caricature. When a Christian does it, it's caricature! It's this dialect, I tell you. As Hartley says, I keep practicing my grand improvements in it, and forgetting to play the part——"

"Look, Mother, you told us to give up our rooms. The last train leaves in fifteen minutes, and besides, Geoff has a ten o'clock rehearsal."

"Oh, go on, go on! You're late for breakfast, late for the matinee, and then you haven't the grace to stay a few minutes and talk this thing over. You know how important it is to me. *Go on!*"

Laurette turns her back, picks up a liner, leans close to the mirror and abstractedly deepens a line by her mouth. She leaves it to her visitors to attempt placatory gestures, say a swift but graceful good-by, catch the train—if they can. She does not help them. She does not even say good-by. Nobody can turn a back more squarely than Laurette.

Peace negotiations having failed, the unhappy group streak for the train, again afoot, in a sodden downpour. Breathlessly they lean back against the damp cinder-smelling plush seats in the last day coach which was already on the move as they swung aboard. They realize that they have been cast into the limbo of lost souls which Laurette reserves for all dullards who attempt to keynote the practical in her presence. Their melancholy is all mixed up with the still pervasive warmth of Mama Kantor, the bright chameleonlike figure of the hotel room, a kaleidoscopic world where allegiance becomes lost among reflections, and where to love passionately is sometimes to embrace a ghost. The sense of vacancy returns; each is separate from the other. The silence is broken only by an occasional skull-shattering sneeze. . . .

To wait for the New York first night, knowing Laurette's state of mind, was like waiting for the start of the big race when one knows that the top-money horse has been having trouble with a tendon during workouts. For the entire tour Laurette wrestled with Mama Kantor.

At the final dress rehearsal before the Broadway opening the company lined up to wish the star well. Moppets and grownups murmured such phrases as "We know you'll be wonderful" . . . "Your greatest triumph, dear Miss Taylor" . . . "Best of luck," etc. At the end of the line stood the patriarch of the group. He took Laurette's hand and solemnly shook his head. "Y' ken't do it!" he said.

Laurette was inclined to agree with him.

But when the curtain rose that night at the Vanderbilt Theatre, the great hocus-pocus had taken place. Mama Kantor sat in her pants.*

"Humoresque" was for Laurette a *succès d'estime* of the first magnitude. There were seventeen curtain calls on the first night. Fellow artists flocked to see the performances. Morris Gest, who brought the Moscow Art Players to New York that winter, left the theatre weeping, and the Moscow Players, who had already seen the moving picture "Peg," came en masse to a performance. These masters of characterization were dumbfounded that one and the same actress could play the two parts. Stanislavsky, moving spirit of the Russian actors, pronounced Laurette America's greatest actress.

Laurette's fellow Americans felt no less deeply.

John Corbin wrote in the *New York Times*:

Here was a creation of great external virtuosity and of far greater spirit within. Her walk and gestures were racial in the extreme,

---

* Edna Ferber commented, "Those bum corsets Sarah Kantor wore under her black silk dress were perfect." Actually Laurette wore no corsets. "I just walked as though I wore them," she told Miss Ferber.

yet always with an indefinable dignity. How it was done escaped analysis, but she positively drooped in the nose, slanted in the eyes, and bowed orientally in the lips.

Charles Darnton in the *Evening World:*

This character study was authentic, real and living, not a thing out of the make-up box and wardrobe room. Not only did the dialect ring true, but the unwieldy figure, the swaying walk and the racial gestures were all part of Sarah Kantor and had nothing whatever in common with Laurette Taylor.

Heywood Broun in *The World:*

The fidelity of the portrait was much deeper than eyes or ears could convey to the spectator. By some other means entirely it came to us that here was a role profoundly believed and felt.

If Laurette had put a pen in the hand of Alexander Woollcott and dictated, he could not have drawn a finer word portrait of what she had tried to achieve.

A performance that is astounding in its rich resourcefulness and now again austere in its tragic beauty. We have never admired her or wondered at her more, and that is testimony from one who in his time has done quite a bit of raving about Laurette Taylor. The illusion she creates remains unbroken until the final curtain. It seems right and true in every inflection of the voice, in every curl of the lip and in every eloquent shrug of the Ghetto shoulders. It is an old woman, her Mrs. Kantor, old before her time from years of grinding poverty, from years of toil in squalor, from years of memories. . . . In the curve of the back, in the brooding tragedy of the eyes, in the immemorial woe that is in the very color of the voice, a race speaks. Her face and body are marked by the years. Yet she never looked so beautiful as she looked last night in the aspiring and prophetic moments of Fannie Hurst's play.

Laurette's personal triumph as Mama Kantor turned strangely sour when it became evident that the public would not support the play. "The Irish and the Jews both must have stayed mad," she commented forlornly.

"Humoresque" played to half-empty houses and closed after three weeks.

Again Laurette does not escape indictment for her choice of playwright.

"We do wish she'd stop her current foolishness," the young Baltimore critic, Robert Garland, wrote while the play was still on the road, "and do something worth while. What an Iris she would make! Or a Candida! Or a Maggie in 'What Every Woman Knows!' Or—but what's the use of crying for the moon? If Miss Taylor prefers Peg to Pinero, J. Hartley Manners to George Bernard Shaw, and Fannie Hurst to J. M. Barrie, the business is none of ours. We'd rather see her as Mama Kantor than not at all."

And Woollcott takes up the old refrain: "From Miss Taylor's best critics—and one might add her severest pals—there have come from time to time the suggestion that she should adventure in plays written by someone other than Hartley Manners. It is probable that they had in mind a few playwrights like Shaw or Sheridan or Barrie. . . . It was most certain that they were not thinking of Fannie Hurst at all."

So Laurette to all appearances shrugged off Mama Kantor, and that same spring barely two months after the closing of "Humoresque" donated her services in "Sweet Nell of Old Drury," the second production of the newly formed Equity Players. Asked by the angrily buzzing Woollcott why, when the Equity Council had given her the pick of any play, she had chosen such "bedizened claptrap," she replied airily, "Because it's spring." And just in case her objectives were still not clear, she elucidated further in a curtain speech on the opening night, "We hope to please the tired businessman—and to make some money." Which they did and pulled the young Equity out of the red after a disastrous season.

Laurette played to the hilt the golden-haired orange vendor, Nell Gwynne, who becomes the mistress of Charles the Second. Her talents as a comedienne never shone with more luster, and the walls of the Forty-eighth Street Theatre rocked with applause. Given her choice of cast, she had surrounded herself as usual with superlative players. She asked Alfred Lunt and Lynn Fontanne, married that spring, to play with her, thus launching them upon their spectacular husband-and-wife theatre career. The period setting and costumes by Woodman Thompson were

lavish, and Hartley's direction "scholarly and brisk." What Woollcott sourly referred to in his review as "a gaudy piece of rubbish
which tottered rheumatically through this town three and twenty
years ago" seemed lusty and thoroughly alive by the time Laurette
and confreres got through with it. It must have appealed a little
to the devil in her to make this paste jewel sparkle like a diamond.
Commented *Variety:* "Sweet Nell, that dear old gibberish of
feathered hats and flowery speeches. . . . In it, our Laurette
makes the unreal seem actual and the maudlin seem gospel truth."

But even though it was spring and Nell was fun, Laurette had
not forgotten Sarah Kantor. To Ashton Stevens she wrote:

> About the Jewish lady I just can't think. It broke my heart for
> awhile and I've left her for Nell Gwynne. It's the first time since
> "The Bird of Paradise" I've played a mistress. Perhaps the public
> won't come to see me as a mistress. They certainly did not come to
> see me as a Jewish childbearer. Thank goodness I read "Humor-
> esque" to you. I was *awfully* good in it, Ashton. I studied them,
> visited them, had one dress me for months and I persuaded myself
> I was one—but never have we played to such awful business.
>
> Do you think the public don't love me anymore? I've always felt
> afraid of that unknown quantity "the Public" and unlike that other
> unknown, "God," they haven't a slight reputation for sticking to
> you—whereas most people say that He is a very good comforter.
>
> Bless you, Ashton, and answer me (about God or the public).
>
>                                                           Lauretta

"Humoresque" was the artistic peak of Laurette's primary
career which was to end abruptly five years later. She did seven
more plays in that time, outstanding among them the pantomime
"Pierrot the Prodigal," "In a Garden" by Philip Barry, and "The
Furies" by Zoe Akins. These were all plays of distinction, and
in each Laurette gave glowing and subtle performances. But her
portrayal of the old Jewish lady remains head and shoulders
above everything else in this period as a bare, austere, blue-
shadowed crag might stand amidst gentle and more verdant slopes.

"Humoresque" stands also at the apex of the single-minded
drive that had been in her from the time she was a child, helping
her over the rough spots, causing her to give hardly a glance sideways at adversity. Nurtured with fierce devotion by her mother

this drive had effectively put blinders on her toward many aspects of life. She was untroubled by them because she did not see them as she reached unerringly for her goals behind the footlights. But with "Humoresque" this single-mindedness faltered. She had realized a mighty ambition and it had proved lonely and unprofitable. In the years that follow she seems to seek her artistic outlets with more restlessness and less assurance. The compass reading of her ambition is not so true. While she makes her own choice of parts and plays, one might imagine that at times the choice is not altogether free but is motivated by the desire to rid herself of barriers never given recognition before. Hartley and Laurette are going determinedly different ways as playwright and actress but she is tremendously influenced by him nonetheless, by his moral prohibitions as well as artistic precepts in the theatre.

As for Hartley, the separation has taken heavy toll of his inspiration although he is much too loyal to say so. If he was pursuing the gay light comedy Laurette mentioned in her letter to Stevens nothing much was being heard of it in the family circle. From the time of "The National Anthem" the tacit assumption between them was that they were working toward a theatre where Laurette could play what she liked as long as she liked. Both of them held to that assumption discussing it very little, but clinging to it as a common goal, with varying degrees of desperation as the years went by, and Hartley produced nothing, or what he produced was inferior and rejected by Laurette.

These years ironically were those of their greatest renown as a couple. They had moved to a red brick mansion at the corner of Seventy-seventh Street and Riverside Drive and there entertained the great and near-great of two continents. Yet these were the years when those close to Laurette were conscious of a mounting avidness of spirit, an intensification of that seeking aspect of her nature that gave such poignancy to her latter years and relationships with people. One felt a pushing forward, sometimes blindly, sometimes purposefully, but always forward; an inborn drive toward specific goals but also beyond that, and more blindly, toward a release as though the strong core of her inner self were molten and constantly under pressure to expand.

As Laurette said herself, she had fame, money, and much love. What now did she seek?

# 50 Riverside Drive

Fifty Riverside Drive, on which the Manners family took a ten-year lease in the autumn of 1922, was a formidable pile of red brick occupying half a block at the corner of Seventy-seventh Street. High, bleak as a battlement with only a four-story bay breaking the severe surface, it did not repudiate grandeur but silently rebuked its more ostentatious brethren with its unadorned mass. The crenelated tower and Gothic spire were not for it. One large stained-glass window alone proclaimed lineage with the opulent era of American architecture; with lofty and membranous stare it gazed northwest up the Hudson like the gelid eye of a matron wishing to give discreet testimony to superior blood. Aleck Woollcott, out for a stroll one afternoon and unaware of the identity of the occupants, stopped before this window with its Romanesque fountain in full eruption midst flowering shrub and clipped yew, and rasped in nettled unbelief to a friend, "There's vile bourgeois ostentation for you!" At which point Laurette and Michael emerged through the front door bundled in identical sweaters and looking about as bourgeois as two circus performers on their way to the tanbark.

The severity of the outer structure swiftly gave way to the warmth of rich interiors. There was a living room with a twenty-five-foot ceiling into which one descended from an upper balcony by way of a long oak staircase. This entrance gave a well-like feeling to the room which was accentuated by the large curving bay along the front, and by the stained-glass window which filtered the daylight through its many hues of green, blue and brown, so that at certain hours everything seemed to swim in aqueous diffractions of light as though submerged under clear water. The walls were covered with fine gold sacking over a vermilion base; soaring plaster arches ended in pediments upon each of which two sculptured knights jousted on muscled steeds.

There was a huge medieval fireplace and where the wall curved into the bay, a pipe organ occupied a raised dais. The tonal attachments were distributed throughout the walls so that the *vox humana* issued rather eerily from beneath the oak stair and cathedral bells chimed from high up on both sides of the fireplace.

To all this magnificence Laurette added the massive Italian Renaissance furniture, carved-wood figures and fruit pieces from the Palazzo Carminati in Venice, and rich antique brocades which she had been collecting since the days of "One Night in Rome." Noel Coward with some justification called it a room of "tortured woodwork" but it was not without charm, and was perfect for the kind of entertaining the Manners family did.

The unusual and impressive entrance into the living room by way of the oak staircase was the delight of Laurette's heart. At her parties, which invariably seethed with celebrities, those who throve on the limelight made this entrance a tour de force, while anyone preferring anonymity felt and often acted like Daniel entering the lion's den. Either way it was a show, and Laurette would seat herself early before the fireplace as though at the theatre, and with unfeigned delight watch each guest cope with the challenge of this entrance.

At one of Laurette's first suppers, Mary Pickford, Alla Nazimova and a famous society beauty, Mrs. Lydig Hoyt, who had recently taken up the stage, arrived in that order. First, Mary comes through the doors, pauses at the head of the stairs, one graceful hand just touching the newel post. "Laurette, what a lovely room!" Then halfway down, another pause. "Charming!" The final descent is all in one little rush, the famous gold curls dancing atop the head, the whole tiny figure buoyant and eager as "America's Sweetheart" should be. Nazimova is next. She does not descend immediately, but stretches her arms out along the balcony rail and gazes broodingly down on the people beneath, a dark shawl about her shoulders. Then she turns, looks back at the arched doors through which she has come and lets the shawl slip slowly from shoulders to waist revealing a completely naked back. "Bee-autiful!" she breathes to no one, and about nothing in particular. Lastly comes Mrs. Lydig Hoyt. Tall. Junoesque. Product of the Junior League and very best schools. Thud. Thud.

Thud. Down the steps like a stevedore. "Sorry, I'm late, Laurette," she calls in a pleasant husky voice, waving her evening bag.

"Julia," shouts Laurette, bursting with laughter, "that's the most honest entrance and the damndest clumsiest one I've seen yet!"

With little persuasion, Laurette gave an imitation of those three entrances many times.

On the second floor was a thirty-foot formal drawing room in the Golden Louis tradition, but as there was nothing formal about the Manners' mode of living Hartley promptly appropriated it for his study. He lined up his bookcases against the gold satin walls, racked his pipes on the Carrara marble mantelpiece, and beneath the two exquisite crystal chandeliers designed by Tiffany, placed his fourteen-foot work table with its litter of manuscripts, files, cigar boxes, and goose-neck desk lamps. The elegant Louis Quinze mirror remained over the fireplace and the heavy satin drapes at the long windows. Sometimes returning home late at night Hartley would sit at this table for a last cigarette, still wearing his fur-collared coat and high silk hat. The elegant and slightly brooding figure reflected in the mirror, beneath the blazing lights of the twin chandeliers, looked for all the world like some forgotten member of the Versailles Conference still waiting to sign a final document.

A small library, which Dwight used as a study, dining room and pantry, completed this floor.

The two upper floors were perfectly arranged for a family dedicated to rugged individualism. Laurette had her suite of bedroom, sitting room and bath at one end of the long corridor which formed the backbone of the shallow house, while Hartley occupied similar quarters at the other end. On the top floor (the fourth from the street) Dwight and Marguerite resided amidst the somewhat tattered glories of their own independence.

A swarm of colored servants ran this loosely articulated ménage. "They have the soft rhythmic tread and gentle voices we all need," Laurette would explain. Laurette's one dictum on housework was that it must not be noticed, and this generally fitted in perfectly with the temperament of the servant assigned to the job; it was not noticed because it was rarely done. There would be an occasional penetration with mop and broom from the lower regions where the servants' quarters were located, but it seldom reached to the topmost floor. Neither did the steam heat or the hot water. Firewood was dutifully hauled to each of the bedroom fireplaces for this, obviously, was a matter of life or death in view of Laurette's peculiar dislike of steam heat until the depth of winter. "I can't understand why you can't keep your fires going," she would say peevishly, if someone complained, happily unconscious in her animal vigor that the small circle warmed by the fire only accentuated the discomfort of the surrounding areas, while halls and bathrooms were uninhabitable. But other than this heroic chore housework was kept to a minimum.

Winter after winter throughout the topmost reaches of the house the pipes would rust up, toilets cease to function, the hot-water faucets dribble only cold. One could wait it out by a roaring fire feeling like Nanook of the North, or descend to the more habitable regions of the lower floors and hope to be taken in by some merciful soul. At times, Dwight, driven by nerves resulting from a late night and forced to contemplate directly these inconveniences, would lean over the vast well of the staircase, cup his hands to his lips and roar into the silence below, "Bring up the humble bucket! We have no water here!"

As likely as not, this would flush out another member of the household, also an inhabitant of the top floor, Hartley's stoat-like secretary. Nobody but Hartley knew just what his duties were. He lived in two rooms with bath at the opposite end of the hall from the children, surrounded by a clutter of old copies of the *New York Times*, English magazines, scrapbooks and news clippings. Mainly he seemed to paste. Any undue disturbance brought him out like a nervous little ground hog. After five years it was discovered he was secretly writing a book on the intimate life of the Manners family and was promptly fired, much to everyone's relief. Nothing more was heard of the manuscript.

Was there such a thing as ordinary life in a household surrounding Laurette? In a way, no. Life at 50 Riverside Drive existed for the sole purpose of accommodating and sustaining Laurette's extraordinary talents and, because it was so dedicated, could not be considered in any way ordinary. If the ordinary served, it was used; if it did not, it was discarded, or perhaps, better to say, ignored. This singleness of purpose was augmented by the fact that Hartley's work was so inextricably bound up with hers that there was no necessity to accommodate two careers, two methods of livelihood. Like a single efficient organism the house respired to nourish its single genius.

The ordinary activities of ordinary people had little reality for Laurette and thereby became somewhat unreal to those who lived with her. Only what was extraordinary was given any consecutive attention, and this tended to make those around her discount matters of everyday living and sum up life almost exclusively in terms of those moments which caught fire from her. It was rather like living by the light and at the speed of a streaking comet.

As children of Laurette—two threads in the unique pattern which genius creates—Dwight and Marguerite devoted themselves to whatever talents they possessed, and like their mother learned to scorn or entirely ignore life's more mundane pursuits. Self-expression was everything; it was the Golden Book of family reading, the leaves bound together and tied by the whole complex of a household woven about this one pursuit to the virtual exclusion of all else. It became the main source of communication. Because Laurette had true genius force, large and small talents were animated and lived by the light of hers, and sometimes when she turned away they died. But brittle or strong, these were the lines and links of family living, and the red brick house on Riverside Drive knew little of any other way of life. Dwight studied at the Art League, designed book jackets, screen silks, did etchings and woodcuts, wrote plays and verse, tooted and banged on any number of instruments. Marguerite laid aside dreams of being a poet—when Laurette found early attempts unpromising—to prepare for the singing career her mother favored. A strenuous schedule of study which included opera, fencing, piano and languages occupied her day.

Daily they rubbed shoulders with those whose talents flashed like beacon lights over a workaday world. Many of their friendships were drawn from this group and the would-be heirs apparent to its brilliance. The ordinary lurked outside and was only sketchily sampled in friendships made at school, or club, or party, and through contact with the "ordinary," talentless, parents of such friends, whose fine qualities of heart and mind and own personal accomplishments Dwight and Marguerite only dimly assessed, so fragmented was their standard of values.

By Laurette's fiat people were sharply divided into two groups, the talented, and the "others." In the latter category were all the twilight contacts made outside the perimeter of her interests. They were not welcome at 50 Riverside. It was a division that sliced ruthlessly through everyday loyalties and made home a kind of royal enclosure where many a friendly tie was perforce severed at the gate. Dwight and Marguerite truncated numerous relationships as "valueless" because they had no value to Laurette. They learned to breathe the rarefied air of her genius even when it meant breathing in painful gulps. They were like aerialists dedicated to the flying swings and taut ropes of carefully promoted talents, aerialists with no feel of the ground and very little knowledge of the long fall.

Like ripples from this central extraordinary character, unordinariness extended all the way down the line even to the colored servants. Though they fell down on the ordinary, they performed the extraordinary almost every day. The hauling of wood to the seven fireplaces was one example. Their day began with a series of breakfasts served on trays, or in the dining room, from nine in the morning until three in the afternoon. The hour for tea fluctuated in kind. When Laurette was playing, there were two dinners, an early one for her, a later one for the family. A buffet supper was generally on the dining-room sideboard to take care of at least half a dozen guests after the theatre.

Laurette was both demanding and indulgent of her colored staff. Martha Smith was her dresser and general factotum of the household for sixteen years. Martha's mother was cook for almost as long. Laurette used to say that Mrs. Smith was "older than God and cooked like all His angels put together." Mrs. Smith claimed that she had been a Southern slave. When Martha grew restive under many tasks and long hours, Mrs. Smith would chide: "Honey, you'se *free*—and that's the sweetest thing in all this here world!" Or she might moan sadly to Laurette after Martha had "sassed" her mistress, "She's a No'thern nigger, M'ss Manners—she don't know how sweet freedom is!"

Sunday tea was open house, but like everything else in the way of entertaining, was casually dispensed. One might drop in for crumpets and cucumber sandwiches and find himself in the middle of a family argument, or be confronted by a milling horde of strangers obviously suffering from complete ignorance as to each other's identity, and not a member of the family in sight. One actor friend—a steady at the Sunday teas—claims that he walked in on such a scene and upon inquiring of one of the servants as to the whereabouts of the family, was told that they had all made other engagements for the afternoon. He goes on with his undoubtedly apochryphal story to relate that Lady Diana Manners had taken up a commanding position behind the silver tea service and was pouring for Phil Baker, while Irvin Cobb lumbered about with a tray of sandwiches, and the Duchess of Rutland tried valiantly to make herself understood by a heavily bearded Russian who spoke no English.

Laurette's Sunday-night suppers were famous. The number of guests was always indeterminate, but supper was generally prepared for twenty or more. These parties went on until three, four or five in the morning, the last guests departing over Laurette's heated protests.

Laurette was the autocrat of every gathering, explosive, tyrannical, witty and swift of mind, irresistibly charming. She could never get enough of anything she liked, a joke, a person, a piece of music, a bit of acting, but was bored, stridently and aggressively so, with what she did not like. She had her own strongly held ideas as to what made a party a success. Above everything, no one was allowed to be dull or "heavy." That was the unforgivable sin. If you had something to say you were to be gay and lively about it, or not say it. Intelligence and knowledge unleavened by wit or personality was not welcome.

Her interest in such subjects as politics, current events, "causes" could only be sparked by an attractive personality. Because she found Herbert Hoover personally a man of great charm ("How he can be so dull in public, I don't know!") she could take an interest in politics when he discussed them, and the warmth of

Eugene Meyer's personality almost persuaded her that finance could be fascinating. But many intelligent and well-informed persons who could easily hold their own in a normal society seemed to disintegrate under the pressure of Laurette's arbitrary dictums as to what was acceptable in her drawing room. Surrounded by the flashy dynamics of Alexander Woollcott, Herbert Bayard Swope, Noel Coward, or the heavy glamour of the Lunts, Nazimova, the Doug Fairbanks, they seemed to turn putty gray in character. And it didn't help to have Laurette baying at their heels like a collie dog after a maverick.

Introductions Laurette considered unnecessary. They were dispensed with. If a well-brought-up guest attempted to introduce two obviously uncomfortable strangers, Laurette's voice would ring across the room, "They can find out who they are for themselves!" Good-bys were also unnecessary. "If you're going, just go—don't break up my party." Seeing a surreptitious handclasp here and there despite this warning, Laurette's full and resonant voice tracks down the offender: "There, there! Stand not upon the order of your going, but for God sake go!"

Laurette was passionately fond of playing games, the spelling games, word games, acting games she had brought from Hollywood. She played them with a ferocity which appalled the more timid. Particularly the acting game. "In the manner of the word" was her favorite. An adverb was chosen, then each guest was asked to perform some particular action, recite, or sing "in the manner of the word." Laurette gave each performance her breathless attention, loudly criticized or warmly applauded, often rising herself to act out the word with certain nuances of interpretation which she felt the guest had missed. Even professionals were not safe from her rigid measure of perfection. Some of the guests— good actors too—felt it the better part of valor to abstain from playing altogether. Others fought doggedly for their interpretations in the face of a mounting barrage of abuse. One such was Marc Connelly who liked to win as passionately as Laurette. A game might come to a complete standstill while Marc and Laurette argued, each giving a more and more fervid performance "in the manner of the word" with neither conceding immortality to the other.

Common fry who wandered into a party unsuspectingly, and found themselves asked to smell a rose "tragically" or dance "hauntingly" in company with such luminaries as Ethel Barrymore, Ina Claire, Alla Nazimova, the Lunts, Leslie Howard and Noel Coward, either staggered through the ordeal with the idea that they could tell their grandchildren about it, or hastily excused themselves to the dining-room sideboard and knocked themselves out with a triple Scotch. Laurette had little understanding of the shy and no tolerance for those who would hide their light under a bushel. Talented people in her drawing room were expected to exercise their talents, not as a matter of exhibition, but as a matter of enjoyment. What, Laurette might well ask, was more enjoyable? The lovely Edith Day must sing those beautiful songs from "Sally, Irene and Mary," or Mary Ellis the "Indian Love Call" from "Rose Marie," or Noel run through his repertoire of tunes. Nazimova must do that blood-chilling scene from her current show "Dagmar" where she tries to escape her murderer; and when she does, not an arm's length from her audience—no footlights, no make-up, no illusion—and fills the room with the same terror she projected from the stage, Laurette looks at her wide-eyed with admiration and breathes, "My God, Alla! I could never do that!"

Skits were popular. Written by Marc Connelly, Geoffrey Kerr, Noel Coward, they generally satirized current plays, current performances. Laurette was never backward about accepting a part.

If Hartley was, as Laurette called him, her "balance wheel" both in and out of the theatre, his touch in a drawing room was light. "Laurie, let the poor fellow be," or "My dear, it's just a bally game!" was all he would say. Her vitality, charm and wit held him spellbound as it did many another and covered a multitude of social sins. He was poor at games and unless specifically urged by Laurette preferred to sit on the side lines swapping stories with a crony, or reviewing all the great boxing events of the age, blow by blow, with the amazing memory he had for such things. But he adored his wife's voracity for fun and people, and in the  middle of a story his eyes would wander across the room to where Laurette was holding forth with all the modesty of a

Zacchini about to be shot from a cannon, smile his sweet shy smile, pause for a moment in bewitched contemplation, completely happy because his Laurie was happy.

Hartley's ideas about proper drawing-room conversation were extremely conservative. Devotees of the new freedom, tackling him, would find themselves under the scrutiny of large expressionless eyes, and quite unable to tell whether the look signified disapproval or obtuseness. Vaguely uncomfortable, they would move away. There were very few meeting Hartley socially, whether it was once or a hundred times, who had the faintest idea what he thought. Many grew restive listening to his stories. Once in Chicago, Freddie McLaughlin, waiting for Hartley and Laurette to arrive for supper at his bachelor quarters and hearing their steps at last upon the stairs, murmured to Ashton Stevens, "Here they come—Anecdote and Antidote."

On the other hand there was no subject Laurette would not discuss if she thought it had valid interest, and one could be quite sure that this interest would release at once a flood of quick, intuitive, highly entertaining remarks, and in one lightning stroke you would have everything she knew, could guess or possibly surmise on that subject. To many of the topics of the day she brought an extreme naïveté and the, at times, inspired intransigence of an Irish Catholic mind. The Freudian vogue left her cold. The concept of life being motivated by suppressed desires was "dirty." To a close friend she wrote loftily after her collapse in "The National Anthem," "I do not believe that an upset of the nerves comes from some thwarted dirty instinct one had when young! As for my reproduction sense (the chief "thwart" as I understand it) . . . that could not possibly be the cause of my nerves, because I reproduced children at an early age and that sense has now been sublimated in my work."

The new freedom in literature startled her. "I get my sex between bedcovers, not book covers," was a phrase she coined and of which she was extremely proud. The play, "The Captive," in which the symbol for Lesbian love was a bunch of violets, spoiled her love of that flower for years; and a fit of prolonged morbidity after reading "The Well of Loneliness," a

novel on the same subject, was dissipated only by the laugh she
got when Hartley pointed melancholically at his toilet one morning and sighed, "Ah, *there's* the well of loneliness."

Discussion of homosexuality was coming into the open for
the first time, and the word "fairy" was the current and smart
colloquialism. Laurette on being told that one of her friends was
a fairy was incredulous. "I don't believe it, but I shall certainly
ask him," was her retort. And she did. And he was. "Well!" responded Laurette. "I don't see why you were so indignant when
I introduced you to so-and-so (a notorious homosexual)."

"Laurette, really darling!" retorted the gentleman. "There
are prostitutes in our circles too, you know."

"Well-r-r . . ." Laurette trailed off; she had come abruptly
to the end of her knowledge on the subject.

This total response to all that captured her imagination made
Laurette not only a highly provocative conversationalist but a
superb audience. She could raise the simplest tale of courage,
love, sacrifice to the height of art by the quality of her listening,
and the smallest talent, if honest, shone by the quality of her
attention. Her own capacity for imaginative truth was so great
that it enveloped and exalted the most minor and homely expression of truth in another.

But these were all projections—away and apart from herself.
Zoe Akins said of Laurette: "Whereas so many actresses are
essentially boring to meet outside of the theatre, because they
draw everything to themselves as a sort of set or background
for their own personality, Laurette did just the opposite. She
was always eager to be drawn away, she would submit herself
to anything that was entertaining, colorful, different. She was
so related to reality that she could not stand to live in it and she
was captivated by anyone who could distract her, lure her away
even for a minute from the awful imposition of reality upon
herself."

This too was a function of the household at 50 Riverside Drive.

One of the realities Laurette accepted grudgingly was the fact
that she now had a grown son and daughter. They were finished with school, and had become an integral part of the household. No longer able to hide them, she switched to the other ex-

treme and became extravagantly proud of them. . . . Marguerite had the most beautiful singing voice and must demonstrate it on command. "She does with the singing word what I do with the spoken word." . . . Dwight had so many talents she couldn't decide which one was greatest. "When he drew," Ethel Barrymore recalled a little wearily, "he was Augustus John. When he wrote verse he was François Villon. When he wrote fiction he was Guy de Maupassant. It's a wonder he survived at all much less stayed the talented, delightful person he is."

This extravagant pride was partly because they were her children, and partly because, if she must have children, they must be nothing short of miraculous in every possible way. "I was *just* sixteen when I had them," she would often reiterate. That was the beginning of the miracle. The rest of it was that they were the *most* beautiful, the *most* talented, the *most* charming and intelligent children anyone ever had. Somehow this superproduction was to sweep before it whatever onus there was to having children at all.

At times, however, she was more than a little wistful about having such grown-up ones. . . . When, for instance, she meets a famous European violinist, and well-known lady's man who is quite obviously worshipful, and wants to ask him to 50 Riverside Drive. It is a shame he has to meet a tall, blonde daughter a head taller than her mother. It is *so* disillusioning! . . . How nice when Marguerite decides not to come to the party but retires early instead. And the musician arrives, bends over his hostess's hand and murmurs, "I hear you have a lovely daughter." . . . All Europeans have a sadistic streak! . . . But then, Laurette has an Irish cunning of her own. "Yes," she lisps sweetly, "she's lovely, and I want you to meet her." Together they climb the four flights of stairs and, just as she hoped, they find Marguerite with long hair down her back, face scrubbed clean of make-up and wearing a nondescript bathrobe, so that it is quite impossible to tell whether she is fourteen or twenty. There follows an uneasy conversation during which the musician is troubled by more than a faint suspicion that he is not in the bedroom of a child, while the daughter tries valiantly to act the part of one, in order to rescue both herself and the guest from the suffocating embarrassment of Laurette's deception. Only Laurette is happy. No illusion is so brief or precarious that it will not serve her better than the truth.

Fifty Riverside Drive had an entirely different rhythm when Laurette was rehearsing. There were no parties then. Those who came and went were mostly connected with the forthcoming play or Laurette's personal preparations for it: producer, press agent, set designer, costumer, masseuse and beautician, language or singing teacher; Aunt Nellie, working and reworking her clothes as Elizabeth used to do. The big living room witnessed the selection of leading roles, informal readings of the script, many a run through of individual scenes. Even after rehearsals were started in a theatre, the house remained closely tied to Laurette's stage activities. Her relations with members of the cast were informal, friendly. Usually they were as welcome at home as on the rehearsal stage. Generally there was a promising young actress to whom Laurette gave special attention, working extra hours at home on scenes, personally supervising clothes and fittings, seeing to it that she "ate properly." The pattern of the relationship first established with Lynn Fontanne, although never again as close, was repeated many times.

The seasoned actors and top-notch leading men with whom Laurette invariably played were always welcome companions.

The Philistines, the "dull little people," those who "live without imagination," to whom Laurette is never cordial, even in her most expansive moods, are now swept from her life. She tolerates only what is grist to her mill, sees only those who can keep life tossing about her "as iridescent and fragile as a soap bubble." She welcomes all the volatile, intuitive forces; the concrete and the completed are not her tools, nor will she spend her energies succoring the unfulfilled. She is creating deep within herself, and everything and everybody around her must serve this purpose or stand aside.

But the house is not unfriendly to those who can contribute to its living pattern. In the late afternoon when family members return from their various activities it is not unusual to find a stray or two—some "glorified bum"—waiting in the living room hoping to be asked to stay to dinner: a lonely young actor, musician, visiting English playwright, or perhaps a homesick foreigner with little English at his command; all drawn as though by a magnet to the warm, generative atmosphere which Laurette, ruthlessly or not, demands as the milieu in which to function as an artist. And if theirs is a vital, stimulating contribution to the pattern, they are more than welcome.

Noel Coward was one of the favorite strays. When he first came to New York from London, his sparkling chain of successes as actor and playwright were still in the future. According to Laurette, "Noel had a great deal of leisure that winter and not much else, and he spent a good deal of it at our house." * The sound of the piano bewitched into melody meant that Noel was in the living room whiling away an hour or so until someone came home. He was a great favorite with the family. Each member in turn would stop on the way upstairs, lean over the balcony, and invite him to stay for dinner. "Thank you, darling, I'd love to," Noel would reply, smiling up at each, the melody never ceasing beneath his roving fingers.

Laurette adored Noel's gift for words.

"He never had to search for the right one. They came effortlessly to his obvious delight as well as to his listener's."

When she bobbed her hair to be in fashion, cutting it herself with that wild improvisation that inevitably gripped her when she got shears in hand, she asked Noel what he thought of the result. "Darling," he exclaimed, "you look like a lousy Shelley."

Later when Noel was back in England and word drifted across the Atlantic that his new play "Hay Fever" was supposed to be an intimate picture of the Manners family, Laurette was hurt. After seeing the play in New York she found it hard to forgive him; the addlepated group of rugged individualists whom he depicted were not her family at all. "None of us," she declared emphatically, "is ever unintentionally rude."

The winter that Laurette and Hartley settled in their new home was a brilliant one in the New York theatre. It was the winter of the visit of the Moscow Art Theatre, of John Barrymore's im-

* "Noel Coward" by Laurette Taylor, *Town & Country*, May, 1942.

mortal "Hamlet," Jane Cowl's miraculous production of "Romeo and Juliet," Jeanne Eagels' triumphant second season as the husky-voiced, swaggering Sadie Thompson in the unforgettable "Rain." And it was that winter that Laurette took her "glorious tumble" * as the old Jewess in "Humoresque," while her shadow flitted across the screens of the nation, younger than springtime, in "Peg O' My Heart." These two performances, seen concurrently, indubitably established her right in an era of greatness to be known as great.

Everybody who was anybody in the theatre came to Riverside Drive. Laurette quizzed them, bedeviled them, adored and insulted them, laughed at their foibles, glowed with their triumphs. She asked Barrymore how he had conceived so flawless an interpretation of the gloomy Dane. Barrymore fastened his mad pin-point eyes on her and drawled confidentially, "Well, I'll tell you, Laurette, he was the kind of guy who kept throwing out these mental boomerangs, and they'd all come back and hit him in the nose, and he'd say"—here Barrymore paused, drew a long finger beneath his elegant nostrils, stared at it incredulously and snarled —" 'Christ! What's that? Blood?' "

Laurette had never greatly admired Jane Cowl as an actress. This opinion was revised sharply after Miss Cowl's performance as Juliet. Thereafter, each time she saw Jane or Rollo Peters (Romeo), she was lavish in her praise, invariably adding with unabated enthusiasm, "But *the* performance in the play is Dennis King's!" Invited to be guest columnist by Aleck Woollcott, Laurette devoted the entire article to a eulogy of Miss Cowl's amazing performance. Her first sentence began: "Now that I have seen Jane Cowl as Juliet, I do believe that Christ walked upon the waters." She could not understand Jane's decided coolness the next time they met.

She considered Jeanne Eagels' Sadie Thompson one of those rarities of the theatre, the perfect meeting of actress and role. At the opening of an art exhibition she saw Miss Eagels across the room and asked to be introduced. The young actress was wearing a black hat with black veil under her chin and Laurette was entranced by the delicacy of profile, the angelic coloring of hair, eyes and skin. As Miss Eagels turned to acknowledge the introduction, she was saying, ". . . and any God damn son-of-a-bitch who

* cf. Burns Mantle's *Best Plays of 1922–1923.*

thinks so is a goddam liar!" Some weeks later at a party Laurette gave for her, Miss Eagels again grew fiery, her husky histrionics quickly drowning out all other conversation. "Hey, Hartley!" Laurette at last called across the room. "Why don't you take Jeanne up to your study and show her your—your—Trollopes?"

Laurette glowed equally with her own triumphs that winter. She was frankly entranced by her screen performance in "Peg O' My Heart." "The slightest lull in the conversation at one of my parties, and I'd have out the projector and screen," she admitted quite shamelessly. Friends became wary of her invitations. Mrs. Charles Dana Gibson, whose husband had just finished a portrait of Laurette, cast a jaundiced eye upon the second or third invitation to dinner at the Manners' house within a brief space of time. "I love you, Laurette, and I love the brilliant dinners you and Hartley give. But I refuse, I absolutely refuse to sit in the dark once more while you unspool your 'Peg' picture." *

Ethel Barrymore, asked by some innocent if she had ever seen the "Peg" movie, breathed, "One whole winter!"

Laurette was the first to broadcast these remarks with an impudent chuckle, and went right on showing "Peg."

Memorable for many reasons, the winter of 1922–23 was most memorable for Laurette because of her meeting with the great Constantin Stanislavsky, actor-director and moving spirit of the Moscow Art Theatre. Their unsurpassed performances of Chekhov, Gorki and Dostoevski were the talk of New York. Upon arriving in New York, Stanislavsky inquired at once about Laurette Taylor. He took the members of his company to see the motion picture "Peg" then playing at the Capitol Theatre. A week later they attended a performance of "Humoresque." Past masters of versatility and character portrayal themselves, they were absolutely astounded that one actress could play two such radically different roles. The portrait of the old Russian Jewess they cheered. Stanislavsky unequivocally declared Laurette to be America's greatest actress.**

Michel Barroy, who idolized both artists, arranged their intro-

---

* cf. Ashton Stevens, *Chicago Herald-American*, Feb. 23, 1945.
** John Golden said of Laurette: "It is her misfortune that she was born in America. In any other country she would be hailed as the world's greatest actress. We never honor our own."

duction. An intensely emotional young Russian ex-patriot, he was
active in the American theatre. The meeting took place at 50 Riverside Drive. Perhaps the vibrations of such a meeting can someday
be recorded and thus be captured and held for posterity: the great
leonine Stanislavsky, with rugged face and keen, kind eyes, de-
scending the stairs to the living room where Laurette awaits him
. . . the moment of meeting when he leans over to kiss her hand,
not formally, but in deep and sincere homage . . . and Laurette
dipping a bit as she always does when pleased, like a little girl
who half thinks to make a curtsy. . . .

They sat on the couch by the fireplace with Barroy between
them as interpreter. Tense with excitement, Barroy plucked the
words from Laurette's lips, translating without pause into Russian,
reversing the process in faultless English as Stanislavsky spoke.
The two seemed oblivious of the interpreter. If they listened, it
was with their subjective minds. The words flowed between
them without halt or hesitancy as though in direct communication; rich sonorous Russian words, quick staccato English words,
while Barroy, white with emotion, pinned little wings to them,
sending them straight as homing pigeons to the ears of his idols.

There were many meetings between Laurette and Stanislavsky.
He would come after the theatre and stay until two and three in
the morning, drinking cup after cup of tea. Occasionally other
members of the Russian troupe joined him, sitting silent and
withdrawn as their leader and Laurette talked. Ivan Moskvin
brought a small flask of a dark liquid which he quaffed from a
liqueur glass, saying not a word.

"They changed the whole look of my living room," Laurette
said. "Even the rather jolly stained-glass window became a som-
berly glowing background for their intent, incredibly sad faces."

The renowned Russian master of acting asked Laurette countless questions as to how and why she did certain things on the
stage. They were things which, to Laurette "just seemed to
come along at rehearsals" and she was at a loss to answer him, but
under his intensive questioning decided she must have a method
and began to expound it with enthusiasm. Hartley, who attended these sessions with a whiskey and soda firmly clutched in
one hand, listened with a mounting look of impish glee.

"You're talking a little through your hat, you know," he told her after one such evening.

"What do you mean 'through my hat'?"

"Because, darling, you have no system, no method—thank God!"

"I have technique," Laurette answered indignantly. "Everybody says a successful actress must be crawling with technique."

"It's a blessing yours doesn't show," Hartley replied.

Laurette was noncommittal. If the greatest living Russian in the theatre thought she had a method, she was going to find what it was, and if she couldn't, she'd invent one.

Then one night Stanislavsky dropped a bombshell. He asked her to play with him and his company. It was the only time Laurette asked Barroy twice what Stanislavsky had said. His proposal was that they do "La Locandiera" by Carlo Goldoni. Laurette would play in English, the others in Russian. The performance would be at the Metropolitan Opera House for a combined Russian-American benefit. Laurette stuttered with excitement when she accepted, and Barroy stuttered hysterically in the translation.

Rehearsals began in absolute secrecy. Every afternoon from two until five the big drawing room was closed to visitors and family. Even Hartley was excluded; Stanislavsky wished to have Laurette completely under his direction. Hartley quite understood.

Laurette discovered that Stanislavsky was absolute master at rehearsals. There was "no laughing, no temporizing; just obeying." Personal ideas on how a part should be played, individual problems, were discussed privately with him by the different members of the company outside of rehearsals. Laurette, used to romping a bit, tried a few amusing remarks which were dutifully passed on by Barroy but met only with toneless "Da's." So she decided to settle down and become as earnest as the rest of them.

The first time she encountered the Stanislavsky method came in a scene where the Italian innkeeper lifts a string of pearls from a chest, holds them above her head, looks at them lovingly, slowly puts them back and closes the lid. Stanislavsky was not satisfied with this bit of business as Laurette did it. He knelt be-

fore the chest and counted: 1 to 4—lid of chest up; 4 to 12—
pearls aloft; 12 to 19—admiring them; 19 to 24 into the chest with
them; 24 to 26—lid closed.

Laurette could not get it right. That night she told Hartley
how unhappy she was. "If I counted, the beads looked like beads,
and the whole scene was spoiled for me. I could not admire them
for the long count of seven, and the quicker they went back in
the chest the better."

Hartley looked solemn. "Why not teach the Russians your
early Irish method?" he suggested.

Laurette was not amused, so he stopped his bantering.

"Do the pantomime of the pearls for me—without counting."

Laurette did.

"Do it again."

Laurette obliged. Each time, thanks to her "early Irish method,"
the beads were pearls.

"It's the same count, Laurie."

"What do you mean?"

"Exactly the same count. You made each move in a fraction
less or a fraction more, but the entire pantomime ended on the
exact count of twenty-six. Do it that way tomorrow."

Laurette did, and Stanislavsky was delighted.

A week had passed when the Russian master came to the house
one evening in a somber mood. He drank endless cups of tea and
began to talk to Barroy in a level continuous voice, staring at his
big sensitive hands folded on the table before him. Laurette knew
something was wrong. It seemed an eternity before Barroy turned
to translate. The management of the Moscow Art Players had
been told of the rehearsals and was strongly opposed to the idea
of Laurette performing with them. It would be terrific kudos for
any actress, and there were several American stars under the same
management who would profit greatly by such advertisement.
Why not keep it in the family?

Stanislavsky had flatly refused to play with anyone but Laurette so the benefit performance was canceled.

Before Stanislavsky left for Moscow he brought a photograph
of himself to Laurette, and as she watched scratched a message

in Russian over almost the entire picture. On the back, while the faithful Michel Barroy translated, Laurette wrote:

> To the admirable, genuine artiste, the supreme Laurette Taylor: I have seldom met actresses who would love art itself more than *themselves in art* . . . You are a happy exception. On the stage the artist in you triumphs over the woman. That is why you can live today with the feelings of a child and tomorrow with the life of a grandmother. . . . You have the most important qualities of a real artiste. That is why you have conquered your delighted, new and immutable admirer
>
> C. Stanislavsky

Concerning these words, Laurette wrote to Ashton Stevens: "I hope it's true. I know the grandmother-child part is. One day I have a long lavender beard and the next I'm so young I haven't cut my teeth or grown my hair. And the reason I love Stanislavsky for writing that is rather *double*—not only is he a fine artist but his is the spirit that kept the Moscow Art Theatre on its knees to art for twenty-five years. And when you meet talent and character, it just does not seem possible. Because (in so many) character makes talent less pliable—and talent makes character too pliable."

\*

# *Hollywood 1924*

The theatre continued on its exciting way through the mid-'twenties. Eleonora Duse made her farewell appearance in "Lady from the Sea" and "Ghosts." Max Reinhardt brought his stupendous production of "The Miracle" to the Century Theatre. "Charlot's Revue" from London introduced the captivating personalities of Beatrice Lillie, Gertrude Lawrence and Jack Buchanan to America. American dramatists brought forth such plays

as "What Price Glory," "They Knew What They Wanted." The
Theatre Guild, prosperous at last, produced "Saint Joan," "Peer
Gynt," "The Guardsman" with consummate skill. To anyone
who loved the theatre these years were meat and drink and a
glorious challenge. Laurette was absorbing it all, and her home
was the center where these scintillating personalities from London, Moscow and America's indigenous crop could meet and
mingle with their peers. But she herself remained for a large part
of the time inactive. And Hartley was not writing.

Their project was still their own theatre, and to achieve this
they had contracted to make two more films for Metro-Goldwyn-
Mayer. "Happiness" was produced in the autumn of '23, somewhat hastily, with no one greatly interested. King Vidor had
again directed, but there had not been the same fun as with
"Peg." King had fallen in love with Eleanor Boardman and Laurette could never quite forgive one of her "crushes" for falling in
love with somebody else.

Hartley and Laurette had scarcely returned when they were
off again in the spring of 1924. The filming of "One Night in
Rome" continued to be just "the damn dull business of making
money." Metro-Goldwyn-Mayer had become big business. The
old delightful informality, the personal touch so important to
Laurette had been largely eradicated.

"A new lot are in charge," she wrote home, "and they began
by telling us how sorry they were to hear we were hard to get
along with."

Laurette was shuttled through the glamour mill: make-up, hair,
clothes, tests. She loathed everything that was done to her. "They
sent a hairdresser to marcel me, and a man to turn my pug nose
into a Prince Rospigliosi. We have been all week doing that. I
look like a lot of other picture actresses, but between you and me
and the family code I won't when we start focusing."

But even the Irish fight went out of Laurette between the
grinding millstones of big business and picture-making. "One
Night in Rome" was the most indifferent piece of acting she ever
did. This fact seemed to fascinate Laurette as much as her usual
excellence. Upon her return home she ran "Rome" almost as often
as she had "Peg"—just for the laughs. One scene in particular,

played at the top of a grand staircase, Laurette awaited with the liveliest anticipation. She had been utterly miserable over her appearance. Her evening gown had a deep décolletage, her hair was tightly marcelled. During the entire course of the scene, employing every possible device, she managed to keep a large ostrich feather fan between most of herself and the camera. She would snap it open to cover a bare arm, spread it across her breast when facing the camera, bring it coyly up to her face on close-ups so that only her eyes showed. Finally when it came time to descend the staircase the fan came first, Laurette lurking behind like a hunter stalking a deer.

Watching this exhibition in the dark of her living room, Laurette would rock with laughter and call out, "My God! I never saw a fan do so much acting!" or hurl insulting advice at her shadowy image, " 'Ere now, my gal, not so busy with the fan! 'Ow abaht a bit of h'acting?" But if her friends laughed with quite the same heartiness she would be cross, and say, "I'm not going to show this picture if you laugh. It's all right for me to laugh, but you can't."

However, the reviewers found her acting "exquisite in its tenderness, command, sympathetic intelligence, and quiet naturalness of expression." One reviewer noted "whilst everybody else has to rely largely on titles, she needs practically none . . . (she is) one of the extremely few actresses who really do understand the difference between stage and cinema, and have learnt their art anew."

Although the actual business of picture-making was dull, the atmosphere of Hollywood still captivated Laurette. In its climate of extremes she was oddly at home. There was a full cup of everything in Hollywood—success, love, luxury, indulgence and adulation; everyone seemed to dance to the piper's tune without ever having to pay him. Basically it was Laurette's creed that, if life was to be lived at all, it should be lived that way, fully, at a high pitch of excitement, and with no fear of consequences. But when she had rushed forth to importune life for just such excitement she had been rebuffed and disillusioned so many times that it had become her habit to find in the world of her fancy the fulfillment otherwise denied. In a subtly abrasive way Hollywood acted upon much that was undischarged in Laurette's nature. The wild, untamed Loretta Cooney, so often beaten down by her father's whip, revolted by the harsh passion of Charlie Taylor, and now locked in the golden cage of Hartley's care, was still very much alive. The many inchoate emotional drives, long suppressed, were at times dangerously close to the surface.

After her work at the studio, Laurette played harder than ever. Many of the old group gathered at her bungalow on the grounds of the Beverly Hills Hotel and at Pickfair. Doug and Mary were away but had opened their place to Laurette and her friends. King Vidor came with Eleanor Boardman, now his bride—"pretty but dull"; the Morgan sisters, Thelma and Gloria; actors Charles and George Meredith; pretty Mary Haggarty of the department-store family; Geoffrey Kerr visiting on the Coast, and several others. New recruits were John Gilbert, just beginning his meteoric rise in films, and his wife, Leatrice Joy. Laurette called this assemblage the Magic Circle.

The strenuous hours of tennis and swimming were resumed, the long evenings of dancing, good talk and games. Gilbert's magnetic personality and inexhaustible vitality added zest to a group that was scarcely in need of it. For the first time Laurette found somebody who could play as hard as she could. These two produced an immediate kinetic impact which accelerated the pace of the whole group and carried it along at a new sustained velocity from day to day.

Elinor Glynn, searching for the ideal Glynn hero, had discovered Gilbert, then a bit player on the Fox lot. His first successes were in the picturized versions of the famous Glynn love stories, "His Hour" and "Three Weeks." Then followed "The Count of Monte Cristo." He had yet to do "The Merry Widow," "The Big Parade" and "Flesh and the Devil," which would make him the idol of millions. Also to come were the series of romantic adventures which would link his name with some of the most glamorous women of his time. He was only twenty-seven when he met Laurette, his marriage to Leatrice Joy was breaking up, and his potential tragedy was already evident to the observant; he expected a great deal too much of life.

The role of movie hero fitted Gilbert only partly. To cut him to size a great deal of quivering flesh had to be lopped off. It is the peculiarly poisonous touch of Hollywood that very often, in the unique processes of molding a star, much that is vital is destroyed while much that is synthetic is peddled as vital.

It could be said of Gilbert what Ralph Block had said of Laurette, that there burned in him "some fever that is entirely a possession of the human spirit, some impetuosity . . . some recklessness . . ." But whereas Block was speaking of Laurette in the theatre, this quality permeated almost every moment and action of Gilbert's stormy and tragically short life. Unlike Laurette he was not afraid of life. Whereas she hoarded every sensation and emotion for the theatre, or at least some dramatic projection which simulated the conditions of theatre, Gilbert lived them wildly, improvidently, recklessly. He was utterly fearless and forthright, abhorrent of sham, enormously quick in sensitive perception and incurably romantic. These qualities he wore like the improvised armor of a Don Quixote and rode forth with his wide adventurer's smile to fight hopeless battles in the thick of life. And there was in him, unmistakably, that incandescence of spirit that will always illumine the romantic idealists, the Don Quixotes of the world.

If Laurette had tried to pick up and fit together the torn pieces of every girlhood dream she had projected into life, she would have constructed an image closely resembling that of John Gilbert. He was the boy down the block to whom she had sent her picture—but this time he didn't send it back; he was the one to whom she had penned crudely printed "Black Hand" notes warning him to notice her—and this time he did; he was all the little boys who had stood entranced by the adorable femininity of the short-lived character "Laurice," the little French girl, so many years ago. He could match the hoyden, the rowdy, the tomboy, and still encompass with the wild ardor of his soul the most timid and abused dream her heart had ever held.

None of this was said, but it was lived day after day: on the tennis courts with Gilbert playing his wild slashing game and Laurette laughing at his intensity; at the Pickfair pool, sparkling like an emerald in the sun, Jack diving "in the manner of John Barrymore," raising The Profile to the sky, quivering his nostrils and lunging with a snarl into the water like Hamlet after the King's conscience; next, Laurette, running the length of the diving board "in the manner of Mary Pickford," tossing imaginary curls, every inch America's sweetheart dashing through the perils of a two-reeler—and at the last minute cautiously wetting one toe. Visiting back and forth on the sets at M-G-M, laughing and whispering, utterly oblivious of others, Laurette in her glamorous robes of L'Enigme and Jack in the bright satins of a circus rider for "He Who Gets Slapped," then supper, then games, then music. When the hardiest souls of the Magic Circle were ready to quit, Gilbert was just beginning. By one trick or other he would start them off again—soft Hawaiian voices chanting behind the hibiscus bushes of the patio, a stringed orchestra slipping up through the dark filling the air with music. . . . Another drink . . . another tune . . .

Each night had the quality of a dream, but instead of fading beyond recall, each night the dream repeated itself and seemed to gain solid rights thereby: the music, the velvet touch of the night air, the voices coming through the dark, laughing, singing; a face caught and held in the soft light of a candle—and gone; the fun . . . the closeness . . . the warm wild spirit of Gilbert magnifying everything, bringing to life a bravura which it seemed suddenly to demand, a color, a pulse and a sense of a thousand unnamed promises . . .

Hartley was always there, but he had grown silent and ruminative, holding himself a little apart from the swift kaleidoscopic company. An occasional sarcasm on Hollywood and its ways, thin and bloodless, fell on deaf ears. He remained meticulously polite and mellowly drunk through the long hours. Life was pressing him too hard for answers he could not give. Always there had been order, always there would be. In the midst of the revelry his eyes, deep deep brown and shadowed with melancholy, would rest on Laurie across the dark of the patio, and it was as though he guarded with that gaze the jewel-like sweetness he had always found in her, and would not look at ghosts or listen to autumnal voices crying in his soul. . . .

Laurette fell in love with John Gilbert. For the first time she felt the boundaries of the world Hartley had so lovingly created as imprisoning rather than protective. Everything she had been afraid of in herself, and had thrust outside those boundaries as harsh and destructive, suddenly wore a new and subtle guise. The reckless, soaring quality of Gilbert's spirit caught up her own and promised not disaster but freedom. For the first time Loretta Cooney felt that she might be in a favorable trading position with life: a dream for a dream.

There were tunes that summer—"Memory Lane," "None But the Lonely Heart"—favorites of Gilbert that the Hawaiians played many times in between their languorous native music and songs. They were to weave into Laurette's heart forever, beyond sentimentality, beyond unfulfilled love; they became requiems in disaster, and associated inextricably with the hurt she gave to one who loved her more than life itself, as she struggled under the bonds that held her passionate nature in a final abeyance.

The last night in Hollywood went by without sleep. It unwound in music and laughter and drinking; dawn and daylight came, a harsh light breaking the final threads of the night's enchantment; the Magic Circle was dissolving. If any of the guests watched as Laurette and Gilbert said good-by, it did not matter. They stood in a burst of glory of their own making and looked not one step further, guileless and cruel as children and as self-absorbed. If Hartley watched, he must have felt close to mayhem at the sight of those two moonstruck pantaloons so ready to destroy what he had so carefully and lovingly built. . . .

The woman gazing out the drawing room window of the eastbound train was not the one who had left Hollywood two years before with a sentimental sigh—Peg, wanting one more waltz in the moonlight, begging to "steal a few hours from the night, dear heart." This face opposite Hartley was withdrawn, almost sullen. He could not speak of what was between them. He had never given words to the raw and inchoate in the human soul. He believed that words were indelible and once spoken their effect could never be erased from the mind or heart; he also believed that what was left unspoken time could take and change and bury, as though it had never been. He held onto these beliefs, desperately now, as husband and wife sat opposite each other day after day on the long journey home and uttered not one word.

About ten P.M. that first night after Laurette had left, Geoffrey Kerr wandered up to Gilbert's hilltop home to find two places still laid for dinner and a distraught Gilbert pacing the floor. Where the hell had Geoff been? He had assumed they would mourn together in a world that no longer held Laurette. After an evening during which Gilbert tried to show Geoff Hollywood Wild Life and failed completely, they ended up at two o'clock in the morning on a roller coaster in Venice which the operator had been persuaded to open up for their exclusive benefit.

"Whether Jack had made some special arrangement with the man, I don't know," recalled Geoffrey, "but it certainly went faster than any roller coaster I was ever on before or since. The outward centrifugal force against the flimsy-looking wooden structure was terrifying. I can see Jack's face now, and hear him grimly repeating every few seconds, 'I hope the goddam thing breaks!' He meant it too."

Wounds healed superficially at least during the long summer months on Long Island. Family routines re-established themselves. Hartley played golf with monotonous regularity—and was as regularly late to lunch. Discussion of why he had not made the fourth hole in three and had missed the putt on the ninth could ripple along and fill the whole of the lunch hour quite amicably. Laurette kept herself busy longing for the food she could not eat; played tennis with Percy Hammond, Grantland Rice, Olga and Sydney Fish; plunged into the ocean; walked in her rubber suit. Michael grew perceptibly older, but late in August hurled a last litter of puppies in the face of advancing time. There was a healing quality in the broad levels of sand and water, the chain of the dunes that lifted along the shore and caught the last rays of the setting sun in ragged irregular cups; the white swans parading on inland ponds; the honeysuckle on post and rail giving out its fragrance. Boundaries smudged and half erased were drawn again under the gentle pressure of the familiar and the well-loved.

That winter, in New York, the games, the supper gatherings, the Sunday teas went on as usual. At times arguments became a little more acrid, and Laurette's undisciplined tongue cut more sharply; her laugh was readier and louder but enjoyment did not always reach to her eyes. Occasionally she did something she had never done before; after the guests had gone she would swing through the pantry door, have another drink, perhaps two. It wasn't that she was drinking more but that she was drinking differently; whereas before it had been an adjunct to fun, now it was a barricade against something in herself that was not fun. There was a tension that grew, and at times freedom from this tension was suborned by alcohol.

The single-minded drive of her ambition had spared Laurette many decisions that less gifted people must make every day of their lives. Many uncertainties about herself and others had been swallowed up by the enormous certainty of her talents and where those talents would carry her. But with the failure of "Humoresque," even the theatre had proved no sure haven. She discovered there were limitations to achievement there, at least in terms of her own satisfaction, and with the knowledge of these limitations came an uncomfortable sense of vulnerability. Fearfully she had looked around in a wider arc at her life. The blinders had begun to slip then, and now, after meeting Gilbert, they slipped even further. Emotional forces which she had thrust aside, or coveted only as material for her work, battered close to the portals of her heart. The dread realities pressed her round. She gave the back of her hand to these realities; she pushed them away with a brusqueness which in time became an unmerciful cruelty. What tenderness she had, already buried deep, was now sewed round with the dragon's teeth of sharp wit and remorseless laughter. Touch Laurette too closely and you found a harsh, cruel woman. The children, once claimed with fierce animal devotion, were now deliberately encouraged in an arrant individualism, a smart sophistication, which rode roughshod over simple family ties and family affection. She could "adore" talent, cleverness, good looks, the weird and the unexpected, but woe betide the one who came to the gates of her heart without such coin, asking only for love.

Years later—the years of her obscurity and poverty—when the blinders were completely fallen from her eyes and she at last looked at everything directly no matter how much it hurt, she wrote of such a woman as she had been, in a play called "Pin a

Rose." The woman had been so hurt in her marriage that she deliberately weaned her two children away from warmth of feeling and family relationships. She explains to the family doctor: "I'm modern. Modern children should have a modern mother. It saves a lot of heartbreak on both sides."

THE DOCTOR: What makes a modern family?
DOROTHY:    No deep roots allowed to grow between them. Every member of this family can pull away from the other without injury to heart, mind, or soul. We have a sort of gentleman's agreement: "Don't expect anything from me and I'll expect nothing from you."

And again in a later scene when the mother tries to explain her daughter's hard-boiled sophistication and apparent lack of feeling to the girl's fiancé, described as "a simple affectionate fellow," she says:

            You see, I brought her up to be an individualist.
BILL:       It looks like a mistake.
MOTHER:     I don't think so. An individualist is not wrought up by the wear and tear of other people's lives. They only have to bear their own.

Laurette, the primitive, was a long way from home when she felt like that.

A change came over Hartley, too. He put away pen and pencils and occupied himself almost exclusively with matters of high finance. In the mid-'twenties there was a new and exciting way of making money. The lush fields of Wall Street were beckoning to professional and amateur alike, and Hartley, in whom the gambling streak had always been strong, began along with millions of others to "play the stock market." He took a considerable part of the "nucleus" which had been earned by the making of three pictures and, without consulting Laurette, for she was not interested in such matters, began buying stocks on margin.

Quickly he became absorbed in this new occupation. He trotted around with such financial giants as Eugene Meyer, Bernard Baruch, Charles Schwab, and many a lesser soothsayer. There was talk of pools and quick profits and buying on margin, and his blood began to course with a new exhilaration. It was better than prize fights which Hartley attended with never less than several thousand dollars staked on the outcome, better than doubling and redoubling at bridge for high stakes. The fever consumed him, quenching other fevers in his blood. Against the advice of Meyer and other friends, he bought large blocks of South American securities. Everything was trumps—for a while.

Supposedly he was writing a play. Laurette would ask him about it. She would wander into his study from time to time, but there would be no sign of a playscript in work on his table; instead there were red and black account books, enormous ledgers, sheet after sheet of paper filled with neat hieroglyphics of numbers and percentages; Hartley's stoatlike secretary in the higher reaches of the house was busily adding up dividends instead of pasting up scrapbooks. Laurette would sit for a while in one of the battered leather chairs and listen to an account of a "killing," a new pool, a new stock coming into the market, and after a bit she would rise and walk away. And Hartley would listen to her steps receding down the hall, over the thick rug of the dining room, and the sound of the pantry door swinging behind her. For minutes after that he would stare at the figures before him without moving, and wonder deep in his heart if they would hold the torrent that was threatening his life.

# *Pierrot the Prodigal*

"What hast thou done with Thy youth?"
*Verlaine*

After two years' absence from the theatre Laurette took a fling at what is perhaps the most difficult of the arts, pantomime, portraying the hapless Pierrot in the time honored "L'Enfant Pro-

digue" at special matinees. In explanation of her choice she said,
"I do not like champions who will not 'champ.' Of course you
do not take on a fellow twice your size, but you might risk a
few pounds! Lady Macbeth is my idea of something I could not
do. Pierrot is my idea of something I might do. And, the populace, now, deserve no less than the Romans. Their thumbs should
have a chance to turn downward."

Alexander Woollcott was so stirred by the beauty and greatness of her Pierrot, so chagrined at the briefness of the venture,
that he burst into a rhapsody over the one and a tantrum over the
other:

We are witnessing in New York just now one of the odd and
exasperating phenomena of the American theater—namely, that
one whom many regard as its best actress, after playing not at all
for two seasons, is now playing for only two matinees a week. Yet
there never was any more reason for the existence of the *Theatre
Sarah Bernhardt* in Paris than there is today for the existence of a
Laurette Taylor Theater in New York.

The discussion as to who is the best actress on the American
stage, always a pleasant occupation for an idle April afternoon,
would doubtless bring up not only the name of Miss Taylor, but
the names as well of Mrs. Fiske, Ethel Barrymore, Emily Stevens
and Pauline Lord. The implicit question is too large, of course. Narrow it and you will find the answer comes more easily. Suppose, let
us say, that you were warned that all the theaters in the land save
one were to be destroyed in one magnificent gesture . . . and that
for the permanent company to occupy that theater during the next
five seasons it were left to you to name the members. Whom would
you name? Well, right off hand, neither do I. But I know the first
name I would choose. It would be Laurette Taylor. A year ago,
two years ago, my choice would have been the same. And I was
never surer of it than when I came away the other afternoon after
watching her performance as the white, moonstruck *Pierrot*. . . .

If Miss Taylor is not the foremost actress of our theater it is
for reasons akin to those which keep John Barrymore from being
generally considered its foremost actor. . . . I am referring to the
fact that his own deep-rooted and curiously sheepish aversion to
the actor's profession, reinforced, as it happens, by the release from
the necessity of acting which the movies give him, have kept his
appearance so fugitive and intermittent in recent years that he is
almost a negligible figure in the panorama of our stage.

And for a hundred complicating reasons Laurette Taylor, too, has assumed a role on our stage which is no measure of the genius she indisputably possesses. To begin with, she has followed neither of the courses which might foster such assumption. She has neither carried her great talent across America as Mrs. Fiske is doing right now in the wig and furbelows of Mrs. Malaprop. Nor has she built herself a stage in New York and by the beauty and vitality of the work she could do upon such a stage summoned America to her door.

. . . Miss Taylor's every feeling about the theater bids her stay in one place—preferably New York. In the troubled trouping of her own young days there must have been born in her a feeling that if ever the gates of New York swung wide to welcome her she would never leave it again. Since then London has been hers for the asking, and it requires no especial shrewdness to suspect that in the back of her mind this minute is a secret ambition to play Pierrot for the people of Paris. But these will be excursions, celebrations. If she is to work out a program commensurate with her remarkable talent and her uncanny skill, it will be worked out in New York in some theater which some one has endowed or she herself has built.

. . . I see no escape from this dilemma except for Miss Taylor to take over a theater in our town, which should be as definitely hers and, in intention at least, as permanent as the Comédie Française or the Metropolitan Opera.*

This article which was reprinted widely must have struck home to Hartley and Laurette. Woollcott was echoing only what had been their most cherished dream. The time was ripe and overripe for its attainment. But nothing was happening. When it came to discussions of this, their mutual goal, there had grown a constraint between them, a reserve which made mention of it painful and unprofitable, as though the dream could not flourish on the arid ground of their spirits' separateness. The long corridor between their rooms—his austere one with the regimented clothes and bottles, and her lacy disordered one of lavenders and purples, and white fur rugs—was not traversed as informally as before. When Hartley came to her room, usually after late breakfast in his room, it would be to discuss tentatively, almost apologetically, some plan for joining a pool, a tip on the day's market, or a suggestion that she might like to invest some of her own money.

* *The New York Sun*, April 6, 1925.

Laurette's arching brows would arch a trifle higher, the eyes become almost cold with deadly disinterest. She didn't know anything about stocks, she said; stocks were another world. She was
just an actress. Money was a bore if you always had to be thinking about it. She preferred the advice of one of his financial-
wizard friends who told her, "If you want to get rich, put your
money in every savings bank in the country." Once Hartley
suggested R. H. Macy's as an excellent investment. "That stock
can't possibly be any good," she told him with sudden heat. "I
go into Macy's basement and never can find anybody to wait on
me!" That is better than the cold eye. That's his old Laurie. . . .
Hartley smiles, waves his cigarette in airy dismissal of the subject, holds her face a moment longer with his gaze, then paddles
off down the corridor in his soft slippers. He won't bother her
any more, he decides; she hates talk of finances of any kind, always
has; he'll roll up the nucleus until he has a nice safe margin of
profit, then he'll hand her the Laurette Taylor Theatre lock, stock
and barrel to do with as she wishes. He hums a little song as he
goes. Everything will be all right. . . .

Laurette had been her old self as soon as she started rehearsals
of "Pierrot"—a bit more than her old self, for there was a new
translucence, a new lyrical quality to her work. Pencil-slim for
the skin-tight suits of the part, she became completely absorbed
in mastering the pantomimic art under director Otokar Bartik,
ballet master of the Metropolitan Opera. Whatever handicap she
felt in losing her voice was forgotten under the spell of pianist
George Copeland's playing of the hauntingly lovely Wormser
score. Her Pierrot moved like thistledown after his light o'love,
Phrynette, chased broken pieces of dreams down the long road
of a wasted youth, begged for reprieve in a world already lost.

"It was like flying," Laurette recalled. "It was the most exciting time I ever had in the theatre."

Was Hartley jealous of Pierrot? Perhaps a little. Somehow
Laurette had winged upward and over the many strictures and
prohibitions which as a result of his training now almost ran in
her blood; not defying them but surmounting them in a burst of
poetic expression which removed her perilously far from his or-

bit. He could not take exception to the lyrical flight, yet he might well wonder what chords and harmonies had been touched in Pierrot's interpreter of which he was not, in literary fact as well as sober truth, the creator.

After the matinees she played a condensed version of the panto-mime with great success at the Palace Theatre. The management, concerned lest the customers feel cheated in not hearing Laurette's famous voice, and also lest the material prove too highbrow, asked her to tell the story before each performance. "I am in a dumb act, but I have no dogs," was her opening remark, and to the audience's delight she proceeded to tell the story in strictly vaude-ville terms. "Her victory was complete," reported *The Morning Telegraph*, "without deviating from lofty standards, she lifted herself into the lightness of the atmosphere of vaudeville."

With "Trelawney of the Wells," which she did in June, Lau-rette's mood changed. The banting and rigid discipline she had imposed for "Pierrot" were thrown to the winds. She indulged an enormous appetite, grew lax about her figure, failed to learn her lines, stayed away from rehearsals on the flimsiest excuses. After the dress rehearsal Hartley was forced to speak some harsh truths.

"You don't like your fellow actors, do you?"

"What!" Laurette shouted, then grudgingly admitted, "Well, I don't like some of them."

"But Laurie, the essence and beauty of Rose Trelawney's char-acter is her love of the other actors at the Wells."

"It doesn't show that I don't love them," Laurette persisted.

"It does, darling," Hartley answered firmly.

On that particular opening night the audience was as star-studded as the cast. A nervous Hartley, Dwight and Marguerite, sat in the fourth row on the aisle. Would they for once see Laurette do something less than magnificent? They had left her gloomy, uncertain, cross. As the time drew near for her entrance they scarcely breathed. Then she was in the doorway, poised there for just a moment, in short claret velvet coat, plumed hat, hands nestled demurely in tiny muff. Fluid oneness of actress and part was unmistakable; there was Rose, loving, breathless, mod-est. The family relaxed. Afterwards, Laurette told them with shining face, "I stood in the doorway and I *was* Rose for the first time, and I knew I'd be all right."

Wrote Stark Young: "The part of Rose Trelawney seemed to have been waiting these many years for Miss Taylor, so great was her pathetic and shy nuance, so subtle her transitions. . . . Her extraordinary talent ran quietly and completely throughout the portrayal . . . what a voice, what a dramatic mask, and what shy precision she has."

The triumph of the evening was hers, shared with old John Drew who was given a standing ovation at the end of the play. Laurette adored John, and she must have managed to love the other actors too, for one critic singled out Rose's tender lines of farewell to her fellow troupers of the "Wells" for this praise: "We have never heard them read as they were last night. Never before have we thrilled as we did at the depth of the words so fraught with love and humanity. . . ."

After the limited engagement of "Trelawney," the family moved to Easthampton, but once there summer routines of diet and exercise were only halfheartedly pursued. Laurette was in the mood to see people. She was on a search for answers. As she functioned less and less in the theatre, her curiosity about people sharpened. They were no longer so much material for her work as material for a haphazard and somewhat affrighted self-study. Gilbert and her feelings for him had stirred up a need to know herself, as once long ago on the little porch at Lake Wonksonk-monk she had felt that need, waiting for Hartley to declare his love. Her basic self was the role in which she was least at home, and haunted by this she darted here and there on myriad explorations, seeking the key to the feelings and emotions of others as a possible answer to her own. But these explorations ended in defeat. She was too honest to pretend to have found what she had not, or take on a role she could not understand. Unlike the theatre where she functioned on an unobstructed plane of full understanding, in life she was boxed time and time again. She gave the impression of one seeking a goal which remained entirely elusive. From a "peak in Darien" she spied from afar with wild cries of joy, but remained the hapless traveler with neither compass nor map for the streams and valleys and unmarked stretches in between. In the simplest aspects of life and relationships lodged her greatest uncertainties.

Her searches at times had all the subtleness of a house detective making his rounds. She was suspicious of all closed doors, evasive answers or determined reticences. She had the primitive's dark distrust of the analytical mind. When she asked a question, she wanted an immediate and uncomplicated answer; to analyze was to hide, to hesitate was to evade. To a married couple obviously ill-matched, she would burst out, "What keeps you two together?" and would expect an answer. Or to a couple overly affectionate in public, "Haven't you got a bed at home?" Everything had to be clear-cut, in place, brought to a conclusion, or it was evasive, dishonest. "I am not a complicated person," she would say, "and I can't live in a complicated way." Almost frantically at times she seemed to line up bits and pieces of other people's emotions and reactions, twisting and turning them to fit them into a pattern that would make sense to her. But they did not make sense, and where she might have found the answers, she dared not look.

In August, 1925, "The Merry Widow" was released in New York theatres, one of the top money-makers of all time. John Gilbert and Mae Murray whirled and twirled to "The Merry Widow" waltz and a whole new set of pulses went out to the lovers of the world from those two dancing shadows.

Laurette watched from a darkened theatre, moonfaced, out of condition from weeks of idling. Afterward there was a telephone call between Hollywood and Riverside Drive. There was nothing clandestine about it, for Marguerite must sit at her mother's side. Laurette and Gilbert prattled on like children, lost children perhaps, but happy children in a world that needed no rationalization. Then Laurette held out the receiver, "Say hello to Jack, Maggie," she begged. On the other end of the phone a high, yet curiously vibrant voice answered the girl's greeting, sought by utter sincerity to tear down whatever barriers there might be to understanding, developed an urgency that came from a sense of the foolishness, the hopelessness of the situation now that a third person had been introduced. Perhaps Laurette felt it too, for suddenly she was sad and troubled. As she and Gilbert said good-by their voices drifted off in wistful half-phrases. Some imponderable had already separated them even before the connection was broken. Laurette's shoulders went up in a hopeless shrug as she stared at her daughter. The lips were petulant. The eyes, large and questioning, were the eyes of a little girl who wanted all the presents under the Christmas tree to be hers, but superficially at least had learnt restraint. There was no need to speak. At times like this a strong empathy between mother and daughter made words unnecessary. Laurette was in love with Gilbert, and Gilbert was in love with her. In her never-never land this was right and as it should be. Only in that wretched world of reality that would never accept her importunities must it be labeled impossible. The dark angel of that world was for the moment Marguerite, but any other symbol would do. There was no resentment on that score. Only a hopelessness. And even a daughter could feel unutterably old, looking at those eyes that begged, always just on the threshold, for life to open its doors and be good to Loretta Cooney.

Back in Easthampton Laurette bants and walks and sweats, doing penance for the easy summer months. She will do "In a Garden" for Arthur Hopkins in November. The family stays late that year, and Hartley, who has frittered the summer away in golf and drinking, grows melancholy as the autumn presses around in the golden sighing sadness that comes to a seashore place. The houses close one by one, the beaches are deserted. An ambient light takes over, filling the emptiness, washing against the shuttered windows, over the lawns and down the quiet lanes. Those who stay are on a short pass to summer dreams. Winter is coming.

*

# In a Garden

Laurette was beginning to swing violently between moods. She gave way to indulgence, grew lax about looks and figure, then abruptly plunged into rigid routines of work, exercise and diet to burst upon her public like grub turned butterfly overnight. It was the same pendulum swing of her childhood, lost moody dreaming, broken by spurts of wild physical activity and sudden vast relish for life.

"In a Garden" was the first serious work of Philip Barry, rising young playwright from Professor Baker's Harvard Workshop, who already had two bright comedy successes to his credit. The part of Lissa Terry, a simple, direct person whose life has become tied up with complicated people, struck a warm chord of response in Laurette. Married to a playwright to whom life is a carefully contrived script in which there must be no "human confusions," Barry's Lissa soon wearies of his blueprinted plans. To the husband's many charted axioms, "Women are so and so," "Life is so and so," Lissa replies passionately, "They are *not!*" To test his theory that every woman in her heart is the mistress of the man who first awakened romance in her, he creates a replica of the moonlit garden in which Lissa spent a romantic hour with a young diplomat. There he arranges a second meeting between the two. The garden weaves its spell until Lissa discovers her husband's plot and, also, that the meeting long ago had been deliberately contrived by the lover. In disgust she leaves them both.

Hartley considered the play the output of a "callow talent."

Although Laurette disagreed, she did have difficulties with her new playwright. At rehearsals they might have been playing prototypes of Lissa and her playwriting husband. Barry was finicky and "literary" about his lines. He would stop Laurette again and again because she was not using the exact word he had written. "It spoils the rhythm you understand, if you use any but that particular adjective," he would call from the auditorium. And Laurette shading her eyes against the lights would glare down into the auditorium and insist that the exact word was totally unimportant. Finally she had him barred from the theatre when she rehearsed.

From then on rehearsals went smoothly. Arthur Hopkins was the ideal director for a good actor. He had little to say, reserving his keen critical faculties for the over-all characterization. The actor was left free to work out his own interpretation. Extremely sparing of praise, Hopkins' highest accolade was to say nothing. Laurette called him "the little man of long silences."

"At the opening in Washington I was terribly nervous," she recalled. "I played the first act in Yiddish, the second act in Irish and by the third act I was longing for the speechless Pierrot. I'd got my voice back, but I didn't know what to do with it. I think Mr. Hopkins was a very patient man to go on with the show."

If this were true—and Laurette indulged in self-criticisms which no one else would dream of—by the time they reached New York she was thoroughly at home in the play and in the part. Robert Edmond Jones' imaginative set by which the living room in the Terry home was transformed into the moonlit garden had a bewitching effect. Louis Calhern who played the lover brought back to trap Lissa, told how Laurette sat on the fake grass of the garden and named the ten things she liked best, then, with his urging, ten more; a lovely speech, strongly reminiscent of the lines by Rupert Brooke in "The Great Lover" which begin, "These I have loved: white plates and cups, clean-gleaming . . ."

"She was afraid she might not remember all twenty," Calhern reminisced, "and I would spread my fingers on the grass and tick them off as she named them. Once, for the devil of it, after she had finished, I said 'And ten more?' She threw her head back, gazed up at the fake moonlight, and went on with scarcely a break naming ten more simple, heart-warming things just as lovely as the ones she had already said. As soon as we came off she turned and gave me a furious slap on the cheek. 'Don't you ever play a trick on me like that again!' she said, and was truly, utterly furious. But the wonderful thing to me was that she was so completely at home in the play, the part, the set, with the man she loved sitting beside her, that it was perfectly simple for her to sustain that beautiful speech. This triumph meant nothing to her, however; she took it as a matter of course, and it in no way lessened her rage at my treachery."

The play was too contrived and high-flown in its language to please the popular taste. In the midst of a booming theatrical season it was a *succès d'estime* but of such short duration that, in spite of the illustrious names and fervent faith of director and star, it hardly left a mark in theatre history. In a rare demonstration of loyalty, however, the first-nighters returned en masse for the final performance. Laurette in a curtain speech thanked them for their devotion and, meaning to be kind to a young and obviously distinguished talent, said, "Perhaps our playwright isn't ready yet, perhaps we did a disservice to his brilliant talent by producing him too soon." Barry, seated in the third row, rose and stalked out. Hopkins met her in the wings, livid with anger. When Mr. Hopkins put on a play, he believed absolutely in its worth, its value to the American theatre; that was the *sine qua non* for producing it. "Never, *never* do I apologize for a play that I produce!" he told her. Laurette gave a little shrug. "*Cio che sera, sera,*" was her attitude. She was not going to break her heart over a play.

That is not to say she did not bring her full magic to Lissa. Hers was, as Woollcott described it, a portrait of "an earth woman, the composition of whose music is full of half-notes and accidentals, . . . who is so fashioned for just living that she could have made an Arcady in a flat under the El." When she looked up at her husband's counterfeit sky, and said, "I want a star—and a baby; and I can't have either," Laurette tore up everything contrived in and out of the script and made the theatre throb with a simple human desire. Her performance "renewed her right to be known in her own land and her own time as a great actress."

In his lectures at the 1947 Summer Theatre Session, Arthur Hopkins had this to say about Laurette:

Miss Taylor had many magic moments . . . but to the end her ways of attainment remained a mystery. She drove to desperation other stars who tried to discover her secret. She did nothing anyone else could make use of. Her gestures were scarcely gestures at all. Her readings were not seemingly aimed for effect. Yet, the effect kept mounting, never wavering, never over-reaching, but always mounting.

Of course, she could not be appraised in terms of acting, for she had progressed from actress to artist. In art, the technique disappears. She became a presence as Duse was a presence, as Booth was doubtless a presence. Presence cannot be imitated.

Her supreme gift was radiance. Even when that unforgetable face was old and ravaged, it could suddenly be illumined by beauty that is not of this earth. She was a star of celestial illumination.*

When John Gilbert came to New York in December for the opening of "The Big Parade," there were no obvious clues as to Laurette's feelings. He was a free man again, having been divorced barely a month after Laurette left Hollywood in 1924. There had been several telephone calls from the Coast, nothing more. Maybe it had all been a bad dream on Hartley's part. The two met again with explosive delight and began a round of dining, theatres, night clubs that was the despair of less hardy companions. Hartley often excused himself for a game of bridge at the Lotos Club or at the home of his old friend, Charlie Schwab. Laurette would call for him on her way home and he would listen politely to tales of the gay doings of the evening. Night clubbing was not his style, and the new decadence in much of the theatre fare he found offensive. Plays like "The Green Hat," "The Vortex," "Cradle Snatchers," all concerned subjects he considered extremely bad taste to discuss on either side of the footlights. "Run along, old thing," he would say to Laurette, "and pick me up whenever . . ." And it might be midnight or later that he would come trotting out through the portals of the Lotos or down the long gravel

---

* Arthur Hopkins, *Reference Point,* p. 93. Samuel French.

Hopkins also said, "Occasionally an actor broke the accepted mold, and at once something extraordinary happened.

"My first revelation was through the then inconspicuous Lionel Barrymore, who was playing a small part with John Drew in 'The Mummy and the Humming Bird' . . . It became something beyond pretense. . . . It happened again when Laurette Taylor was playing a secondary part in 'Alias Jimmy Valentine.' There was no analyzing the effect, or the way of its attainment, but obviously if hers was acting, then no one around her was acting."

drive of Schwab's Riverside Drive château in response to the cab-
man's ring, seemingly quite exhilarated by his evening of cards.
Laurette, ceaselessly fascinated by the enigma of his character,
would slip him a sideways glance and giggle and say, "Hartley,
you are a one!" And Hartley would reply, "What do you mean,
old dear?" And they would proceed home strangely amicable.

Texas Guinan, who greeted the customers with a euphoric
"Hello, Sucker!" was the rage that season as a night-club hostess.
Laurette, planning a party at the 300 Club, was surprised to have
Hartley voluntarily forego his game of bridge for the evening to
join the group. She explained rather elaborately that she was certain he would be bored if not downright offended by this particular smoke-filled den of vulgarity. But no, Hartley was quietly
insistent that he come along. As the group crossed the dance floor
Texas was standing in the center brightly spotlighted. Instead of
her customary greeting she let out a yell, grabbed Hartley's arm
and pulled him into the spotlight. "Hartley Manners! You old son
of a gun!" she trumpeted. "Where the hell have you been?"

Hartley smiled with shy pleasure, shook her hand decorously
and murmured, "Good evening, Texas. How are you?"

Then he proceeded on his way at a sprightly trot which he
sometimes assumed in moments of keen enjoyment.

Laurette could talk of little else all evening, but try as she
would, she could wangle no information from him as to where and
when he and Texas had known each other. All he would say was,
"Why, darling, I knew Texas when she could shoot the spot out
of an ace at twenty paces. Very good shot! Very good, indeed!"

But Laurette was a willful person, and she had had long training in going after what she wanted despite all opposition. There
came the day which Hartley hoped and prayed would never come;
the day she asked for a divorce. She and Jack had talked it over
and they wanted to marry. Jack's wildest romanticism was tied
to an ideal of a family hearth, and this was the only kind of
romanticism that the Cooney, Dorsey, Catholic Laurette could
accept. These two pantaloons had discovered they were family
people, so the logical end to their infatuation was marriage.

Hartley had had months to prepare himself. He did not have a writer's eye for nothing. He had watched the pantry door swinging after the parties were over; he had seen the eyes unlit by laughter; he had heard her as the wife, Lissa, cry out against the charted axioms, the neat literary concepts about life, passionately defending the "strange irregular rhythm of existence" such axioms deny. He had watched her as Pierrot, releasing the pure essence of a lover's heart. Although he never could imagine that he would hear the words now being said to him, he gave no indication as to how cruelly deep was the wound of those words. He asked no consideration of himself, nor did he berate her for a fool, as well he might have. What he said was said quietly and with finality. "No, Laurie, Peg O' My Heart cannot have a divorce. You must remember your position in the theatre and the love and respect in which you are held by the public. You cannot throw all this over for an infatuation, ruin everything you have fought so hard to achieve for the sake of a flashy movie actor."

That was all.

Had he castigated her, had he pleaded for his own happiness, she would have defied him; she was still the girl who could tie a pink bow on a whip raised against her, and she was still the woman who had buried the last trace of tenderness toward suffering when she buried her mother many years before. Hartley knew Laurette well. She relished her prestige. She lived and breathed in the theatre. He gave her her choice: to risk everything for a passionate intrigue—how forlornly little she knew of such a flowering!—or to maintain herself in the "life of her imagination" which had created for her such golden vistas of adventure and fulfillment, and had never betrayed or let her down.

. . . When she told Gilbert, it was in the voice of a little child who has had such a hard time over a lesson that no emotion is left for its recitation. Gilbert can't understand. He is terribly hurt —hurt as only a heedless, headstrong lover can be. A complete romantic, he would throw everything over for this love, but he senses in Laurette a reserve, a sudden calculation too canny for his warm blood. It is as though she said, "I am no fool," and by implication made him one. And so there is a blight on tender leaves, but the roots have already gone deep and displaced more fragile growths. There is a wreckage that must be accounted for. . . .

Gilbert has the better part of it, for he can fly to a new love and believe with all his romantic soul that this time there will be happiness. And this he does. In the tragically few short years that are left him, his name is linked with the most beautiful and glamorous women of his day. He marries and divorces, draws the scarlet thread of his romances through page after page of Hollywood history: Greta Garbo, Ina Claire, Virginia Bruce, Lupe Velez, Marlene Dietrich. There are those who felt he loved them all, and there are those who felt he loved only Laurette. But Laurette has made a choice; she has closed a door and left herself but one avenue of escape from the chaotic and unresolved world of her own emotions.

From now on when she reads about Gilbert in the papers— a series of escapades, a flight to Europe, a new amour; when she hears his voice on the phone, thin but vibrant, asking with such wistfulness how things go with her—is she happy? When his public laughs him derisively from the screen as he speaks his first lines in talking pictures, and his career tumbles in ruins around him; when gossip tells of his drinking and quick dissolution under failure, Laurette feels a piercing sorrow. Earthbound, she looks at the moon and wonders why she did not make the trip; she is Pierrot again, and in her Pierrot's white troubled face "is the mute eloquence of a thousand old unhappinesses." But she has made her choice.

Laurette's sense of sportsmanship in private life was not notable. She made the rules. If she found herself on the losing end, she thought nothing of charging that the rules had been switched, that someone was cheating. She was never wrong. In the theatre where she was infallible this presumption of rightness was wholly justifiable; and there her real infallibility made her generous.

But the scene with Hartley was not staged behind a proscenium arch. She was not generous about it. She felt vaguely that he had got hold of an extra trump somewhere that she hadn't known anything about, and she resented it. She let him feel her resentment. She packed up and announced she was going away; but before leaving she let him know that there was much that was not right between them. That his increasing preoccupation with the stock market did not please her, that they had not sat with a playscript between them for three years, that he had discussed no idea, no character, no outline of work in all that time, that she could not live in cubicles, moral, domestic or any other kind. And she ended by throwing one of his favorite quotations in his face, "There are more things in heaven and earth, Horatio, than are dreamt of in your philosophy . . ."

His "my dear child," the hurt creeping into his eyes—for he was not a man of iron—only made things worse. She locked her heart against him and she went away.

It was a winter of ten-foot snowdrifts in Boston when Laurette arrived for the first of several visits at the home of John Hays Hammond, Jr., son of the world-famed mining engineer and himself an inventor of such brilliance and virtuosity he has been compared to Thomas A. Edison. He had not yet built his fabulous Gloucester Castle where Laurette was to enjoy brief respites from the many days of despair that were to come, but was ensconced in its more modest forerunner, surrounded by the early Gothic, Byzantine and Tenth Century art treasures that he was collecting.

On first hearing of Hammond from Lester Donahue, Laurette had not been kindly disposed toward him at all. She had expected Lester to play the score for "Pierrot," but he was under contract to demonstrate the newly invented Hammond piano. Its completion and the "Pierrot" production happened to coincide.

"Who the hell is this man and his piano?" Laurette gracelessly demanded, and Lester by way of answer took her to the Algonquin to meet him. Under the inventor's potent charm Laurette's truculence soon vanished and they became great friends. His insatiable curiosity and enormous imagination, which seemed to be able to project the most fantastic dream into the future as solid fact— and in the course of his career did just that with hundreds of inventions—immediately created for Laurette that wider world she hungered for. Like Laurette he abhorred bores and filled his home with "glorified bums" who ran the gamut of creative activity from poetry and music to television and frozen foods.

Gloucester Castle—the fabulous structure with its hundred-by-sixty-foot Great Hall, medieval chapel, Roman swimming pool, and rooms filled with the art treasures of Europe—was to become Laurette's "room with a view" at some of the most crucial moments of her life. This first week end at Hammond's gave her a chance to breathe, to expand, freed momentarily from the sense of crushing reality which had been building since the scene with Hartley; a reality which threw open not the smallest window upon the future.

Fifty Riverside Drive seemed lifeless by comparison. Some thread had broken that had given meaning and unity to the life that was lived there. A sense of this, still largely undefined and not communicated from one member to another—how gloriously independent they had all been!—had sent Laurette's children off on paths and activities of their own. Marguerite had gone visiting in Chicago, suddenly sick of the long grind of work and in revolt against the musical career so carefully planned by Laurette. Dwight had taken a studio at Columbus Circle in the old Loew's Theatre building and spent hours at his drawing and painting. More and more frequently his nights were spent there, while his small study at home overlooking the Hudson drew dust.

Hartley was a man in a dream. He had one trump left to play. One morning during that long, snow-filled winter of 1926 he walked into Laurette's sitting room, where he was so seldom welcome now, and told her, "Laurie, I have been very fortunate in the stock market. I have made a lot of money, more than we will ever need. I can sell out, now, today, and we can do what we have always wanted to do, have our own theatre, play the plays we want to play—occasionally mine, if they please you, but also the best of the modern; Molière, Shakespeare. . . . There is nothing to stop us now. We are no longer in bondage, thank God, to the Shylocks of the commercial theatre."

What day this was that he made his speech, what haunted night Laurette had had, what regrets, what guilts had been eating her soul, it is impossible to say, but she turned on him with a ferocity he never forgot and with no glimmer of affection or understanding in her eyes blurted out, "I'm sick to death of this talk of money, money, money! I'm not interested in money. I married a playwright, not a stockbroker!"

In retrospect it was from that moment that Hartley dated the disintegration of the family and the life they had shared. Months later, when suffering, physical and mental, had broken down his vast inner reserve, he confided to Dwight and Marguerite, "Something died inside of me when Laurie said that. I didn't care any more, because she didn't. Everything we had planned for was dust. I walked out of the room. I never looked at a market quotation again. I never called my bank, I never called my broker. A year later many of my stocks were worthless. In time I was forced to arrange a loan at the bank to cover shrinking margins. It really didn't matter. Everything I cared about had gone long before that."

Perhaps Laurette could have made a more expansive world for herself, gone her own way, discarding the world Hartley had so lovingly created for her protection, leaving him to his own preoccupations. Marriages have existed on such a basis. She had resources far beyond his if she dared use them. But now her most positive moods were riddled with a sense of guilt. She had hurt Hartley and she knew it, and could not really forgive herself that. But she was too proud to say she was sorry, too stubborn to admit that the decision not to marry Gilbert, partly at least, had been her own. From now on everything she does is undermined by a sense of guilt. Her revolt against Hartley and the things he stands for is almost entirely negative. It has become a deeply ingrained habit with her to look upon everything that is not lit by the sun of his approbation as somehow wrong, "not done," destructive, to approach with suspicion anything that has not passed by the guard of his love. Many things within herself, now, do not pass this guard; she knows it full well, and she gazes at these things darkly and in secret, and in great trepidation of spirit. The burden of guilt builds and builds and finds no release. How welcome the hard stone floor of All Saints Church would be, the priest to hear her confession, bury it in the bosom of the Holy Ghost and not break faith with her! But it is not so easy for Loretta Cooney any more. And life in its inexorable fashion will press her down even further until she faces her own nature with honesty and resolves herself not alone as an artist but as a human being.

For Laurette was a great artist, and what she was to go through was to make her, by virtue of a hard struggle fought and won for her own soul, a great human being.

\*

# *Her Cardboard Lover*

The whole Gilbert episode, cataclysmic in her life in many ways, Laurette buried, put away somewhere in the vast storehouse of feeling to which only her acting furnished the key. This was not a determination on her part, a noble desire to spare Hartley further grief, or even the feeling of a need to dissemble; it was simply the closing over and sealing of a wound, a process as automatic and unconscious as breathing. For entirely different reasons, as different as their two natures, husband and wife behaved as though nothing had happened. No breath of scandal touched their lives. Those few who were cognizant of the Gilbert-Laurette affair had taken it lightly, as just another "crush." Only Gilbert, Hartley and Laurette knew to what depth it had gone.

That spring Laurette sat watching Elsie Janis and her mother pack their trunks for Paris. In the round brown eyes, the cherubic face—too cherubic because of many pounds of excess weight—the petulant look about the mouth, Elsie thought she detected signs of common everyday variety of marriage fatigue. Under questioning Laurette admitted she had been "scrapping" with Hartley and nothing seemed right.

"So why scrap, you wild Irishman?" Elsie asked. "What you need is a vacation from your family. Come along with Jenny and me to Paris. It will do you good."

Well, why not? Laurette thought. A play Gilbert Miller had

given her to read, "Dans Sa Candeur Naive," was running in Paris; if she needed an excuse that was it.

On hearing her spur-of-the-moment plan, Hartley developed pressing business of his own. There was a possibility of a production of "The National Anthem" in London. He'd hop over to see about it and perhaps they could meet for the return journey. Within a week of each other they sailed, and reporters noting the separate sailings wondered if a story was brewing.

As soon as Laurette was in Paris her spirits revived. She was fired with the ambition to bring "Pierrot" to the French so that she could speak to them in a common language. But then she saw "Dans Sa Candeur Naive" (Her Cardboard Lover) and forgot everything else. This was the play she would do in New York. As if by magic the excess weight began to melt away. She had Molyneux design the gowns, shimmering silks and satins for the ultra-sophisticated Parisienne, Simone Massoubre. In Paris this lady, *sans gêne*, who smokes, drinks, takes a lover, and runs around *en déshabillé*, seemed utterly possible—an entirely new step, new road for Peg O' My Heart. Her elation was contagious. Elsie gave a big party for her. In the midst of the celebration Hartley called from London. He had concluded his business, and would she consider returning on the same ship instead of separately as had been the original plan?

Laurette came back from the telephone with that dipping walk which signified only keen pleasure. She guessed she was a real "family guy" after all, she told Elsie. "Imagine, here in Paris, the city of free love," she chuckled, "and me so delighted to hear the voice of my legitimate spouse! Think of all the new things we're going to be able to tell each other, thank God, now that we have been separated for a while."

Full of plans and high spirits she boarded the *Mauretania* at Cherbourg, to join Hartley for the homeward trip.

Nothing was ever really right about "Her Cardboard Lover." Hartley was shocked by what he termed the tawdriness and vulgarity of the play Laurette had chosen. Under his aegis Laurette had never smoked, never kissed, never undressed, never sat on a bed, never been a mistress. The part of Simone Massoubre required all of these things and quite a bit more. He spoke of this with great gravity. He asked her not to do the play. He said she would break faith with a public who looked to her for clean, decent plays; that no matter how much she disliked it, millions had enshrined her as Peg and would never accept her in such a vulgar, licentious role.

She didn't see it that way at all. The part was a challenge, the very opposite pole from Peg, and that was where she wanted to go. Was she to be haunted for life by Peg? Imprisoned forever in one deadly role? "If I am only to be remembered as Peg, you can write on my tombstone, 'Here Lies a Disappointed Woman.' "

To call the play "a cheap bedroom farce" was ridiculous! "It is most subtle comedy, and Leslie [Howard] and I will play it like a couple of children."

When Hartley found she could not be dissuaded, he ceased his criticism, but Laurette knew how painful her decision was to him. Some of her positiveness slipped away under his disapproval, and some of her Paris slimness went with it. By the time rehearsals started at the end of August, the snug Molyneux gowns were a trifle snugger.

George Cukor directed "Her Cardboard Lover." Although still in his early twenties and at the outset of his career, he already possessed that unfailing sensitivity in handling temperamental stars which was later to gain him fame and fortune on the movie sets of Hollywood. He was keenly aware of the many handicaps visible and invisible which Laurette had to overcome to play Simone. "She had reached the age where undressing on the stage inevitably took artistic toll," he recalled. "She knew it perfectly well and she had to fight hard to overcome the knowledge. Besides this she was essentially a modest woman. Her strict training, Catholic upbringing—all this made it very difficult for her." To her artistic credit, she did achieve the lady. Recalling this achievement years later, Cukor's eyes lit with admiration.

"Rarely have I seen such a performance!" he said. "Simone was a passionate, foolish, neurotic woman and was realized by Laurette with extraordinary subtleness and absolute command. She was comic, distraught, light as a feather, and heartbreaking all at the same time."

The play opened on the road in October, 1926. Review headlines were what one might have expected: "Laurette's on the
Loose in a Comedy"—"Miss Taylor Cutting Up Didoes"—"Behaving Outrageously"; and the general consensus was summed up
by Robert Garland's comment in *The Baltimore Daily Post:*
"Watching her, Peg O' My Heart would die of shame." But he
goes on to say:

> Dying, she'd enjoy it. For, in "Her Cardboard Lover," Laurette is
> swift and fresh and charming. . . . Deftly, she outlines the char-
> acter of Simone. Surely, without fumbling, she walks up to Jacques
> Deval's weak-but-willing lady and deposits the spark of life within
> her. Honestly, disdaining hokus-pokus, she endows Simone with
> height and breadth and thickness.

The dominant feeling, however, was that Peg was miscast. One
thoughtful gentleman, who had followed Laurette's career since
"Seven Sisters," hitched his pince-nez high as he gazed at the
double bed in the second act and sighed, "In many ways, in many
ways this play is miscast. Miss Taylor should have something
rowdier!"

There are always those who, visiting a celebrity backstage,
will try to find just the right word to conceal their true feelings.
From every side came silken murmurs, "so sophisticated, dear Laurette" . . . "delightfully daring" . . . "dejeune" . . . "risqué."
John McCormack after seeing the play sat in brooding silence,
hands folded across his chest. Finally Laurette asked him point-
blank, "Well, John, tell me now, what did you think of me?"
John shifted his magnificent head to one side, stared dejectedly
at her for a long moment and sighed, "I don't like to see you in
dirty plays, Peg."

Laurette, of course, flew into the fight. This fight was her own.
"It's that Peg again. Will I never bury that girl? All my friends
are raising their eyebrows, 'Laurette, how can you!' But I say, why
not? If a writer finds the times changing, and the public demanding a type of thing he has never written, he would be rather silly
to sit back and say 'I won't write.' He must jump right in and
swim with the tide. And so must an actress. I like the part. I think
I like it better than any part I ever played."

She was bucking her friends, bucking Hartley, bucking the

critics, and while still on the road she began bucking the producers, Gilbert Miller and Al Woods. They were catching the general virus that Laurette and the part were somehow at loggerheads. They began to be rather pointedly obtuse about certain changes Laurette suggested in the script. Finally, after Washington, Baltimore and Atlantic City, the play was closed "for revisions." Rumor had it that they were searching for another actress.

While waiting for the supposed revisions, Laurette met one of the managers of the Keith-Albee circuit who remarked, "Haven't you a first-class sketch in which you can play our houses, Miss Taylor? Our managers are clamoring for you since 'Pierrot.' "

"Haven't I a sketch?" came back Laurette. "Of course I have a sketch. I'm going into rehearsal tomorrow morning."

"That's great!" said the delighted manager. "Can you give us a dress rehearsal next Thursday?"

Laurette rushed home to find Hartley taking a cat nap on a sofa. "Hartley, I want a sketch ready for nine o'clock tonight— a vaudeville sketch that will run twenty minutes. Two characters —I'll learn my lines tonight and we'll engage Richie Ling for the other part. Now don't say it can't be done because I have the idea already. There'll be just two characters, a man and a woman."

Hartley raised himself to a sitting position and as he brushed at the sift of cigarette ash shrouding his vest, Laurette outlined her plot. A few minutes later he was in his study and at eight forty-five that evening had completed the sketch which he called "The Comedienne." The dress rehearsal on Thursday went over with a bang, and Laurette was offered forty weeks consecutive bookings at one of the highest salaries ever paid a star. She notified the booking office, however, that two weeks would be the limit as she expected to reopen in the "Cardboard Lover." The sketch was booked straight into Chicago with an engagement at the Palace in New York to follow.

Teamwork between husband and wife was restored in this emergency. It was like old times to be on the road, perfecting a show together. Laurette wrote her children from Chicago:

> The sketch went over better than anyone anticipated. The notices were all good as the one enclosed . . . and we have been in the papers every day. Mrs. Fairbank (Mrs. Kellogg Fairbank),

Ashton Stevens, Freddie McLaughlin, etc.—Gosh! it has been nice
to see them and it's grand to be playing again.

    Will be in Monday morning. Love

                                              Mother

    The sketch opened at the Palace two days after Christmas and
was called "a sparkling little comedy just right for the holiday
season."

    Eventually Laurette had to face the fact that she had lost Si-
mone. She charged breach of contract and was awarded four thousand dollars in damages. Jeanne Eagels took over the part and
opened on the road at the beginning of the new year. Ironically,
when the role lost the honest, innocently forthright quality with
which Laurette had endowed it, the play disintegrated into just
another bedroom farce and went to a quick and undistinguished
grave.

    Hartley did all he could to soften the blow and set to with a
will to turn "The Comedienne" into a three-act play. He wrote
under killing pressure, realizing the psychological importance to
both of them. It was not a good job. Barely a month after playing
the Palace, they were back in Chicago with the three-act version.
Still in process of rewriting, the show opened. Lines were half
memorized, costumes arrived only in part, scenery was unset.
Quite unlike "Happiness" which had hustled into the breach with
a smile, "The Comedienne" died on the threshold with a grimace.
Laurette wrote home from Cincinnati in March: "Nothing has
gone right, so I thought I would spare you. The papers do not
like the play. We close here this Saturday and return to New
York. The play is to be re-written. . . . It's very depressing.
However, as that fine old Italian 'L'Enigme' used to say *Cio che
sera, sera.*"

    Undoubtedly Laurette could have faced these ups and downs
philosophically if she had evaluated them simply as an actress.
There are few stars who, like the brightest planets, do not know
the dark and frosty spin away from the sun of public approbation.
The experienced actress learns to expect such changing fortunes,
and part of her armor—and glory—is her fortitude on such occasions. But Laurette was involved in more than the ups and downs

of a career, and the armor of the actress was not sufficient to cover the wounds of growing personal catastrophes. She was making the mistake she had warned other actresses not to make; her own problems were beginning to dominate her work. The revolt against Hartley which led her into the "Cardboard Lover" was personal; the hurt pride of her demand for an immediate vehicle when it failed was personal; and the devils of guilt within her would be appeased by neither success nor failure, but pushed her ever closer to the brink of a pit that was black and bottomless and held no light.

*

# *Delicate Justice*

In the 1920's the consumption of alcohol beyond the bounds of sociability was looked on by most as an inordinate love of liquor, as basically offensive as gluttony. Although Dr. Sigmund Freud's theories were beginning to percolate into the various fields of human behavior, alcoholism was still the stepchild of psychoanalysis. In the popular mind the alcoholic was funny, pathetic, or disgusting; few looked upon him as mentally ill.

Laurette had not taken spontaneously to drinking. She had been carefully schooled in drinking by Hartley along with the other social graces. With her vast enthusiasm and high animal spirits she never depended on liquor for stimulation. In a day when the relationship between psychic pressures and alcoholism was little understood, Laurette was the perfect example of how indistinguishable the fusion of the two could be; so perfect, that in the years when she began to drink to excess many who had known her long and intimately never suspected that drinking had anything to do with her increasingly erratic behavior. She was basically primitive, violent, a creature of instinct and appetite, and these elements, largely nonfunctioning in life, had found their only outlet in the theatre. Even in the theatre under Hartley's influence they had been drastically curtailed. Now as she became a stranger to the theatre she became a stranger to herself. What had been the glorious light of her talent became a blackness in her own soul. And it was drinking that tripped the switch on this blackness. She was not so much possessed by alcohol as by the negative forces accumulating within her which alcohol released. Only a psychologist would have interpreted as alcoholism the sudden shifts from affection to abuse, from delight to anger, from sociability to morose solitude. For that matter, was it alcoholism? In the beginning it took very little alcohol to set these forces in motion, and there were none of the usual indications of drinking; she did not reel, or grow incoherent, or silly. The words "inebriated," "tight," "drunk" were quite inappropriate to describe the effects of alcohol on Laurette. The sole indication might be the glaring eye, the accusative speech, a progressive "bossiness," a torrent of abuse, suspicion, ridicule, launched without provocation; or, if the demon within her were in a more benign phase, extravagant praise, an almost mawkish adoration of the slightest talent, an insistent pleading to be diverted, entertained, carried somehow to a dizzy brink of comprehension by a song, a story, a brilliant or witty dissertation; and if this were done, the face would swamp with wild delight, until in the end it seemed almost that she begged to be rescued from delight just as a moment before she had begged to be rescued from boredom. For there was in these days no containment for Laurette in alcohol or anything else; whatever demon it was used her as only one who has a great capacity for life can be used. It roamed the many rooms of her being, where her joy and laughter dwelt as well as her sorrow and confusion, and it ended by wrecking them all.

This drinking with a difference had begun after Laurette's return from Hollywood in 1924. Whether it was responsible for her moodiness at the time of "Trelawney," her abstentions from rehearsals, the savage thrusts of her tongue as she wounded others, the fitful indifference to her enemy fat, it is not possible to say. The drink may have come before or after: an attempt to forget an unpleasantness, or not to face one. As there was only this heightening and exaggerating of some of her more unpleasant characteristics with none of the classic indications of overindulgence, the fact that drinking was in any way the problem was almost completely disguised. Even when alcohol became the dominating force, which very soon it was to be, few recognized it as such. Many of Laurette's friendships were destroyed before those involved had any inkling of what destroyed them.

Lynn Fontanne was one of the early victims. She and Alfred were enjoying great success in their acting partnership which had begun with Laurette in "Sweet Nell of Old Drury." They were the darlings of the newly formed Theatre Guild, and under the banner of that organization had done brilliantly "The Guardsman" and "Arms and the Man." It was natural for Lynn to stretch her wings a bit before her one-time mentor, but Laurette did not take kindly to the exhibition. If Lynn attempted to take the center of the stage at a party or offer an opinion different from Laurette's, there would be a sharp, "See 'ere my girl, come off it!" or maybe just a plain, "Shut up!" To Laurette, Lynn remained the skinny girl in the hat with the velvet streamers whom she had taken under her wing. If reminded that Lynn was very much a star in her own right, she was likely to answer, "I can't help that —she's not as good an actress as she used to be." When drinking, this "self-indulgent" honesty became downright abuse. Lynn left many of Laurette's parties in tears with Alfred glowering Teutonically at her side and muttering, "There is no reason for you to put up with such abuse, Lynn! We will not go there again." Finally Lynn could take no more, and left one evening, vowing never to return.

Such scenes were entirely blocked from Laurette's mind the following day. If she thought to apologize—vaguely conscious that she had been guilty of some breach of good conduct, but closing out all memory of the deadliness of her attack—she was shocked by Lynn's unforgiving attitude. Thus was misunderstanding compounded between them.

Lynn never connected these scenes with alcoholism until years later. One night in 1949, while making up in her dressing room for the part of the eighty-year-old lady in "I Know My Love," she talked to Laurette's daughter.

"To my knowledge I never saw Laurette drunk. People told me she drank, but I said I had never seen her in that condition. It never occurred to me that the hate she poured out on me was her drunkenness. . . ." Lynn put down the grease stick with which she had been drawing the purple cords of age on her neck, and gazed into the mirror before her as though it were a corridor into the past. "Now, you are telling me something . . ." she murmured, "now you are telling me something . . ."

Time was running out on love, friendship, the small ties of affection and kindly habits that bind people together; alcohol has no mercy on these things; they wither and die under its breath.

At home, scenes between mother and daughter became progressively more violent, the "princess-complex" hurled with increasing fury, fantastic accusations of flirting or being secretly in love with this actor or that author week-ending with the family at Lockdune; the attack provoked by incidents as negligible as a conversation indistinct to Laurette, or shoulder touching shoulder at a picture show. While later, she might grasp Marguerite's hand, hold it against her breast in what seemed honest bewilderment, and say, "What is it, Marguerite? Are you mad at your mama for something?"

Marguerite's singing voice had been pre-empted by Laurette and had to be trotted out at her command. At three or four in the morning in a smoke-filled room, crowded with some of the world's greatest entertainers, Laurette, first pleading, then wheedling, and at last grown scornfully abusive, would want to know why Marguerite refused to sing. "What does it matter what time it is, whether your stomach is empty or full, whether you're tired or not? Just get up and sing! Sembrich at seventy can sing on a full stomach. Melba would sing any time, anywhere. Come on, come on—'Le Prophete'—'Bohème'—'Louise.' Nobody sings 'Depuis le Jour' like Marguerite, believe me! Oh, for God's sake, come on —sing!"

Hartley and Dwight knew full well the reason for the wildly erratic behavior but neither discussed it with Marguerite. They did not speak of it to each other, nor did they face Laurette with it, being perhaps all too eager not to face it themselves. Laurette aided and abetted them in this with all the force of her imaginative powers. As alcohol possessed her more and more, she began to build an elaborate fantasy world between herself and this stark fact. Rightly or wrongly, Hartley and Dwight went along in the deception; in a way it might be said they were half deceived by it as Marguerite was wholly deceived. Laurette was highly skilled in the erection of a fantasy world. She had had years of practice. So persuasive could she be that others found themselves accepting it over the evidence of their senses, and so strong a hold did it exert on her own mind that time and time again she could pull herself out of a bout of drinking, alone, with bedroom door locked, quell her shaking hand, steady her raw nerves, and sally forth to look others straight in the eye and convince them, and herself, *it was not so*.

In April of 1927, directly after the closing of "The Comedienne," they had gone to Easthampton. In the rambling frame house the night stillness would be broken by sinister mutterings and angry cries from the third floor which Laurette had appropriated for her sleeping quarters, and the floor boards would creak and groan under a constant restless movement, undirected and purposeless. At breakfast, looking pale and worn but exceptionally tidy, face powdered and lipstick in place, Laurette would tell of the recurring nightmares she suffered or of an acute illness that had passed with the dawn, and in bright, animated fashion discuss various reasons which might have caused the one or the other. Hartley and Dwight would murmur in an abstracted manner, seemingly anxious to let the matter drop. After constant repetition the show wore thin, but both performer and the two in the audience who knew its fraudulence clung desperately to it nonetheless, seemingly helpless to do otherwise. Perhaps there was nothing else to do.

The wildest of fears began to obsess the one member of the family ignorant of the truth. The unreasonable demands and accusations, the sudden savage scenes of jealousy and rage, the eyes black with hate, could mean only one thing; under some psychic compulsion that was almost madness Laurette had come to loathe and despise her daughter. So strong did the conviction become that on hearing the strange nocturnal movements, the ominous mutterings, Marguerite, filled with a nameless terror, would rise and barricade her door. Finally, leaving home seemed the only way to salvage what was left of a relationship riddled with fear and misunderstanding, and strained beyond further enduring.

That Marguerite chose acting as a livelihood in branching out for herself, thereby repudiating the carefully planned and tirelessly promoted musical career, did not make her decision any easier for Laurette; this was clearly an act of defiance; the theatre was the one field which Laurette passionately objected to her entering.

Oblivious to all that had led up to Marguerite's decision and a final shattering scene over the removal of her belongings, Laurette sent the following letter to a summer-stock theatre on Staten Island:

> Darling:
> We have had *no violent* scenes! We have had differences of opinion about four or five times during this long association—and that's a very low batting average for families. I love and have loved you very much indeed. I miss you terribly. Of course one knows when a child comes through the agony of birth with you, that another agony of that same two parting will come later. That's inevitable.
> Live your life, darling (as you always have incidentally). . . . Don't bother about my life. The years will not diminish no matter how many times you touch your toes or walk in a heavy sweater:— and "*Cio che sera, sera*" is a comfortable lazy way to look at life.
> I'm your good friend, my dear, even though I am your severest critic. Don't answer this. Just think of the pleasant wonderful times we have lived together.
> You need me in my capacity as a mother and an actress. And I need you. You and Dwight are the two things in the world, the two reasons why I go on living. Never a scene ever, is what I promise you. Again I say, live as you please, but don't throw away my love (you won't find an awful lot of that around). . . .

Three months later Laurette sent word from 50 Riverside Drive that she was gravely ill and begged her daughter to return. The illness actually was not serious; a bad case of poison oak which had swollen her face to the size of a pumpkin, and nothing more. But she was insistent that Marguerite remain home. It had been very "humiliating," she explained, not to be able to say just where her daughter was when people asked. So when Laurette was sufficiently recovered the family returned to Easthampton. It was there that Marguerite learned the truth. Her reaction was not only dismay but incredulity that the issue of Laurette's drinking had not been faced.

When she brought up the subject, Hartley was painfully embarrassed, horrified that anyone should suggest mentioning it to Laurette. . . . Marguerite did not quite understand the situation; the recent, many, and unhappy scenes with her mother would make her judgment hasty and ill-advised in this matter. By far the best thing was for the family to give no indication whatsoever that anything was wrong. Laurette would get hold of herself after a while and all this unpleasantness would be forgotten. . . . In this Dwight heartily concurred.

As if in answer to this negative policy, Laurette grew progressively worse. The nights in the frame house were unspeakable. Each conspirator lay in bed frozen with misery and horror listening to the sounds emanating from the third floor, sounds which seemed to come from hell and under. It was as though one side of Laurette fought to suppress all knowledge of her mounting disintegration, while the other racketed wildly through the hours of the night crying out in loud inhuman voice on the vistas of damnation it had come to know.

Each morning the drawn faces, the hollow-eyed stares around the breakfast table, gave testimony to what was not to be discussed. It was a strange household, living out an illusion which day by day grew more unnatural and unreal.

On one such morning there came a breaking point, not dramatic, or violent, but rather from utter impoverishment of will on the part of everyone to carry further the shadow-thin deception. But, of course, Laurette tried. She sat at her place at table, hair drawn back in neat gold buns, a deathly pallor under the swift improvisation of make-up. Clearing her throat and lifting her coffee cup with shaking hand, she began her story. . . . The haggard faces, averted eyes of the others told *their* story. The knowledge shared by them all seemed to raise a solid wall against this, her last illusion. Laurette's grasp of fantasy faltered. . . . no one was heeding . . . she was playing to an audience of nonbelievers. Quickly she rose, flung down her napkin and left the room. No one spoke. Almost automatically Marguerite rose and followed. In the living room, with shades still half drawn, mother and daughter faced one another. Grasping Laurette's arms, and holding her gaze steady on the dead-white face, Marguerite blurted out what had never been said before in that house, "Mother, what are you going to do about this drinking?"

A blow across the face could not have evoked a more violent reaction. Laurette trembled from head to foot, drew herself up taut with rage and indignation.

"You *would* say that to me," she spat out, "because you hate me! Hartley and Dwight would never, *never* say such a thing, because they love me. But you hate me! You despise me!" It was a voice skilled in delivering the full weight of an emotion and it did not fail her now.

Marguerite managed to stammer, "I don't hate you. I want to help you. I——" Then under the pressure of emotion too great for words, she turned and fled onto the broad porch.

How long it was before Laurette followed, Marguerite did not know. The screen door banged and she turned to face whatever further recriminations were to be. But instead Laurette came directly toward her, straight-legged, enormous-eyed, like a frightened child. Quickly she pressed her head down against Marguerite's breast, seeming suddenly pitifully small and helpless in light kimono and heelless slippers. It was a gesture both of contrition and utter exhaustion, and for a long time she did not move. Then came the small muffled voice pleading, "What *am* I going to do, Marguerite?"

Convulsively Marguerite pressed her close, and Laurette's own arms crept around her daughter's waist. Thus they stood for a long time without speaking as though, somehow, in the intensity of their embrace they could obliterate the past and stem the awful flood of the future.

Was that moment a haven? Could she have turned and, with the help of those who loved her, begun to find her way in reality? It is useless to speculate; for she did not. The habits of a lifetime were too strong. Later when reality was far more cruel and could no longer be avoided, when Hartley lay dying, she had to take that step. Day after day she was forced to face everything she hated and feared in life. When she tried to run away she ran like Joyce's hero, Stephen Daedalus, with the sense of mortal sin on her soul, the dead weight of guilt for the unhappiness she had brought Hartley in his last years. For ten years after he died she was to run —a terrible race—until at last she turned and faced herself, as she would not now, except for this brief moment when she caught her breath on the sunlit porch of Lockdune.

Hartley worked long and desperate hours on a new play that summer. Each time that Laurette had acted since her return from Hollywood she had stopped drinking, dieted, exercised, and behaved in exemplary fashion. Between plays she ballooned out, ate voraciously, grew restless, unpredictable, began to drink. But she had never broken faith with the theatre.

With this for inspiration—and little more—Hartley finished "Delicate Justice" in August. It was unbelievably poor. Laurette's role was that of a faith healer, known only as The Visitor, mysterious, Portialike, who sought to expound deep wisdom and help solve the problems of others.

What Laurette thought when he read it to her can only be conjectured. There must have been as much desperation in her listening as there had been for him in the writing. Instinctively she knew the theatre was her salvation, and the supremely important thing just then was that Hartley had written a play for her.

There wasn't a great deal of time to slim down, to work off the bloat which she had let gather on her bones throughout that tortured summer. Again they stayed late into the autumn and with grim determination Laurette plodded the lanes, sweated under her electric sheet, dove into the ocean, and let the waves swirl her back and forth on the shore as she lay face down, arms out, holding her breath beneath its salty goodness.

The notices after the opening in Philadelphia made it all too plain that "Delicate Justice" had been manufactured by a harassed and tired brain. In all the years of denunciation of Hartley as playwright these notices set a new low: "Inane and sprawling play,"— "talky, obvious and inept." As usual it was "poor Laurette Taylor doomed to dwarfish and twaddling vehicles year after year" and this "the worst of all."

Hartley was already numb. He had been through weeks of rehearsals with a cast growing progressively more resentful of Laurette's "big star" ways. Morning after morning she failed to arrive
at the theatre, then sent peremptory messages to the company to
meet in the evening at 50 Riverside Drive. There reclining on a
couch, taking little interest in her own scenes, she swooped down
on the mistakes of others, as Noel Coward put it, "with all the swift
accuracy of a pelican," interfered with Hartley, squabbled over
minor points in the script. It was quite evident to him that she
was drinking in secret, but the members of the cast knew nothing
of this. Hartley had to employ all his tact and skill as a director to
keep the company working together.

One spunky young lady in particular, Jessie Royce Landis,
fresh from playing leads in Detroit stock, seemed to call forth
Laurette's ire. "No, no, no," Laurette would say after the girl's
every reading at the first rehearsal. "That's not right at all, Miss
Landis," until Hartley was forced to step in. "Laurie, Miss Landis
had no opportunity to see the script before rehearsal and is reading
cold. Naturally she is nervous."

At one of the last rehearsals in New York, Laurette broke into
a long speech with the remark, "You have a habit of running your
words together, Miss Landis." Miss Landis blew.

"You have no right to say I have a habit of running my words
together, because you don't know. I may be running my words
together *now*, because I am nervous, but you haven't known me
long enough to know if I have a *habit* of doing it. I can show you
notices where I have been praised for my clear diction. . . ."

"Well, well, well . . ." said Laurette as she let her voice trail
off in mock surprise.

One day seeking a new opening scene, Hartley asked Jessie to sit
at the piano and sing a few phrases of "I Love You Truly." As
the pure, liquid tones poured forth Laurette walked onto the stage
as though drawn by Circe's call. "Why are you wasting your
time as a dramatic actress when you can sing like that?" she
breathed. "Sing the whole song, Jessie. . . . Hartley, she's to sing
the whole song."

From that moment forward Laurette's attitude changed. It was
as though a door tight shut had unlocked in her heart. Music could

always do that, even at this late date when she was beginning to isolate herself more and more from others. This friendship became fast and enduring. It was bolstered by the unfeigned respect Laurette came to have for Jessie as an actress, but it was music that had unlocked the door.

But the friendship grew among the many thorns of the ill-fated production of "Delicate Justice." It was unlike Laurette not to settle into a part. The play, essentially shallow and false, never caught her imagination sufficiently to give her that push forward into the creative regions of her mind where she stopped being "difficult" and began to function. Hartley could only hope. . . .

When it came time to entrain for Allentown where the play was to open, Laurette made some excuse and stayed behind; she would take the next train and be there for the dress rehearsal. But with the cast assembled on stage and waiting, Laurette still had not arrived. The door to her room at 50 Riverside was shut and locked and there was silence behind it. On the long distance telephone Hartley spoke to his stepdaughter in a tight, exhausted voice, "If she breaks faith with the theatre," he said, "it is the end." It was his first direct admission that Laurette was drinking, and it was wrung from him in an agonizing hour.

Finally Laurette came, penitent and shaking, barely in time for the opening curtain. The result was a performance keyed to a tension that was well-nigh unbearable to anyone knowing the situation. Hartley watched with Marguerite, sitting far back in a box. Laurette made her performance a tour de force to hide its several weaknesses—lines unmemorized, nerves controlled only by the greatest effort of will. It tingled along the spine. It was like watching a magnificent race horse overreaching, courting disaster with every stride. The man in the box sighed heavily from time to time and chewed distractedly at his under lip.

The notices meant nothing to him; he was past caring; but to Laurette they were the sharp prod she needed into positive action. She spent her fury on the critics. She took firm hold of herself and with the company worked heroically on cuts and revisions. But it was too late. The play limped on to a Chicago opening and there received its *coup de grâce*.

# The Furies

Dimly Laurette sensed the near treachery to what was more deeply
ingrained in her than anything else: her loyalty to the theatre. That
winter she began a series of abortive efforts to control her drinking. She went to a doctor who said it was all a question of a healthy
body making a healthy mind. "Take care of the body, my dear,
and the mind will take care of itself." She thought that a splendid
idea. She took a body-building course complete with electric
cabinets, internal baths, special diet. It helped that the doctor was
a good bridge player and a gay and amusing companion. But only
for a while. At Hartley's request she consented to see a well-known
psychologist who journeyed up from Washington for a series of
conferences, but quickly convinced him that he could not help her.

She talked for hours to Father Francis Patrick Duffy, renowned
wartime chaplain of New York's Fighting 69th, a long-time friend
of both Hartley and Laurette, but she argued with him as she had
argued with her grandmother. The Church had been very shabby
about recognizing her marriage to Hartley and she was not inclined to listen to the Church. It was a silly thing to say you were
living in sin with a man you loved because you'd first divorced
a man you hated. "That's living in sin," she would say, "to live
with a man you hate." And if the Church was that silly and mis-
guided, it couldn't help her with this problem. She even went
to a convent for a while to find peace in those holy surroundings,
but after the first dramatic appeal of the seclusion and the gentle
kindliness of the nuns, she was thoroughly bored and left. She
would be wondrously "good" for a while and Hartley's tired
face would light with hope; then—crash!—doors would be locked
and silence descend, and the world would come to an end for
everybody in that once gay house on the Drive. She was beginning to use drinking as a whip to make life jump around for her,
to form odd caricatured patterns of despair, tension, hope, con-

fusion, embarrassment. That was better than life's being just goddam dull, which it was beginning to be when she was not in the theatre. If life was going to have the effrontery to menace her with its dullness, its funlessness and threat of old age, she would menace it right back on her own terms. Laurette was sulking, a luxury she thought she could afford. She still thought she had enough control of alcohol to use it for her own ends. The theatre remained her undefiled refuge and despite her near treachery she would keep it so.

When Laurette began rehearsals of "The Furies" in February 1928, the rumor was already abroad that she drank. She obstinately refused to admit the existence of this rumor even when it had become a flaming banner head in the minds of theatre people as soon as her name was mentioned. When she absented herself from the first reading of the play without adequate explanation, the management promptly went into a funk. They went to Alice Brady, explained the circumstances and asked if she would consider the role. The forthright Alice replied, "Well, I drink too, you know. I'd like to do the play—you bet I would—but I drink too, and Laurette would be simply wonderful in the part." Abashed by this frank appraisal of the situation the producers retired for further consultations. Laurette continued in the role.

Zoe Akins had written "The Furies" for her. Originally it was conceived in terms of music which was to be integrated with the action and dialogue, but somewhere along the way this concept had been lost and the music dispensed with. Laurette, however, continued to think of it in musical terms. Her imagination was caught up by the vaulting and lyrical quality of the prose, and in the mystery-thriller plot she fervently hoped she had found the prescription for good "box-office."

Shorn of the music the play's hybrid nature became manifest, but it had some arresting moments of drama by a craftsman who gave the theatre "Déclassée," and the Pulitzer Prize winner "The Old Maid."

Said Gilbert Gabriel: "Miss Taylor achieved the subtlest and most glowing piece of playing many of us have seen her do in many years." The play's "curious and inverted beauty" held Woollcott fascinated throughout the evening, "an evening to which the returning Laurette Taylor brought a sensitive, honest and beautiful performance that was touched with a loveliness of which the secret will die with her."

As though sensing she would be a stranger to it for many a day, Laurette lingered long in the theatre during the rehearsals and run of "The Furies." She felt a protection within its walls which could no longer be conjured up in the world outside. George Cukor was again directing. He knew her vanity, capriciousness, her high and mighty airs covering the pitfalls of her ignorance and insecurities, and that once in harness these things dropped from her as though they had never existed. Zoe Akins too was her good friend. "Zoe lets my imagination breathe," Laurette would say in chuckling admiration. Others of the company were as congenial: Alan Campbell who played her son, fresh-faced, whip-smart, and not yet exclusively devoted by marriage to the wit of Dorothy Parker; Estelle Winwood, calm and sagacious as Athena's owl under the paranoiac stare, the lisping vague delivery.

Albert Carroll, mimic extraordinaire, came nightly to perfect the take-off of Laurette which he was to give in the "Grand Street Follies." She liked to see him sitting in the shadows backstage, sinuous and catlike as a Beardsley drawing, following her every move with insolent smile, a small pad for note-taking on his knee. Eventually she traveled down to Grand Street to watch the strangely accurate witchery of his Fifi Sands. Several nights later Estelle Winwood saw Laurette shaking out her white chiffon gown before going on stage. "What's the matter, darling?" she asked. "Is there anything wrong with your dress?"

"No," replied Laurette, "I just wanted to make sure Albert Carroll wasn't in it."

It was in the weird, imaginative expansiveness of others that Laurette felt most at ease. This was the climate in which she still could breathe while every other aspect of life seemed closing in on her.

Fifty Riverside had stripped itself of these reaches. She did not ask the reason. She could whip up the dull into the dramatic by "behaving badly"—the ubiquitous phrase that for the next

ten years adhered like a gray fungus to the subject of her drinking—and she did; but it meant torturing emotions, it meant lines
of suffering drawn deep on beloved faces, the pained silence, the
averted glance, the hurt withdrawal. She could fill the house with
guests and demand in payment from each the last ounce of dis-
traction and excitement; but after it was over, the household sank
to an even lower level of exhaustion and emotional bankruptcy
from which it became each time more difficult to stir into dynamic action.

Hartley sat at his writing table wrapped in his winter coat with
the fur collar. It was three A.M. and he had gone to his study at
midnight, but the sheet of paper before him was blank. There had
been a brief spell of spring weather weeks before and Laurette
had ordered the furnace turned off. Now it was cold again, a
raw windy cold, but no one had thought to order the furnace
started, and Hartley had not bothered to keep the fire going in
the marble fireplace of his study.

"The Furies" had closed after forty-five performances. Laurette had asked him to write a comedy. Next season she would
play light comedy, nothing else—either his or someone else's—
but only comedy, with "no moral, no message, no preachment."

In response to a soft knock on the door, Hartley called a quick
"come in," but did not change his position, which was that of a
man who for a long time had sat immobile staring into space.
Marguerite entered on a familiar sight: the slightly hunched
figure in the chair, cigarette smoke columning into the still, cold
air above the dark head, a single desk lamp shining down on
the white, unmarked paper. Above, the ghostly chandeliers re-
fracted the light from their many crystal prisms like faint messages
from a more stately world.

The children had taken to visiting with "Jartley" when they
came home at night, no matter what the hour. The thin thread
of light under the study doors was a comforting sight in a house
which often now was cold and silent and cheerless. Hartley welcomed their company. Intimacy with his stepchildren, which
had once embarrassed him, now seemed a source of comfort.
His vast reserve had broken a little in the last few months and

he confided in them shyly, almost apologetically; it was the slenderest bridge of communication but infinitely dear to Marguerite and Dwight, for they had come to love him deeply.

Supposedly he was at work on the comedy which Laurette had requested. But there was nothing to show for it. Night after night one or the other of the children found him thus, a drift of ashes over his vest, ash tray piled high with stubs, the unmarked paper before him.

This night his eyes were heavily shadowed. He seemed crushed down under the silence of the house around him, a silence which had built up for days since the last hardy guests of a Sunday-night supper had straggled out into the dawn, and Laurette, with the high excitement still on her face that people and parties engendered, had gone to the pantry and from there to her room, shutting and locking the door behind her.

Even though he had come to detest the parties they were better than this silence. There was a horrible finality about it as though all in the house had been buried alive in one grave. He spoke out in his despair. "Everything has gone from this house," he said, his large mournful eyes lifted to his stepdaughter's face. "That is what alcohol does. When it comes into a home everything goes, love, affection, loyalty, all decent human feeling—it leaves nothing. That is its terrible curse."

He hunched his shoulders high, folded one cupped hand over the other, and with a faint turn of his head indicated the unlit dining room at the other end of the hall. "I sit here and listen to that pantry door swinging . . . swinging. It is the knell of everything we have built together—and I am absolutely helpless. . . ."

Laurette was taken to a sanitarium late that spring. For the first time she was surrounded by total strangers hired to care for her, to whom she was just another case. There was no torture on a beloved face to be dramatized; no pained silence or numbed acquiescence to be elicited by tales of nightmares or mysterious attacks of illness—"no beautiful stories to go with some beautiful tears"; just the hard impassive faces of paid attendants who cared not one whit for such things. She was delivered at last into the hands of that vast horde of the unimaginative whom she had loathed all her life, the maw-worms who fed on human misery, who wait for some weakness to reduce the glories of one's spirit to the grubbiness of their own. They had a passport at last to her impregnable country: her drinking, her inability to master alcohol. Once within the four walls of that sanitarium, not one shred of imagery, or drama, or even caricature of human emotion was left; nothing cloaked the horrid fact that she was a drunkard, and as a drunkard the Philistines possessed her at last body and soul.

It jolted her as she never had been jolted before, and added to that was the physical torture of the so-called cure. She was afraid of death, and for days thought she would die. She was afraid of ghosts, and for days she saw ghosts. With eyes wide open she stared at them; her mother's face forming in the mirror behind her own, like a pale floating medallion in space; her mother beckoning to her with a death-pale hand from a bed of roses.

\*

# Summer 1928

Chastened by the experience of the sanitarium, Laurette picked up the scattered pieces of normal living with a new solicitude. Even dieting and reducing seemed almost pleasurable. One of her favorite quotations was Voltaire's "No one has a full capacity for two passions," and now to strip her life of all thought but a physical ideal of herself, and of all activity except that which propelled her toward the desired goal, was a kind of Lenten preparation, a purification which cast out all other indulgences and appetites.

It was good to leave the town house immediately and retire to Lockdune where the broad lawn swept to the edge of the pond and, beyond, the rugged guardian dune rose against the sky, "a

silent rebuke to all action" as her son called it; good to hear and
see and smell the ocean once again as the combers rolled in stately
rhythm on the distant beach. "The place never looked lovelier,"
she wrote Marguerite, recuperating from a back injury at the
upstate farm of Jane Peyton, then Mrs. Samuel Hopkins Adams,
"like places in England. All swept clean at night and laid in the
sun in the morning." She was on her egg, soup and tomato diet;
alone in the house except for Mary, the maid. Hartley was in
New York with the faithful Martha "having daily sessions with
the dentist and nightly sessions with a new play." Dwight was
in Boston rehearsing a new play of his own. It was better to be
alone for this reducing business. "It is much easier if you don't
have to order food or smell food or see it. Whatever little Mary
eats in the kitchen certainly has no tempting odor."

Since the episode on the porch at Lockdune the relationship
between mother and daughter had remained close and affectionate except during the periods of drinking. Then Marguerite invariably became the focal point for her mother's lashing tongue
and wildly improvident accusations; but now while she was making a determined effort at control, and with distance lending
enchantment, Laurette wrote often and warmly to her absent
child.

"I think of nothing but health and beauty and you feel darn
selfish about that when other people are around you. Of course
it's damnable from twilight on—but Michael and I go to bed at
8:30. I read until sleep comes and wake up when I please. Look
like nothing at all but can feel my jawbone coming through the
fat." She has been lucky about the books in the Easthampton
library. One story in Theodore Dreiser's "Chains" makes a deep
impression. "It's about evil spirits that followed at the elbow
of over-indulgent people because they could get the flavor of
too much eating, drinking, loving or murder from those humans.
They had no place to go and unless they could find someone
living, practicing the same vices, *they* lived as deaf and blind
things. It is written creepily, and to think of a lot of small things
feeding on me gave me half my determination."

Then there was a life of Voltaire. She was inspired by "a man
who worked incessantly on nothing, he was so sickly. A man who

at 73 said, 'I've only one tooth left and I'm saving that for Fréron' (his great enemy). It seemed a rebuke." And lastly, "a most amusing and side-splitting" biography of Balzac. "It is the epitome of fun. His conceit was so thorough, so real, and of course, he was enormous. All the caricatures of him in the book frightened me— and they did give his enemies such an advantage for lampooning."

She is living in books and through books with her old avidity. Hers is an imagination that must always have food, and project in imagery the eyeless and mouthless hungers—"the deaf and blind things." Never, never must these possess her again, drag her down to that nethermost hell where all that is corrupt turns upon the human spirit and tries to destroy it.

The letter ends wistfully, "My dear, as Voltaire said at eighty, there's not much fun in collecting years. Your Mommer."

The next letter is more cheerful.

"This is the seventh day of electric sheets, touching toes, dying of hunger and thirst, and I have lost seven pounds! That tomato, egg and soup thing is marvellous . . . but, what a life! I have read script after script and am trying to pick a success as well as something I want to do. There is no lack of offers, thank God—but—if I continue to surprise myself with myself, as I have done this week, I can wait for something magnificent."

She sees no one. Hoyti and Olga Wiborg are away. Percy Hammond has been ill. She misses her children. She writes often of small inconsequential matters. "Michael has had an operation on his posterior and is now able to sit down without jumping up immediately. For some reason (known only to God) the operation on that end restored his *voice!* He now howls to get in and screams to get out. . . . I've started painting *'Aunted Annie* and *'Appy Annie,"* (the canoes) "and I seem to take the color better than they do.

"I'm hungry but happy. Hartley came down for the week end with Martha. After twelve days of Mary I was glad to see him and after twelve days of me Mary was glad to see Martha." And so it went.

Hartley finished the play. "A very light comedy for a very *light* comedienne," Laurette wrote. It was not her play. He was taking it to New York for Billie Burke's consideration. "Greta

Cooper, Bertie (Dr. Eskell), Mary Morley and Charles Mac-
Arthur were here over the 4th," the letter continued. "The house
is empty now and I'm back at the old grind."

In New York, at Dr. Eskell's suggestion, Hartley had X-ray
pictures taken because of a cough which had become chronic
in recent months. Later he was surprised upon answering the
phone to hear the doctor's voice tight and urgent, advising that
he not return to Easthampton. More X-rays and further extensive
examinations would be necessary. Hartley mildly remonstrated.
Eskell talked on, and in a worried, rambling discourse mentioned
cancer. Politely but firmly Hartley terminated the conversation,
told Martha to close the house and took the next train for Easthampton.

The X-rays had indicated cancer of the esophagus.

Laurette was full of plans when he returned. She had lost
eleven more pounds, she wrote Marguerite, and was pleased with
herself. They would be in Boston on the sixteenth of July for the
opening of Dwight's play, "Trevalyn's Ghost." Later she was
going to Jack Hammond's "when she looked better." Ben Hecht
and MacArthur were writing a play for her based on the last days
of Isadora Duncan, but she thought it very "cheerless" and was
determined to do comedy next season. She had sent a play of her
own about a mermaid to Jed Harris, and he had liked it and
thought Ina Claire could do it. She was really getting back in
stride. The Irvin Cobbs had bought a house next to the Percy
Hammonds and they were all playing golf together.

Hartley seemed a little blue. She thought it was because negotiations with Billie Burke had fallen through. "But he has a grand
idea now," she wrote her daughter. He would not return to the
city but would work on it at Lockdune. It was more like old
times than ever, Hartley working through the night on a new
play, her jawbone coming through, flesh firming and skin clearing as it had not done in months. Yes, she could afford to wait for
something "magnificent" now, and this time it might very well be
Hartley's.

Then she was told. The doctor, upset by Hartley's disappear-
ance and refusal to communicate, telephoned from New York.
"I don't think anyone should ever be told," she wrote years later.
Certainly she should not have been; at least not that way.

What was she to do?

It was Hartley now who spun the tight, sacrosanct dimensions of a make-believe world that was not to be invaded by disastrous reality, and it was Laurette, pushed with dreadful finality from her own refuges, who must stay outside and watch helplessly and with terror in her heart. In numerous telephone calls the doctor importuned her to get Hartley back to New York at once. . . . Did he realize what was wrong? . . . Had he said anything? . . . Was he sleeping? . . . Was he eating?

To all of which Laurette replied in that voice of high indignation she used when reality strained credulity: Yes . . . yes . . . yes . . . Hartley was living in his usual methodic way. He was working every night on his new play. He rose at eleven. Ate what breakfast he could. Played eighteen holes of golf. Ate lunch if he could. Rested in the afternoon. Ate dinner if he could. Played bridge in the evening or read in his study. To all suggestions that he finish his medical check-up, he was politely noncommittal, or gently insulting: "Bally doctors!—never get through with you!" or something to that effect. What could she do?

Well, insisted the doctor, was she sure that he was sleeping? How was she to know that? She didn't sleep with him. "To Hartley's intense astonishment," she wrote Marguerite, "I slept in the same room with him for four nights, explaining that it was to keep him from being depressed about the possibility of having more X-rays taken. It really was to see if and how he slept. Well, he slept from eleven on with the same old snore he has had for fourteen years."

This letter, the first after hearing the news, and following a month's silence, was determinedly chatty in tone and quite vague as to just what was wrong.

"I really didn't write before because it seemed wicked to alarm people until you know there is cause enough. God knows Life's end is bad enough without anticipating it every time one has an extra cough . . . or an extra back like yours, darling . . . or is extra thin like Dwight, or extra old like Michael." The letter closed: "The blots you see, Maggie, *are not tears.* We had the King, Queen and Ace of thunderstorms last night and there isn't a dry piece of paper in the house. We treat windows as though they couldn't close. We are about to have another so it seemed

economical to write before the paper became wetter! Affectionately Your Ma."

"Every morning," she was to write later of this time, "you
open your eyes and wonder why your heart is so heavy . . .
then—it descends on you. . . . A blackness. An impotent fury.
Every morning of every day! You think if *I* wake up in blackness what depth of darkness would envelop him if he knew!
You dress, you eat, you face a man who now, in his heart, wishes
he could find the reckless honesty in you again. . . ." Or does he?

Ritualistically, just as he plays his golf, works on his play, takes
his afternoon nap, Hartley sits down three times a day to meals.
In a pitifully short time what he calls his "smoking cough" catches
him. He murmurs a ritualistic excuse—cigarettes or handkerchief
left in his study—and leaves the table, dabbing at his lips with a
napkin. Laurette watches him climb the stairs humming a tune.
She finishes the meal alone, or perhaps he rejoins her later, drawing on a cigarette, one eye closed against the smoke, chatting
lightly of this and that.

There are days and weeks, two months of this in all, before
he can be persuaded to return to New York. Every day Laurette
faces the reality that Hartley is dying, and she must face it alone,
burying the secret somewhere inside of her, playing along with
him now as he once had played along with her in a grim game of
make-believe, torn between the conviction one moment that he
knows, and the next that he does not know what is wrong.

All her life she has fled from illness. When her children were
ill, she could not bear to be around them. If it were a minor indisposition, it made her angry as an inconvenience and a nuisance;
if it were major, it frightened and depressed her and she stayed
away. She visited Dwight but once in the hospital when he had
an appendectomy and that was when he was well on the way to
recovery. She loathed the smell in hospital halls, she explained,
the sight of sick green faces and all the apparatus of the sick-
room. "Marguerite comes because she's just a bit *morbid* about
such things."

But every day now Laurette must face these things, sit opposite them in dreadful intimacy—death which she is afraid of, illness which she loathes. She cannot lash out at them, repudiate

them, because they have become the inseparable companions of the man she loves. They have put their marks on him; the tiny blue bruises under each eye, the transparency of skin, the drawn delicacy of the whole face, as though a waxen mask has been pressed upon it to reveal the fineness of the bone structure beneath. He has the "priestly" look of their first meeting, and she thinks she sees in his enormous eyes a plea. But what is it for? —Honesty or deceit?—Truth or lies? She cannot tell.

She begins to drink. There are days when her expression is sullen, when her eyes stare murderously into space, and she is silent and immobile as though locked in combat with an invisible enemy. It is alcohol all right. But it isn't touching anything. The nerves of course, but not the brain—or at least that part of the brain that contemplates reality. Nothing touches that now until all the senses are blacked out; and it is the first thing to come alive and begin again its lidless stare.

Marguerite came home in August. Dwight was in and out, taking all he could and fleeing to parts unknown until he gathered the stamina to return.

No sooner was her daughter in the house than Laurette released in one overpowering flood all the undischarged emotions which had been suffocating her. Marguerite became the whipping boy, the villain of the piece. As if under a giant emetic Laurette disgorged her fear, her cowardice, her revolt. She laid upon her child the corroding guilt she felt for Hartley's illness—a judgment for her sins; the mistakes which a frustrated Catholicism would not allow her to confess; the overwhelming sense that it was too late to make amends, that the love and gratitude in her heart had been hopelessly tarnished and were unworthy of the man whose life had been one of unsullied devotion. There was no door open for escape from these things and she could no longer bear them alone. The empathy between mother and daughter worked two ways; it could give understanding and communication, or it could be merely the extension of all that was unresolved and black in the one or the other. Now Laurette flayed the blackness within herself, projecting it into the crepuscular image of her daughter.

In loud hysteric voice she accused Marguerite of unfeelingness, hardness, deceit, hate, ingratitude—all those things that were eating her own soul. She stood in the shadow of death and beat her breast as one done grievous wrongs and asked to carry too grievous a burden. She filled the room with rage and hate until the girl shrieked back at her accuser, and felt as though some evil force were turning her heart to stone at a time when she wished only to be loving and forbearing, and give what support she could.

It was a household strung to the breaking point.

Hartley removed himself from an emotional turmoil he no longer had the strength to sustain, or control. He was always, and to the end, the tender one, and even as he suffered and starved and knew in his heart he was dying, he tried to bind up the wounds of those he loved. Lying on his study couch where he had retired after an unsuccessful attempt to swallow a morsel of food, he heard below the voice that could place a whisper in the last row of a theatre balcony. "Every day of my life I have to face a man who is dying, *dying*—do you hear me?—and you stand there and ask me to have some control!" and only a few seconds later he was pressing the head of a weeping girl against his breast, and murmuring, "You mustn't upset yourself. Laurette is not herself. She does not mean the things she says. You must go back with Jane and Sam where you are happy. Everything will be all right, my dear."

The visit was catastrophic. Finally the situation became so unendurable that in a brief interlude of co-operation from Laurette, the house was closed and the family moved up to the city.

Once in New York, Marguerite persuaded Hartley to see Dr. Charles Green, the osteopath who had successfully treated her injured back. By manipulation he made it possible for Hartley to take his first solid food in over two months. Returning from the first treatment Hartley went directly to the pantry and presently the smell of frying bacon permeated through the swinging door. When Marguerite investigated she found him holding a plate heaped high with milky soft scrambled eggs and several pieces of crisp bacon. "Come in, come in," he said as he proceeded to eat every morsel, glancing up now and then with the old impish sparkle and chuckling delightedly.

For all the seeming obliteration of the senses, alcoholics have deep within them some survival pulse which seems to warn of acute dangers other than the slow destruction they have chosen for themselves. An alcoholic will remove high heels to negotiate a flight of stairs, will carefully stay away from windows from which it is easy to tumble. There is also a curious sapience which allows them to register the exact climate around them; and when on their own terms, they decide life is once more tolerable without alcohol, they will spontaneously give it up and make their bid to return to normal life. The day after Marguerite left and Hartley took his first food, Laurette abruptly stopped drinking and began to take care of herself. Again the prolonged abuse of her body, followed by sudden abstinence, had nerves rubbed raw and mind filled with terror and thoughts of death, but with a new doctor in attendance she buckled down heroically to a strict regime of dieting and exercise.

"Laurie has had nothing since the day you left," wrote Hartley to his stepdaughter, "is fasting under observation, has lost a pound a day and is beginning to look more like she used to." And later to Jane Adams: "She has not the slightest indication to 'go bad.' I am sure that last attack frightened her. . . . When you see her don't refer to the unhappy days. Let them rest. This cure looks very hopeful; assume it is going to last."

His concern for Marguerite continued. She was by now seriously ill and faced an operation. He wrote to Sam Adams: "Do assure Marguerite of her being taken care of by me. I would like to see a more sympathetic understanding between mother and daughter. I do not think it is hopeless." And to the faithful Jane: "I cannot thank you and Sam enough for all you have done for Marguerite. The poor child has had a wretched time. You have done your best to make it easy for her."

His optimism about Laurette was short lived, as was his new found ability to eat. After six weeks the esophagus closed.

The eminent surgeon who was called in remarked that he would prefer to operate on people without imagination; that a highly developed imaginative faculty was more apt to be responsible for an operative failure than the operation itself; in effect, that it is possible for imagination to kill people. These words haunted Laurette. They expressed what was to her the intolerable fact, that life was essentially merciless on those born with imagination.

The operation was supposed to give Hartley three years of borrowed time. "Enough perhaps," thought Laurette desperately, "to write a great play." Actually it gave him less than three months.

He was alarmed and frightened by what was done to him. He was given no time to prepare himself. There was no time. He was rushed through X-rays, explorations. The final operation was immediately imperative. The surgeon was right, what was done to him broke him in spirit rather than in body, abused the deepest precepts of his nature, his fastidiousness, his modesty, his vast personal pride and reserve. The man who had played eighteen holes of golf every day with the shadow of death on him, who worked every night on a new play, whom friends saw swinging down Fifth Avenue with his silver-headed cane, head high and step jaunty, even when he and those around him knew he was doomed—this man now was broken and afraid because there had been taken from him the intangible bastions of his life. Laurette knew better than anyone else what this meant and inwardly wept for him and knew he would not survive.

He was under opiates most of the time. He was put in Marguerite's room on the top floor with nurses in attendance day and night. The house was empty and silent in those days. Lights burned day and night in wall brackets, forgotten, as in the corridors of hospitals, or as if lit by some searcher in a house that is not occupied. A few of the faithful came, those who had known the party days when the big room below stairs was filled with laughter and song, but not many. Jessie Landis was always there, and Jessie would go upstairs and stand at the foot of Hartley's bed and sing the songs he loved. Toward the end when he could scarcely speak, he would see Jessie and whisper, "Girl—sing." And Jessie would sing his favorite "There Is a Lady Sweet and Kind" and always he would smile a pleased and grateful smile— for he indeed was a gentleman sweet and kind.

Dwight was there through day after day of the agony, pale and distraught. Marguerite came, toward the end, from a hospital in Auburn, accompanied by Sam and Jane. Laurette was like a wild thing, one moment a defiant fury raging at everyone, the next sullen and withdrawn, lying for hours on her bed like a wounded animal.

The house seemed to hate illness as Laurette hated it. It too seemed to have grown sullen and cold and silent. In that room four flights up was the whole concentrate of its life shrouded in pain and drugs; and when the drugs failed, there was loud crying and terror and sorrow. Sometimes in the dead of night Hartley would cry out in an enormous voice, "MURDER! Help! MURDER!" and the whole house seemed to shudder and lie supine under that cry. And those in the rooms below would grip whatever their hands could find, or their own flesh, and hang on and pray to God to lift the horror and suffering from that house.

But when Laurette came to visit him only delight suffused his face. What did it matter that she did not come for days, sunk in her own opiate against suffering? Those time spans were gone for Hartley. Life *was* in her presence; it was *not* when she was gone. Like a child he reveled in her smile, her quick gay sallies, the tomboy chuckle, the lyrical Irish talk. He took no note of the battered and bloated face, the bloodshot eyes, the trembling, scarred hands, but saw only the core of that wonderful sweetness that had always been his.

She would put her face close to his and smile that wonderful smile, and everything dissolved in her nearness; his fear and pain and loneliness. "Come with me, Laurie . . . come with me. . . ." he whispered once with terrible clarity. And Laurette curled her lips in a smile, rumpled his dark locks and answered lightly, "Come where, Hartley—you silly guy? I'm with you, darling, right here." And because he wasn't supposed to excite himself (she'd seen the chart the nurse kept: "11.15 P.M.—crying, calling for his wife. 2.30 A.M.—crying, calling . . ." on and on between the notations of injections), she would put a finger to his lips and say, "Hush, now, darling. . . ." And then she would be gone, walking straight-legged down the hall, like a little girl sent on an errand and now returning—back to her room, back to her world of make-believe that was becoming so shredded and tattered and poor a hiding place.

There were whole stretches when time did not exist for her between those visits, but when it did, she came to him.

One day as Laurette sat beside him, he said to the nurse, "You don't always speak the truth, but tell my girl the truth now."

The nurse said, "What truth, Mr. Manners?"

He turned and put his hand on Laurette's cheek. For days his hand had been going past any object he tried to reach, but this day it came directly to her face. He gazed at her earnestly for a long minute and whispered with great tenderness, "Tell my girl it will be a long time before I see her again."

Tears were not for Laurette. No tears, ever. "Nonsense!" was her sharp reply; then to mitigate the sharpness she put her cheek against his and whispered close to his ear, "Nonsense, my darling!"

Revolt, fury, guilt and despair tore her to pieces when she was away from him, until a merciful oblivion came. But when with him, she brought only the ineffable sweetness of her nature, that sweetness which he loved so dearly and had enshrined in his heart forever. And surely it was his to claim, for in all their life together he had nurtured and loved it, and held it above corruption.

It was a gloomy evening in December; Jane, Sam, Dwight, and Marguerite, keeping the death watch, were gathered in the well-like living room waiting for dinner. Dr. Devol had remained upstairs with Laurette. She was being difficult, stubbornly insisting on returning to Hartley's room where she had been only a few minutes before. The doctor was trying to dissuade her: Hartley was unconscious, had been for a number of hours, no immediate change was expected; she should have her dinner. Joining the others, Dr. Devol said he hoped he had persuaded her.

But he had not. As soon as he was out of sight Laurette darted up the stairs swiftly and stealthily. Some sixth sense told her she must hurry if she would be in time. As she entered the room Hartley turned his head toward the door but did not open his eyes. Quickly she went to his side and took his hand and, as though he had waited only for that moment, he gave one long shuddering sigh and life went from him.

When Devol found her she was standing talking quietly to the face on the pillow. Death had erased all marks of suffering from the wide brow, the deep-set eyes. There was a look of great serenity, of dedication, the "priestly" look which Laurette had always found so beautiful.

No one could have behaved worse in the days that followed. Laurette would have nothing to do with the barbarisms of a funeral. Those who came to perform the final duties were obstructed and excoriated by a woman who seemed to be waging a singlehanded battle against the world. She would see no one, she would do nothing, and anything anyone else did was wrong. Somehow she got through the church service dry-eyed and bitter. Father Francis Duffy said the Mass, a truly priestly gesture for his good friend Hartley Manners who, although living outside the Church, had, according to Father Duffy's noble conscience, observed its Christian precepts all his life. But religion brought no solace to Laurette. She was on the outs with religion and with God, as well as the world. When years later she would remark, "I could never understand why Hartley was taken away from me. I mean to speak to God about it when I see Him," she was not being humorous or quaint. She meant it. She had a score to settle with God. It was a very personal matter.

After the funeral everyone was sent away from the house on one excuse or another. Marguerite and Dwight returned with Sam and Jane to Auburn; Laurette would join them in a day or two when she had settled a few things. The servants were dismissed. Then she called the Salvation Army to take away Hartley's clothes and personal belongings; even the fourteen-foot writing table was to go, but it was too big to be moved. After that, she hired a couple of men and had them carry all photographs, press books, letters, programs—every item she could find which represented her life with Hartley in the theatre—and pile them in the service yard behind the house. Alone once more she poured kerosene over the pile and set a match to it. The bonfire went on for hours. She made several trips to the house returning with more papers which had been overlooked and added them to the flames; anything that escaped did so only because it escaped her frenzied search. Once a policeman looked in. She told him what she was doing and he went away. "Someone should have stopped me," she wrote later, "but who was to know I was quite off my head?"

After that she took a taxi to Macy's, bought gay lounging robes and pajamas for Sam, Jane, her children and herself. That night she boarded the midnight train for Auburn. Hidden under her voluminous cape was the ancient and decrepit Michael. It was two days before Christmas.

On Christmas morning the members of the Adams' household gathered for breakfast clad in the flamboyant robes Laurette had brought them. Laurette looked around the table with bright desperate eyes. "My God," she announced in a harsh voice that was meant to be humorous, "you all look like wax figures in a store window! And not a bit gay!"

She was fast running out of ideas about what to do next. Each step away from the beautiful face lying so peacefully on the pillow was a step into chaos. Everybody seemed to know what to do but Laurette. Her children knew enough to follow the coffin out of the church with some semblance of composure—"Where did you learn to be so *sensible* in the face of sorrow?" . . . Jane knew enough to make out lists of the right people to ask to the funeral—"Just like a social tea!" . . . Letters had to be written, flowers acknowledged, the right things said, the right amount of gratitude shown; there was always someone who knew about these things and could do them properly. But Loretta Cooney had no ideas at all. She had burnt every remembrance of the world she had lived in with Hartley—for why should there be bridges to a world that is gone? Like a frantic impressario filling in for some suddenly canceled production, she had ordered, bossed, railed at everybody around her, bought costumes, demanded lights full-up, gaiety, laughter. Now she was taking stock of her handiwork: the lifeless figures, the failure to come in on cue, the total lack of comprehension between herself and those around her. Under her categorical imperatives life refused to assume the faintest aspect of meaning. . . .

Laurette's nostrils flared with the hopeless anger of the vanquished and the eyes that had known no tears darkened.

"I'll be a fool without Hartley," she announced with stark finality. "Just a God damn fool!"

*

# April Child

"Aries people are determined to think
and reason out their own methods and
ways, as they become confused if asked
to follow other people's minds or suggestions."

*Pasted in early scrapbook
belonging to Laurette.*

In theatre annals of the next decade Laurette's life is to remain
virtually blank. After sixteen years on Broadway this "star of
celestial illumination" abruptly disappeared from the theatrical
skies. "Following the death of her husband, Laurette Taylor
went into retirement" was the ubiquitous phrase used by polite
journalists. Gossip had more unkind things to say: she was
through, a hopeless alcoholic, the theatre would see her no more.

Laurette would in time refute that prophecy and make perhaps the most extraordinary comeback in theatre history. But
even this is not the measure of her story. The potential of its
greatness lies hidden in the ten dark years of obscurity. For in
these years, no longer against a make-believe background but
against the background of life itself, Laurette struggled to master
the one role which had always eluded her—that of her own self.
No columns of praise, no critical accolades, no achievement
awards are given for such a struggle; nor can her success be properly judged by the tenuous hold she was at last to achieve upon
the territory to be conquered. But in terms of human values it was
to be her greatest triumph and shines with undiminished luster
above the far easier conquests of her theatre career.

She did not immediately tackle the part. She sulked. She lied.
She wove her fancies; gave herself to fits of boredom interspersed

with bursts of disciplined activity. Consistently and over long periods, she drank.

Drinking was the over-all pattern. Into it were worked tentative designs during brief periods of self-discipline and sudden purposefulness. But the designs break off, are left unfinished, and the same monotonous pattern—gray, designless, shroudlike—covers the hours, the weeks, the years, and is the more horrible because it conceals life, not death.

It is doubtful whether Laurette's purpose was to destroy herself with drink. She had too much vitality and enthusiasm for that. It was rather as though the initiative was wrested from her, and the creative forces so powerful within were inverted into a negative pressure which pushed her down to the lowest darkness to which a human soul can descend. She made no attempt at first to vanquish these forces. She seemed to harbor a vague idea that she was "getting even" with life for the dirty trick it had played on her.

In time she became lonely and frightened. Her magnificent stamina began to desert her; she was hounded by remorse and in her basically Catholic soul believed herself damned to the nethermost Hell; doubly damned because she was convinced that she would never see Hartley again. Propped up in bed one Sunday morning shaking with the aguelike tremors of the alcoholic she raised enormous battered eyes to a visitor, Buff Cobb, and said with stark despair, "Hartley's gone into the light, Buff. I know it. And I can't follow him. I'm in Hell, and I'm going to stay there. I can't get out. And I'll never see him again."

There is no charting of such inner turmoil. One can only trace the surface patterns that form, break up and realign themselves, giving some indication of the deeper stresses beneath. Essentially it was Laurette's fight and in moments of clarity she knew that it must be made alone and in her own way. In this her greatest show she was both actor and audience. She it was who called "Bravo!" and "Shame!" watching the bad parts with lackluster eye, sitting suddenly bolt upright and fascinated when the piece moved dynamically; turning her back on it altogether when it bored or overwhelmed her with disgust.

There were would-be saviours, of course. Some rode in on

bold white chargers only to ride quickly away when they found not a languishing princess in a lonely tower, but a virago of despair, a dragon snorting fire from a thousand heads. Some came with real love and labored selflessly to help. Laurette accorded them at first the most touching devotion and gratitude. Then suddenly she would be bored; gratitude, affection, the last modicum of interest were abruptly discarded like the wig, make-up, and costume of a role she had played too long. Some made it their business not to know that anything was wrong; they were there when the lights were lit and the drinks were served, and stayed away when the house was dark and silent. And there were those in the theatre who never lost the vision of her genius, and gave her every opportunity at their command to come back. But until ready she spurned them all. Psychologists, priests, doctors, as well as friends and family played only minor and inconsequential roles. She told them all when she had become just the least bit friendly with the truth, "I have to lick this myself, and I'm going to lick it with a glass in my hand."

The fanciful was still her bulwark against the harshness of reality: She did not have to play in the theatre any more because Hartley had left her all the money she needed. This was, or at least soon became, fancy, not fact. Hartley's will, made at the peak of their early success with "Peg," reflected the generosity of a man who had made several million dollars. It called for the payment of numerous bequests in England and the United States and a lifetime annuity to Annie Dunne in London. The principal was to be left in trust to Dwight and Marguerite with the income to go to Laurette while she lived. His estate actually approximated two hundred and eighty-three thousand dollars. Loans from New York and London banks consumed over half that total. The bequests, taxes, administration, and miscellaneous debts reduced it further, leaving about fifty-six thousand to be placed in trust.

But the trust income, plus play royalties, Laurette considered quite inadequate to her needs, and a year and a half after Hartley's death she asked the children to release the principal for her use. With no more than a telephone call from Laurette's lawyer as legal advice, the release was signed by the children, but not

without considerable misgivings as to the wisdom of their act.
This was in the summer of 1930 when the value of the estate
had further shrunk due to the stock-market crash of 1929. Nevertheless, for all her dislike of financial matters, Laurette displayed
uncanny judgment in disposing of family assets. In the September
before Hartley died she accepted a handsome offer for the remaining lease on 50 Riverside Drive which little more than a year
later would have become a white elephant. Lockdune was sold
for cash. In July, 1931, a year after the principal of the trust was
released, the talking-picture rights of "Peg" brought sixty thousand dollars from Metro-Goldwyn-Mayer. In all, this gave her
about one hundred and seventy-six thousand in available funds.
But in less than three years the money was gone. All that remained then were the royalties from Hartley's plays, "Peg" royalties for the most part, rolling in year after year, as high as
twelve thousand dollars annually, rarely below four thousand.

But such sums meant nothing to Laurette. Nor did the rate
at which she spent them bother her at first. She lived in the
mañana of the alcoholic: tomorrow would be different. The right
play would come along, the right role, the right producer. Her
potential earning power was terrific whenever she was ready
to put it to work. She ignored the fact that Broadway gossip
was beginning to stick. The whispering chorus, "We can't trust
her,"—"we can't take a chance," she did not hear. Was she not
always briskly on hand to discuss scripts, the details of a contract,
why she would or would not play a part? Could she not look as
wonderful as ever after a week of treatments at Elizabeth Arden's,
and a diet of soup and tomatoes? The weeks that her phone did
not answer, that business appointments were cancelled by a harassed lawyer who "knew nothing"; when a frightened colored
maid said anything that came into her head about the "flu" or
"called out of town" or—Laurette's favorite—"motoring in the
country" to impressive personages arriving with contracts under
their arms or in full evening dress for dinner; these weeks did
not exist for Laurette. She was back at her old stand of self-
delusion, the old hocus-pocus which she prayerfully hoped would
work in life as successfully as it worked in the theatre.

She had a car, a chauffeur, a country place at Sneedan's Landing across the Hudson, a vast musty apartment on Madison Avenue to house her Italian furniture, rich brocades and Steinway piano. When in the mood she entertained lavishly at both places. Any suggestion that the family fortunes had radically changed put her at once on the defensive. That Dwight and Marguerite must now pursue a livelihood no longer as a matter of artistic bent but as one of cold necessity was a fact that she could not and would not face. "Why Marguerite thinks she must live in a cheap little room and *grub* for a living is beyond me!" was the way she summed up her daughter's modest beginnings in the field of journalism. Any mention of necessary economies in front of Laurette's friends elicited an airy, chuckling, "Marguerite likes to indulge the fancy that she is a poor working girl." Dwight, married in 1929, was also having his financial troubles, but she passed these off by excoriating his "practical-minded" wife, who had taken all the fun out of him and made him so "damn solemn" about the business of earning a living. To admit that her children were in financial difficulties would be to shake the bastions of her fanciful world. She preferred not only to ignore but to deride the fact.

"I rattled around in my enormous apartment, then I went to Europe and rattled around in expensive hotels" was the way she described the year after Hartley died. On the European trip her long-time friend, Mary Morley, accompanied her. "Wandering through Europe," wrote Laurette later, "I grew to have a deep appreciation of Francis Thompson's 'The Hound of Heaven.' Only it was the memory of Hartley that 'hounded' me: 'Through the valleys, up the mountains——' I went to the churches, stayed in their quiet, lit candles, tried to get comfort where I had been taught to look for it. I never saw the face nor heard the voice of Jesus. Nothing appeared above the candle glow except Hartley's face. Nothing except his voice came through the stillness: his voice, and his eyes asking, 'What *is* the matter with me, Laurie?' "

In London after a dutiful and blankly uninformative luncheon with Martin and Annie Dunne, during which she decided they could not possibly be Hartley's kin, she looked up old friends: Gerald du Maurier, Noel Coward, Edith Evans, C. B. Cochran. Lynn and Alfred Lunt were playing in "The Guardsman." Grace

George and William Brady were there. It was all the same world, but it was a world without Hartley.

She still sought answers, demanded explanations of why life should be so cruel. Because her friends had written plays, played great parts, spoken suavely, effectively, often touchingly to millions, they must know something, have some crumb of philosophy to give her. But du Maurier was as bewildered as Laurette by life's unkind quirks, and could only gloom companionably as they sat together in his dressing room at Golders Green where he was trying out a new play. "Family—children—that sort of thing—don't help much," he commiserated. "Nice when they're babies; but then when they're older, they yawn down their noses at you. You know how it is—come in at two in the morning and if you speak to them, tap their lips and yawn, 'Wha' faw-w-ther?'" And he and Laurette suddenly laughed together like naughty children taking off their elders.

Noel was terribly kind. You could "let down your hair" with Noel, pour out your troubles. But after a while he grew impatient. "My dear Laurette," he remonstrated, "Christians astonish me. The more they believe in a beatific future the more they weep when a loved one goes to it. A pagan and his pagan relatives are the happiest people. They die easily . . . because they have no regrets for the past and don't believe in the future." * This was the echo of the brash young Gerald at Herbert Tree's dinner many years before when she had first come to London. Sorrow and loss were then abstracts to him, too. She might have, for just a minute, felt a little older and wiser than Noel. But the feeling didn't last. Everyone knew better than Laurette. She knew, as she often put it, "jes' nothin'."

She grew bitter about her friends—except those few who had patience with her "idiotic seeking" as she called it.

"It is tragic," she wrote later, "how patient people can be if you're visibly smashed . . . a broken back or something. And what a nuisance you become if your broken soul is stumbling about before their eyes." Lynn's defection she never understood and dated it quite arbitrarily from the time her career went into

* "Noel Coward" by Laurette Taylor. *Town & Country*, May, 1942.

obscurity and Lynn's zoomed. There was great bitterness on both sides.

London was haunted by the voice and face of Hartley. The memories were too strong, and from time to time, without warning, she slipped into the confused misery of drink. But she was not at all difficult or belligerent. With a heartbreaking docility she would accede to Mary's pleas to relinquish theatre tickets, call off engagements, stay in her room, and there, heroically, would battle alone until her demon was under control. She was on some kind of search and it buoyed her momentarily from giving over entirely to alcohol.

There was a brief stay in Italy. More people to see, more questions. In September they sailed for home. Laurette barricaded herself in her cabin, ate scarcely a meal. The search was over and she had found no answers.

One old friend had left her in the spring of '29. Michael, deaf, semi-blind and rheumatic, never resigned himself to the loss of his master. After Hartley's death, all Michael's waking hours were given over to a ceaseless pacing, a hopeless search for the one who was gone. Finally, Laurette could bear it no longer and took him to the veterinarian in Easthampton who had been Mike's friend for many years.

"There's nothing really wrong with him, Mrs. Manners," said the kindly little man, "but Mike is old and infirm and very tired. Suppose you leave him with me, and one of these days—after a good dinner and a stroll in the sun—I'll put him quietly to sleep."

After some hesitation, Laurette agreed. As they talked, Mike wandered into an adjoining room, where for a time the tap-tap of his long claws had been audible, but now there was silence.

"I'll say good-by to him," Laurette told the veterinarian.

"Wouldn't you prefer to spare yourself that, Mrs. Manners?"

"Oh, no. Mike and I have been together seventeen years— I'll say good-by to him, if you don't mind."

Just inside the door they found him, on his side, dead. Laurette didn't cry. Instead she spoke to him in the soft brogue of Peg which he loved so well. "Shure, Michael, ye always knew when to take your curtain call," she told him proudly, "and ye knew when to take the last. It's a grand exit ye've made, Michael . . . believe me."

Boredom was very real with Laurette. She was never one to while away time over a manicure or shampoo, dawdle in shops or at luncheon. Routine matters of living were anathema and most of her extraordinary life she had been spared them. Her life had been geared to the single drive shaft of the theatre and when that shaft ceased to turn, there were periods of almost no auxiliary motion whatsoever. With alcohol, these periods could be prolonged indefinitely. Gradually they were taking over her life.

In the back of her mind was an honest belief that she could return to the theatre whenever she wished, and with this eventual grace hers for the asking, could in the meantime behave as outrageously as she pleased. But there was another factor that was cruelly deceptive. It was when life beckoned most persuasively, when excitement lit her eyes, laughter and good fellowship warmed her, and success seemed within easy grasp that she would turn and walk into her room and lock her door on the world. The prospect of a good play, congenial company, some event which set off to best advantage her charm, wit, the extraordinary radiance which drew people to her—these were the pressures that catapulted her into the abyss. It would seem that she could not accept this image of herself, for was it not this image, this bubbling, joyous and reckless creature reaching out for life with so vast an appetite, which had betrayed Hartley?

The hound that chased her was far more apocalyptic than she knew.

*

# Alice-Sit-by-the-Fire

Early in 1932, William A. Brady arranged for a group of theatre people to appear before a Congressional Committee in Washington in protest against a Federal excise tax on theatre tickets, and rehearsed them carefully in their statements. It was Laurette's first contact with an audience since Hartley's death. As usual she proved a delightful and persuasive speaker. "I could feel myself capturing and holding them," she recalled. "When it was over, I told Bill Brady I wasn't through as an actress."

Then and there they began laying plans for her return. Whatever doubts Brady had dissolved in her radiance.

That night Laurette's daughter, visiting at the Beekman Place apartment, was awakened by an ecstatic "Marguerite, Marguerite!" There at the foot of the bed, coat still on, handbag clutched characteristically in front of her, eyes shining like lamps from under a bizarre piratical electric-blue hat, stood Laurette. Waving the bag from time to time to emphasize a point, she gave a rhapsodic account of the day's events. "They loved me—and how they laughed!" she chuckled. "Carter Glass came up afterwards and told me if there were a few more speakers like me, the theatre would be tax free forever! He's a darling fellow, talks like a gangster out of the side of his mouth in the queerest rasping voice —but a darling! And you should have seen how his face lit up. Oh, it was fun!"

She ended with a verbatim account of what she and Brady had said on the train, and then, with her lips curling as though over a particularly delicious morsel of food, murmured, "Mm-m-m-m, but it was wonderful to find myself talking theatre again!"

Yet she turned, with that incandescent look still on her face, went directly to her room and began to drink. By the next morning the bright vaulting spirit had been obliterated and in its place was a hulk of insensate and glowering despair.

Brady, in blissful ignorance, and with the magic memory of Laurette delighting the tired and overworked members of the Senate Committee, went enthusiastically ahead with his plans to revive Barrie's delicate and tender comedy, "Alice-Sit-by-the-Fire."

On the opening night, four years to the week and day since she had last appeared on Broadway, the hosannas rose to the theatrical rafters. The rejoicing over her return and the rejoicing over her performance filled columns of newsprint. "She does not tamely remind us," wrote Brooks Atkinson, "what a superb actress she is. In every scene she seems to be creating something fine and rapturous that has never been seen before. To have Miss Taylor back is a wondrous thing." The ovation on her first entrance "threatened to tear apart the walls of the Playhouse." The welcome was not only for the artist but for the woman who had thrown off despair, conquered her demons and was back. "It was peculiarly thrilling to sense the immediate, almost pell-mell cordiality she established with the audience," wrote Gilbert Gabriel. How happy she was to be with them and how happy they were to see her! "Please God," wrote Atkinson fervently, "may she never be absent again."

Celebrations were fervid. A party at Beekman Place was a "must" on the list of all who loved to skim the cream off success. She was drinking "socially" along with everybody else. To close friends she said, "Don't worry. I'm all right." Even the most pessimistic had thought all along that the theatre was the only therapy Laurette needed. She was back. She was triumphant. All was well. But almost immediately there was a pitch of excitement too high for comfort, and although the drinking was social, there was too much of it. One evening, after the play had run several weeks, Laurette failed to appear at the theatre and money was refunded at the box office. The next night she played, after broadcasting a few highhanded excuses for her absence.

The rumors began all over again. . . . Brady had been a fool . . . she was totally unreliable. . . . To refute them she gave a large party for Mrs. Patrick Campbell, asking several members of the press. Aleck Woollcott brought along Brooks Atkinson, hoping to dispel the latter's forebodings after the one-night closing. It was not a reassuring evening. From the outset Laurette was not in control of herself. Guests straggled in, having been asked to come at different hours, and a huge spaghetti dish covered a multitude of omissions at what was supposed to be a banquet.

Mrs. Campbell as usual took the center of the stage. George Bernard Shaw's letters to Ellen Terry had recently been published and Mrs. Pat was mellifluously deriding them. "Love letters!" she snorted. They meant absolutely nothing. Her letters from Shaw were vastly more interesting. Dipping into a large evening purse, she continued, "I happen to have here one of the letters——"

"*Happen!*" clucked Woollcott, who was enjoying the debacle of the evening quite as much as he had been prepared to enjoy its triumph. "She's been carrying that letter around for twenty years!"

Mrs. Pat ignored him. She leaned over to the hostess whose drooping head gave no indication of conscious attention, grabbed Laurette's hair at the nape of the neck and thrust the letter under her nose. "Here, r-r-read it, Laurette!" she commanded. There was a painful pause. Abruptly Mrs. Campbell released her grip and Laurette's head fell forward. "*I* will read it," she said, glancing about with the perverted sense of triumph she seemed to derive from the humiliation of others. And read it she did.

Later in the evening Mrs. Pat again singled out the hostess, loudly bemoaning the advancing years. "I'm sixty-nine, Laurette —just think of it—sixty-nine!" If still expecting no coherent response, she was quickly disillusioned. Laurette even in her worst moments could display amazing resilience. Sassily and quite suddenly her normal self, she came back with, "Well, don't worry about it, Stella. You don't act a day over ten!"

The resilience was momentary. Several nights later she arrived at the Playhouse obviously in no condition to go on, but over every protest insisted on playing. It was a terrible evening on both sides of the footlights.

Frightened, she fought for control through a sleepless night and the next afternoon was at the theatre sober, but was told the matinee had been canceled. Besieged by reporters, Laurette insisted she had not the faintest idea why the performance had been called off; they would have to ask Mr. Brady. Later, when Brady's announcement that he had withdrawn the play was read to her over the telephone by a reporter, she had nothing to say. Also without comment she forfeited her bond for good conduct and was five thousand dollars poorer.

The reverberations of this catastrophe reached far beyond the limited confines of Broadway. They even penetrated to a modest white-frame house in Far Rockaway, Long Island, where a kindly, keen-eyed little woman lived with her daughter. A few days after the closing of "Alice-Sit-by-the-Fire," the secretary in Mr. Brady's outer office looked up to see this alert little body standing before her desk. She wished to know Miss Laurette Taylor's home address. The secretary was sorry but it was against the policy of the office to give out such information. The visitor protested that she was a relative and must get in touch with Miss Taylor at once. Brady stepped out to have a look. "How do I know you're related to her?" he growled, cigar in side of mouth. "By my nose!" responded the little woman tartly. Brady studied her nose. "By God, that's right!" he said, and gave her the address.

It was Nellie Tye, Elizabeth's favorite sister, and mother of Mabel, the cousin of whom Laurette had always been so fond. They had not seen each other since the days when they had happily cut up Mr. Goodman's beautiful dresses for "The National Anthem" and resewn them closer to Laurette's fancy. Nellie had come every day then to Riverside Drive and watched with bright incredulous eye the high, wide and handsome doings of Elizabeth's girl in her heyday. Laurette admired Nellie for her Dorsey spunk and independence, and had never forgotten her devotion during Elizabeth's last illness.

She admired her now, standing in the darkened hall of the apartment, determined to tackle this family problem which had filled her with grief. "Oh, Loretta, aren't you ashamed of yourself! Whatever got into you to do such a thing? What is the matter with you, now—with all that you've had out of life and raised to be a God-fearing girl—carrying on like this?" It was the robin-bright eye of her mother, the quizzical turn of head, and under the scolding chatter the fierce loyalty that had surrounded

Laurette as a child. Nellie had come to help. Laurette knew that. The whole flooding remembrance of her mother must have invaded her consciousness. But she said not a word. Instead she turned with strange enigmatic smile, walked up the stairs, into her bedroom and locked the door.

. . . All night long she must have tried to piece together two measures in her life, like two strains of music in jarring dissonance from different songs. There had been the Dorsey guts, and there had been the dream-come-true with Hartley—and then lost. The Dorsey guts were no more like the dream than a woman's silks are like her bone marrow. Now she possessed neither. Whatever the measures had meant, they had fallen away into silence. There had been no union, no higher harmonic from the two. Thoughts of desuetude and death plagued her, and no amount of alcohol could match them with oblivion. . . .

Nellie spent a harried night, sitting bolt upright in a hall chair wondering what to do. In the dawn her fitful sleep was broken by the rattling of the chain-bolted door as it was opened from the outside. Long, black fingers inched through, fumbling at the lock, and a rolling eyeball appeared at the crack. "I'se just the colored maid," came a hoarse, conspiratorial voice, "tryin' to get in." Nellie, nerves a-tingle, unbolted the door.

The two were in the kitchen making coffee when Laurette strode in carrying a full bottle of Scotch. Nellie drew herself up, a solid mass of indignation. "What are you doing with that?" she demanded.

"I thought we'd have a drink," Laurette replied, a glimmer of mischief in her eyes.

"You'd do better pouring that down the sink and having coffee with me," said Nellie tartly.

Laurette walked directly to the sink, up-ended the bottle and allowed the contents to gurgle slowly down the drain. Then with the same mischievous look and dipping walk she used when pleased with herself, left the room.

Undoubtedly, in that odd inverted fashion she toasted the Dorsey guts. And undoubtedly she wished to God she had those guts to make the fight that was before her. . . .

Nellie needlessly chided herself that she did not stay. But

there was nothing anybody could do. Nellie's simple, prayerful life had never been shaken by such revolts and doubts as tore Laurette apart. The magnitude of the problem, the disorder and hopelessness of Laurette's existence appalled her, and she did the only thing she could do—went back to her home on Long Island and took up the chore which Bridgett had so long and faithfully performed: daily prayer for the salvation of Laurette's soul.

*

# *Enchantment*

When Laurette ceased drinking after the fiasco of "Alice" and began to rationalize what she had done, it went like this: "For whom was I acting? To whom could I talk afterwards? . . . I found it stale and profitless without Hartley around. . . ." No, she was through with the theatre, acting bored her. She would use her knowledge and experience to write plays and fiction. Hartley had been very encouraging when she was working on the mermaid play that last summer in Easthampton. Yes, that was what she must do. One had to be much more self-sufficient as a writer, and that was what she must learn to be now that Hartley was gone. In the theatre she missed him too much. "He was my anchor, my blanket, my top judgment and the closeness of our bond was the theatre. . . ." Yes, the only answer was to go into an entirely new field of creative activity where the memory of Hartley was not omnipresent.

She set about her new career with dogged determination. A small portable typewriter is introduced midst the opulent grandeur of the Italian antiques, the time-toned brocades of the upstairs studio room at Beekman Place. It is as incongruous in its surroundings as is Laurette sitting before it in the early morning hours enveloped in loose lounging pajamas, glaring at the keyboard with smoldering belligerence while two pecking fingers slowly marshal the black letters. "The mechanical thought-killer," is the name she gives it. As with most actors the morning hours are the least inspired, she feels not at all sufficient and in the evening, when life begins to pulse, from past habit she wants people around her. It is so much more fun to bounce ideas off people than off an unresponsive piece of paper. However, she keeps at it. She begins to revise the mermaid play "Enchantment," and starts on some Irish fairy tales.

She does not lack for offers in the acting field despite theatre people's badly shaken confidence. Movies, radio, the stage are all possibilities, although hedged with requests for a posted bond, flat-out demands for "good conduct," or the more subtle squeeze play of "financial reasonableness" on her part; all of which infuriates her and is an excellent excuse for withdrawing from negotiations at the last minute.

It is a lonely time. The only self-discipline she has known is the theatre, and to apply it now in solitude far from the theatre's warmth and hubbub is hard, well-nigh impossible; the monastic, soul-searching hours of the writer are the antithesis of the happy "rag-picking" she used to do along the busiest highways and byways with Hartley. To be alone, with only the faltering little hammers of the typewriter to cut a path of escape, is more like suffocation than self-expression. Time and again she would flee the cold, dead little machine on the card table and seek companionship with her "glorious bums," lose herself in the sparkling chatter and gaiety of theatre people, the music and beat of the theatre world. But it was a brittle hold she had even on this world. She passed through the lighted rooms, the crowds of her fellow artists, a strangely separate figure on a ceaseless quest; a quest that was the more heartbreaking because she seemed to stop abruptly in excited expectation before each burst of laughter, each well-told tale, each warm persuasive personality, like a child who peers in bright windows clutching her pennies, devouring with her eyes the many trinkets on display, not knowing what to buy or if to buy at all. And in the end, confused, she passes on until there are no more windows but only the dark street, and she is frightened and once again, alone.

One night at a party she spied an actor friend across a crowded room and involuntarily called his name. There was something in the voice that was like a cry for help. As he turned she sped to him, clutched his arm with wild illogical gratefulness, and with no other preliminaries, cried, "You can help me, José, I know you can help me!"

Laurette had met José Ruben many years before when he accompanied Sarah Bernhardt on one of her farewell tours. They had remained good friends through the years. Currently he was playing in the highly successful "The Cat and the Fiddle," which he had also directed. She had great admiration for his ability. His performance of Oswald in Ibsen's "Ghosts" remains one of the classics of the American stage. He possessed much of Hartley's all-round knowledge of the theatre, the same ineluctable standards of performance; there was the same gentleness and patience without the moral rigidity. Whether she thought of any or all of these things when she called to him, why she seemed to see the flutter of Salvation's robe behind his swart Gallic figure is unfathomable, but his response was immediate; he had heard the stories of her drinking, he sensed the desperation of her plea. What could he do to help? What did she want of him?

The next morning she brought "Enchantment." He did not find the play too promising, but anything that could perform the miracle of restoring her to the theatre would be magnificent for that reason alone. They began to rework it together. Gradually he won her over to the idea of playing the part of the mermaid, Crystal, which at first she had not even considered. She began to look her beautiful self, face and figure slimmed and firmed; her ambition returned in full force. Meanwhile, George Cukor, now a motion-picture director, made tests of her in scenes from "The Harp of Life." It was a gorgeous test in everyone's opinion and did much to restore her confidence.

Then came an opportunity to try out a new play by S. K. Laurens, "Finale," in summer stock, and Laurette felt, with José directing, she could make a success of it. To do this he arranged with Max Gordon for a leave of absence without pay from "The Cat and the Fiddle." They drove up to Stockbridge ahead of time in Ruben's car, rehearsed intensively. Although nervous and on edge Laurette got through the engagement. In September they played another week in Westport, Connecticut.

These two engagements, successfully completed, seemed to be the best possible therapy for Laurette. She was sure now she would bring "Enchantment" to Broadway and was full of plans for a production. Robert Edmond Jones must do the sets and the costumes, José would direct, of course. . . . It was hard to have to tell her that his leave of absence was up. His financial sacrifice had already been considerable and he did not feel he could forego a lucrative road tour. Laurette became quite obtuse. The mention of money she considered a venal concern in the face of such glorious prospects for her return to Broadway. If he truly had her welfare at heart he would stay, not leave her alone at a time like this. . . . This was all she knew, and any other attitude was quite incomprehensible . . .

Even before he had gone, she began to drink. The rapturous, translucent Laurette disappeared before his eyes, the months of devoted care and work were destroyed overnight.

Ruben left to be away a year, heartsick at his failure.

But Laurette had stored away a little bit of new knowledge from this association. She was at her "rag-picking" even if unconsciously so. Ruben had the breadth of tolerance toward human fallibilities characteristic of the Gallic temperament and had gradually lured Laurette to a little more tolerance of herself. "Laur-rr-retta," he would say, giving her baptismal name a rich Latin sound, "what is it to drink a little? Why is it you are so afraid of little pleasures that you must make them into big sins? —*Ce n'est pas important, ma petite!*" Laurette needed desperately to have her devils exorcised instead of locked away in cupboards, and it was this good friend who first opened the doors a tiny crack and made her look at them with less fear.

In a letter to Cukor, written in January, 1933, she told of her new, more expansive feeling toward life. "I have been seeing a lot of people who have been around for years. Hartley and I never knew them really. I find some of them most unexpectedly charming—I suspect it's because I'm more charming; having decided to bury the Irish gloom along with St. Patrick's snakes and pretend I had a very vivacious French father."

After Ruben's departure she had gradually got herself in hand and gone about the promotion of a Broadway production of "Enchantment" alone. Although her mentor was gone, she had regained her lost confidence step by step. Harry Moses scheduled the play for a spring opening, Robert Edmond Jones directed in addition to designing costumes and sets. The incredible Laurette, looking every inch the timelessly young Crystal, rehearsed with a catlike grace and cold enchantment that was something entirely new in her repertoire.

Her name went up in lights on the marquee of the Plymouth Theatre for the opening April 18, 1933. At the last minute there was a postponement. A few days later Moses announced the abandonment of the production.

To the outside world Laurette disappeared after each such episode. People shrugged and wondered. Few knew of the desperateness of the battle, and when she emerged again it was hard to find the scars.

After each downfall she pulled herself up again. It was the same solitary operation that the descent into oblivion had been. Laurette's glorious constitution was beginning to feel the abuse, and there were many times when a nurse had to be brought in; but as soon as she could say "no," the nurse went. The sight of the white-capped attendant represented total defeat; and it was from this nadir that her fighting spirit began to rally. The very first maneuver in the battle was to throw the nurse out. From this point on she proceeded to take care of herself in the same way that a hurt animal does, slowly, methodically, in complete solitude and with single-minded purpose. Begun shakily and requiring a tremendous effort of will, the restoration nonetheless went forward systematically step by step until the goal was reached. Once embarked upon there was no backsliding, and there were no short cuts—no sedatives, no drugs—for Laurette had a mortal fear of drugs and never used them in the mildest form. The task was heroic and took the invulnerable stuff of a fighter.

The ubiquitous companion of Laurette's dark years was her colored servant, Marie; Marie the primitive, the childlike, tall and lean as a Masai, naturally laughing and trustful, who took Martha's place when the latter retired after sixteen years of service. Marie had two choices when Laurette began to drink:

to be locked in or locked out. By hook or crook she tried to get herself locked in. Then she bided her time, stepping light, saying nothing, keeping quietly out of sight. If by chance she were locked out, she would arrive faithful as sunrise day after day to see if the bolt had been slipped on the door, which was Laurette's tacit admission of need. If it were, in she would go for the duration.

From her barricaded position Marie would issue dramatic bulletins to the world outside. "The marshal's at the door!" she would announce in a hoarse whisper over the phone. "He's poundin' on the door—what'll I do?" or, "Can't smile at that groceryman no mo'—he's MAD!" or, "Gertrude (the laundress) she's not like me, Miss Margaret; she works for *money!*" And sometimes with wild displeasure: "Now she say I stole her jewelry. Why does she want to accuse me like that? She know I can't get no justice in the courts!" But her anger would not last. Marie understood. She had seen her people lie and steal and kill in revolt against the soul's adversity. She knew Laurette suffered and she understood. The bill collector, the threatening landlord, the outraged dignitary, were familiar figures in Marie's world. Instinctively she gave the soft answer, the placatory excuse. And when Laurette turned her world right side up again Marie was the first to rejoice, with a joy that was sometimes hard to differentiate from her mourning. At the sight of her mistress, emerging fresh as a rose from her bedroom, Marie with long legs together would jump up and down uttering small shrill cries like a mating bird; the same exhibition that, like as not, heralded the approach of ten dinner guests whom Laurette had invited and totally forgotten. When the happy days came, Marie skittered around the apartment putting things shipshape, whistling at her work, calling out bits of news which Laurette had missed, brewing countless cups of coffee, welcoming the first visitor with a shining face. She would even go so far as to scold a bit if Laurette dallied before coming to the table for her supper. "Now you know that soufflé won't stand!" she'd chide, blissfully happy that so temperamental a thing as a soufflé could once again raise its head in the household.

Marie stayed for almost five years. It never occurred to her to find an easier mistress to serve. Through Marie's simple primitive nature, her childlike devotion, Laurette reached down from time to time and touched the earth and grounded the lightning in her soul.

After each determined attempt at a comeback, the wreckage piled higher; wreckage of friendships, broken promises, bad faith, unhonored contracts, unpaid bills. Laurette dared not look behind. She went forward. There was always a morning when she sat at her desk in a room rich with the scent of Elizabeth Arden beautifactions—a smell as intrinsically a part of Laurette's renascence as the vernal breezes are of spring—and took up the business of living; letters in a bold hand explaining her silence; telephone calls imperiously abrupt concerning appointments broken, bills unpaid. More and more alone, self-sufficiency for which she searched so desperately receded into the distance like a will-o'-the-wisp. She trusted fewer and fewer people. Suspiciousness grew on her year after year. Having no memory of events for weeks on end, she brazened out her lack of knowledge by accusations of bad faith on the part of others, disloyalty, neglect and concomitant offenses. She still could not be wrong. Always she must find some weakness in others to explain each debacle. She was a long way from facing herself and from becoming self-sufficient.

Her correspondence with George Cukor during this period reveals the troubled mind, the desperate clinging to half-truths, the imagined need for a Svengali to bolster her faltering will. But also it is clearly evident that no amount of adversity and insecurity softened her demands as an artist.

When negotiations developing from "The Harp of Life" movie test ran into a wall of unexplained silence at the time of Ruben's departure, Cukor wired and wrote to know what had happened. Was she ill? "Yes," fibbed Laurette. "I had an honest illness sent me by God. Not me, myself." But negotiations are going forward, she continues. Her only concern is to be sure that he will direct. "I cannot face my first acting picture without you. Never would I have made that test—that gorgeous one—without your guidance. I would rather do a play or radio (both of these are very much pending) until you are free. You see, having broken my confi-

dence in myself in one way, I lost it in all ways. As I know
now, Brady was a mistake. I also know that it is important for
me to have implicit faith in a director and a great satisfaction in
pleasing him. How will I know for a certainty you will do the
picture?"

But the motion-picture producers were not overly enthusiastic
about "The Harp of Life." They wanted Laurette, not the play.
She writes again:

"I really am at a loss to understand being offered the Silver
Cord mother when the Harp has a bigger and better mother to
show the world. . . . It is certain in my mind that the Harp is
the play for me in talking pictures."

Her royal insistences do not go down well with the powers
that be in movieland and George finds it hard to smooth her way.
She demands John Barrymore and when they offer Lionel she
says no, because "Lionel isn't as good an actor as John—now."
When informed that George is fulminating because she is "too
damn bossy" she writes in quick penitence, "You seem to think
I insisted on Barrymore. Of course you know that was only a
suggestion I hoped might come true. No *insistence* on *anyone*
for that matter." She wants to please George. She trusts him.

After the failure of "Enchantment" to open, the picture deal
again grows cold. The Broadway whispers swell to a chorus:
"She's finished!—she's through!" Several weeks later Laurette
takes her battered world by the scruff of the neck and sets it
upright. Brightly she writes to Cukor that she is boarding a
Grace Line boat for California; her play is to be rewritten and
will be done in the fall. Actually she has purchased the production from Harry Moses, who has relinquished all rights; any interest in producing it now is entirely her own. But this is not
mentioned in her letter. She goes on to say: "RKO called and
asked me to play the mother in 'Little Women.' I said 'no' of
course. Really, George, it's beyond my understanding! I make a
marvellously attractive test and they offer ugly 'Silver Cord'
mothers or apple pie ones like 'Little Women.' It's beyond me
why I should think either of those parts an opportunity! However,
darling, that has nothing to do with anything, except I want to
see you before I start back. With love, Laurette."

Laurette visited her son and his growing family who had been living on the Coast since 1932, when Dwight adapted his Broadway hit "Gay Divorcée" for the movies. That production followed by "Top Hat" had not only launched the famous Fred Astaire-Ginger Rogers team but established Dwight as a top-flight film writer. Laurette was spunky and gay, extravagantly proud of her son, enjoying again the Mad Hatter atmosphere of Hollywood, unawed and disrespectful. At a swank preview she commented to an AP man about the star, a reigning M-G-M queen: "She has a face like a baby's bo-hind—two expressions, either wet or dry."

In every possible quarter she plugged "The Harp of Life" but apparently to no effect. To sell Hartley's plays along with her services was as hard as ever, and there is no doubt, too, that rumors of her unreliability were quietly closing doors on all sides.

When she sailed in July, Cukor sent champagne to the boat. Laurette cabled him: "Dear George. There is nothing I hate more than sweet Italian champagne."

\*

# *Fighter's Odds*

These were the darkest days of all. There were no offers. Only old George Tyler, watching a new theatre he could no longer understand, treasuring the memory of Laurette's glory, agreed to do "Enchantment." But it was just one more plan that went down under a flood of alcohol. How bravely she pulled herself up from the abyss, but how hopeless seemed the short agonized periods of work at the typewriter before the awful silence settled again.

Laurette's finances were in a terrible state. Rent and servants were unpaid, business affairs in a tangle, nurses' and doctor's fees eating up every bit of available cash. Merchants and others, hopeful of an eventual comeback, had extended credit, large sums which could not possibly be paid unless she got back in the theatre and utilized her tremendous earning power. She still persisted in the illusion that her drinking was a well-kept secret, still tried to prove by sheer dint of suppressing the facts that alcohol had nothing whatever to do with the increasingly erratic and snarled pattern of her life.

Laurette's lawyer, once Hartley's, for whatever reasons of his own, went along in this illusion. He scheduled business appointments, canceled them when she did not show up, did what he could to avoid the penalties for more flagrant breaches of good faith, and never indicated he was aware of the reason for her capricious behavior. When asked by a harassed member of the family why he had complicated matters by pursuing certain negotiations on schedule when he had every reason to believe she would not appear, he coldly replied that he considered it "none of his business" that his client drank; he may have been *told* that she drank, but he did not know from personal experience that she did, and he did not want to know. Because he never admitted that Laurette was menaced by the disaster of hopeless alcoholism, he never made it his concern or responsibility to provide a hedge against such disaster. Dwight and Marguerite felt it was from such an ostrich-like position that he had engineered the signing away of the original trust. Needless to say Laurette was delighted by his loyalty to her illusions as well as her needs, and as her suspicion of others grew he became, perhaps, the only person she trusted implicitly.

In the meantime, Marguerite and Dwight, desperately trying to fill the financial gaps, placate those unpaid, and protect Laurette as best they could from the consequences of alcoholic irresponsibility, finally recognized one clear fact: the signing away of the trust fund had been a grievous mistake. In a belated attempt to correct the error they decided to bring joint action to re-establish in trust whatever assets remained in the estate.

Laurette was incredulous, indignant. The action would result in publicity that would splash her name over the front pages of every newspaper, ruin her reputation! Her lawyer rallying to the fight tried to prevent the move with every means at his command. The daughter would be cut from her mother's will. (Laurette never admitted Dwight was involved.) His client had finished a new play and a summer-stock engagement was imminent; this would crush her resolve, perhaps fatally retard her return to the theatre.

But the chronically optimistic view no longer seemed valid.
There had been many crucial opportunities in the six years since
Hartley's death, and each had dissolved in failure. Was this not one
more fantasy woven across the hard realities? One more subterfuge
to continue her self-destructive way which could lead only to
utter destitution? Wasn't it their patent duty to protect her from
any further squandering of her assets? There would be no publicity. The hearing would be held in chambers with no reporters
present. Marguerite and Dwight decided they could not in good
conscience put off the move any longer.

The hearing took place, July, 1934, in the Surrogate Court before Judge James A. Foley. It came too late. There were only bills,
the royalties from the plays, and the small trust fund set up for
Annie Dunne. This fund, the understanding judge insisted, over
the objection of counsel for Laurette, be held in trust upon Annie
Dunne's death instead of coming to Laurette direct so that she
would be assured of some small income for the rest of her life.
Grasping the seriousness of the situation and irritated by the refusal
of Laurette's counsel to recognize anything but his client's immediate wishes, the judge, solely upon his own initiative, further
ordered that upon Laurette's death the trust should be divided
equally between her two children. This, he stated, seemed to be
only fair as partial restitution for their dissipated patrimony. After
the hearing he called Marguerite aside, took her hand and said with
obvious concern, "I'm sorry, terribly sorry to hear all this. I had
no idea that things were so bad with her. This was the best I could
do."

After the court action—a move which embittered her to the
bone—Laurette did none of the things expected of her. She did not
go to pieces. She went ahead with the summer-stock engagement,
completing it successfully. Carried along on a wave of positive action, she moved her belongings from the expensive East River
duplex to more modest quarters on the top floor of an apartment-
hotel at 14 East 60th Street. There was a brisk flurry of telegrams
between Laurette and Cukor on movie possibilities. If the wave
seemed too high, too fast, to be sustained, those who watched
clung to hope nonetheless.

What was the answer to Laurette's buoyancy? Partly hurt

pride; partly determination to show how deeply she had been maligned. But perhaps the most significant clue was to be found in the play which had been presented at Ogunquit that summer. Written in the blackest days of 1933–34, "At Marian's" told the story of an alcoholic. Many aspects of it were Laurette's story thinly disguised. It was not a very good play and parts were extremely muddled in thought. Produced as a comedy, the audience had found it heavy and depressing. But that, at the moment, was not the important thing. What was vastly important was that Laurette had written direct, hard-punching lines about an alcoholic, and spoken them herself; that while still denying such a problem existed in her own life, she was telling of the weaknesses and fears that destroy an alcoholic, of the ugliness and utter degradation that comes with drink. One excerpt from the play shows how far she had traveled down the long road toward facing the truth about herself at last.

In a letter to Charles, her tennis-playing fiancé who has been unable to see her for days, Marian breaks the news that she is an alcoholic. She does not spare herself in the description of what that means. "Did you have to be so damn graphic?" Charles asks miserably, then reads aloud excerpts from the letter:

> I have been *low sick* like any other drunken woman . . . *only* I have a house, Webster (the maid) and money to make it look less horrible. Understand, I don't drink in a gay fashion with a lot of people in a cabaret or at a dinner table—mine is the most degrading, lonesome, swishing up of anything alcoholic! I don't care about *anybody or anything*. How Webby manages me I don't know—but without her I would be a mess living *in* a mess—

The letter concludes: "I wanted you to know—it's not nice, it's not pretty."

Charles comments: "You didn't spare yourself any, did you?"

Marian: "A half truth is half sister to a lie."

The woman who wrote that was beginning to fight with everything she had.

But then, without warning, the wave broke in a smother of broken engagements, incoherent, halting lies on the telephone, then recession into the all-engulfing silence. Laurette the effulgent, Laurette the child of hope and light, was gone. The procession of nurses took up again like paid mourners at a funeral service that is never concluded.

Communication between members of the family was infre-quent. Dwight, busy in Hollywood, assumed without complaint the more pressing financial burdens. Marguerite, closed out by resentment and anger since the trial, had problems of her own trying to support herself and maintain a shaky marriage to a charm-ing but impecunious ex-playboy. One day close to Christmas Laurette's doctor telephoned Marguerite at *Fortune* magazine. He was in great distress. The latest nurse had walked off the job in a state verging on hysteria and refused to return. Laurette was a very sick woman. She had flouted every order; he could no longer take responsibility. What could be done? He did not know. He had exhausted every resource.

Laurette did not recognize Marguerite as she bent over the bed. Barely able to speak she clung desperately to her daughter's hand, murmuring over and over again the name of the nurse. She had apparently been alone and helpless for hours. Frightened, Marguerite called her own physician at once, but because of the baffling ethics of the medical profession was able to persuade him to look in on the case only unofficially. His diagnosis, also unofficial, was that Laurette might die at any time of inflamma-tion of the brain; she should be taken to the hospital immediately. Then another medical ethic further blocked action. No patient who can indicate dissent, even by a shake of the head, can be re-moved to a hospital except by court order. Laurette was virtually unconscious but one had only to say "hospital" and her head turned determinedly from right to left. With this unhappy situa-tion medical ethics left Marguerite to cope alone.

Under emotional duress one is liable to make major tactical errors. Of all people, Marguerite sought out Laurette's lawyer for advice—the same who had made it none of his business to know that Laurette drank. He was still smarting from the recent hu-miliating defeat in court. Rising to the full height of his outraged sensibilities, he announced that Laurette's daughter might be so heartless as to seek commitment of so glorious a talent, but never would he be party to such a thing.

Possible court action for Laurette's protection had been discussed by Marguerite and Dwight as far back as 1932 after the closing of "Alice-Sit-by-the-Fire," but the harsh realities of commitment with all its ego-destroying implications had frozen their resolve, and nothing had been done. Now the ugly word was thrown gratuitously and with brutal abruptness into a conversation the sole purpose of which was to seek aid for a desperately sick woman. Marguerite, aghast, asked if there was not some other way by which a terribly ill person, deprived of the aid of both nurse and doctor, could be gotten to a hospital for proper medical care? Surely something less drastic than commitment proceedings could be arranged? "My advice to you," responded this monument of self-righteousness and self-imposed ignorance, "is to return home and be a loving daughter to your mother."

The interview later compounded misunderstanding between mother and daughter. Seemingly dogged by an unsuspecting naïveté, it never occurred to Marguerite that the talk would be relayed to Laurette as an attempt, frustrated by the lawyer, to bring commitment proceedings. The knowledge that this is what transpired came several years later in a letter Laurette wrote to Dwight: "It would have been a shame if Marguerite had been able to do what she tried to do . . ."

Marguerite, now desperate, searched frantically until she obtained a nurse who would take an alcoholic case without a physician in charge, then got in touch with the psychologist whom Laurette had consulted before Hartley's death. The next morning he stopped in briefly to size up the situation. The nurse had tidied things up and done everything possible for Laurette's comfort, but her physical condition was virtually unchanged. The psychologist agreed to return in twenty-four hours when it might be possible to persuade Laurette to enter a hospital. His words on leaving were, "She is very ill. It still may not be possible to talk to her but I will do my best."

The following day he was astonished to have Laurette open the door. She was dressed in her fanciest pajamas, hair caught neatly back with two combs. The nurse was nowhere in sight; if still in the apartment she was there by sheer force of character. Laurette did not open the door wide, just a few inches. The face was battle-scarred and badly puffed but carefully sicklied o'er with a pale cast of powder; eyebrows brushed, brown eyeshade daubed on upper lids and a mouth drawn with lipstick in a rough extemporaneous hand. It was a fighter's face, pugnacious in its ruin, punch-drunk but not licked, ready for the next round, the next blow; a brutal, suffering face but one that still challenged all comers. "What are you doing here?" she asked indignantly. "I did not send for you." Whatever he said was unconvincing. She told him to go away, she did not need him.

With slow deliberation Laurette closed the door in his face, thrusting out her jaw and glaring belligerently through the crack until the last possible moment. It was as though she wished to impress upon him finally and forcefully, so that there would be no possibility of misunderstanding, that she had not asked for help and did not want it from anyone.

This extraordinary ability to fight her way back alone was one of the phenomena of Laurette's make-up. There was a heartbreaking and hopeless gallantry about it. It was fighter's odds of a thousand to one. And even as she threw all her handlers from the ring and began punching the referee, one hoped and prayed that the final decision would be hers.

But the strongest constitution cannot stand such abuse indefinitely. This last episode was a grim warning she did not take.

Laurette abhorred hospitals, sedulously avoided them and was positive that if taken to one she would die. A young doctor called in to see her during the Ogunquit engagement, asked with youthful earnestness for her full medical history. "That's easy," replied Laurette, "I've had two babies and two teeth out."

But by the spring of 1935 she was a very sick woman. She had developed severe anemia and lost forty-five pounds. Dr. Edmund Devol minced no words: her condition was dangerous and she must go to the hospital at once.

Laurette begged for time. At last she had a really magnificent opportunity. The faithful George Cukor was to direct John Van Druten's "The Distaff Side" in pictures, and had arranged for tests to be made of her as Evie, the part played by Sybil Thorndyke on Broadway. George was in New York, a rehearsal scheduled for Sunday at her apartment; Carol Stone, Estelle Winwood and Laurette had been working on the scene for weeks. After almost two years of inactivity things were moving again. She must not miss this opportunity and there must be no mention of illness to Cukor. Against his better judgment Dr. Devol conceded and the rehearsal went through on schedule with the doctor standing by.

The next morning, April 1, 1935, her fiftieth birthday, she was taken to the hospital for an emergency transfusion. An operation was postponed until blood count and weight could be built up. In the meantime a blood donor stood by. Another hemorrhage, according to the doctor, probably would have been fatal. Laurette knew this, knew that behind the excessive bleeding there was a possibility of cancer. Although terribly frightened, she faced these possibilities with a new fortitude. She would not allow Devol to communicate with her children, but fastened her mind on life, not death, and prepared to meet alone what was ahead.

Her main concerns were that Cukor not misunderstand the sudden disappearance into a hospital and that the opportunity to play Evie not be lost. "Dear George," she wired on April third to the Coast, "came to Woman's Hospital on my birthday. Nothing serious. Should have come before our rehearsal but the doctor knew it would break my heart. I wanted to tell you everything so you would have complete confidence and understanding . . . Am writing . . ." And in the letter: "I weighed 110 pounds when I came. This is the eighth day and I weigh 117. I'm glad, because at this rate I'll be fit for the tests in two weeks, I should say. It's a great piece of luck my face being round—you can always put a diaper on bones."

The rest of the four-page letter is devoted to the scene she will play in the test; subtleties of interpretation, possibilities for humor, suggestions for dress for all three characters.

The operation took place April tenth. There was no malignancy. The next letter is two days later. She is planning to rehearse as soon as she gets home, and thinks she can make the tests by the end of April. "My face, as I told you, looks the same. In fact, this rest and right food have taken the tired lines away as well as that pinched look of sickness. Anyone in your concern who wants to know about me can either telephone or see Doctor Devol."

The fear of misinterpretation of her illness still plagued her.

Devol asked if he might write Cukor of her amazing recovery.
Laurette jumped at the suggestion. In his letter Devol paid high
tribute to the courage she showed at the Sunday rehearsal. "With
an alarmingly low blood count and a hemoglobin of less than
twenty, so weak she could scarcely get out of bed, she struggled
through make-up, set the stage as it were before a crackling log
fire, and went through, heaven knows how, that very trying rehearsal."

Eager to speed his patient's recovery, both mentally and physically, and knowing how much she banked on the opportunity to
make the picture, he poured his optimism and enthusiasm into
the letter:

> Her comeback has been nothing short of miraculous. Her spirits
> are gay and hopeful and each day she shows in every way more
> satisfactory gains. I have never known her more eager to get into
> harness than she is at present. My belief is that she will now go
> steadily forward to gain the lost time, of which she is so deeply
> conscious.
>
> Mr. Alexander Wollcott, who went in to see her yesterday, tele-
> phoned me with great enthusiasm about his visit with her. He thinks
> she is the greatest living American actress.
>
> No doubt Mrs. Manners has written you of her progress, and her
> hopes, but I felt it might be a comfort to you to know from her
> physician of her present condition.
>
> Sincerely yours,<br>Edmund Devol

Laurette is home by the seventeenth and talks with Mr. Altman
who is to make the tests. "Would it be time enough two weeks
from today, the thirtieth?" she writes George. "And how soon
could you get me word back as to my suitability to the part?" She
plans to sail to California rather than go by train, and has made
a deposit for reservations on the *Santa Paula* sailing May twenty-
fifth, and arriving the eighth of June. "I must go by boat. For the
*first time in my life*, George, I have been near death—really.
. . . So the boat trip (I thrive on boats) is necessary." If the test
is a success would he let her know in plenty of time?

> How I wish you could fly here and spend a day making the tests.
> If they are not satisfactory I shall always feel it was because you
> were not here to light me. Will I go one day—(the twenty-ninth

say) for hair and make-up and the next day for scenes? Shall I comb my hair different ways or just the way *I* like it best? In the scene with Carol Stone I shall wear a plain well-cut negligee (no pajamas I suppose? Not even sedate ones?) In the scene with Estelle a dress such as you suggested, something chic, well-cut and simple. . . .

If you are not going to direct the picture or anybody's mind has changed about me, let me know immediately—so I don't fasten my mind on those tests, and can go about another proposition that has come up here.

. . . My face is full and only has a 'sick look.' A girl from Arden's is coming everyday to massage that away.

The dates are set with Mr. Altman, make-up and hair on the thirtieth, the playing of the scene on the third of May. Mr. Altman had asked that the scenes be cut a little. "I told him that I would like to ask you about that and he said, 'Never mind, you had better do them as Mr. Cukor rehearsed them.' "

At the same time she is plugging for a test of a young actor, John Meredith, who played Charles in the initial production of "At Marian's" in Ogunquit. If Cukor is interested, she will write a duologue and make the test with him. "I assure you George that John was surprisingly good as Charles. You know I'm a wise bird about acting."

She is devoting every hour to getting well and ready for these all-important tests. The Elizabeth Arden girl comes each morning for massage. At noon she walks to the Tavern in Central Park, has her lunch of almost raw meat, vegetables and fruit, sits in the sun for a while, walks home. From two to four she dictates letters or works on scripts. Carol Stone and Estelle Winwood arrive at five for rehearsals. Occasionally there is bridge at night, but usually, exhausted, she drops into bed directly after supper. "That is my day—with my brain racing and ready to go, and my body not yet willing to keep pace. . . . I am looking awfully well, George, really, except for a sort of sick look in my face. . . ."

The day is drawing near and she has not heard from George. There is a mounting concern over lighting:

He (Mr. Altman) told me how he took Sybil Thorndike and asked me if I had any suggestions. I told him you arranged the light in my test so that there was very little movement—so as to have a

good light *all the time* during the duologue and to give free play
to the expression of the face without it looking haggard through
going into a bad light. He then said you had mentioned that to him
but that *movement* was so essential to a scene. . . . George dear,
would you make your wishes quite clear to him?

The test could be a younger woman than fifty—I had my children just six months after I was sixteen—and (don't laugh) I could
have been a late baby with my mother. This is written (as everything I write you) only as a suggestion, my dear. I know the value
of the "lust of the eye" in Hollywood particularly.

As to the test from my play—do let us do that. I have written a
scene that shows my pantomime gift and John's figure! Entirely
different acting than Evie—

These assertions of my different talents are only made, George,
because I feel the necessity (in these particular tests) of showing
"my all"—so I convince M-G-M I am as good as you have "tooted"
me—because they are the people I want to go with *and only* because you are with them: because of the humor and understanding
between us about acting.

Am well, untroubled, and only hope no sick look shows in my
face. There is very little when I look in the glass.

There is a report from Altman to Cukor, May fourth, that the
make-up test went well and Laurette was pleasantly surprised
when she saw it. The actual dialogue test was to be air-mailed to
the Coast May eighth. "I gave Miss Taylor every co-operation.
As you said Miss Taylor is a little difficult but before the test
was over she said she was greatly pleased—and I take it this is quite
an admission from the great Laurette. I think she did a swell job
and I hope it comes out as well as it looked."

Laurette's last letter is undated. "Dear George: Have you seen
the test? Was it awful? Don't be afraid to tell me. I want to know.
I'm no longer proud . . . if you hear of anything in Hollywood
for me let me know, won't you? With much affection. Laurette."

Laurette did not sail for Hollywood. Whatever the logical or
illogical reason, there was no official report on the tests and this
silence reached her with all the mercy of a two-edged sword.

There was one herculean attempt to turn disaster to something
immediately constructive. She picked up the phone and called
Day Tuttle who as a stage-struck youngster had admired her back
in Easthampton days and who was now running the Westchester

summer theatre with Richard Skinner. She has rewritten her play "At Marian's" in a lighter vein and suggests that they produce it with her in the title role. She would bring the script out to Mt. Kisco that very night for them to read.

Skinner and Tuttle were at the station to meet her. Scanning the coaches as the train slowed down they saw her face briefly at a window "a little white and pinched and questioning." Then she was coming toward them along the platform "a trim jaunty figure with its self-confident undulant walk." They both agreed she looked marvelous. There was only "a kind of whiteness in the face" that was somehow disturbing. . . .*

For ten days Laurette was the center of the life of the young and eager Thespians who made up that enterprising summer theatre, and seemed to thrive on the admiration and keen interest she evoked from them, most of them fifteen to thirty years her junior. Tuttle and Skinner began enthusiastically to make plans for the future; "At Marian's" would not only be done at the Playhouse but they would take it to New York.

"It's going to be the beginning of great things in the theatre for all three of us," said Dick Skinner.

"I think so, too," replied Laurette, jubilantly linking arms with her young benefactors. "The beginnings of great things in the theatre again. For all three." *

Rehearsals began and for four days she commuted to Mt. Kisco. Then she shut herself up in the apartment at 14 East 60th and no one could get to her. The telephone was off the hook, and no amount of clamor or pleading at her locked door evoked an answer. The Playhouse had been sold out on her name. At the eleventh hour "The Patsy" was substituted. The day before the opening Laurette called. She was ready to come out and rehearse and open the next night. Tuttle said he was sorry, they had had to make other arrangements, it was too late, etc. etc. She kept saying yes, yes, yes, in a subdued voice, "I quite understand . . ." Then she hung up.

In August she played at the Casino Theatre, Newport, under the auspices of the Actor Managers', Inc. The play: "At Marian's."

* "Recollections of Laurette Taylor" by Day Tuttle. *Theatre Arts;* March, 1950.

The audience: brilliant. It was like old times. The Newport elite gave box parties; Mesdames Hugh Auchincloss, Cornelius Vanderbilt, Hamilton McKay Twombly, Walter Belknap James. Laurette and Hartley had always thrilled to their plushy audiences. There was a special air of quiet celebration; the return of the prodigal daughter. Knowledge that Marian's fight was Laurette's own added to the warmth of their welcome. It was what Laurette loved, "quality applause—affectionate as well as admiring." It comforted her heart and gave her courage to forget past mistakes.

She played again in January in Miami, at the invitation of the Walter Hartwigs who had their winter theatre there.

Again she had slipped, but this time had not hit rock bottom. Despite bitter disappointment and extreme loneliness, the landscape of her life seemed perhaps not quite so bleak, not quite so fearful as her "overexercised imagination" had made it, now that she spoke the truth, and looked at the truth through Marian's eyes.

*

# *Eloise*

In the summer of 1936 a strangely solitary figure, swathed in voluminous silk crepe slacks and jacket, could be seen walking to and from the beach at Ogunquit. In the small New England community used to the sight of actor-folk this lone figure seemed to stand apart from the bustle of the summer theatre and drama school run by the Hartwigs.

To a few of the middle-aged natives "Peg O' My Heart" was a warm memory of their youth, and they were surprised to learn that this rotund little woman in tentlike habiliments was the Peg of that past era. But to most the reference was more vague—some old-time actress, so they were told, who had been living in retirement for many years.

In the profession it was different. Otto Preminger, arriving in America from the European theatre, was to learn immediately and unequivocally that Laurette Taylor was, bar none, America's finest actress. But the information was invariably accompanied by a shake of the head; the tragedy was she could not be depended on, not one producer dared take a chance on her. It was too bad, but there it was. Her sister actresses were unanimous in proclaiming her "top gal" as Helen Hayes put it. Ethel Barrymore, Katharine Cornell, Ruth Gordon, Tallulah Bankhead, all handed her the palm. "I simply have never seen anyone like her on the stage," stated Ethel. "What she did was indescribable."

As to the students in the school, they were a whole new generation come of age since Laurette had played the last of her successes on Broadway. In their theatre history she occupied an equivocal position; it was far less durable than that of those hardy souls who had literally trouped their way into the permanent pages of the drama, more tenuous because her vehicles had lacked the enduring quality of the classics, or even, according to the critics, that of good playwriting. There is nothing more ephemeral than theatre fame, and Laurette's refusal to troupe once she achieved stardom, or to play in any but her husband's plays had shrunk the memory of her with this new generation of drama students to the dimensions from which she had been so determined to escape: a personality actress with a one-part success, "Peg O' My Heart."

When she talked of the theatre to these young people—and she came often to visit with them—they glimpsed a fabulous past: special performances for the great Bernhardt, exciting tales of the legendary Stanislavsky, stories of the theatre's pageantry by one who had been in the thick of it. Her legend took on body then, but still they must have wondered as they sat in a half circle at her feet and turned eager faces up to hers: what of her style— her technique? Would these not appear outmoded now, cloying, mannered, overblown? The very essence of her acting was an "immediacy" which could not be forecast, and was difficult to look back on except as an emotion engendered in the beholder; those who had seen her found it impossible to describe, and those who had never seen her found it impossible to imagine.

But the students were delighted with Laurette's friendliness, her laughing breathless stories in which she herself took unqualified delight. She attended all the student plays, freely criticized their work, with uncanny precision pinned down the weaknesses and strengths of their performances, and to their oft-reiterated question, "Miss Taylor, have I talent?" always gave a blunt answer. They were thrilled when she strolled down to the converted garage, where the students gathered every night, bringing along the Broadway star from the current show.

Laurette was living alone in a cottage close to the ocean, writing a new play. She was doing her own cooking and housekeeping and sticking to a strict schedule of work. A reporter that summer wrote of her "somewhat reserved manner" despite her friendly smile; another of the "curious seeking quality" of her glance. Harold Clurman was to capture perhaps better than anyone else some of the qualities which the more sensitive of these youngsters felt as they gathered about her, drawn by a magnetism, a central fire, that was unmistakable.

> What distinguished Miss Taylor just as much in her failures as in her successes was the quality of her talent. She expressed a constantly tremulous sensibility that seemed vulnerable to the least breath of vulgarity, coarseness, or cruelty without ever wholly succumbing to the overwhelming persistence of all three.
>
> She was staunch even when she appeared broken. She suggested a kind of mute devotion and loyalty to what she loved even when everything conspired to batter her. . . . Laurette Taylor seemed to be the victim of a thousand unkind cuts so minute that no word could describe them, no poet make them pathetic. She seemed always to be weeping silent tears, and her slightly bent head or averted eye were unspeakably moving because they were gestures so brief as to appear wholly imperceptible. Her voice was like buried gold whose value we could not guess; her speech flowing and ebbing in strange unequal rhythms was like a graph of her soul in its bursts of tender feeling and recessions of frustration and confusion. A luminous confusion composed her aura. It shone brighter for its ambiguity and its refractions. It warmed us deeply because it was generated from the unrhetorical sources of an ordinary woman's being rather than from any studied glamour. There was always something surprising about it, and no one appeared more surprised

by what she sensed and experienced than Laurette Taylor herself. Her face was always suffused with a look of startled wonder, at once happy, humourous, frightened and innocent." *

Among the drama students was a wisp of a girl with a pale heart-shaped face and beautiful but large hands to which she seemed not yet to have grown up. She wore her dark hair in two pigtails and her face was innocent of make-up. Excruciatingly shy, she had a way of flitting about backstage like a sweet but terrified wraith. Spying her one day at a rehearsal Laurette leveled a forefinger, asked bluntly, "What's that girl doing here?"

Laurette took a dim view of anyone with too many drawbacks to overcome choosing the theatre as a career, and this shy wispy student struck her as poor material. The girl was Eloise Sheldon, age sixteen, who had left Radcliffe College in her second year determined to have a career on the stage.

Shortly afterwards Laurette saw a student one-act play, "The Miners," and revised her opinion as to the girl's possibilities. "She made me laugh and she made me cry," said Laurette, and decided then and there that Eloise possessed that mysterious thing, "quality," on the stage. From then on Laurette saw everything she did and criticized her work freely.

One day as Eloise walked offstage from a rehearsal Laurette was standing in the wings. "How's my little girl?" she asked, and put her hand against the cheek of the pretty childlike face. It was a gesture of great tenderness, spontaneous, unguarded, existing of itself, yet it was to build a bridge to a whole new world and bring back the lost components of trust and simple affection to Laurette's life.

In the years to follow Eloise was often to witness the brusqueness, the outright cruelty of a woman who had estranged many with an undisciplined tongue, but it was never to be directed against her. There was a need that loneliness had brought out, a kindness and tolerance that had never been there before for those who lacked confidence and needed love before they needed either approbation or criticism. Eloise became the focal point of this new understanding, a winter growth, but from soil well harrowed and ready for the seed.

* Harold Clurman, "Death by Entertainment," *Tomorrow*, March, 1947.

Through the fall of that year the friendship grew. Eloise was working on a Hilda Spong Scholarship at the American Repertory Theatre on Fifty-ninth Street, and at the end of each day made a habit of dropping in at Hotel Fourteen for a visit. Laurette was applying herself to writing, leading a life of great simplicity— a lonely life—in the disordered eyrie on the topmost floor. The playscript "Of the Theatre" was taking final shape, the story of an old actress who sits in the audience and exchanges views with young drama students rehearsing on the stage.

The theatre, except for an occasional first-night party, had largely removed itself from Laurette's life but she was determined to hold on to it as a playwright at least. She tried to believe she did not want to act any more, no longer cared one way or the other about being an actress, but there were times, as when she saw John Gielgud's "Hamlet" and mingled with old friends and compatriots at the reception afterwards, when she wasn't so sure. When Gilbert Miller offered her the co-starring role with Cedric Hardwicke in "Promise," a Paris import, Laurette took it.

What happened was one of those malign quirks of fate which so often and so cruelly trip the foot of the embattled alcoholic.

A few days before the opening Laurette was hurt in a taxi accident on the way to rehearsal. The left side of her face was smashed and swollen. A doctor was called to the theatre. There were different accounts of what followed. "No one suggested I go home as Hartley would have done," Laurette wrote later. "Instead I carried on with a partly bandaged face. The doctor told me that by the time we opened, my nose would still be swollen and as I was to play an extremely attractive, chic woman, I'd have nightmares about a chic hat above a swollen nose. Instead of doing something constructive about it, like giving up the part or asking for a postponement—Hartley was my constructive side—I continued rehearsing in the theatre and trying to conquer my jitters at home. I wasn't successful. I still think it would have made a lot of difference if I had been sent home to rest that first day. . . ."

Miller's version, told a fellow producer, was slightly different. The nose had been injured, true, but it was well on the mend. Three days before the opening Laurette arrived at his office and stated flatly that she could not act with Cedric Hardwicke, who never "looks you in the eye." Then she went home. When she did not show up for further rehearsals Miller went to her apartment, walked in unannounced, and found her drunk. He canceled the play and brought suit for damages.

It was not altogether the debacle it appeared. Laurette was learning to turn her defeats before they became utter routs. She finished her play, took it to her friends, the Walter Hartwigs. That summer she and Eloise returned to Ogunquit and "Of the Theatre" was produced with Laurette in the role of the old actress. Eloise stage managed, Jack Kirkpatrick directed.

In the fall of '37, Eloise was back at the American Repertory Theatre. One evening when she stopped for the customary visit, there was no answer to her knock. At two o'clock in the morning a frightened floormaid telephoned from the hotel, begging Eloise to come at once. She was let into the apartment with a passkey. Not until then did Eloise learn of Laurette's drinking. She made a bed for herself on the couch and spent the rest of the night there. So began the long, thankless vigil by an alcoholic's side, the patient nursing and care. She had loved the turbulent, shining and childlike quality of Laurette; now she sensed the loneliness, the despair, the mute longing for companionship. There was no need for words. When Laurette was well, Eloise moved her few things into the apartment and stayed on.

As to how she slipped so easily under Laurette's embattled defenses, when so many had failed, Eloise's explanation was characteristically modest and simple: "You see I knew her when she was old and afraid, and you have to let the screen down sometime."

They promoted the fiction that Eloise had a room down the hall but actually she continued to sleep on the living-room couch. Not until several years later did she move into an adjoining one-room apartment with door connecting. They had a working agreement that Eloise was to type Laurette's manuscripts in return for lessons in acting. This was a happy arrangement for both, as neither had any money to spare.

"That was the winter the manuscripts kept coming back," Eloise recalled. "She could take the disappointments but not always the high spots."

In the clear mirror of Eloise's devotion Laurette faced herself with more honesty than she ever had before. She could recount her sins of omission and commission with a new humility and wonder openly where she had gone wrong. "She was conscious of the many complexities in herself and others," Eloise recalled to Marguerite after Laurette's death. "When as a family you were all together, I don't believe your mother had ever known any feeling of insecurity about herself. When I came to know her she was feeling that, and only just admitting it. And you know that insecurity about yourself makes you understand much more about other people." And yet in many ways it was impossible for Laurette to change. "I've seen her so touched by something," Eloise continued, "and so abrupt about it because she was so touched." What change there was, was only within limits; it was narrow and tenuous, and when any pressure was put upon her, she was the same old Laurette, impatient, confused, shrugging off emotional closeness because it was too difficult to handle.

The life with Eloise was the antithesis of theatre life. Every morning Laurette was up at seven preparing the breakfast. By nine she was at work. She had started a long semibiographical novel on her grandmother Bridgett and the Dorsey family. Her recollections of famous people had been added to, and several of the sketches submitted to various magazines. Also begun was a fourth playscript "Pin a Rose" written under a nom de plume— "*pomme de terre*" as she called it—a man's.

When Eloise took a job at the Experimental Theatre run by Antoinette Perry and Brock Pemberton, Laurette became interested in the work of the young drama students. She coached, put on several sketches, staged her own play "Of the Theatre," again taking the part of the old actress. This led to a guest appearance on Rudy Vallee's radio show. There was a definite stir of interest along Broadway.

But Laurette bided her time. There were elements in her life which for the moment needed cultivation and care and were far more important than immediate theatre prestige. Instinctively she knew this. Her work with the students and companionship with Eloise, the simplicity and routine of her daily existence were creating spiritual reservoirs of strength. Long ago, when her heart was closed and black with the bitterness of Hartley's loss, John

Hays Hammond, Jr. had said to her, "You try to hold love to you, Laurette. That's wrong. Love should be a channel; it should go out and out and on and on. . . ." She was beginning to learn the truth of this, and the learning, momentarily at least, dominated and directed her life.

Laurette's next two excursions into acting were tentative and inconclusive. Hope Lawder asked her to play at the Spa Theatre, Saratoga Springs. The play picked for her was St. John Ervine's "Mary, Mary, Quite Contrary." Laurette remembered Mrs. Fiske as being amusing in the role. When audiences found Laurette only mildly so, she shrugged philosophically, "Mrs. Fiske was funny in rubber boots. I'm not."

Tuttle and Skinner drove over from their thriving Westchester Playhouse to see the performance. Delighted that Laurette was on her feet, they whisked her off to a restaurant and the three talked "Candida" until the early hours of the morning. Although only a tepid admirer of Shaw, and having often expressed the opinion that "Candida" had only one act, the last, Laurette agreed to do it. The guarantee she asked was extremely small, her attitude "down-to-earth" about what she was worth to any producers until she proved herself. "Don't expect me to draw the way Ethel and Fonda and Leontovitch can," she told them, "I've been out of circulation too long. I'm not really worth more than one hundred and fifty dollars a week to you boys until I show you I can deliver the goods." *

Brooks Atkinson reviewed the performance in part as follows:

> Some time having elapsed since Laurette Taylor has been visible and audible to the Gotham playgoer, there is a chance to renew fond acquaintance this week. She is now playing Candida in Shaw's comedy of that name at the Tuttle and Skinner Westchester Playhouse. It is a little difficult to discover just what her ideas about Shaw's second-best heroine may be, for her performance is still in the tentative and submissive stage until the last act, when she takes command and suffuses the stage with the warmth of womanly acting. During the first two acts she casually passes through the play.

* "Recollections of Laurette Taylor" by Day Tuttle. *Theatre Arts*, March, 1950.

. . . The young people in tonight's audience . . . were not seeing a great actress in one of her best parts or characterizations. But
they had an opportunity to discover how liquid human speech can
be when Miss Taylor pours her voice into it.

It was a curiously equivocal notice, and very unlike those
Laurette garnered when her talent was working full power. She
had often said in the past that there could be nothing else in one's
mind when acting a part but the part itself; personal considerations
must not exist. "The true actor acts all the way from his toes to
the top of his head because he is imagining he is completely another person. So if I am this person how can I be affected by
anything that touches Laurette Taylor?"

It is not too wide of the mark to guess that Laurette Taylor's
Candida was affected by several things happening to Laurette
Taylor. She was all too conscious of the fact that almost everyone
had lost faith in her, that she had hurt Tuttle and Skinner and
that "Candida" was in part, at least, restitution to them. In studying herself as a woman she gave only half of herself to the woman-
liness of Candida. At week's end when Tuttle brought her the
modest check of the guarantee, she caught his eye in the dressing
room mirror and said with chuckling delight, "Well, we did it.
*This* time we did it." * It was a human rather than a theatrical
triumph, and at the moment she relished it far more.

That autumn Herman Shumlin gave her the script of "The Merchant of Yonkers," adapted by Thornton Wilder from the Viennese. She liked it and went to his office to discuss it. Then Shumlin
told her there were rumors abroad that she could no longer remember her lines; that he had the greatest respect for her talent,
but as a businessman it was up to him to protect the money that
would be in the production. Would she be kind enough to study
the part and audition it for him? Laurette blazed, "Certainly not!
I'm no amateur!" and left the office. He never heard from her
again.

The interview was a shattering blow both to pride and her new-
born confidence, and made acute the deep suspiciousness of others
that had grown through the years. She got home in a terrible

* "Recollections of Laurette Taylor" by Day Tuttle. *Theatre Arts;* March,
1950.

state of mind. To Eloise she cried in gaunt despair, "If they say you drink or take dope, you can get over it. But when they say you're forgetting your lines, you're *finished!*"

*

# *Outward Bound*

Bill Brady had been in show business a long time. His training had been the rough and tumble of the road during the 'eighties and 'nineties, the hardy nursing bed of many of the theatre's great showmen. As a boy he sold papers in San Francisco and was a peanut-butcher on the Southern Pacific at the same time Charlie Taylor was riding the SP engines to Los Gatos. Later, as itinerant actor and producer he toured the same circuits and used the same pirated versions of the classics as Charlie Taylor, employed the same ingenuity to keep actors fed, the bill collector happy, and the audience coming in. He was playing Faust in Asbury Park when Charlie brought his moonfaced ingénue, Loretta Cooney, there in "Child Wife." They shared notices in the Asbury Park Press. Maude Adams worked for him in Rider Haggard's "She" for six dollars a week. He gave David Warfield his first job on the New York stage. In his plushier days, when recognized as dean of big-time showmen, it took little urging to start him talking of those early times. He loved the fight of them, the vigor and virility, the quality and fortitude of the show people who had been schooled in them and gone on to become the burning lights of the modern Broadway stage. His admiration was for those who had come up the hard way, his scorn for the Johnny-come-lately who had never known the early rigors of show business.

Like many a rough-talking, rough-acting man, he was a sentimentalist at heart. When he stopped Laurette Taylor's son on Forty-eighth Street one day in the autumn of 1938 and asked how his mother was doing, whether Dwight thought she would consider playing for him again, he was not just thinking back to "Alice-Sit-by-the-Fire," or back to the opulent years of her undisputed reign on Broadway, but far, far behind that. He knew what had made stars of her caliber shine. He had a plan to set her shining again.

Dwight, after six years in Hollywood, was producing a comedy at the Vanderbilt Theatre opposite the Playhouse. Brady sauntered over during a break in rehearsals. He was thinking of reviving Sutton Vane's "Outward Bound" as part of a repertory program and wondered if Laurette would be interested in the role of Mrs. Midget. Out of the side of his mouth, and with customary ferocity of expression even when at his most benign, he growled a battery of questions. Could she be trusted? What were her feelings toward him since "Alice"? Was she friendly? Did Dwight think she would do the part?

There was only one answer to the last question in Dwight's mind: she *should* do it. And he thought she was ready. What she needed was encouragement, the sense that the theatre wanted her again, that theatre people were friendly, believed in her. "You go ahead with it from your end," he told Brady, "and I'll do everything I can from mine."

"Outward Bound" is an eerie fantasy of a shipload of people who discover to their surprise and horror that they are dead and bound for Eternity. Mrs. Midget, a dowdy self-effacing little charwoman, at first snubbed by the other passengers, becomes something of a heroine after their destination is known. During the voyage she discovers that the drunken wastrel aboard is the son whom she has helped support out of her savings but refrained from seeing lest she bring him shame. While others meet the Examiner at the end of the journey with varying degrees of bluff, pleading, guilt or defiance, Mrs. Midget asks only the favor of being near her boy and continuing to work for him. " 'Ave they good jobs there?" is one of her first inquiries of the Examiner about the Great Beyond. When told that her wish will be granted she gasps, "It's 'Eaven, that's what it is, it's 'Eaven!"

Laurette was offered the part by actor Bramwell Fletcher as production executive for the newly formed Playhouse Company. Whether by design or happenstance she was not told that Brady had any connection with the organization. She was thoroughly pleased and excited. Mrs. Midget was not a starring role but she thought it a very good one, and besides was convinced that as originally played by Beryl Mercer in 1924, the little Cockney scrubwoman had fallen far short of her possibilities for pathos and comedy. Further, she was delighted to learn that the company planned to establish itself as a permanent repertory organization, keeping its productions on Broadway throughout the year. Her answer to Fletcher was a quick and decisive yes.

Then she learned that Brady was behind the venture. Almost at once she began to waver. Her thin reservoir of confidence, badly depleted by Shumlin, oozed away. Without explanation she shut herself off from her new associates, was "out" when they called. When Dwight got to the apartment she had begun to drink.

With maddening, supercilious logic she began to explain why she was not going to do "Outward Bound." The billing was wrong, the salary inadequate. When she accepted she had no idea Brady was associated with the company. She had no confidence in him whatsoever. It would be a serious mistake to appear under his auspices again. . . .

Dwight no longer tried to suppress years of mounting fury and launched a stinging blast. How long was she going to live under a dead man's shadow? Long before Hartley died she had torn herself to pieces trying to live by his standards instead of her own. And she was still doing it. She had set him up as some kind of god, judging the rights and wrongs of her conduct by him, trying to be a lady when she was not a lady, polite when she was not polite. All of which was not important. It was high time she realized that the power of the combination had not been in Hartley's education, his gentility or knowledge of the art of good behavior but in her own earthiness, her honesty, her closeness to the sources of feeling. These had been her contribution, and it was when Hartley had put these ingredients into plays like "Peg" and "Happiness" that he had been at his best.

Ignoring her rising anger, Dwight went on deliberately. In many ways Hartley had done her a great disservice. He had overprotected her, failed to face facts and make her do so, clung to artifices and pretensions which were valueless and which had only added to her confusion, making it harder for her to accept herself as she was. It was high time she gave up her blind adoration, saw the relationship in its true light, and recognized her own worth as an individual apart from Hartley or anybody else.

Laurette's fury broke in a storm of abuse. "Why you—*you traitor!* How dare you talk about Hartley like that after all he did for you? How dare you call him——"

The telephone bell shrilled through the apartment and Dwight answered gruffly. It was the Brady office. They had been unable to get in touch with Miss Taylor for the last day or two. Was there anything wrong? Nothing at all, replied Dwight. She was busy with costumes and hair, last minute appointments before rehearsals started. She would be there on Monday then? "Yes, absolutely. Tell Mr. Brady for me that she's fine, just fine. All set."

"Now," said Dwight, hanging up, "I've given my word to Brady. I've staked my reputation in the theatre. And if you don't care anything about yours, you can think of mine for a change. I'm just getting started again and I can't afford to be made a liar."

It was almost curtain time and he was needed at the Vanderbilt; but before he went he wanted one thing clearly understood: if she didn't go through with this engagement he was through, once and finally through with her.

Laurette could feel herself crowded on all sides. She had to make a move in some direction. She was afraid to go forward, deathly afraid, for behind she must leave the last remnants of Hartley's protection—prohibitions mostly that were meant to be kind— and the featureless terrain of alcohol that asks no effort, harbors no loves, spurns those who come with love to help. The one she adored above everyone had castigated her, spoken heresy against her other great love, and now was walking out. She would lose him, not only now, this minute, but if she failed to carry through with "Outward Bound" he would not come back, ever. She knew that. All the forces of darkness that had battered her for ten years battered her now, and she cried out that if he left she would hurl herself from one of the long balconied windows to the street. Her face was distorted with despair, her demon sat between her brows and there was no light in her eye but the light of her own private hell. . . .

Dwight deliberately turned and walked from the room. He took the slow, old-fashioned elevator down the fourteen floors, walked slowly through the lobby and down the few steps to the street. . . . There was no gathering knot of people under the lamplight . . . no dark dead form smashed upon the pavement. . . . He filled his lungs with the cold air of December. He knew that a victory had been won.

On Sunday he was back. Laurette greeted him, scrupulously neat, hair caught back with two barettes, a dark blue sailor jacket he had given her buttoned over wide slacks. "She looked like a battered old sea-captain," Dwight recalled, "but she was sober." With shaking hands she lit a cigarette, and in the ravaged, still-suffering face the smile was sweet. "I'm all right," she told him. "I'll be at rehearsal on Monday."

On that first Monday members of the distinguished cast noted in Laurette an extreme nervousness which seemed to increase on succeeding days. Bramwell Fletcher was directing and playing the part of her son. She found fault first with one thing then another. She could not take direction from the stage. Hartley had always felt it was a grave mistake for an actor also to direct; someone should be watching from the auditorium. After several days there was a worried consultation with Brady, and Otto Preminger was brought in to take over direction of the play.

Preminger already had made himself a reputation in America for handling difficult temperaments. He had been schooled in Europe in the best tradition of the Viennese theatre, and while still in his twenties had taken over the dramatic seminar in Vienna from the hands of Max Reinhardt. Hedy Lamarr and Luise Rainer had been his pupils. His first assignment in the United States, to which he had fled when the totalitarian governments began to strangle all creative expression in Europe, was the direction of the declining and debt-ridden John Barrymore in a bit of persiflage called "My Dear Children." When Barrymore stepped to the footlights in answer to the first night applause his words were these: "The credit is due to Otto Preminger who has been a demon of tolerance and a tower of patience."

Brady informed Preminger of his experience with Laurette in "Alice." In putting her in the role of Mrs. Midget he realized that he was taking a long gamble. However, Preminger was not to worry. Brady's wife, Grace George, would sit at the back of the theatre and be up on the lines to take over if Laurette quit.

It was soon evident to the new director that something other than ordinary nerves and the frictions of first rehearsals had put Laurette on the defensive. Her attitude was constrained and unhappy, her manner toward him reserved and suspicious in the extreme. Shortly after taking over he invited her to lunch and told her quite frankly what he had heard—from Gilbert Miller, from Shumlin, from Brady.

His frankness brought forth her own. "I know Grace is sitting at the back of the theatre—and I know why she is there," she said. "It's humiliating and disgraceful! I won't go through with this—they don't expect me to—and I won't." What's more, she told Preminger, she didn't think they had expected her to when they gave her the role. "They'll get all the publicity that goes with my name—good and bad—and then they'll put Grace in the part."

Laurette admitted she was bitterly disillusioned, licked. No one would give her a chance. She told Preminger her side of the Shumlin story. "If he had no confidence in me why did he send me the script? And if he sent me the script then he must have thought I could do the part." And now Grace hiding in the back of the theatre, learning the role of Mrs. Midget! It just wasn't fair play! Laurette was notoriously a "poor study"; her method of tackling a part had always been to learn the lines at the very last, but now they were saying she had no memory, that she was no longer capable of memorizing a role.

"Look," said Preminger with quiet authority, "I'm in charge now. I assure you no one will play your part but you. I will see to that. No one will study your lines. There will be no understudy. But if I do this for you, you must come through for me." He added, "I will give you all the cuts and changes. Take them home and don't return until you know your lines—whether it is a few days or two weeks. When you have memorized every word, come back."

In three days Laurette was back, letter perfect. The other actors were still reading from the script. It was a psychological boost of inestimable importance.

From that time on Laurette was at every rehearsal, keenly interested, friendly, enthusiastic. Preminger let her give suggestions freely, took her to lunch, discussed scenes, actors, production details, large and small. In every possible way he tried to promote the sense of her importance to the production, of his complete confidence in all matters. She throve on it.

It was like the old days with Hartley. Their views on acting were amazingly similar, the Viennese-trained director, and the melodrama-trained Laurette. "She had an uncanny ability to put her finger on a central weakness of another actor," Preminger recalled, "and she could be very sharp about it." Then he added with a smile, "She was not in any sense a mild woman." As to her drinking: "It would have been quite hopeless to approach her with a promise-me-you'll-be-a-good-girl technique. There was a demon in her that would not be boxed like that. It was in part what made her so weird on the stage—surprising you with unexpected phrasing and accent; the fluid, the unexpected, this was the nub of her inspiration. To approach her with a program of being good, of never touching another drop, was to try and box her demon. She would never allow it. I knew this at once."

Laurette called him M'sieur Printemps, kidded him about his still heavy Viennese accent, imitated the wiggle of his fingers over his head when he grew excited about some new idea. She was happy again. The theatre was as it had been in the days long ago. Grace folded her tent and quietly stole away. There was no understudy for Mrs. Midget.

As the day of the opening approached Laurette seemed confident and untroubled. At dress rehearsal she was satisfied to see that the mechanics of the part were right without giving a performance. Eloise, at the theatre each day helping Bramwell Fletcher with incidental producing chores, had yet to feel the full power of Laurette's genius. So, for that matter, had Preminger.

The day of the opening he called an early rehearsal and kept the company at the theatre most of the day. Laurette protested; Hartley never had more than a line rehearsal in the morning and dismissed the company. Preminger considered this gravely. "I think it is better we do it this way," he said quietly. Fletcher had several tasks for Eloise outside the theatre but she refused to go. "You can fire me if you want to," she said, "but I'm not going to leave Laurette." At five o'clock the company was dismissed for supper. Laurette and Eloise had been going to and from rehearsals in the subway to save money, but Laurette considered this occasion sufficiently momentous to throw caution to the winds. "This time we take a taxi," she announced; "my luck can't be bad forever."

By the time they were home she was sick with nerves, but dined well on rare steak as Hartley had taught her. The tension, she told Eloise, was not because of any doubts about herself but a reflection of the tension she anticipated on the other side of the footlights as to whether she would go through, and the worry lest this tension affect the other actors. By the time her make-up was on, however, she was calm.

In pork-pie hat, black alpaca cape and tippet of fur, holding a capacious knitting bag, Laurette made her entrance backing cautiously through stage door left. Most of the cast was assembled onstage and had received their hand. On sight of the nondescript little figure sidling backwards through the door the audience burst into thunderous applause. Laurette turned to say her first lines but it was of no use. The ovation continued, gathering momentum. People shouted and whistled and wept; they beat their feet on the floor; here and there groups rose, until finally the whole audience was standing. The humble shawl-wrapped figure bent a little at one knee, thrust one high-buttoned shoe tentatively forward, then drew it back. The hands with the knitting bag fluttered uncertainly up to the throat and down again. Still the demonstration went on. It was obvious that Laurette was shaken—shattered, almost—by the prolonged ovation, but also evident was the delicate poise, the established inner equilibrium of the artist that cannot be swayed by emotional turmoil within or without. She tried to stop them in every way she knew how; she fumbled with the cheap handles of the knitting bag, swung it down at her side, pressed it high over her heart; her hands moved in small patterns of humility and service, essentially the gestures of Mrs. Midget. But it was hopeless. A floodgate of welcome and homage and rejoicing had opened and the audience would not, could not, stop. For ten solid minutes shock waves of sound buffeted the tiny figure on the stage.

Somehow, finally, Laurette managed to say her first line, then quickly moved to a chair, plunked herself down, drew two large knitting needles from the bag and began to knit. It was a gesture both humble and commanding, humorous and apologetic. The tender and moving quality of it reached out like a quieting hand and drew the audience ever so gently under the spell of the self-effacing Mrs. Midget.

At the end of the play there were twenty-two curtain calls and Laurette made three grateful little speeches; not much, just murmurs between the thunderous acclaim. Several times she held her hand over her mouth as though trying not to shout back, the incredible brows arching high with excitement. There was no false humility, but pride and gratitude and a kind of shared astonishment on her face, as though she said to her audience as she stood there looking out, "Yes, the truth is wonderful, isn't it? The most wonderful thing in the world! It was in me all this time. I'm glad I could bring it to you again." And beneath her artist's pride her heart was melting with the warmth of the affection that came flooding across the footlights. They remembered. They cared. They loved her. The metamorphosis was complete.

Afterward, in direct contact with the stream of wellwishers backstage, emotion overcame her. Putting her arms around Theresa Helburn, Laurette wept, "Oh, Terry—it's back! The theatre's back!" Later, walking to their home for supper arm in arm with Vincent Price and his wife the lovely Edith Barrett, she said, "It really wasn't a very good performance." Still not humility; just a bob curtsy to that inner vision, not quite lived up to under the unusual stresses of the evening.

Although no starring part, Mrs. Midget indisputably became one by virtue of Laurette's superb performance. "Not because she makes any attempt to transform the work into a starring vehicle," said critic Richard Watts. "On the contrary her playing is both quiet and modest. It merely happens that she is one of the finest actresses in the world."

John Anderson tried to be more analytical. He went twice to see the play, particularly giving attention to what he called Mrs. Midget's "incredible scene" with the Examiner. "God knows it is not the dialogue of the scene, but the curious suspension of it, and it is this . . . which Miss Taylor has seized upon for one of the most heartbreaking passages of acting I have ever seen. Seeing her begin it with a tremulous ballet of her hands, I tried to watch sharply enough to sleuth out the magic of such spellbinding, and then gave up, too misty-eyed, I'm afraid, to detect anything that can be explained."

Of all the praise showered upon her Laurette liked Anderson's the best. "That is, or should be, an actress's heaven," was her comment, "to create a *complete* illusion and none of her spectators be able to detect how it is done, and as the play progresses give up trying." *

Pleaded Brooks Atkinson who found her portrait of Mrs. Midget "an evocation of light," "Please, Miss Taylor, be careful at the street crossings, and don't catch cold at this aguish time of year. There is no point in wasting a gleam that is precious in a somber world."

Mrs. Midget performed the service Laurette had devoutly hoped for: brought her back in triumph to the theatre and, despite the smallness of the role, re-established her at once in the top bracket of stars. And the Broadway to which she returned was far from mediocre. New and old names flashed from the marquees, drawing capacity audiences. Although many of the plays were only fair-to-middling, individual performances were exerting magical power: Raymond Massey's Abe Lincoln, Maurice Evans' Falstaff, Robert Morley's Oscar Wilde. Tallulah Bankhead had the greatest role of her career as Regina, in "The Little Foxes"; new laurels came to Judith Anderson as Mary, the Mother of God in "Family Portrait." Katharine Cornell shone in "No Time for Comedy," Katharine Hepburn in "The Philadelphia Story," and there was the compelling vigor and magnetism of Ethel Waters in

* "Critics" by Laurette Taylor. *Town & Country.* March, 1942.

"Mamba's Daughters." In all this brilliance, "a gallant little body in shawl and pork-pie hat" reached out with disarming humility and utter persuasiveness and laid claim to her niche in theatre history. "In her meager moments on the stage," a future chronicler was to say, "she created a character so sensitive and moving, so tender and pathetic, that critics still mention it as one of the few eruptions of histrionic genius in our time."

With the success of "Outward Bound" Laurette became the best "copy" in the world, the story of a comeback. Everything she said and did was of interest, and to the delight of reporters she talked freely of everything—her youth on One Hundred and Twenty-fifth Street, Grandmother Dorsey, struggles in Western stock. She admitted the ten blank years after Hartley Manners' death. "Something happened to me then. Instead of treasuring the things that reminded me of our happiness I destroyed them." For ten years the theatre, life, people, meant nothing. She had tried to escape all three. "The opening night of 'Outward Bound' I found I cared very much indeed for all three—particularly the theatre." Yes, she had authored several plays, none of which had got to Broadway, and had just finished another under a pseudonym on which a producer had taken an option. He didn't know she was the author. No, she wouldn't play in it: "They'd either say I was a good actress who couldn't write, or a good author who couldn't act. I wouldn't give them that chance." Oh, yes, certainly she intended to act again. "But this time I want to find the play as well as the part."

There was one keen disappointment which came with success. The Playhouse Company abandoned their original plan to do repertory in New York. "Outward Bound" was to run through the winter, summer and fall of 1939—one of a handful of plays to vie successfully with Mr. Whalen's World's Fair out on the Long Island flats—and late in November begin a tour of Eastern cities. It seemed Laurette was never to attain her dream of repertory in New York.

In the spring of 1939 she received the Barter Award for the season's outstanding performance which was presented by Mrs. Franklin Delano Roosevelt. In January, however, had come the honor she treasured most, an invitation to give a command per-

formance at President Roosevelt's Birthday celebration, to be
followed by supper at the White House.

Laurette worshipped Franklin Roosevelt. Here at last was a
man in high office of incomparable charm and humor, who *used
his facial muscles*, had a gorgeously flexible voice, and was a
raconteur and speaker of rare brilliance. He was her ideal. There
was a distinct tremor in her voice at the conclusion of the show
as she stepped to the footlights to salute him with, "Happy Birthday to you, happy patriot,"—a tremor which had perceptibly
deepened when she realized she was within one word of Al-
Smithing her hero with "Happy Birthday to you, Happy Warrior!"

As time for the White House supper drew near each member
of the company gave way to nerves in a different way. With
the bravado of the desperate Laurette announced that she intended
to tell the President two funny stories, both against himself. "For
God's sake, you can't do that!" Florence Reed warned her. "Oh,
yes I can," Laurette retorted. "Look where Nell Gwynn got
with Charles the Second, telling him funny stories!" If she heard
another voice under her own determined accents . . . *Curb your
sense of humor, Laurie . . . have respect* . . . she did not heed
it.

When suppertime came the company and other guests gathered
at the entrance of the dining room. There were ten tables, and
there seemed to be no place cards. Laurette had hoped for a buffet
supper, where she could bring a plate to the President and in that
way sit beside him. Now she did not know how to accomplish
her goal. As there were no stars in the "Outward Bound" aggre-
gate, Mrs. Roosevelt might solve the problem of precedence by
asking the guests to seat themselves. Laurette thrust her right
foot forward, determined to run for it if this happened . . . *Dignity, Laurie.* . . . "That word with the porcupine quills, Mr.
Manners—the divil take it!"

"Miss Taylor," said Mrs. Roosevelt, "will you kindly sit on the
President's right?"

Laurette shifted her balance back to center and with gracefully gliding step—every inch the poised actress—took her place
beside the President.

Otto Preminger who sat at the same table told how, pale and

excited as a child, she scarcely took her eyes from Roosevelt's face during supper. She told the two stories when the appropriate time came and Roosevelt threw back his handsome head and laughed long and heartily at both. "Nell never made Charles laugh more!" she would recall proudly. If the spectral Hartley were still around, he must have smiled, for this was the essence of the Laurie whom he loved.

After supper, Laurette, in fascinated pursuit of her hero, failed to note the other guests mounting a broad staircase, and instead virtually crashed her way into the small private elevator which carried Roosevelt and his wife upstairs to the President's study. Mortified by her mistake she pressed her ample person against the elevator's wall and managed to stammer, "I'm so sorry, Mr. President, I thought the others were following."

Gravely the President replied, "I think it is delightful of you to ride, Miss Taylor, when you can walk."

\*

# *The Scolding Hills*

". . . you simply do not understand innocence.
She will be afraid of nothing; she will not even know
That there is anything there to be afraid of.
She is too humble. She will pass between the scold-
ing hills,
Through the valley of derision, like a child sent on
an errand
In eagerness and patience. Yet she must suffer."
*"The Cocktail Party"*
*T. S. Eliot.*

The five years following "Outward Bound" were in some ways the most difficult of Laurette's life. Now she wanted to be in the theatre but could not find the play. There was no money. Her extremely modest salary had gone to pay long-standing debts, provide for barest needs.

Laurette had never put a discount on her talent, and she did not now. She was deeply shocked while in Chicago to see John Barrymore in "My Dear Children." "I can't bear to see him exhibiting his decline!" she cried to Ashton Stevens. It did not matter that as a man of honor he was expending the last ounce of his strength to pay incalculable debts. It was beyond her imagination to cheapen and hold up to ridicule God-given talent for any reason whatsoever. She was emphatic about her own. Hers was not to be wasted on inferior plays or find an easy vehicle in which to display itself. To those who urged a degree of compromise to keep her busy and happy in the theatre, and financially solvent, her answer was adamant and final, "No. This time I must come back at the very top. I must have both the play and the part." This was the iron in Laurette's soul. It had carried her over many a rough route, and now it was to take her to the summit.

There was no scarcity of scripts; they poured in. "Nothing but pipe-smoking tobacco-chewing horrible old women," was the way she described the parts. "I don't have to play that sort of thing. I can wait." To Preminger she confided, slipping momentarily back into the comforting world of illusion, "Hartley left me an annuity so I can afford to wait for the play I want."

Guthrie McClintic sent a script, urged her to do it. "You'll make the play, Laurette."

"I'm tired of making the play," she replied irritably. "I want the play to make me."

In the meantime she and Eloise had resumed their Spartan life. Laurette was at her typewriter every morning at nine. Spurred on by the interest and advice of Doubleday's Thomas Costain she began reworking her novel; also she was continuing her recollections of famous people. When Eloise obtained a few small acting jobs out of town Laurette journeyed to the tryouts. Theatre people—Ruth Gordon, Richard Aldrich, Charles MacArthur—welcomed her warmly, sought criticism and help, prodded her with the universal query, "Laurette, in heaven's name why aren't you acting?" The answer was always the same, "Because I can't find the play."

It was known that she was practicing her philosophy of moderation in drinking, but how well no one was quite sure. The Busch-Feketes, husband and wife, after seeing "Outward Bound," dramatized "Embezzled Heaven" with Laurette in mind. But the Theatre Guild was wary and decided on a wait and see policy. If Laurette was aware of the skepticism she gave no sign. Salary offers consistently below her worth were the cold shadow of this skepticism, but the shadow in no way dissipated the bright inner knowledge of her supremacy as an actress. She waited.

With the Japanese attack on Pearl Harbor in December, 1941, the lives of most Americans changed abruptly. Laurette's was already austere, cut to the bone in luxuries and superficialities. Eloise became a volunteer hostess at the Stage Door Canteen, later took a paid job working long hours, and Laurette was more than ever alone. But she plugged away at her writing, participated in a number of war-loan drives on the radio, coached young drama students. There was a dogged fortitude like Bridgett Dorsey's which became more and more evident as the dreary years went by, and like Bridgett, Laurette kept her troubles to herself.

For company she got a lively cocker spaniel called "Mr. Smith" who further shredded the antique upholstery and ruined the rugs. One morning Eloise got a call to come at once. "Mr. Smith," Laurette announced abruptly, "is having a fit." She raced home to find the cocker quite well if his usual uncollected self. It was Laurette who was having the "fit." In spite of Mr. Costain's enthusiasm the publishers had turned down the reworked novel.

Seeing her less and less frequently, and hearing of no forthcoming activity, Broadway began once more to have its doubts. The years were passing as they had passed after Hartley's death, after "Alice-Sit-by-the-Fire." Inevitably the question changed from a direct "Why in heaven's name aren't you in the theatre, Laurette?" to the more oblique one to Eloise, "How is she behaving these days?" At the few gatherings she attended Laurette came to know the fishy eye of the one-time idolator, and there were some in the seats of the mighty who, once and for all, scratched off her name from the lists of those who could still be useful to them. But Laurette waited.

At Hotel Fourteen her bedroom closest held only the necessities of a wardrobe, and the jewel case given her many years
before by Hartley contained a jumble of cheap costume jewelry.
Piece by piece the exquisite sets of emeralds, rubies and sapphires
had been sold. The cavernous dark-panelled living room with
light slanting in mote-filled shafts through leaded windows began to look like some reliquary of the past. Ben Ali Haggin's
large oil portrait of Laurette, elongated and elegant with Michael
on her lap, reflected the style of another era. The photographs
of favorite actors and others, some of the most famous faces in
the world, were stained, neglected, frames held together by tape,
glass fronts broken or missing. The rich antique brocades of the
enormous Italian chairs were tattered and worn. Gazing sorrow-
fully at them Laurette exploded to Eloise, "I can't cover them in
gingham, God damn it!" All around her and in her mirror was
growing evidence of the attrition of the years. Her robust health
was gone, an unhealthy fat clung to her bones. Despite the success
of "Outward Bound" and the creative readiness of her spirit
she was in danger of sinking into the pathetic twilight of the old
actress, poverty, illness and obscurity. But she waited.

Her interest in young drama students did not lag. She coached
at the American Theatre Wing and directed several productions.
Though she was learning a patience in teaching which she had
not possessed before, her tongue remained sharp, her tutoring
direct and succinct. To a pretty young Miss busily preening before the footlights Laurette would say, "If you are on the stage
just to show off your little breasts and little waist you should
choose another profession." To a neophyte overly conscious of
awkward arms and hands, "Don't cuddle the furniture." And to
another who has studied posture and is busily striking attitudes,
"Never be graceful on the stage. Never think of the way you are
going to sit down or get up—just do it." And to another bent on
exhibiting a basic likableness, "Don't try and curry favor with the
audience; you must do what is true to the part and stand or fall
by it."

One night at the Chamberlain Brown Drama School a young
girl playing a scene from "Peg O' My Heart" blew her lines. From
the auditorium in the soft delicious brogue of Peg came the miss-

ing speech. It had been over twenty years since Laurette had spoken those words in a theatre.

When Marguerite, who had re-married and was living in California, wrote early in 1943 that she was expecting a baby, Laurette's response was immediate, close and affectionate as though no gap had ever existed between them. "I am very glad indeed about the baby," she wrote. "No matter what happens later, they are the wonders of the world—and I always thought you should know that wonder." And in July when the baby was born: "Marguerite Coutant Courtney! What a name for an opera singer! . . . People say you forget all about the pain and inconvenience of birth; that's not true. It's only that the wonder wipes out anything else. . . . It's wonderful, Maggie darling, that you have this baby—Wonderful! Much love, Your Ma."

One brisk December afternoon, in 1943, Irvin Cobb's daughter, Buff, encountered Laurette on Fifth Avenue busily shopping for Christmas toys. She was bubbling with excitement at the prospect of spending Christmas with her grandchildren who, upon the birth of Marguerite's baby, numbered four. Yes, she was going for a long, long visit, she told Buff, and really get to know them all. Barely were the holidays over when Buff met her again on a New York street. "Why Laurette!" she exclaimed. "Back so soon? I thought you were going for a *long* visit with your grandchildren!"

"I know," replied Laurette with ill-concealed pugnacity. "But they didn't like me very much, and I didn't like them."

Thus bluntly Laurette summed up a visit which in some ways was little short of a fiasco.

Its timing could hardly have been less opportune. Dwight's marriage had recently broken up, and he had his hands full caring for his two young sons, Jeffrey and Andrew, and daughter Audrey. Competent help was almost unobtainable because of the war. Gas rationing made it difficult to get around, and with her son working long hours at the studio Laurette was, perforce, largely isolated throughout the day with the three children.

Try as she would the role of grandmother fitted her not at all.

Instead of being gentle and sweet and affectionately discerning, she challenged her grandchildren's ideas, pried into their minds, badgered them for entertainment when their father was away, competed for attention when he was home. She was more like another child, some grotesque contemporary who had bullied her way into a position of power and was demanding an allegiance they found no reason to give. At best the feeling was one of armed truce.

With Dwight and Marguerite her behavior was not much better. Jealous possessiveness of her son made her an open critic of his children. The old unreasoning competition with Marguerite still operated, although now the gaze would slip impishly sideways—the gamin, ready for a chuckle now that such behavior no longer called forth the "princess-complex." It was a good-natured relationship with a knock-about sense of fun and fellowship, but the depth and warmth and tenderness of it had been lost long ago, sluiced away to strangers on the other side of footlights.

Whatever the shortcomings of her family relationships, however, they did not defeat her. Nor did the fat which had become formidable. Whereas once a few extra pounds would send her in hiding, now looking half Bedouin, half pirate in enveloping cape and wide brimmed hat, she sailed down the aisles of swank Los Angeles shops and boulevards with so jaunty an air that all eyes turned to follow with a fixity of expression usually reserved for Hollywood's sleekest celebrities.

She saw old friends Hedda Hopper, Elsie Janis. At her specific request Marguerite asked King Vidor to cocktails. If conscious of his deep shock at her appearance she gave no indication but told her stories, fluttered her hands and flashed her beautiful smile, dominating the occasion with the old dynamic charm which still managed to triumph over the barricades of gross flesh.

There were several conferences at the studios but after each a vacuum developed. A producer sent a Clifford Odets script which Laurette liked enormously, but as soon as he saw her the producer cooled. Privately Dwight was told what he already knew: there was no photographing that amount of fat.

In despair he burst out to his mother, "You say you want to act, but how in God's name can you expect to act looking like that?

You're neither hippy, nor bust-y, nor jowl-y—just cylindrical like a snowman. It isn't even the Marie Dressler kind of fat that you can use in character parts!"

Laurette was momentarily nonplused, then shot back, "But what can I do? I eat nothing, and still I get fat!" It was true. She had lost her magnificent appetite; food no longer interested her; yet her enemy sat on her bones seemingly in a final triumph.

Bored and restless she began to drink large amounts of beer, the alcoholic beverage to which she now limited herself. It increased the bloat but the drinking seemed in no way compulsive. There was a resilience of spirit, the resilience of one who sees clearly a goal and holds unshakably to a path despite all obstacles besetting the way. Pressures, defeats, failures that once had her on the run, failed utterly now to shatter her morale.

In spite of all its difficulties the visit was a period of integration. It was a period of acceptance; of the bleak limits of her ability to succeed in family relationships, of her lost looks and youth, of her own standards of conduct without reference to how well or ill Hartley might think of them. And she accepted with amazing philosophy the general indifference of the movie moguls of Hollywood. It could have, and very probably did, occur to her that she might never be given another chance to act in a play or motion picture worth playing; it could very well have occurred to her that she was in serious danger of professional extinction; but she was undaunted by any of these realizations and conjectures.

The clue as to how she felt is perhaps to be found in a letter written to Marguerite after her return to New York. She spoke of the "wonderful time" she had had, her concern for Dwight and his broken home, her companionability with Marguerite and joy over the infant (the one grandchild spared Laurette's competitive aggressions because of tender age); then she wrote: "I drank more than I have for years but I felt fine then and now—and not afraid —that's what used to kill me, being afraid."

It was the old Laurette who had met Buff on the street and delivered the callow appraisal of her grandchildren. But it was the new Laurette who on hearing that her life-long friend Irvin Cobb was dying went and sat by his bedside. "It threw me back

a little to that time of waiting at our house," she wrote, but she
kept on with the visits nonetheless. "I hope mine comes in the
ocean quickly, and no one finds my body. Have you seen 'A Guy
Named Joe'? That's my faith since Hartley died. . . . Do see it.
It's a wonderful picture and a wonderful faith for Christian or
heathen."

Again, Laurette was showing an emotional stability, this time
in the face of illness and death of which she had been incapable
before. There were many things of which she was now no longer
afraid and that was a good feeling; the feeling of being "fine and
well."

Dwight had made it abundantly clear that Laurette had one
problem and one problem alone. From New York she peppered
him with wires about the Odets script. Had they cast it? Had he
heard anything further from the producer? She got no replies. Instead he sent her the name and address of a New York physician
who had been recommended for his success in reducing over-
weight patients. The financial arrangements were taken care of;
all she had to do was present herself for a course of treatment;
after that there would be time enough to discuss parts and plays.
On St. Valentine's Day with only grudging good grace Laurette
set out for the offices of Dr. Paul De Santo.

Dr. De Santo was dark, good-looking. He combined a quiet
friendly manner and nice sense of humor with a delightful freedom from professional pomposity. Laurette liked him at once.
He found her condition mainly glandular. Under his careful medical guidance she lost fifty pounds within a few months. Jaw-line
grew firm, and enormous eyes with a new sparkle began once
again to dominate the curving upward lines of the face. Eloise
thrilled to see her stride from the doctor's office as though she had
found there not only health, but hope and optimism.

Still there were no plays and no money. Script after script came
into her hands but she was appalled at the poverty of language
and ideas, at the coarse horrible old ladies held up to her as worthy
successors to the clear-souled Mrs. Midget. She was redoing
the rejected novel for the third time and adding to her reminis-
cences of famous people. "My fingers are calloused and weary

from writing on stories that lately haven't turned into money," she wrote Marguerite.

In the fall Eloise went off on the road in Mary Coyle Chase's "Harvey" which was to introduce a six-foot rabbit to Broadway and bring back old-time vaudevillian Frank Fay in the greatest role of his career. But for Laurette it seemed that all her effort, all her slimness, all the waiting was for nought; the play, the part, did not come along.

She was ready as never before to exercise her full powers as an artist. Guilt, remorse, self-deception were behind; even her claims to a place at the hearth of human affection were modest and she did not press them. Her gift was from God, and she had kept it well. All common ills and ill-fortune faded away in the light of this knowledge. Humbly now she stood before the doors of the theatre with this, her one treasure, asking to enter. Long ago she had said: "I think that the germs of greatness are born in one, but that the courage of cultivation is a matter of conscious effort. The instinct of self-preservation must be in a large measure killed, and the sense of giving substituted." In her hands was the gift to be given. Surely the enigmatic future would grant the last shining wish of this battered child who stood so unafraid upon its doorsill?

\*

# *The Glass Menagerie*

One day in early November, 1944, Eddie Dowling stopped by the apartment and left a script by an unknown author. Laurette sat up most of the night reading it and could hardly wait for dawn to call Eloise in Boston. "I've found it, Eloise! I've found the play I've been waiting for!" she cried jubilantly.

It was "The Glass Menagerie" by Tennessee Williams.

She was down at Dowling's office that same morning. "I wasn't

too coy about business arrangements. When you haven't played
for a while and the absolutely right part comes along, that's all
that matters." *

Sometime before, Jessie Royce Landis had given a dinner party
to which she had invited Laurette and George Jean Nathan, unaware of a decided coolness between them. Nathan's criticism that
Mr. Manners had never written a play which could "possibly
interest anybody over eleven" burned in Laurette's memory.
Nathan, on his part, had never had much use for Laurette because
he felt she had largely wasted her talents in her husband's plays.
On this particular occasion they decided to be charming to each
other. "And," reminisced Jessie, "I know of no two people who
could be more charming once they decided to turn it on." They
sat on the couch all evening and nothing and no one could pry
them apart—although there was some stiff competition from other
luminaries like Sinclair Lewis.

When Nathan read "The Glass Menagerie"—his primary interest being the role of the daughter Laura for Julie Haydon—
he told Dowling there was only one actress to play the nagging,
down-at-heel, ex-Southern belle, Amanda Wingfield, and that was
Laurette Taylor.

Tennessee Williams was twenty-nine when he wrote "The
Glass Menagerie." After graduating from the University of Iowa
he kept himself fed and writing by taking odd jobs all over the
country. His first three-act play, written on a Rockefeller grant,
was produced in Boston where it was promptly hooted from the
stage as obscene. There was a stint of work which jumped him
from eighteen dollars a week as an usher in a Los Angeles theatre
to $250 a week at a motion-picture studio. He spent one and a
half months on a Lana Turner picture which won him ignoble
oblivion as far as the studios were concerned, but a full stomach
and an opportunity to do his own work for the remaining four
months of his contract. This work was "The Glass Menagerie." It
fell into sympathetic hands when it came to Eddie Dowling.

Eddie Dowling in his youth had been a song and dance man
and a producer of light musicals such as "Sally, Irene and Mary,"
"Honeymoon Lane." More recently he had made himself an

* Helen Ormsbee, *Herald Tribune*, April, 22, 1945.

enviable reputation as a sensitive actor-producer of such fragile and lovely plays as William Saroyan's "The Time of Your Life" and Paul Vincent Carroll's "Shadow and Substance." With them he won critical benedictions, literary awards and artistic fame —but little money. When "The Glass Menagerie" came to him he already had tucked under his arm a playscript with "commercial possibilities" with the backing to put it on from Louis J. Singer, Wall Street broker, a moody newcomer to the ranks of Broadway producers.

After reading the Williams' play, Dowling could feel his practicality slipping and asked Singer to release him from their arrangement. "I've found a play I love. I don't think it will earn a dime but it will make me very happy to do it," he explained.

"Have you arranged for backing?" Singer asked.

"Not yet."

"You've got a partner," said Singer.

Laurette, the third of this triumvirate, came back to the realm of the theatre a half-forgotten legend. New eyes looked at her with curiosity, old eyes with skepticism unburied. Hadn't she "retired" again after "Outward Bound"? Few knew what those years of retirement held; many had grave suspicions. Dowling had his doubts in spite of Nathan's recommendation. Williams, on hearing her name in connection with his play, was astonished; he thought she was dead. The only memory he could dredge up was that of walking past a moving-picture theatre in St. Louis as a boy of ten and reading the announcement of the silent film "Peg O' My Heart," starring Laurette Taylor. He had not gone in. He imagined she was "very old" and again was astonished to find her so youthful, "a quality of youth," as he put it, "that had nothing to do with face or figure but an outreaching spirit that was entirely youthful." As to the rest of the company, they were for the most part twenty to thirty years Laurette's juniors, and she was a creature walking into their midst from some dim page of theatre history, her quality unknown, the legend, the rumor, the woman, the actress, all more or less nebulous to be filled in by the actuality of her presence.

Anthony Ross, the Gentleman Caller, had played "Outward Bound" in summer stock with her and had better firsthand knowledge than the others. The excessively shy Julie Haydon knew only the legend and was in semi-speechless awe of it. The others studied Laurette with frank curiosity. They were Margo Jones, assistant producer and director, young Randolph Echols and Willis Gould of the production staff, and Mary Jean Copeland, understudy to Miss Haydon, who was to become Mrs. Anthony Ross.

There was nothing nebulous about the way Laurette took hold once she made up her mind that "The Glass Menagerie" was her play and Amanda her part. "It's a beautiful—a wonderful—a great play!" she told Williams emphatically. "And Amanda an absolutely true characterization." That one little word *true* said everything. "You can have all the other adjectives," she once said. "Just call my playing *true*, and you have showered me with compliments."

She found the author guilty of an artiness in the writing here and there, and an oversentimentalizing of the mother. Both character and play were much too good for such trimmings, she said, and began energetically cutting the script down to its "bare and beautiful bones." Her interest did not stop there. The part of Laura the crippled daughter fascinated her, and Laurette gave it almost as much attention as her own. "Actually she directed many of the scenes, particularly the ones between mother and daughter," Williams recalled, "and she did a top-notch job. She was continually working on her part, putting in little things and taking them out—almost every night in Chicago there was something new but she never disturbed the central characterization. Everything she did was absolutely in character."

Her script of the play was heavily penciled, but when some later tried to say that she had made the part of Amanda by her editing as well as her playing, she replied, "What nonsense! Amanda was always there. After all, you don't bother to operate on a corpse."

It was Laurette's great good fortune to find Williams with his fresh, dynamic approach to the theatre, the high literary quality of his writing and his genius for three-dimensional characters just when she needed him most. But it was also Williams' great good fortune to find Laurette. For his was the inestimable advantage of having Laurette's acutely trained eye and ear entirely at the disposal of a play she believed in and deeply respected.

The plot is extremely simple. Amanda Wingfield, the frowzy, decaying Southern gentlewoman, struggles in dire poverty in a St. Louis alley flat to put spine into a shiftless, frustrated son, and a fragile, crippled daughter who spends her time with a collection of little glass animals. Amanda nags and lectures, fitfully moons about her glamorous girlhood among the magnolias and jonquils of the South. To escape her shrewish outbursts the son shows every sign of running away as his father did years before. The only action is when Amanda browbeats him into bringing home a young man for dinner as a possible suitor for the morbidly shy Laura. When it turns out that the Gentleman Caller is already engaged to be married, the little family sinks back into despair and the son leaves home.

Called "a memory play," a narrator spoke of these events standing to one side of the stage, while the scenes in the shabby St. Louis flat lit up and faded as in memory they might. Dowling played Tom Wingfield, the narrator-son, and was director-producer.

Williams had had little direct contact with actors before "The Glass Menagerie." They were unknown and rather terrifying elements necessary to the promulgation of a play. From the outset his extreme diffidence at rehearsals brought forth Laurette's most forthright responses; but artistically they understood each other perfectly, and this understanding was the amalgam of their friendship. Speaking of their relationship Williams said, "I cannot say that I ever got over the awkwardness and the awe which originally were present, but she would not allow that to stand between us. The great warmth of her heart burned through and we became close friends."

And Laurette in describing the author would invariably start out, "Tennessee is a *very* sensitive fellow!" Then she would tell of exchanges between them. "He came up to me when we first started and said so diffidently, 'Miss Taylor, Ah hopes yo' don't mahnd mah sayin' so but yo' Southe'n accent is a little thick.' 'All right,' I said. 'How would you like it if I copied you?' He said that would be fine." From then on she would tell him at rehearsals, "Talk to me, Tennessee, just talk to me. Don't explain how to pronounce the words, just keep talking." Later when she met Williams' mother Laurette told him, "Don't worry, Tennessee, I'll never go quite as Deep South as your dear mother."

In one of the play's most effective speeches the word jonquil cropped up a dozen or more times. "It's just too many jonquils, Tennessee," Laurette said. "Can't you cut a few?" "Laurette," he answered solemnly, "it's got rhythm. Ah need all those jonquils." "I took the lines home and sort of sang them to myself. Tennessee was right. Not a jonquil came out."

Although she took the most energetic interest in rehearsals, in everything and everybody that had anything to do with the play, and warmed the nervous author's heart with her understanding and respect for his work, Laurette gave little indication of what she was going to do with the part of Amanda. She was up to her old trick of watching the others, seemingly much more interested in them than her own part, neither learning her lines nor her business. Tony Ross tried to pump heart into the others by recalling how magnificent she was, but as time went on he began to worry along with the rest. As Laurette sat hunched over her script, peering nearsightedly at the lines through a large magnifying glass, murmuring through her speeches, or walking about like one achieving a hesitant, tactile familiarity with a world and people not yet clearly seen, Dowling was heard to murmur more than once, "That woman is crucifying me!" Intermittently he talked of procuring another actress for the role. Even Eloise worried. When it came time to leave for Chicago she wanted to give up her part in "Harvey" and go with Laurette. But Laurette would not hear of it. "We may need that money you're earning," she cautioned; "this play hasn't opened yet."

She seemed blandly unconscious of the discomfort of the others. There was the joy and buoyance that always came to her with the exploration of a character she was to play. Amanda fascinated her. She could see whole facets of the woman's life before the action of the play started and after it was over, "and that, Hartley taught me, is the test of a good part." The outer aspect of this inner search concerned her not at all. When Tony Ross in a later interview remarked that "like many great actresses" she did not "give" at rehearsals, she was indignant. "How dare you say such a thing!" she demanded. When Tony held his ground and insisted it was true, she grew thoughtful and replied, "Well-l-ll . . . how can you *give it* before it has grown inside?"

It was a bitterly cold morning in December when "The Glass Menagerie" troupe disgorged from the train into Chicago's barn-like Union Station. The impression was hardly that of a winning team. With scarcely a nod at one another they scattered in all directions. Dowling and Singer went off arm in arm, ignoring the feminine star who stood hesitant and alone on the platform. Julie, hatless and pinched-looking, flitted by as insubstantial as a puff of steam from one of the locomotives. Tony Ross, six-foot-three of protest against the cold and early hour, passed somnambulistically. The anxious author, who had forgotten something, dove back into the car and emerged again to feel the bleakness of the station like an unfriendly slap—a dismal portent of his play's reception. Desperately he longed for the sight of a familiar figure and at last saw one. With his poet's sight he limned the picture not only of the figure before him, but something of the inner essence of the spirit which inhabited it:

It is a short and nearly square figure in a peculiar costume, like something rooted from the bottom of an old wardrobe trunk. The coat is grey muskrat, but the many small pelts of which it is composed, are not enjoying the most pacific relation. Discord threatening disunion is at work amongst them. Almost down the upturned collar of this coat is a very broad brimmed hat of the type that is worn by cinema buccaneers. Between these two defensive perimeters is a pair of eyes that are much too bright to be described as brown and a cloudy profusion of hair that is lighter than auburn. This is the figure of a star. Her name has been famous. It is still a legend, but the face in the station passes without recognition. The figure passes without assurance among the jostling swarm. The brightness of the eyes has bravery but not certainty. The motion of the figure is hesitant; for a moment it even appears to be lost. One hand which does not wear a glove is clutching a very large purse as if it contained a more secure world than that of a teeming station. . . .

"Laurette!" I called her name and she turned and cried out mine. Then and there we joined forces. The station diminished to a comfortable size; the bitter cold thawed a little; we moved off together with a feeling of a union deeper than physical, more than accidental, to find a taxi.

Catch one we did! It was Laurette who hailed it with an imperious wave of her ungloved hand, hesitation all gone as she sprang like a tiger out of her cloud of softness; such a light spring, but such an amazingly far one! *

Laurette's undiminished enthusiasm for the play heartened them all. Tony Ross squired her to dinner almost nightly. To his worried queries about the part of the Gentleman Caller—a single long scene toward the close of the play—she answered, "It can make you if you play it right." And it did. She fussed over the wraithlike Julie with some of the same tigerish concern Amanda shows for her daughter in the play, urged her to eat properly, dress warmly, and over Julie's faint protests that she never wore hats, insisted on buying her one as protection against Chicago's icy winds. She worked on their scenes together, tirelessly striving to eliminate the rather sepulchral quality of Julie's crippled Laura, bring it into clearer focus as a character of flesh and blood. They shopped for their costumes together, Laurette turning dressmaker just before the final rehearsal when she found Laura's second act dress too "bosomy" for the character. At first Laurette doubted the sincerity of Julie's quivering and devoted responsiveness but finally came to believe in it. "Julie really loves everybody," she would say to visitors backstage as Julie sat adoringly beside her. Then add, thumping the frail girl admiringly on the knee, "And you know, she used to be the most awful actress, but now she's good!"

There was a story that went the rounds that on the curtain calls in Chicago, Julie insisted on taking Laurette's hand and kissing it, although repeatedly warned by Laurette not to, and that, finally, exasperated Laurette drew her hand away and slapped Miss Haydon soundly on the cheek in full view of the audience. This story was vehemently denied by Laurette. "True, she kissed my hand and I told her not to, but what I did was pull my hand up as she held it, chucking her lightly under the jaw. It's ridiculous to say that I slapped her."

The spirits of the company were not improved by the fact that Chicago rehearsals had to be held in the smoking lounge of the Civic Theatre because of difficulties in working out a complicated lighting system. Not until the dress rehearsal did the company play on the stage, in the Mielziner set, and with the background

* Claudia Cassidy. *Chicago Sunday Tribune*, Sept. 19, 1948.

music created by Paul Bowles. But through all the difficulties Laurette continued gay and altogether sure. She had decided reservations as to Dowling's interpretation of his part, finding it, as she had Julie's Laura, unreal and bloodless, and it irked her not a little that an actor of fifty-three should be undertaking the role of her son; but she conceded that he was a fine and sensitive director and there was no sign of the trouble that was to cloud their relationship later on. Bubbling with fun she told her old friend Ashton Stevens on the telephone, "It's a wonderful play—wonderful. Just four characters, you know. Yes, four—two people and two ghouls."

Finally on Christmas night the dress rehearsal came. The audience consisted of the four hundred members of the soldier-cast of "Winged Victory" then playing Chicago. Under the spell of the set, the lights, the music, the beauty and magnetism of the lines, all integrated for the first time, "The Glass Menagerie" came to life. Audience and players were carried away by the pulsing reality, the beat of life itself which seemed to emanate from the blue-shadowed St. Louis alley and the tiny flat where the Wingfields struggled with their mean and hopeless existence.

"To make those guys rave," recalled Tony Ross, who had been a soldier and a member of the "Winged Victory" company, "it had to be good. The phony was something they couldn't use." As for Laurette, in the words of the author, "She brought everything together and gave a performance for the first time and the impact of it was stunning! I could never have imagined it. I never saw anything like it in all my life."

Contrary to the supposed jinx of a smooth dress rehearsal, the opening night was another superb performance. That "tangible, taut and tentacled play" as critic Claudia Cassidy called it, "gripped players and audience alike, and created one of those rare evenings in the theatre that make 'stage struck' an honorable word." *

The buoyancy of spirit which seemed to stem from complete faith in the play, and an unshakable assurance about her part and herself, carried Laurette through the opening without a hitch. When Randy Echols gave her the last call for the curtain and stuck his head in to wish her luck, she was bending over a dark and sodden mass of material in her wash basin. Passing him a moment

* "On the Aisle." *Chicago Sunday Tribune,* January 7, 1945.

later on her way to the stage she thrust the dripping mass into his hands with the command, "Here, dry this." It was the dressing gown she was to wear in a later scene of the first act. She had decided the color was wrong and dyed it. The sweating Echols constructed a dryer of bits and pieces backstage, played lights on it, fanned it, blew on it, went quietly mad as Laurette launched into Amanda's opening speech.

Almost without exception the Chicago critics hailed "The Glass Menagerie" as an event of first importance in the theatre. All were unanimous in saying that Laurette, in the best role of her life gave the greatest performance of her life, not to say of the century, and was backed by superlative performances by each of the other players. Ashton Stevens wrote that fifty years of first-nighting had provided him with few jolts "so miraculously electrical" as the jolt of Laurette Taylor's performance as the bubbling down-at-heel mother. But the public did not come. The second night there was barely four hundred dollars in the house; the gross on the week was thirty-six hundred. "You see, neither of us old hams has drawing power," was Dowling's ill-considered comment to Laurette. But the drama critics returned again and again. Claudia Cassidy attended three times in three days and went back for more—"a risky business in the realm of make-believe." Stevens practically lived at the Civic Theatre the first week. "When people ask for him I have him paged there," commented Kay, his lovely wife.

Appalled that Chicago should have one of its rare opportunities to preview a play of the first magnitude before a Broadway run and exhibit such abysmal apathy to the event, the critics began to beat the drums in columns of daily newsprint. Civic pride was involved. Weren't Chicagoans always complaining about getting second-rate shows? Second- and third-best casts? Here they had a play and players of the rarest and highest order and they would not support them. Led by the veteran Stevens, Claudia Cassidy, Henry T. Murdock, they began a campaign of exhortation. Columnists took up the cry; editorials were written. It became a crusade. Half anesthetized by such moribund fare as "Goodnight Ladies," "Twin Beds," "The Waltz King," it took a bit of doing to wake up Chicago theatregoers to what was going on at the Civic Theatre which had never housed a hit. But finally it worked. Just as Dowling and Singer seriously considered closing a costly flop, receipts began to climb and romped to capacity at $17,800 for the last six weeks. Toward the last of the run customers were turned away from the box office by the hundreds at every performance.

Laurette was the toast of the town. "By virtue of the fact of 'The Glass Menagerie' and Miss Taylor's presence in it," crowed Stevens, "Chicago for the moment is the center of the theatrical world. She is courted now as no other American actress since Adelina Patti. . . . The town's most distinguished writers, players and social big shots nightly crowd her spacious dressing room." Actors, directors, producers stopped off on their way through Chicago, or came expressly to see a performance rumored to be nothing short of miraculous, and went away to spread the word. Fellow professionals flocked to the Sunday night performances; Helen Hayes, Ruth Gordon, Cornelia Otis Skinner, Ina Claire, and innumerable others, made it abundantly clear that they considered Laurette the greatest living actress. "Flowers to the living, I calls it," purred Stevens, "and I loves it to the heart's core."

Everyone was eager to wine and dine the resurgent Laurette. Faces long lost in the past re-emerged to bask in the sun of her success. With an eye to what seemed to presage a triumphant return to Broadway, many a note and bouquet came from New York. Now and then she felt the bite of cynicism. On one fulsome message of congratulation from an erstwhile close friend which ended, "Across the years," Laurette added in an impatient scrawl "and after *all* these years!" But she did not look backward for long and rarely with bitterness. This success was too sweet, too highly prized after the five difficult years she had waited to achieve it.

If there was no scheduled party Laurette could be found holding court in the Pump Room, at the grill of the Hotel Sherman, or any of a number of eating places close to the Loop. The cast of "The Winged Victory" voted her their "Pin-up Girl" and she gave them a photograph of Amanda wearing the ancient taffeta dancing dress. They crowded her dressing room after per-

formances, and each evening a patrol of soldier-actors sought her
out wherever she went. They were always welcome.

Her own personal Gehenna seemed to have been left far behind. She feared it no more. With a limit of two drinks during
the many midnight feasts, she served notice on alcohol that she
had it licked. Quite obviously alcohol was no longer necessary
to a spirit again bubbling joyously from its own wellsprings of
happiness. Tony Ross, her favorite escort—"How that fellow
eats up life!"—recalled the party she gave for the "Winged Victory" cast the night of its Chicago closing. "We went to supper
at an all-night bistro called the Singapore. At five o'clock in the
morning Laurette, enjoying a huge plate of spare ribs, glanced
around the table and remarked that some of the boys were looking a bit weary. With the hardiest survivors she left the restaurant
at eight."

In all this jubilance there was a cloud no bigger than a man's
fist. Two or three weeks after the Chicago opening Ashton Stevens
called her on the phone. He was stern. She was hurting the chances
of the play by this public feuding with her co-star Dowling. The
New York columnists were picking it up. "You don't want to
get to New York and have them talk about a backstage fight between two Irishmen instead of the play, do you?" he chided. There
was a deep silence on the other end of the telephone. "Laurette!
Have you hung up on me?"

A little voice came back, "No. You're the first one who has
talked to me like that since Hartley, talked honestly to me. That's
the trouble Ashton—I must have honesty. I'm going right down
to the theatre tonight and make up with Eddie. I'll be nice to him
tonight, Ashton, I promise."

Actually she didn't feel she had not been nice. She had praised
him lavishly as a director. She had also told him he was far too
old for the part, and too mannered. She had, as was her way, picked
to bits the parts of his performance she thought were not true or
wrong for the play. When she felt he had elaborated to the point
of farce on the scene in which Tom returns home drunk, her protest was vigorous and direct. She didn't call that feuding. She
called it honesty and an honest concern for the play. When
Dowling was noncommittal in response, it only confused her.

Then she would hear from others that he was hurt by her criticism, deeply wounded because she talked behind his back. In she would stamp to his dressing room. "How dare you say I talk behind your back? I've never talked behind your back! I've never said anything I haven't said to your face. I've told you about that monkey hat you wear on the back of your head, that makes you look like a monkey. I've said that to you since the first day you put it on. I've told you and *told* you about those ridiculous pauses —'She touches my—' and you pause and wonder why you get a titter! For God's sake say *shoulder* and *then* pause. I've told you that again and again!"

But now, as Ashton scolded her, she was quite contrite. That evening, to Dowling's astonishment, Laurette began a series of lunging advances. She decided the safest and most friendly subject was Dowling's son who was away at war, and kept asking how he was. Dowling was more taken aback by these explosive gestures of fraternity than by the fights. Finally, Laurette gave up and blurted out, "Ashton told me to make up."

At first she did not take it too seriously. She had had many a spat in the theatre and everybody had ended up the best of friends. As Stevens put it, "She was most traditionally Irish. She loved hard and hated even harder. God loved her loves, and the Devil had conditioned her as one of the world's most amusing haters. She was so witty about it that I sometimes envied her enemies." *

Those who felt her enmity, however, were not always inclined to find her hate so amusing. After her outbursts at Dowling the air never cleared. In time she won his cordial if unspoken dislike, and no one was more surprised and hurt to find this was so than Laurette. She thoroughly enjoyed a good fight; denied one she became peculiarly weaponless and vulnerable.

From the first there had been irksome misunderstandings about billing, contract arrangements. What was the status of "The Glass Menagerie" company? Were they in Chicago on preliminary tryout to a New York opening? Or were they, as to be inferred from some publicity releases, acting in the initial production of a repertory season? The company wanted to know— Chicagoans wanted to know. And Laurette wanted to know. Still

* Ashton Stevens. *Chicago Herald-American*, December 10, 1946.

deeply suspicious of the good faith of others, such misunderstandings did not improve her relations with Dowling. Not able to
have it out with him in a good head-on scrap either on business
or artistic matters, Laurette's blood boiled over. "It's like wading
through molasses to try to talk to him!" she snorted.

After the Chicago opening matters were not improved. To
share stellar honors and not share equally in all the adulation does
not smooth out backstage tension between feuding stars. Dowling
received unstinted praise both as producer and director but to
Laurette, unquestionably, had gone the lion's share of the acting
honors. In his testier moments her co-star was heard to murmur,
"That old woman should kiss my feet for what I've done for
her!" But instead of showing a seemly gratitude for the opportunity he had provided she was going around saying what a lousy
actor he was. It was hardly conducive to a beautiful accord between the two.

There were apparent slights, which Laurette took far more to
heart than she would have an outright disagreement. When Mayor
Kelly arranged an after-theatre supper honoring "The Glass
Menagerie," Laurette innocently inquired of Dowling the place
and hour of the event, and was told that only Dowling had been
asked. Shortly thereafter Louis Singer asked Laurette how she
was going to the affair. When she reiterated Dowling's statement,
Singer turned to him in astonishment, "Why of course the whole
company's invited, Eddie, you know that!" Laurette did not wait
to hear the explanation. She alone of the company did not attend
the supper.

But in the jubilant days of the Chicago triumph all this seemed
relatively unimportant; the Taylor-Dowling spat was no more
than a columnist's titter.

Laurette felt that she had only one thing to worry about and
that was how New York would receive "The Glass Menagerie"
and her performance as Amanda. She knew that too often for
comfort the Main Stem had reversed the decision on a play that
got "raves" on its out-of-town opening. The very brassiness of
the peans of praise rising out of the West might conceivably be
building up critical headaches in New York. Fear of the New
York opening grew in Laurette as she rode the delightful roller

coaster of Chicago's adulation and praise, and occasionally there was a sensation in the pit of her stomach that did not always come from that exciting ride.

*

# *The Postman Rings Twice*

"The Glass Menagerie" opened at the Playhouse on Forty-eighth Street, Easter eve, 1945, the day before Laurette's sixty-first birthday. That street and that theatre held many ghosts: the gentle, ill-fated Alice, betrayed by the personal despair of her creator; Mrs. Midget, tremulous and unassuming, who slipped so modestly into the hearts of her audience. Across the way at the Cort, Peg had cavorted full of Irish talk and high spirits thirty-three years before, and now came Amanda—"Peg grown old" as Laurette called her, grown shrewish and still talking, only this time with a Southern accent instead of Irish.

Laurette was backing a playwright and a play as well as a part, as she had those many long years ago. Some had not agreed with her choice then, but she had never questioned it.

It was fitting that in her dressing room at the Playhouse that evening was a large framed photograph of Hartley Manners, the man who had put her on top on Broadway, under whose nurturing and guidance her talents had glowed and grown and known only success.

None of these ghosts bothered Laurette any more, neither Peg nor Alice nor Mrs. Midget, nor the ghost-haunted eyes of the man in the picture. She looked on them all now as links in the chain of her experience leading to this moment when she was ready to pour the full maturity of her powers into a play and a part which she believed to be eminently worthy of her best. This surely was reward for all she had been through, and what the man in the photograph had always wanted for her.

With minor exceptions Laurette had been triumphing every time she stepped on the stage for fifty years, and shouts and cheers are pretty much the same—at least in the telling. But this time, as she finally took her bow alone at the play's end there was to be detected in the audience's acclaim no admixture of affection, personal tribute, or even warm welcome, but only one solid roar of recognition for the perfection of the art she had shown that night.

The reviewers spoke with a single voice as to the masterpiece of her portrayal, and with only a rare dissent here and there as to the importance of the new playwright, Tennessee Williams. To Chicago's brassy trumpets they loosed a full orchestra of praise.

Stark Young wrote in the *New Republic:* * "The play gives every one of the four characters it presents a glowing, rich opportunity, genuine emotional motivations, a rhythm of situations that are alive, and speech that is fresh, living, abundant and free of stale theatre diction. The author is not awed by the usual sterilities of our playwrighting patterns. . . . The part Miss Taylor plays . . . is the best-written role I have seen in a play for years. All the language and all the motifs are free and true; I recognized them inch by inch, and I should know, for I came from the same part of the country, the same locality and life. . . . Behind the Southern speech in the mother's part is the echo of great literature, or at least a respect for it. There is the sense in it of her having been born out of a tradition, not out of a box. It has the echo and the music of it."

This was praise indeed from the author of "So Red the Rose," one of the finest novels ever written about the traditional South, and Laurette felt more than vindicated in her choice as she read it.

"What Miss Taylor does with these matters," continued Mr. Young, ". . . is almost impossible to convey with anything like the full, wonderful truth. Here is naturalistic acting of the most profound, spontaneous, unbroken continuity and moving life. There is an inexplicable rightness, moment by moment, phrase by phrase, endlessly varied in the transitions. Technique, which is always composed of skill and instinct working together, is in this case so overlaid with warmth, tenderness and wit that any analysis

* April 16, 1945.

is completely baffled. Only a trained theatre eye and ear can see what is happening, and then only at times. . . . She is the real and first talent of them all."

Burton Rascoe found it a play that "hurts you all through. It arouses in you pity and terror. That, according to Aristotle, is what tragedy is for: it is supposed to drain you of these emotions, so you can go on living. 'The Glass Menagerie' certainly does that. . . . I can't say anything adequate as to Miss Taylor's creation of The Mother. You can't describe a sunset. She was there—a simple, sanely insane, horrible Mother, pathetic and terribly human and terribly real. . . . I never hope to see again, in the theatre, anything as perfect. . . ."

This inability to describe what Laurette did, even by the most articulate, had plagued the critics from the outset of her career. Faced with her consummate portrayal of Amanda, the chronic difficulty was compounded. It made one reviewer cry out,* ". . . some permanent record should be made of 'The Glass Menagerie' if only so that we will not have to beat our grandchildren in order to make them understand how wonderful Laurette Taylor was . . . is. For Miss Taylor gives a performance that will justify the existence of the theatre for a long time to come, that is the pure distilled essence of great acting from the first to the last moment, from the aborted gestures to the consummated ones, from the rambling, unemphasized monologues to distinct diatribes of frustration and spite. When she wasn't on the stage we found ourselves wondering what she was doing back there in the kitchen . . . and you know, there isn't any kitchen backstage at the Playhouse."

They tried to tell something of the fluency, the subtlety of the emotional transitions, the unexpected accents of speech as she putters about the wretched St. Louis flat mumbling and complaining—"a mumble that can be heard at the top of the gallery"; the dreary monologues about her girlhood which have become dull with repetition, even to herself; the fleeting moments when she successfully recaptures her "white-columned" past as in the jonquil speech, which begins: "That was the spring I had the craze for jonquils. Jonquils became an absolute obsession . . ." In that

* *Cue.* April 7, 1945.

one word *obsession* was somehow captured both the intensity and
the hopeless fragility of the youthful dream. Again as she stands
on the stoop with the crippled Laura, gazing up at the new moon
and for a moment knows hope—"and over her face flit all the
lovely ghosts of girlhood when seventeen gentlemen callers came
riding to pay her tribute." And again when she lifts the skirt of
her ancient blue taffeta and recalls a waltz in a moonlit garden
with one of her swains; the sordidness of the present drops away
in the swift wave of nostalgia, and you see her as she was, listening to a whisper of love among the magnolias. "She has but to
mention youth to summon it," wrote John Mason Brown. Which
was not hyperbole but solemn fact.

. . . There is the torture of a mother's soul when her son tries
to make her face the truth about Laura, that she is a cripple and
"different from other girls . . ."—the small fluttering movement
of the hands, the body drawn tautly back, as though by holding
herself physically away from the son pleading at her knee she can
hold away the truth he is forcing upon her. The machine-gun
propulsion of her words as she turns on him in tigerish fury and
frustration and asks "Why? Why? Why?" Not as three questions. "On her tongue they become one word, composed of three
desperate syllables, each one of which is equally stressed and
equally stabbing."

. . . And finally, as she calls after the fleeing Tom, "Go then!
Then go to the moon—you selfish dreamer!" The voice, never
raised, almost mumbling still, seems to track him down, course
along the dark alley like a desperate hound released from the
cage of a frightened but unconquered heart.

And so it went; unfathomable masses of material which compose
a human soul dredged up, laid out for all to see, yet done with
gestures, intonations, cadences, changes of mood and expression
so swift they seemed improvisations of the moment, fading away,
never to be recaptured or repeated, gone as life is gone in the very
moment of its living. This quality of immediacy, of evanescence
was the essence of Laurette's acting. In a profession that builds
few monuments, hers was the least possible to build. Legend would
not remember her for beauty, style, or noble stature, for voice
or profile, for tricks of speech or gesture. What she did came

from within and was transferred to the beholder by means other than those recordable. Her one commodity was truth, and the feel and texture of truth as it passes from one person to another is the most ineffable of experiences. In the most impermanent of the arts, her art defied all record.

And yet there was an immortality of sorts. Many who saw her took away new conceptions of truth, new penetrations and insights as to what acting in its highest expression can mean. She was a source, a spreader of light. Perhaps the author of "The Glass Menagerie," who came to the theatre with no preconceived notions of what the theatre should be and very little idea of what contribution an actor might make, has said best what the art of a great actress can mean:

> In this unfathomable experience of ours there are sometimes hints of something that lies outside the flesh and its mortality. I suppose these intuitions come to many people in their religious vocations, but I have sensed them more clearly in the work of artists and most clearly of all in the art of Laurette Taylor. There was a radiance about her art which I can compare only to the greatest lines of poetry, and which gave me the same shock of revelation as if the air about us had been momentarily broken through by light from some clear space beyond us.*

Laurette's own triumph of the opening night was enhanced by the triumph of the author and the play in which she had so much faith. On the twenty-fifth curtain call the reluctant Mr. Williams was persuaded to show himself at the side of the proscenium arch and bowed low to Dowling and Laurette, presenting a modest behind to the cheering audience. It was a great evening.

There had been another side to the triumph of that opening night, seen only by the small band of Laurette's fellow workers backstage. They had witnessed at first hand the power and glory of art combined with the frailty of the human vessel that carries it, and the juxtaposition had been too much for their pent-up emotions. As Laurette finally stood alone upon the stage and the shouts and cheers rose to a crescendo, they clutched each other in

* *New York Times,* December 15, 1946. "An Appreciation," by Tennessee Williams.

the wings and wept; not only wept, but according to one of their number they "bawled."

The company had left Chicago on a Sunday. The following Saturday, the morning of the opening, rehearsal call was for ten thirty A.M. Laurette arrived pale, outwardly composed but inwardly distraught with nerves and exhaustion. All week her sleep had been fitful. The imminence of what was perhaps the most crucial moment of her career, had taken toll. Presently she began vomiting. At noon Randy Echols begged Dowling to let her go home and rest, but he would not hear of it. Perhaps he had a legitimate fear of "that bottle" as he called it, but if so, he was the only one who harbored such a fear after the smooth four months' run in Chicago. The all-too-familiar scenes were run through time and time again. There were still difficulties with the set, and light cues were intricate and demanding. When Laurette was not onstage—and the talkative Amanda was onstage for two hours of the two hour and twenty minute show—she was hanging over a bucket that Echols had placed in the wings.

"It seemed incredible to us," recalled Tony Ross, "that by curtain time Laurette would have the strength left to give a performance. We went home for a few hours for supper, but Eloise told me Laurette could eat nothing. When it came time for the first curtain Mary Jean and Julie helped her to her place at the table. Eloise had got the night off from 'Harvey' to dress her. As the lights dimmed on Dowling at the end of his opening narration and began going up on the dining-room table we could hear Laurette's voice, 'Honey, don't push with your fingers. . . . And chew—chew!' It seemed thin and uncertain. Slowly the lights came up full, and as she continued to speak her voice gained strength. The audience didn't recognize her at first, and by the time they did she was well into her speech, and kept on going right through the applause. They soon quieted down." Thus they had seen Amanda launched. "The bucket stayed in the wings," continued Tony, "and the few minutes she had between scenes, she was leaning over it retching horribly. There was nothing left inside of her, poor thing, but onstage—good God!—what a performance she gave!"

Tears were on Laurette's cheeks as she took her bows that night and her smile was fragile and elusive. With the bang she wore to make Amanda appropriately "low-brow," her hands holding out the ruffles of the ancient blue taffeta as though she might break again into the waltz of her girlhood, she looked like a great ruin of a child gazing timorously upon a world she found to be infinitely pleasing.

Back in her dressing room among the flowers and the telegrams was a bottle of Scotch from George Jean Nathan. The next day she sent him a wire: "Thanks for the vote of confidence."

For talents which Robert Garland labeled, "mature and magnificent, memorable and completely perfect, hypnotic and four-dimensional, out of this world and incredible, heartbreaking and, to put it bluntly, superb," * Laurette won the unanimous vote of the Critics Circle for Best Actress. (The play won on a divided vote.) Next came the Donaldson Award, arrived at by a poll of two thousand theatre people; then the annual *Variety* poll (unanimous); and on December 6, 1945, she proudly shared honors with General Dwight D. Eisenhower, Mrs. Franklin D. Roosevelt and others who received the Newspaper Guild's awards for outstanding accomplishment at its huge Page One Ball. In January, 1946, there was another command performance at the birthday celebration of her idol, Franklin Delano Roosevelt.

About all the fuss and honors Laurette's comment was, "It just goes to show that the postman can ring twice." She was in immediate demand for everything: radio shows, speeches, benefits, cocktail parties, dinners, charities, interviews. Wrote Garland: "In star dressing rooms from Times Square to Columbus Circle, Miss Taylor once more is Queen. Following each afternoon performance comes a reception. Following each night performance comes a levee."

After the first wild whirl of events she sat down and dispatched a hasty note to Stevens in Chicago:

Other people can write, other people can phone you, but this "glamour puss" (one of your craft thought that one up!) goes hay-

* *Pictorial Review*, April 8, 1945.

wire with praise . . . and until she stops kicking the clouds around
can't write, phone—or think. Blame makes me belligerent. Praise
weakens me . . .

Tallu came back and said I must have a concealed phonograph
record playing my Southern accent. "Never before," she said, "has
a Northerner done anything but bastardize the speech of the dear
old South. How come such perfection from an Irisher?"

Was I pleased.

I'll write again, Ashton, when my temperature goes down.

LAURETTE

The tag "Glamour Puss" stuck, and backstage Laurette became "Old G.P."

She was almost more pleased with her conquest of the Southern accent than any of her other highly touted accomplishments.
An outspoken Broadway star, who was in the minority in not lik-
ing the play, and vituperative as to the performance of Dowling,
reported, "Laurette kept needling me about what I thought of her
accent. When we strayed away from the subject she'd bring me
back with 'Pretty good for an old Irish biddy, eh?' It finally
dawned on me that the Southern accent had been the one real
chore—the only one—of that whole magnificent performance.
And because it had been hard, *this* she considered her crowning
achievement. The rest she simply took for granted. The fact
that in the telephone conversation you saw and heard the person on the other end of the wire, that she carried the whole goddam show on her back, was no trick at all, not worth mentioning.
But that accent! She'd worked on that, and she was pretty pleased
with it. No one who is just good, just excellent, could have that
attitude about one minor facet of a performance. That's greatness!"

The few who questioned the authenticity of the accent were
Northerners. Garland, a Baltimorean with more than a trace of
an accent himself, rushed backstage to ask in which section of
the South Laurette was born, to which she replied, "Suh, Ah was
bo'n in the Suth'n section of New York City."

About her performance of Amanda she insisted all the to-do
was really not deserved. "She's written so truthfully, she plays
herself." To Ward Morehouse she confided: "I find I don't know

any tricks any more. Acting is really so simple and my advice to young people is not to be a bedroom thinker—wait 'til you get to the theatre to do your acting. In playing Amanda you're riding on the audience's shoulders." *

Just as with Peg, she never deviated from the conviction that Amanda was so superb a part that any good actress could play her. When the road company opened in Pittsburgh in the fall of 1946, and the notices spoke enthusiastically of Pauline Lord's performance, Laurette, already ill and retired from the show, wired Tennessee Williams in New Orleans: "What did I tell you, my boy? You don't need me."

Laurette emerged from the triumph of "The Glass Menagerie" like one who had broken from a chrysalis. Not the avid enjoyment of regained success and security that might be noted in Chicago, but a more lazy ambling flight over familiar terrain; a relaxed recognition of what she wanted and did not want from life; what she loved, and what no longer interested her; what she was and what she was not. There was a renascence of the Tom Sawyer quality. There was the gamin whose love of life was frankly lusty rather than ladylike. There was still, miraculously, the shimmering young girl peering over life's portal, eyes shining with wonder, taking in the show that life is, still sitting bolt upright when the drama excited her or withdrawing when it beat too strongly upon her "butterfly imagination."

In Chicago she had struggled with a throat ailment which for a time made it difficult to speak, but this had momentarily disappeared. Although her vigorous health was no more, she could still make good her boast that she was going back to God with everything He gave her—tonsils, teeth, appendix and all.

She made a declaration of independence from all ghosts, and a declaration of a new self-honesty. Earl Wilson, *New York Post* columnist, who dubbed her Glamour Puss, and whose specialty in trade was to ask blunt questions and crassly expose the feet of clay of current Broadway idols, took Laurette to supper after a performance. He inquired about her drinking. She replied and he wrote: "After Hartley died I went on the longest wake in history. I'd drink anything. It was a kind of hell. . . ." There was

* "Broadway After Dark," *The New York Sun*, October 12, 1945.

indignation among Laurette's friends. Why should he bring up so
unpleasant a subject, exhume what was past and done? What's
more, he had gone on to report that during the interview Laurette
had not only taken her own double Scotch but absent-mindedly
drunk his. A close relative fulminated that in Hartley's day no
columnist would have dared print such an impertinence. Laurette
was unperturbed. "Nevertheless, that's what I told him and that's
what I did," she said.

More seriously she spoke to a reporter of what she had learned.
It was wartime and in many a home a loved one had been lost.
Out of her own experience she had this to say, "Tell them there
is no escape from grief. They have to stand and face it. . . . My
blind and blundering efforts to forget my husband's death made
me a nuisance to my friends, a burden to myself. If anything like
that were to happen to me again I'd never sneak out from under.
I know now that you can't outrun sorrow. You just have to learn
to bear it."

The true dimension of herself seemed to give her pleasure. No
longer did she wish to "take life by the throat and ask it what
the hell it means." No longer did she feel the need to race com-
petitively by the side of every super-charged ego, or nip at the
heels of the laggards. She went her own way, kept her own counsel, behaved as she wished to behave. She could take or leave the
adulation that came with success. She did not forget the values
learned in her lonely years: the fickleness of fame and fame's
friends; the strength of the Dorsey pride which helped her make
the fight; the discipline of the theatre and Hartley's training which
provided the ultimate handholds out of the abyss; the loyalty of
youth that gathered around the central flame within her when it
burned low and in secret, instinctively drawing close, evoking its
warmth; the companionship of Eloise, a small flame of its own
guiding her back to the paths of everyday life. These were the
solid blocks of her happiness. The rest was a passing show.

It was the recognition by the youth of the theatre that gave
her triumph a special luster. The much-discovered Laurette was
discovered once again. To these young actors and actresses, who
had come to maturity during her absence from the stage, she was
as new as tomorrow's sun, the revelation of what many of them
had groped for blindly; of their world and their time. The little

troupe of "The Glass Menagerie"—Julie, Tony, Mary Jean, Randy and Bill—was the immediate expression of this; they adored her, looked on her as contemporary, guide, friend, and she in turn treasured their devotion and admiration. But beyond this small nucleus was a far wider circle. There were young men and women throughout the theatre world in the process of launching their careers, or already embarked upon them to whom, by their own statement, Laurette was the first to reveal the true meaning of the theatre. Said Norris Houghton: "I have heard such unanimous adulation of an older actor by youngsters in the profession only among the neophytes in Moscow who worshipped at the feet of Stanislavsky and Kachalov and Moskvin." *

For the first six months of the New York run she was still an indefatigable partygoer. When one superlative host, whose parties she had often attended in the 'twenties, materialized backstage to invite her to a soiree in her honor, she could scarcely wait until his back was turned to explode, "My God, I thought he was dead!" But of course she will go. To Tony Ross, who inexplicably seemed to think he had something else to do that evening, she elaborated, "But it's a party, Tony. Mr. X is giving me a party!" When Tony still seemed bothered by the earlier engagement Laurette, standing a step or two above him on the stair landing, bent down, hands on knees, face close to his, and repeated with lip-molding emphasis as though he had suddenly gone deaf, "But you don't understand—it's a party—Mr. X gives the most wonderful parties! Of course you can go!"

She was not unconscious of her eminence on the theatrical scene but dismissed it with the air of one who had worn the ermine so often that she now preferred to drag it carelessly behind like a wrap that is no longer needed. At the many gala events she liked to arrive early, perch on a high bar stool or stand near the door to watch the celebrities and current glamour girls make their entrance. "Tell me if you see Eleanor Holm," or "Has Judy Garland come yet?" she might say tugging at her escort's arm, blissfully unconscious of the groups of people gathering to point her out and whisper her name.

Her witticisms made the rounds of Broadway. Some she

* Cf. Norris Houghton, "The Art of Laurette Taylor," *Theatre Arts*.

claimed, some disclaimed. "That's good," she'd say, when a story which she purportedly had authored was repeated, "but I didn't say it."

The fact that she and old-timer Frank Fay had swept the board of acting honors fascinated her. To Buff Cobb she said, "Just think, two Irish Catholics—Frank Fay and me—tops on Broadway!"

She had not actually returned to the Church but had finally buried the hatchet over the Church's non-recognition of her marriage to Hartley. Catholicism and herself she now treated as separate powers, being respectful but in no way allegiant. Vaguely she felt that the triumph of her struggle against drink had won a thousand indulgences for her soul, and that her passport to Heaven did not require the stamp of any formal religion.

After the New York opening a new contract was drawn, increasing Laurette's share of the box-office receipts and giving her a five per cent interest in the producers' net profits from all sources. In November she wrote to friend Stevens, "Everything is now monotonous in its rich prosperous rhythm. Our manager brings the statement *before* the performance. It's always the same to the last cent. Ah me! I'm just a poor little rich girl."

Two ideas obsessed her once the success of "The Glass Menagerie" was firmly established: to make money so that she would never again know poverty, and never again to allow the rumor of drink to becloud her name. She would not give up drinking; that, she stated emphatically, was the sign of her true conquest of alcohol; what she was determined to prove was that she could drink and control it.

As to the money, now that she had it, she followed the long ago advice of Hartley's astute financier friend, and started accounts in various savings banks. She had little interest in clothes. In Chicago, having no maid and not wishing to bother with laundry, she had bought things as they were needed. In New York she stocked up on loose lounging robes, contented herself with several versions of her "cinema buccaneer" hats. But she was childishly proud of her ability to buy what she wanted. When her daughter came East in the early spring of 1946 and found the New York winds bleak, she said with ill-concealed pride, "Let me lend you a fur coat. I'm rich. I have three."

Doors firmly shut suddenly opened. Her recollections, "Stars That Crossed Mine," were to be published in December and she was busy on the final draft. Another publisher was interested in the novel. An article on John McCormack had sold to *Town & Country*. "Enchantment" was under consideration by Billy Rose on George Nathan's recommendation. "Fun With Stella," her latest play, was finished and under option to a producer. The postman had decidedly rung twice.

Mostly she spent her money refurbishing the long neglected apartment. The Italian furniture at last achieved the rich brocades it cried for. The dressing rooms were redone; Eloise put up shelves for the glass menagerie; Laurette covered the big, comfortable chairs. Then Eloise's tiny apartment was tackled, material bought, cut and sewed, chairs upholstered, curtains and matching pillows made. "She didn't bother with a pattern," Eloise recalled, "just cut and pinned free hand, and everything came out perfectly in the end."

Automatically she took up the old responsibilities that came with success. Sister Bessie, whose violent financial reverses Laurette had unfailingly cushioned with generous checks in her heyday, once again became her charge. She could and did weep over the responsibility now, but unquestioningly took it on. Part of her frugality, too, although she never spoke of it, was undoubtedly a determination to make up to her children for any financial deprivation they might have directly or indirectly suffered at her hands. Laurette's strong, stubborn and silent pride came straight from Bridgett Dorsey.

In November, in a letter to Ashton Stevens recounting "O.G.P.'s" many activities, Eloise had written, "Around the theatre all is peace and love. Laurette comes trotting off the stage in the blue dress, starts to come into the dressing room, turns quickly in midstream and starts up the stairs. 'I guess I'll go up and fight with Eddie during the love scene,' she says happily. But nope. They don't fight. It's nothing like Chicago, everybody tells me."

The overwhelming success of "The Glass Menagerie" in New

York muted temporarily the troubles between its co-stars. Laurette unhesitatingly called Dowling a great director and credited him with achieving some of the play's finest scenes. Dowling on his part was genuinely moved, and publicly exulted over the triumph of Laurette's comeback, seemingly happy that he had been instrumental in it. The confidence they had placed in one another was gloriously vindicated by the reception of the play which one critic predicted would run for twenty years on Broadway. She even conceded a point on his acting—a small one. When scheduled to fly to Chicago on a Sunday for the opening of his production "St. Lazare's Pharmacy" and fly back for the Monday night performance, Laurette protested. In a letter to Ashton she explained her concern: "Perhaps Eddie being such a good be-medalled Catholic thinks he can control the weather—but I think it's unfair to everyone for him to take that chance. No matter what opinion of his performance I have, he's identified himself with this play."

Slights, imaginary or real, were now shrugged off with a laugh. In one of the periodic accountings of the show's expenses there appeared an item: Flowers—$5.oo. Her lawyer, puzzled, inquired, "Do you use fresh flowers in the show?" "Why, no," answered Laurette. "We've had the same old gray crackling jonquils since the play opened in Chicago." What's the explanation? Slowly a look of incredulity suffused Laurette's face. "Wait, now"—her voice rose in disbelief—"Eddie and Singer sent me flowers when I won the Critics Award. Do you suppose . . . Yes, that's it! The five dollars is *my* share of the bill!" Such a thing might have hurt in the Chicago days, but now it was just another funny story to the Glamour Puss of Broadway.

But one central fact remained: she had no respect for Dowling's performance. Her intolerance of what she considered bad acting had not softened with the years, and it was as an actor that she must see him night after night. Hartley had tried to school her tongue, and with the timid, the student, the sensitive actor-in-the-making she had learned patience. But with a supposed peer she still saw no reason for mercy. If Dowling had enjoyed any illusions as to Laurette's opinion, her forthright comments and blunt attacks in Chicago had soon dispelled it. Now there was an armed truce; he avoided discussion, and Laurette perforce must hold her tongue. But she did not forgive him his artistic sins. Further, she never quite recovered from what she considered the ridiculous indignity of having the fifty-three-year-old Dowling playing her son. "If I have to look into that face once more and hear him call me mother, I'll explode!" she would say with the sharp intemperance that bad theatre invariably promoted.

When Erich Remarque came backstage and asked, "Tell me— this Dowling—he is your lover, perhaps?" Laurette was dumbfounded. "Of course not!" she replied indignantly. "What on earth makes you think that?"

"But why else would he have the part?" persisted the puzzled novelist. "He is much too old!"

Denied a good scrap offstage, she would punish him onstage if he overplayed or introduced extraneous business. When he began spitting out his coffee in the breakfast scene Laurette was infuriated and plainly showed her disgust to the audience. Their delighted response to Amanda's revulsion made Dowling careful to mind his stage manners.

Dowling did not take kindly to such censure or to the stories floating around Broadway, nor was the situation eased by the fact that Laurette continued to receive the lion's share of the adulation despite co-star billing. Yet he had the Irishman's gift of circumlocution when faced with matters he preferred to ignore. When Laurette attempted to clear the air, quite as eager to fight out their differences as to discuss acting faults, she would be put off with a placatory "Now, now, lass," which only made her hackles rise further. Onstage the scenes of vitriol with her son at times edged higher, grew sharp with accumulated frustration. One night she advanced on him like a ravening tiger to begin the excoriating speech, "You're going to listen, and no more insolence from you! I'm at the end of my patience!" A few embellishments of her own made it quite clear she was unburdening long-thwarted impulses under the drawling accents of a Southern belle. Afterwards, to a gape-mouthed witness in the wings she muttered, looking greatly refreshed, "I had to do it. You can never get him to face you off stage."

It is to the credit of both as actors that their turbulent relationship failed in any way to muddy the beauty of their scenes together. Many considered these scenes to be among the most sensitively realized of the whole play. When a backstage visitor, who knew of the feud, remarked on this fact with considerable wonder, Laurette expostulated, "Oh I wouldn't do anything like that!"—meaning that even in anger and frustration she would not lay hands on the essential integrity of a scene. And to Dowling's credit as a sensitive artist, neither did he.

The feud was a source of secret merriment backstage. Laurette was an entertaining scrapper and this scrap relieved the inevitable monotony of an extended run; at times she was egged on by those who knew her love of a good fight. While still buoyant with success, and not as yet seriously ill she tended to shrug off the feud and go her own merry way. But to Dowling it was not amusing. His resentment grew. To keep his mind "sweet," he confided to Fulton Oursler,* he began to write prayers during the scene where Laurette scolded him. But the breach did not heal.

There was always laughter and chatter in the Number One dressing room on the ground floor, fleet figures whisking in and out; the "kaffee klatch" Dowling called it. This devotion on the part of the entire company to his co-star in the face of their differences, could not have helped matters. From his quarters one flight up he must have sensed a powerful and solid allegiance, which in time, and under the circumstances, could only have been interpreted as dark conspiracy. "Give the Irish a miserable thought," Laurette once said of her fellow Hibernians, "and they create an Ibsen drama."

* *Reader's Digest*, January, 1951.

# "Blow Out Your Candles, Laura . . ."

The Glass Menagerie.

After the play had run almost a year, the throat ailment which had been troublesome in Chicago returned to plague Laurette. She tried to ignore it but over the weeks again experienced increasing difficulty in producing her voice. "Maybe it's the Southern accent," she would say lightly. "I've never had any trouble like this before." She began the steam inhalations first used in Chicago, was careful to "baby" her voice before each performance. There were periods of relief when the throat seemed almost normal, then the muscles would begin to ache and the two-hour stint of Amanda's ceaseless prattle would leave her whispering and exhausted. A throat specialist warned of serious damage to vocal chords if she persisted in playing while the condition was acute. She would not listen. She dreaded the rumor of alcoholism shrouding her name, and one missed performance was all that was needed to resurrect it.

The little coterie backstage drew around more solidly than ever, banded together to shield her from unnecessary strain and annoyance. Once, when a favored group managed to crowd into the dressing room, the lanky Tony loped in, face wreathed with concern, waggled a finger at Laurette and with his other hand pointed dramatically to his throat. "Remember . . ." he warned in a voice almost as husky as her own, then backed out, casting glances of marked disapproval like a gaunt Savonarola amongst the unredeemed.

One night bobby-soxers chanted in the alleyway outside the window demanding to see her. Laurette was sunk in a deep up-

holstered chair smoking a cigarette, apparently oblivious to the
commotion. Cousin Mabel was there—she had seen every play
Laurette ever did. "They're bobby-soxers calling for you, don't
you hear?" Mabel asked. Laurette cocked her head and listened.
"M-m-m," she said in a hoarse whisper, "me and Frank Sinatra!"
Then, suddenly weary, "Close the window, Mabel."

With growing concern the troupe watched Laurette's onstage
efforts to transcend her affliction. Evident were the muscles moving under jaw and along the throat before each speech, preparing to do the impossible. And they did. Amanda's discontented
mumbles and diatribes susurrated along the farthest row in the
balcony; every syllable of a nostalgic discourse found its way to
the listening ear. But the strain of eight performances a week under such conditions was taking its toll.

As time drew on an acute colitis set in, causing hands and body
to tremble; attacks of nausea left her weak, the eyes grew bloodshot and swollen with lack of sleep. No one had to tell Laurette
that the symptoms were identical in appearance with severe hangover, nor that unfriendly eyes noted them with cold distrust. She
dragged herself to the theatre time and again when she should have
been home in bed. Once again she was running from an apocalyptic hound, this time clutching to her breast the shining treasure of her good name which she had fought so hard to re-establish.

She cut down on all outside activities, accepting few invitations
and entertaining only close friends at home. But the loyalty and
devotion of the group at the theatre she welcomed . . . Randy,
Willie, Julie, Tony and Mary Jean. Their small, devoted services,
their fierce loving protectiveness made the effort of coming to
the theatre worth while. To them she became an inspiring symbol, the living embodiment of a flaming spirit triumphant over a
body which daily was losing strength and resilience.

Dowling remained aloof from the general concern. An old suspicion hardened his heart. Was the star really so ill? Or was an
old craving destroying her health? More than once he objected
to the congregating in Miss Taylor's dressing room—the "kaffee
klatch" was interfering with the show. More specifically and in
less guarded language certain members were told "not to talk to

that woman" during a performance. If this was meant to benefit Laurette only Dowling interpreted it that way. There was immediate indignation and resentment. Smoldering animosities flared. Half-seriously, half-jokingly, the order was flouted. Doors were closed now, and the laughter behind them, the indignant voices, angry whispers, only made matters worse. The conspiracy which he had imagined, Dowling had at last brought down on his own head.

When neither Singer nor Dowling made any move to celebrate the anniversary of the play's opening, Laurette took the other members of the company to see Mary Martin in "Lute Song." "That girl can do anything she wants to in the theatre!" she often said of Mary. Afterwards they all had supper at the apartment. It was the last time the group was to be together. A few nights later Laurette arrived at the theatre so ill that she requested the curtain be held until sure she could play. Dowling ignored the request, ordered it rung up on time. Laurette played the first scene, then Laura Walker, the understudy, took over. Mary Jean upbraided Dowling. A week later she was fired. Randy Echols and Willie Gould immediately handed in their notices; Mary Jean had protested for all of them; Dowling could reinstate her or lose his staff. Dowling stood his ground.

Laurette was too ill to fight; and besides this was not the kind of fight she understood. She had fought over everything else: contract, billing, box office statements, her fair share of the profits —and the bills; she had come to expect no special consideration as a star or person from either Singer or Dowling, and had learned to battle for her rights as Hartley would, coldly, methodically, through lawyers, expecting no quarter and giving none. But now she would not fight; she was too ill, and it was all too small and petty. All she knew was that the solid little world backstage which had given her so much pleasure and comfort had been destroyed. Now there was nothing but the long, taxing performance, and a silent corroding hate poisoning an atmosphere that had once been carefree and serene. "For the last six months of the run," stated Dr. De Santo, "she was so disgusted she didn't care whether she ever went to the theatre or not."

On week ends she began to drink more than was good for her.

The effect was out of all proportion to the small amount taken; heart palpitated, breath came short, and exhaustion racked her body; but in spite of De Santo's warnings she would not give it up. With joy in the theatre gone, health broken, this domination of her ancient enemy, on her own terms, was the only triumph left. Never did alcoholism take back the reins of her life; sick and disheartened as she was Laurette rode into the final storms, master of her destiny. It was a mad, weird triumph—some might say, a Pyrrhic victory—but to her it was sweet, and her very own.

Eloise gave up her part in "Harvey" to help. She weeded out the long line of visitors, became dresser, secretary and general buffer for the ailing and despairing Laurette. To husband the last bit of nervous force for her performances Laurette would speak not a word all day. On many nights the throat specialist would be in her dressing room to make sure that she used her medication, spoke to no one; then he would step out front and marvel at a performance that showed not a single flaw. Yet as soon as she was within the concealing shadow of the wings, hands and body began to tremble.

Only the obsessive fears of being labeled an alcoholic and once again sunk in poverty drove her on. A few times with the straight bang of Amanda in place, the sloppy first-act robe tied about her ample frame, inhalations and medication taken, she started for the stage, then shook her head and turned back; voice and strength were gone and no amount of will power was of avail. Laura Walker would take over.

"Sometimes when she was so terribly ill," recalled Eloise, "it used to break me in two to realize what people were saying." Wrote that "sensitive fellow" and staunch friend, Tennessee Williams, in a beautiful appreciation after Laurette's death:

> Gallantry is the word that best fits those human qualities which made Laurette Taylor so intensely lovable as a person. I do not think it is realized how much she sacrificed of her personal comfort and health during the year and a half she played in "The Glass Menagerie." She remained in the part that long because of a heroic perseverance I find as magnificent as her art itself. It is not necessary to mention the mistaken reservation some people had about her ability to remain long with a play. But Laurette was painfully

aware of that reservation and determined to beat it. She did. She was neither a well nor a strong person at any time during the run of the play and often continued her performance when a person of ordinary spirit would not have dared to. . . . I have never seen her physical suffering affect the unfailing wonder of her performance.*

As the throat specialist had feared, a growth established itself on the vocal chords and an operation became imperative. On June 3, 1946, she exercised the option in her contract and absented herself for four weeks. The operation was performed in the doctor's office; the growth proved nonmalignant. Though grateful for the respite, Laurette's exhaustion was still deep. Fear forced her back before she was ready. More and more obsessive had become the conviction that her share of the profits would be withheld if she did not play.

In the first sweltering days of July word came that Jane Adams lay in a coma at the hospital in Auburn and little hope was held for her life. Laurette was deeply affected by the news. During the weeks of that long hot summer her mind turned again and again to the bedside of her friend, and a brooding melancholy descended. In her recollections she had written: "When I was in trouble Jane was always there. . . . She is a woman of outspoken opinions, deep consideration and a capacity for friendship that I have never met since. Without my mother, Jane and Hartley, I would be a banshee wandering the world wailing its call of disaster."

When Jane died on September ninth, Laurette's grief was mute and boundless.

The play went on through the midsummer heat. High blood pressure added to Laurette's misery. Offstage there was progressively less discipline, less and less will to perform daily routines. She should go to the dentist but never went; she should buy new clothes but never bought them; she should eat but did not, only perhaps creamed chicken or a curry, or other highly seasoned dish the doctor frowned on, and then when it was cooked she really did not want it; a bite or two and the fork would go down on the plate. She should stop drinking entirely, but would not.

* *The New York Times*, December 15, 1946.

The effect of one drink was immediate and distressing, riddling what was left of her physical stamina. The hours of her day became shapeless with exhaustion, but night after night in the theatre the performances threaded themselves like perfectly matched jewels, reflecting only the glory of an artist who had reached perfection.

She knew that rumors of drinking were spreading willy-nilly, and she was haunted by that other fear that Dowling and Singer would retaliate for her absences. "They'll cut off my royalties, they'll find some way to keep the money from me, if I don't go. Oh, yes they will," she would burst out illogically. "You don't know them the way I do." Driven by these fears, nothing could stop her from playing, and gradually the last ounce of her strength was being poured into the chattering Amanda who glowed like the Phoenix above the ashes of Laurette's existence.

For her last performance Laurette could not walk unaided to the stage. Coming off she would stretch out both hands to Eloise who would guide her past the props and stays back to her room. Yet that night Eloise and Julie stood together in the wings and wept at the diamond-cut beauty of her performance.

With the closing notice on the call board and only a week to run, Laura Walker played the next several performances. Laurette begged to return for the final show, but the doctor ordered her to the hospital instead. Her blood pressure was dangerously high, the nausea had become constant.

After two weeks of rest and special diet she wrote to Marguerite, "I'm beginning to feel really like one of the fighting Irish again." But it was a hollow boast.

Months before, Eloise had been married to a Naval officer prior to his being ordered overseas. A baby was on the way and she was now with Laurette almost constantly. During August they frequently drove to the ocean in the car Laurette had purchased for her. Laurette would lie stretched on the sand listening to the diapason of the surf, occasionally feeling the shock beneath her tired body as a comber struck hard against the shore. There had always been a feeling of renewal from this rhythm, this pounding, vibrating closeness with the sea, but now it did not

come; only a sense of slowly unwinding like a spool of thread
over the ledge of eternity.

One stifling night they drove to One Hundred and Twenty-
fifth Street to see if the Cooney home was still there. They went
up Fifth Avenue, skirted Mount Morris Park where the curfew
bell still hung in its tower, looming against the sky like the skeletal
remains of another time. The rows of once smart houses remained
intact, still retained an air of discreet prosperity. On One Hundred
and Twenty-fifth Street they turned west. It was surprisingly unchanged except for the hordes of humanity swarming the pavements, lounging in doorways and open windows; many of the
four-story brownstone fronts still stood, converted to shops and
rooming houses. Number 52 was there, its brownstone steps
sheared away and the original entrance bricked over. Lights shone
in several windows. Laurette looked for a long moment without
speaking. She had not seen it since Charlie Taylor had taken her
away as his bride. They drove past P.S. 24 on One Hundred and
Twenty-eighth Street, past the quiet gray mass of All Saints
Church, still the most impressive structure in the neighborhood.

They did not drive out again after that evening. It was as though
Laurette sensed that in drifting back to the place of her childhood
she had closed a circuit, and in that circuit the meaning and purpose of her life was contained.

September came. Over and over during the stifling days she
would say to Eloise, "I want to live just long enough to see your
baby." As much an expression of spiritual as physical exhaustion,
it sprang involuntarily to her lips.

One might hope that a new play would catch her imagination,
rally her interest; or was it right to wish that for one whose life
had become only work? Or one might pray that the small tentacles
of the new life which Eloise carried would wrap around Laurette's
heart, draw her back from the fatal drifting; but would this be
mercy for one who had lived so turbulently and was now so tired?

Sharp waves from a busy world buffeted her indifference. Plans
were afoot to do "The Glass Menagerie" in pictures. This would
be the crowning opportunity to pin her fame to the immortality
it deserved, for all time capture the fluidity of gesture, speech, expression which had eluded analysis. She could ask her own terms.

London was clamoring for a production and made it quite clear that the date waited only on Laurette's availability. Could they know when she would be free?

Randy Echols and Bill Gould brought the playscript of "La Folle de Chaillot" by Jean Giraudoux. Laurette felt a tingle of excitement as Eloise read the literal translation aloud. The legend of a delightfully lunatic old woman who defeats the enemies of Paris was both comic and compassionate and offered a supreme opportunity to exercise her mastery of that thin line between the absurd and the sad. She wanted to give her young friends a success, and saw an unusual chance for Julie Haydon to introduce a new brand of comedy in the role of Constance. She told the two neophyte producers to go ahead, find the financial backing and she would do it.

But when Zoe Akins called from the Coast about another play Laurette had begun again her mysterious drifting. "I've just turned down fifty thousand dollars for a movie," she said in a weary faraway voice. "I don't know what I want to do. I've got hold of a good play for next year, but I don't know if I'll do it—I really don't know what I want to do."

She puttered around the apartment waiting for the baby to be born. She was knitting a crib blanket of indeterminate length in all the colors of the rainbow. She wanted the baby to be her special care. It would be like starting all over again, and perhaps with this baby, this little family under her wing, she would not make quite so many mistakes. One night when Laurette was unusually low in spirit, Eloise brought back the old delighted smile with the announcement that if the baby were a boy she would name him Hartley.

Late in October the child was born. Labor pains started at midnight and Eloise tried to move around her apartment quietly, but almost at once Laurette was in the room, watch in hand, issuing orders, bustling her off in a taxi. For the next twenty-four hours the nurses were kept hopping by Laurette's incessant calls to the hospital.

For a brief period after the baby came home she seemed to be rallying her forces around the newcomer, a lovely little boy. There was nothing but the child on her mind. She would sit for hours holding him, talking to him, planning for him, reminiscing about her own babies—how happy she had been with her first, how proud and ignorant. . . . How she had pushed Elizabeth and Bridgett from the room at bathtime, saying she would care for her own infant, and how after soaping him the small wriggling creature had flopped off her lap into the tin tub at her feet, face down, and paralyzed with fright, she had screamed for the two women hovering outside the door. . . . Talk—talk—talk—— She was talking against the time of action. For all the sweet embroilment of the tiny life, she was hanging back, reluctant to be pulled again into the stream of life.

After meeting the challenge of the baby's birth Laurette seemed unable to go further. The simplest routines became oppressive. She could not rest. Eloise would hear her bedside radio playing throughout the night. Because she would not eat, Dr. De Santo was feeding her intravenously. She complained of the baby's crying and in the next breath declared she would die if Eloise and the baby left her. Eloise was rapidly squandering her own strength caring for the tiny Hartley and Laurette. It was a racked household—one life riding the strong flux of primal energy, the other swirling aimlessly on an ebbing tide. De Santo, deeply concerned for the health of all, finally insisted that Eloise take the baby for a month's visit at her parents' home; they could be back by Christmas.

The last few days before their departure Laurette was in bed most of the time. Eloise would bring the baby to lie beside her, and Laurette was happy just to watch his tiny movements, stroke the soft curve of his cheek, cradle the petal-pink heels in her palm, and chatter to him half joshingly, half sentimentally of the hazards and joys which lay ahead.

As the time came to part, Laurette was cheerful, talking of plans to go to Florida, relax in the sunshine until Christmas, of the contract she had signed only a few days before to do "The Mad Woman of Chaillot" ("La Folle de Chaillot"). The terms were fabulous. With its success—and she did not doubt it would be a great success—she would be a very wealthy woman again. There would be no more worries for any of them, little Hartley, Eloise, herself.

But this was more talk. Her strength was gone. To those who watched her it was evident she would never play eight performances a week again. "Four months before she died," De Santo reported, "I would have said she could play again, but her health deteriorated rapidly at the end. There was nothing really fatal about her illness, but there was a fatal lack of desire to fight."

While dressing Hartley for the journey Eloise was shaken by the presentiment that she would never see Laurette again. When the plane was delayed in take-off for four hours, she sat clutching the squirming Hartley, fighting back an overwhelming desire to return and stay by the side of the woman she loved so deeply.

Laurette did not leave her bed again. Tony Ross telephoned to find her voice weary and distant. Letters and cables from London, progress reports from the jubilant young producers of "Mad Woman," a flurry of business instructions from her lawyer, last-minute vacation arrangements for Florida, harried a woman who had turned her face away. Nothing could stop her now. The small ecstatic parabolas of growth in the baby who had lain in her arms and who would return in a few weeks, were too fragile, too tenuously new, to tie her with strong bonds to life. She was tired. She wanted to go on now, to the end, not back to the beginning. In her own primitive way she had made her peace with God and was convinced she would rejoin her beloved Hartley in a world of radiance and kindness and gentleness; a world that would no longer demand her tortured understanding but enfold her, as on this earth only the theatre had enfolded her and given her peace.

Her only dread was the shadow of the hell she had lived in for ten years falling upon her again: the loneliness, the poverty, and, most dreadful of all, the procession of nurses—symbol of her grimmest defeat—taking up vigil once more over her prostrate body. "If you bring a nurse into this house, I will die," she told De Santo after Eloise had gone. But what was he to do? Poison had spread throughout the system. Exhaustion was complete. She was too weak to care for herself. Two and three times a day he came from his office close by to warm a cup of broth, try to persuade her to eat; in the evening he would stop by with his wife, staying until after midnight.

At last Laurette could not rise from her bed unaided; the nurse was inevitable. She came, on December 6, 1946, a week after Eloise left.

·In the small, darkened bedroom Laurette lay, withdrawn and uncommunicative. She watched the white shoes tapping efficiently over the floor, the starched straight back, the cap with stiff upthrust wings seeming to fling out the challenge, "*Now*, we'll see who's boss!" An old rebellion flared deep in Laurette's soul.

The nurse was really kind and generous, picked with care by De Santo, but in the rustling authoritative figure Laurette saw only the total bondage of mind, heart and spirit from which she had fought so long and desperately to free herself. Again she was delivered into the hands of the Philistines and had no strength left to escape.

Just twenty-four hours later, as the long winter shadows reached into her room, Laurette, propped up on her pillows, asked for a drink. Was there a familiar flint-eyed look, a murmured something about doctor's orders? It was an old tiresome pattern. She had fought so hard a battle, come such a long way, won such victories in her soul. Why should this lone tattered standard of her darkest ordeal be the only banner left flying on this the last battlement? Laurette glared back, stubborn and unyielding. *She would like a drink.* . . . She had won over it so many times before . . . it was the least of her enemies now. . . .

She heard the nurse's steps returning. Reluctantly, Duty bent over her, distant and disapproving, holding out a glass. . . . The bitter liquid passed Laurette's lips and fleetingly she felt the small triumph of being no longer afraid . . . she was not afraid of anything any more. . . .

A high agonized cry rang through the apartment as a mighty pain clawed at her breast. It echoed out into the hallway, beat emptily against the closed doors of the corridor and faded away down the long shaft of the elevator. Then the voice that could place a whisper in the back row of the topmost gallery was still. The heart that held the paradox of so much and so little understanding, that had been so meager with itself, so generous in the art it served, was at rest at last.